Designing Hyper-V Solutions

Deploy Microsoft Virtualization and VDI solutions using real-world Hyper-V configurations

Saurabh Grover

[PACKT] PUBLISHING

enterprise 88
professional expertise distilled

BIRMINGHAM - MUMBAI

Designing Hyper-V Solutions

First published: August 2015

Production reference: 1040815

Published by Packt Publishing Ltd.
Livery Place
35 Livery Street
Birmingham B3 2PB, UK.

ISBN 978-1-78217-144-7

www.packtpub.com

Credits

Author
Saurabh Grover

Reviewers
Vikash Kumar Roy
Lai Yoong Seng
Oleg Sokolov
Milan Temelkovski

Commissioning Editor
Andrew Duckworth

Acquisition Editor
James Jones

Content Development Editor
Natasha DSouza

Technical Editor
Prajakta Mhatre

Copy Editors
Ting Baker
Yesha Gangani
Vikrant Phadke

Project Coordinator
Vijay Kushlani

Proofreader
Safis Editing

Indexer
Rekha Nair

Production Coordinator
Melwyn D'sa

Cover Work
Melwyn D'sa

About the Author

Saurabh Grover is a technical consultant who specializes in Microsoft Platforms, Virtualization, and Cloud Computing with Microsoft Azure. He has over 11 years of experience with Microsoft technologies and has achieved many industry-admired certifications, including Microsoft Certified Solutions Expert (MCSE) for Server Infrastructure and Private Cloud.

He currently works for a Fortune 50 technology company and is involved with the implementation and support of Hyper-V solutions and other Microsoft technologies that provide technical and operational insights into research and development and businesses.

Outside his professional role, Saurabh likes to travel to new locations and enjoys photography as a hobby. He tries to take great pictures.

Acknowledgement

The list is long and it's hard to convey thanks by merely using words. This is my first major attempt at writing, and like any other first-time author, technical or nontechnical, I am equally excited and wish to express my gratitude to everyone who has contributed to my success. However, keeping the text's depth in mind, I will mention some of the people who have made a lot of difference.

Thanks to my teachers, who carved the intellect in me and provided me with enough boost to match up to the escape velocity. Mrs Rita Bhattacharya and Mr Subroto Roy, I would like to thank you from the bottom of my heart for instilling confidence in me when I needed it the most.

I'd like to thank my ex-counterparts, the late Satya Ramachandran, Richard Pulliam, and Surinder Singh. Satya was an inspiration and a friend. He and Richard were the first to get me up close and personal with the Microsoft Server world. Incidentally, I received my first official training on Hyper-V from Satya. Surinder is the the go-to guy when you are dwindling with technical ramble and need at least someone who can hear and clear your thoughts. Thanks Surinder for listening!

I would also like to extend a big word of thanks to my friends who are established authors and have always encouraged me to write. Prasenjit Sarkar, who is a VMware vExpert (yes, you heard it right and this book is about Hyper-V!) and a noted author; and Pratik Dasgupta, who is a storyteller.

For the team at Packt Publishing, a big "thank you" to all of you rock stars! The acquisition editors, James Jones and Kevin Colaco, for giving me the opportunity and providing me with timely feedback and guidance; the project coordinator, Sheetal Sarkar, for keeping a stopwatch and ensuring that I didn't lose track; and the content editors, Shaon Basu, Pragnesh Bilimoria, Natasha Dsouza, and of course, Sweny Sukumaran (the patient one), for ensuring that my scribbles made perfect sense. I am grateful to my technical reviewers, Alessandro Cardoso, Vinicius Apolinario, Yoong Seng Lai, Milan Temelkovski and Oleg Sokolov, for their friendly advice on points that required attention.

My final thanks go to my family. Well, I just can't thank them enough, as there's nothing without them: my mother, Shashi Grover, who has been the pillar of my life and has taught me to never get overwhelmed by obstacles; my brother, Sanchit Grover, who has been my relentless life support and has introduced me to the binary world of computers; and finally, my wife, Ruhi, whom I married while this book was underway.

About the Reviewers

Vikash Kumar Roy has been associated with IT for close to 16 years. In his IT career, he has worked on various platforms and domains. Currently, he has gained expertise on end user computing. Prior to this, he designed and delivered solutions on server virtualization.

> I would like to thank my guru and my boss, who helped me learn and deal with every challenge in my current job and previous job.

Lai Yoong Seng was awarded the sixth Microsoft Most Valuable Professional (MVP) for Hyper-V in 2010. He has more than 14 years of experience in IT and has joined a Hyper-V and System Center specialist, Infront Consulting, in Malaysia. He specializes in Microsoft Virtualization and has started blogging about this technology (www.ms4u.info) and presenting at local and regional events. Lai is the founder of the Malaysia Virtualization User Group (MVUG), which provides a one-stop center for people who want to learn about Hyper-V, System Center, and Azure. Previously, he was actively engaged as a technology early adopter (TAP) and tester for System Center Virtual Machine Manager 2012, System Center 2012 SP1, Windows Server 2012 R2, System Center 2012 R2, Azure Site Recovery, and the upcoming Windows Server and System Center vNext.

Besides this, Lai has been a technical reviewer for *Windows Server 2012 Hyper-V: Deploying Hyper-V Enterprise Server Virtualization Platform, Hyper-V Network Virtualization Cookbook, Hyper-V Security, Learning System Center App Controller,* and a video called *Building and Managing a Virtual Environment with Hyper-V Server 2012 R2,* all by Packt Publishing.

Reviewing a book takes a lot of effort, process, and determination. This would not have been possible without help from my family, colleagues, and friends. I would like to thank my parents for being understanding and patient and helping keep all the stuff together while I was reviewing a book.

Finally, a very special thanks to Packt Publishing for giving me an opportunity to contribute to this book.

Oleg Sokolov is an enterprise software engineer with more than 10 years of industry experience in developing embedded systems and desktop software. He lives and works in Nizhny Novgorod, Russia.

For the last few years, he has been focusing on custom software development based on Microsoft infrastructure solutions, such as the integration of industrial measuring systems into enterprise IT environments. Oleg has good experience in Microsoft products and technologies, such as Windows Server, SQL Server, System Center, Exchange, Hyper-V virtualization, and so on.

In 2014, he founded a company called QuickSoft (`quicksoft.su`), which develops custom software solutions that help automate internal business processes for enterprises.

Milan Temelkovski is an enterprise ICT support engineer with over 15 years of specialization in Microsoft and HP platforms. He started working with Microsoft Server from Windows NT and has been deploying, troubleshooting, and teaching Microsoft products since then. Milan is a member of the IT-Pro group and a regular speaker at group events. You can contact him at `milan.temelkovski@outlook.com`.

www.PacktPub.com

Support files, eBooks, discount offers, and more

For support files and downloads related to your book, please visit www.PacktPub.com.

Did you know that Packt offers eBook versions of every book published, with PDF and ePub files available? You can upgrade to the eBook version at www.PacktPub.com and as a print book customer, you are entitled to a discount on the eBook copy. Get in touch with us at service@packtpub.com for more details.

At www.PacktPub.com, you can also read a collection of free technical articles, sign up for a range of free newsletters and receive exclusive discounts and offers on Packt books and eBooks.

PACKTLIB

https://www2.packtpub.com/books/subscription/packtlib

Do you need instant solutions to your IT questions? PacktLib is Packt's online digital book library. Here, you can search, access, and read Packt's entire library of books.

Why subscribe?

- Fully searchable across every book published by Packt
- Copy and paste, print, and bookmark content
- On demand and accessible via a web browser

Free access for Packt account holders

If you have an account with Packt at www.PacktPub.com, you can use this to access PacktLib today and view 9 entirely free books. Simply use your login credentials for immediate access.

Instant updates on new Packt books

Get notified! Find out when new books are published by following @PacktEnterprise on Twitter or the *Packt Enterprise* Facebook page.

Table of Contents

Preface

Virtualization of workloads is no longer a new concept, and organizations are willingly adopting and promoting server and desktop virtualization. OS and software vendors have already realized the drift and efforts that are being made to develop workloads that can be ported seamlessly to a virtual machine platform, other than being hosted on a physical server.

The latest server virtualization platform (Hypervisor) release from Microsoft, Windows Server 2012 R2 Hyper-V, is not only economical and user-friendly but also a robust and resilient solution. Hyper-V is now one of the top contenders in the server virtualization area, and is already leading in some markets.

This book is a handy and easy-to-follow guide that describes the concepts of virtualization and the Hyper-V design approach. Each topic is explained sequentially to help you build an understanding of Hyper-V and thereafter deploy a fully functional and robust solution, alongside a disaster recovery failover plan. I'm looking forward to all of you becoming Hyper-V experts!

What this book covers

Chapter 1, Introducing Release 2.0, introduces Windows Server 2012 R2 Hyper-V and provides an overview of the Hyper-V architecture and licensing requirements. This chapter also explains the concepts of virtualization and cloud computing, and lists the features that the new hypervisor platform brings to the fore. Then it covers a feature set comparison with other leading hypervisors on the market.

Chapter 2, Planning and Deploying Microsoft Hyper-V, provides you with some design guidelines for Hyper-V deployment. It also covers the installation of a new Hyper-V host, considering both the GUI and server core options. Then we cover scenarios involving the upgrades of legacy Hyper-V hosts and migration of workloads to the new Hyper-V platform. Finally, this chapter gives you information about Hyper-V management methods and configuring various Hyper-V settings.

Chapter 3, Deploying Virtual Machines, helps you design and deploy new guest machines, as well as explaining virtual machine conversion principles for both physical to virtual (P2V) and virtual to virtual (V2V) conversions. This chapter also teaches you about generation 2 virtual machines and their benefits over generation 1 virtual machines.

Chapter 4, Hyper-V Networking, covers the virtual networking fundamentals and benefits of the new Extensible Virtual Switch (EVS). It then discusses how the EVS design leverages Hyper-V Network Virtualization (HNV), and talks about various switch extensions and their functions. This chapter also focuses on Windows Server 2012 R2 NIC teaming and QoS.

Chapter 5, Storage Ergonomics, discusses the virtual storage options for guest machines. This chapter has a focus on virtual hard disk offerings, VHD and VHDX, and a setup walkthrough for guest clustering with shared VHDX. It also covers Virtual Fibre Channel and Virtual SAN setup walkthroughs, and discusses the basics and limitations of pass-through disks. Finally, you get an insight into Storage Management Initiative Specification (SMI-S), and a bonus section for configuring a Windows Standards-based storage management service that allows integration with SMI-S providers, both with the Windows File and Storage Service console and Virtual Machine Manager 2012 R2.

Chapter 6, Planning a Virtual Machine's High Availability and Mobility, provides you with the knowledge to set up a VM's high availability and mobility, namely quick, live, and storage migrations. This chapter also gives basic training on Windows Failover Clustering and Cluster Aware Updating (CAU), and tells you how to configure them from a Hyper-V perspective. Finally, there's handy information on configuring Cluster Shared Volumes (CSV) and Scale-Out File Server (SOFS).

Chapter 7, Building a Secure Virtualization Environment, focuses on security considerations and best practices for protecting a Hyper-V infrastructure. Besides providing suggestions to protect the hypervisor and management OS, this chapter also trains you on protecting communications in a VM's high availability and mobility scenarios. Moreover, it provides an insight into the free Microsoft utilities that assist in implementing a secure Hyper-V solution.

Chapter 8, Hyper-V Replica, discusses disaster recovery planning for Hyper-V through the Hyper-V Replica. This chapter goes in depth and covers major aspects for setting up and designing VM replication. It concludes with an insight into Microsoft Azure Site Recovery (ASR).

Chapter 9, Backup and Recovery Strategies for Hyper-V Solutions, covers Hyper-V backup strategies and best practices. It also provides an overview of the Windows Server Backup (WSB) feature and its improvements in Windows Server 2012 R2. We see how to use the WSB feature as a reliable backup and recovery solution if an organization does not wish to invest in an enterprise-level backup solution. This chapter concludes with an insight into Microsoft's System Center Data Protection Manager 2012 R2.

Chapter 10, Building a Virtual Desktop Infrastructure, discusses the basics and benefits of RDS and the Microsoft VDI. This chapter also lists the benefits of Hyper-V for VDI, and provides a walkthrough of a standard VDI deployment.

What you need for this book

This book focuses on Hyper-V and how to leverage other Windows Server features to build on its high availability, resiliency, scalability, and recoverability. If you wish to approach the labs and the scenarios discussed inside the book, all you need is a computer (workstation or server) or two that are Windows Server 2012 R2 certified as per the *Windows Server Catalog* website, and a Windows Server 2012 R2 edition with a trial license for Hyper-V Server 2012 R2.

Who this book is for

This book is intended for a wide audience. It is meant for IT admins and consultants who are either planning to adopt virtualization or migrate to Hyper-V as a suitable hypervisor platform. It is also for architects who wish to gain greater insights into the intricacies of the low-cost yet robust and reliable solution of Hyper-V.

The book will train you on virtualization and Hyper-V. However, a working knowledge and experience in managing Windows Servers and a fair understanding of networking and storage concepts is expected here.

Conventions

In this book, you will find a number of text styles that distinguish between different kinds of information. Here are some examples of these styles and an explanation of their meaning.

Code words in text, database table names, folder names, filenames, file extensions, pathnames, dummy URLs, user input, and Twitter handles are shown as follows: "To keep things simple, we will refer to the location as `C:\ClusterStorage`."

A block of code is set as follows:

```
Name                    : HClus1-Team2
Members                 : {Ethernet 2, Ethernet 6}
TeamNics                : HClus1-Team2
TeamingMode             : Lacp
LoadBalancingAlgorithm  : HyperVPort
Status                  : Up
```

Any command-line input or output is written as follows:

```
Set-VMHost -VirtualMachinePath "D:\TestLab" -
VirtualHardDiskPath "D:\TestLab"
```

New terms and **important words** are shown in bold. Words that you see on the screen, for example, in menus or dialog boxes, appear in the text like this: "As the selected method is ADDS, the next screen is **Active Directory Credentials**."

> Warnings or important notes appear in a box like this.

> Tips and tricks appear like this.

Reader feedback

Feedback from our readers is always welcome. Let us know what you think about this book—what you liked or disliked. Reader feedback is important for us as it helps us develop titles that you will really get the most out of.

To send us general feedback, simply e-mail feedback@packtpub.com, and mention the book's title in the subject of your message.

If there is a topic that you have expertise in and you are interested in either writing or contributing to a book, see our author guide at www.packtpub.com/authors.

Customer support

Now that you are the proud owner of a Packt book, we have a number of things to help you to get the most from your purchase.

Errata

Although we have taken every care to ensure the accuracy of our content, mistakes do happen. If you find a mistake in one of our books—maybe a mistake in the text or the code—we would be grateful if you could report this to us. By doing so, you can save other readers from frustration and help us improve subsequent versions of this book. If you find any errata, please report them by visiting `http://www.packtpub.com/submit-errata`, selecting your book, clicking on the **Errata Submission Form** link, and entering the details of your errata. Once your errata are verified, your submission will be accepted and the errata will be uploaded to our website or added to any list of existing errata under the Errata section of that title.

To view the previously submitted errata, go to `https://www.packtpub.com/books/content/support` and enter the name of the book in the search field. The required information will appear under the **Errata** section.

Piracy

Piracy of copyrighted material on the Internet is an ongoing problem across all media. At Packt, we take the protection of our copyright and licenses very seriously. If you come across any illegal copies of our works in any form on the Internet, please provide us with the location address or website name immediately so that we can pursue a remedy.

Please contact us at `copyright@packtpub.com` with a link to the suspected pirated material.

We appreciate your help in protecting our authors and our ability to bring you valuable content.

Questions

If you have a problem with any aspect of this book, you can contact us at `questions@packtpub.com`, and we will do our best to address the problem.

1
Introducing Release 2.0

Technology has a way with change and change is necessary. We have witnessed many advances in the world of computing, with improvements and innovations being released at the drop of a hat, be it the room-sized hard drives squeezed down to thumbnail-sized memory cards, or mainframes giving way to distributed traditional servers and then to virtualized workloads. With virtualization at its fore, cloud computing has now taken the IT world by storm. Microsoft has become a major stakeholder in it with its earlier releases of Hyper-V Server 2008 R2 and Azure. Later on, it grabbed the attention of medium and enterprise businesses with Windows Server 2012 Hyper-V. Now it has put its best foot forward with the Release 2.0 of Windows Server 2012.

In the forthcoming pages, we will look into the Hyper-V architecture, which will help you understand what runs under the hood and realize what to fix if the setup does not deliver as expected. We will also look at the technical prerequisites, scalable options, and features introduced with Windows Server 2012 R2 Hyper-V.

Some features are new to this hypervisor platform, while others are improvements to earlier offerings with Windows Server 2012 Hyper-V, with more support for Linux VMs now.

There is also a basic overview of the licensing aspects and the **Automatic Virtual Machine Activation** (**AVMA**) feature released with Windows Server 2012 R2. It's imperative to understand the licensing requirements when designing a solution and ensure that you pay for what you use.

A discussion on Hyper-V always invites a comparison with the market leaders — VMware's ESXi servers. After almost a decade of catching up, Microsoft has delivered a product that matches up to its worthy competitor. We will close this chapter with a comparison chart of VMware's latest offering, ESXi 5.5, and Citrix XenServer 6.2 in order to show the features' differences and similarities.

In this chapter, we will broadly discuss the following topics:

- An insight into virtualization
- Cloud computing
- The Hyper-V architecture and technical requirements
- Features of Windows Hyper-V 2012 R2

An insight into virtualization

Before we proceed further with the technical know-how about Windows Hyper-V 2012 R2 and the concepts of virtualization, it's necessary to know where it all started and how it grew into what we see today.

Virtualization – how did it begin?

The origin of virtualization dates back to the 1960s, when IBM was building its mainframes as a single-user system to run batch jobs. Thereafter, they moved their focus to designing time-sharing solutions in mainframes, and invested a lot of time and effort in developing these robust machines. Finally, they released the CP-67 system, which was the first commercial mainframe to support virtualization. The system employed a **Control Program** (**CP**) that was used to spawn virtual machines, utilizing resources based on the principle of time-sharing. Time-sharing is the shared use of system resources among users of a large group. The goal was to increase the efficiency of both the users and the expensive computer resources. This concept was a major breakthrough in the technology arena, and reduced the cost of providing computing capabilities.

The 1980s saw the debut of microprocessors and the beginning of the era of personal computers. The demerits of mainframes, primarily their maintenance cost and inflexibility, saw personal computers and small servers move into the main scene. The low cost of implementation, performance, and scalability with networked computers gave rise to the client-server model of computation and pushed virtualization to the backseat. During the 1990s, the cost of computing soared again, and remediating the rising costs made the IT industry come full circle and revisit virtualization. There were several disadvantages of client-server technology that showed up with time, primarily low infrastructure utilization, increasing IT management costs and physical infrastructure costs, and insufficient failover and disaster management.

The 1990s saw the rise of two major players in the virtualization history, namely Citrix and VMware. Citrix started off with desktop virtualization and brought in the concept of remote desktops along with Microsoft, then known as **WinFrame**. Even since it was released, WinFrame has evolved into MetaFrame and Presentation Server, and nowadays it is called XenApp. VMware introduced server virtualization for x86 systems and transformed them into shared hardware infrastructure, which allowed isolation and operating system choices for application workloads, as well as defined rules for their mobility.

Virtualization – the current times

The reasons for the return of virtualization to industry-standard computing were the same as they were perceived decades ago. The resource capacity of a single server is large nowadays, and it is never effectively used by the installed workloads. Virtualization has turned out to be the best way to improve resource utilization and simplify data center management simultaneously. This is how server virtualization evolved.

Virtualization has a broader scope nowadays and can be applied to different resource levels. The following are a few ideal forms of it:

- Server virtualization
- Storage virtualization
- Network virtualization
- Desktop virtualization
- Application virtualization

Let's look at their purpose and meanings, though in this book, we will focus primarily on server virtualization, and towards the end the focus would shift to desktop virtualization.

Server virtualization

In an ideal situation, a role/application would be installed on a Windows-based server (or any other OS platform), which may have been a blade or a rack server. As and when there was a further requirement, the number of physical servers increased, which also raised the requirement of real estate, maintenance, electricity, and data center cooling. However, the workloads were mostly underutilized, thereby causing a higher **OPEX** (short for **Operational Expenditure**).

Server virtualization software, better known as a **Hypervisor**, allows the abstraction of physical hardware on a server/computer and creates a pool of resources consisting of compute, storage, memory, and network. The same resources are offered to end consumers as consolidated virtual machines. A virtual machine is an emulation of a physical computer, and it runs as an isolated operating system container (partition), serving as a physical machine. At any point in time, there could be one or more than one virtual machine (VM or guest machine) running on a physical machine (host). Its resources are allocated among the VMs as per their specified hardware profile. The hardware profile of a VM is similar to real-life hardware specifications of a physical computer. All running VMs are isolated from each other and the host; however, they can be placed on the same or different network segments.

The equation for hosting the VMs is dealt with by the virtualization stack and the hypervisor. The hypervisor creates a platform on which VMs are created and hosted. The hypervisor ensures the capability of installing the same or different operating systems on the virtual machines, and sharing the resources that are deemed fit by hard profiles or dynamic scheduling. The hypervisor is classified into two types:

- **Type 1**: This is also referred to as a bare-metal or a native hypervisor. The software runs directly on the hardware and has better control over the hardware. Also, since there's no layer between the hypervisor and the hardware, the hypervisor has direct access to the hardware. Type 1 is thin and optimized to have a minimal footprint. This allows us to give most of the physical resources to the hosted guest (VM). One more advantage is decreased security attack vectors; the system is harder to compromise. A few well-known names are Microsoft's Hyper-V, VMware's ESXi, and Citrix's XenServer.

- **Type 2**: This is also referred to as a hosted hypervisor. It is more like an application installed on an operating system and not directly on the bare-metal. The hosted hypervisor is a handy tool for lab or testing purposes. There are many merits of the Type 2 head, given that it's very easy to use and the user does not have to worry about the underlying hardware — the OS on which it is installed controls the hardware access. However, this is not as robust and powerful as Type-1 heads. Popular examples are Microsoft Virtual Server, VMware Workstation, Microsoft Virtual PC, Linux KVM, Oracle Virtual Box, and a few others.

The following diagrams should illustrate these concepts better:

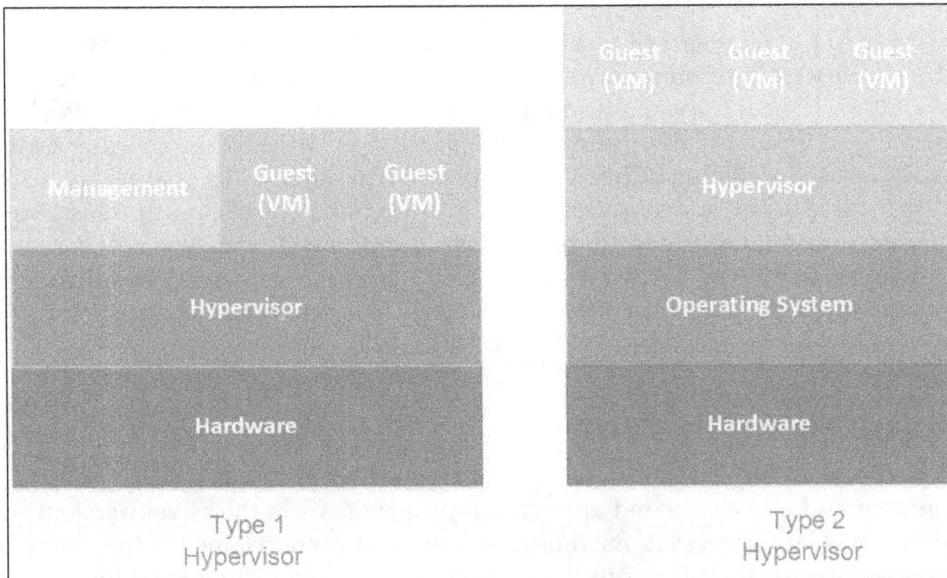

Figure 1-1: Differentiating the Type 1 and Type 2 Hypervisors

Storage virtualization

Storage virtualization allows abstraction of the underlying operations of storage resources and presents it transparently to consumer applications, computers, or network resources. It also simplifies the management of storage resources and enhances the abilities of low-level storage systems.

In other words, it introduces a flexible procedure, wherein storage from multiple sources can be used as a single repository and managed minus knowing the underlying complexity. The virtualization's implementation can take place at multiple layers of a SAN, which assists in delivering a highly available storage solution or presenting a high-performing storage on demand, with both instances being transparent to the end consumer. One closest example is offered with Windows Server 2012 and 2012 R2, called **Storage Spaces**. Storage Spaces enables you to abstract numerous physical disks into one logical pool.

> For more information, refer to www.snia.org/education/ storage_networking_primer/stor_virt (*Storage Virtualization: The SNIA Technical Tutorial*).

Network virtualization

Network virtualization is the youngest of the lot. Now, with network virtualization, it is possible to put all network services into the virtualization software layer. It introduced **Software-defined networking (SDN)**, which uses virtual switches, logical routers, logical firewalls, and logical load balancers, and allows network provisioning without any disruption of the physical network while running traffic over it. So, it not only helps utilize the complete virtual network's feature set, from layer 2 to 7, but also provides isolation and multi-tenancy (yes, cloud!). This also allows VMs to retain their security properties when moved from one host server to another, which may be located on a different network. **Network Virtualization using General Routing Encapsulation (NVGRE)** is a network virtualization mechanism leveraged by Hyper-V Network Virtualization.

Desktop virtualization

Desktop virtualization is a software technology that separates a desktop environment and any associated application programs from the physical client device that is used to access it. Each user retains their own instance of the desktop operating system and applications, but that stack runs in a virtual machine on a server that is accessed through a low-cost thin client. The fundamentals are similar to those of mainframes, which were later inherited by **Remote Desktop Services (RDS**; also known as **Terminal Services**) and finally evolved into true desktop virtualization, called **Virtual Desktop Infrastructure (VDI)**. In principle, VDI is different from a remote desktop, and it is expensive. In VDI, users get their own small VMs from the desktop pool (Windows 7 or 8), whereas in the case of using a remote desktop, it's a shared environment with desktop experience of a Windows Server. In RDS, users can't customize their user experience as with virtual machines or real desktops.

Application virtualization

Application virtualization allows applications to run seamlessly on unsupported platforms, or along with their own older or newer conflicting versions on the same device. There can be two variants for this, namely hosted or packaged:

- In a hosted app virtualization, servers are used to host applications and allow users to connect to the server from their device. A good example of this is RemoteApp.

- In a packaged app virtualization, as the name indicates, an application is packaged with a pre-created environment that assures the execution of the app on a different operating system from where it was packaged. In practice, you may run a Windows XP application on a Windows 7 or 8 desktop without having to customize the app as per the newer platform. A few contenders can be Microsoft App-V and VMware Thinapp (integrated with the VMware Horizon Suite). One more example is Citrix XenApp, but that has been discontinued by Citrix.

Cloud computing – raising the bar for virtualization and automation

Cloud computing is one phrase that has captured everyone's imagination in the 21st century. The debate on the topic of whether cloud computing is really a revolution or an evolution won't settle anytime soon. However, during the last couple of years, there have been multiple new start-ups based around this "new" form of technology, as well as some big players joining the league of service providers on the cloud.

Cloud computing is a way of delivering hosted services. However, it is more than just outsourcing, as it has to offer more flexibility, scalability, and automation. Another interesting aspect is self-service, wherein the consumer can request a VM on the fly, build an app and host it on the cloud, or request an infrastructure. Then the service gets provisioned in a transparent way. Of course, with the abilities, limitations, and possibilities with cloud computing, vendors have coined their definitions for the same, which may send wrong signals to the end consumer.

The **National Institute of Standards and Technology (NIST)** is the federal technology agency in USA that works with the industry to develop and apply technology, measurements, and standards. It published its definition of cloud computing, which has general acceptance among cloud adopters and IT gurus.

The link to download the documentation is `http://csrc.nist.gov/publications/nistpubs/800-145/SP800-145.pdf`

As per NIST, the cloud model is composed of five essential attributes, three service models, and four deployment models.

Attributes

Every cloud model has these five attributes, regardless of the deployment or service models:

- **On-demand self-service**: Consumers can request and get services provisioned without any intervention by IT teams or service providers.

- **Broad network access**: There is support for most kinds of client platforms over the network.

- **Resource pooling**: Providers pool their resources and allocate and remove the allocation to the consumers as per their requirement. This process is transparent to the consumer.

- **Rapid elasticity**: Consumers notice that resources are available in abundance. These can be committed to them as and when required and released accordingly.

- **Measured service**: Optimization and metering of resources for chargebacks.

Service models

Cloud computing services can be availed primarily as per the following service models:

- **Software as a Service (SaaS)**: This service model enables a consumer to use an application hosted by the service provider on the cloud rather than deploy it on their premises. Applications using this service model are messaging and collaboration apps, Office apps, finance apps, and a few others. Google Docs and Microsoft Office 365 are good examples of this model.

- **Platform as a Service (PaaS)**: This service model grants more flexibility to the consumer, and they can upload and deploy a custom app or database. They also get to control the configuration of the application-hosting environment. Cloud Foundry, one of the subsidiaries of VMware/EMC, is a PaaS provider.

- **Infrastructure as a Service (IaaS)**: In this model, the providers offer a subset of infrastructure that may consist of both virtual and, at times, physical machines, with complete control over the OS and installed apps and limited control over the storage and other networking components (host firewalls). There are a few contenders in this league, such as Amazon Web Services, Rackspace, and Microsoft Azure that provide both PaaS and IaaS service models.

Deployment models

A cloud environment setup is determined by factors such as cost, ownership, and location. So, there are different deployment models for different sets of requirements. The following are the deployment models for a cloud-based implementation:

- **Private**: A private cloud is provisioned and dedicated to a single consumer. It can be managed by the organization on premise or off-premise, or it can also be run and managed by a service provider. Microsoft System Center suite of products assists the customer to set up an in-house private cloud with manageability over hypervisors from different vendors, namely Hyper-V, ESXi, and XenServer.

- **Public**: A public cloud is provisioned and shared by many tenants and is managed by the service provider off-premise.

- **Community**: A community cloud is a rare collaborative environment spanning across participants with a common objective. The participants are consumer organizations, and they put their resources under a common pool. This model is managed and maintained by one or more members of the community.

- **Hybrid**: As the name indicates, this is a merger of two or more cloud models, and the usability is decided by the consumer. In principle, the cloud models are unique but connected by proprietary technology, and allow portability of relevant data between the models.

Cloud computing has generated a lot of excitement in recent years. However, it is still less mature than regular outsourcing. Nonetheless, the winning bid from cloud models lies in the concept of automation and self-service, giving the consumer the freedom of choice and manageability.

Moreover, we have seen some new acronyms being coined around service models in recent times, in addition to what has been stated earlier, such as XaaS and NaaS. For example, XaaS, or anything-as-a-service, makes the **SPI** (short for **Software/Platform/Infrastructure**) model converge as demanded and delivers it as a service. NaaS, or network-as-a-service, is based around network virtualization and allows provisioning of virtual network service to consumers. This is just an indication that cloud computing is changing and will be changing the face of IT in the times to come.

Windows Server 2012 – the 2.0 Release

The year 2012 saw one of the biggest platform and system management releases from Microsoft Windows Server 2012 and System Center 2012. The new face of IT and new expectations and requirements from customers made Microsoft develop a mature product in Windows Server 2012, with an objective to "cloud-optimize IT." There were notable advancements made in the hypervisor's third release, Hyper-V 3.0, and the virtualization stack.

Windows Server 2012 was focused not only on virtualization and cloud aspects, but also on improvement of other OS aspects and their integration with Hyper-V, Azure, and VDI. Here are the names of a few important ones: dynamic memory management and smart paging, domain controller cloning, automation with PowerShell 3.0, SMB 3.0 with a Scale-Out File Server over the cluster shared volume (which has found many use cases), Storage Spaces, data deduplication, VHDX, IPAM, NIC teaming, Hyper-V Extensible Switch, Hyper-V Replica (MS's answer to VMware's SRM), and so on.

Windows Server 2012 and Hyper-V Server 2012 swept the market. However, there were still some missing pieces in the puzzle. Windows Server 2012 R2 (Release 2.0) was released in October 2013, with some key improvements to Hyper-V and other aspects. For starters, R2 brought back the forgotten **Start** button to the Metro UI. There were also significant improvements from the networking and storage perspectives:

- **Networking**: With a clear focus and vision for Cloud OS, Microsoft has worked hard towards improvement in this division. New PowerShell cmdlets have been included for Windows networking roles for better automation and control. Windows Azure has progressed from being just a PaaS provider to an IaaS as well. Windows Server 2012 introduced the capabilities of hosting a multi-tenant cloud. With R2, Microsoft took network virtualization further. Windows Azure Pack for Windows Server and System Center 2012 R2 Virtual Machine Manager provide virtual network creation and management.

- **Storage**: Microsoft has been focused in order to provide better manageability and control over storage options for admins. Many noteworthy features were brought in with Windows Server 2012, namely SMI-S, data deduplication, Storage Spaces, iSCSI Target Server, and DFSR enhancements. In R2, we saw classic improvements to the former listed features. Data deduplication is now supported on CSV and proves to be a boon for VDI setups. Storage Spaces allows storage tiers, which facilitate movement of data between faster or slower media, based on the frequency at which the data is accessed. Moreover, the old and reliable replication engine, FRS, along with the VDS provider has been deprecated.

Windows Server 2012 Hyper-V (R1/R2) – the challenger or the new champion?

It has been a late realization, but after a decade of research and understanding customer requirements and post multiple releases, Microsoft has finally come out with a stable, feature-rich, and yet economical virtualization platform in the third release of Hyper-V. The software vendor's goal and vision, as per their data sheet, is to provide a consistent platform for the infrastructure, apps, and data – the Cloud OS. They are almost there, but the journey up to this was an interesting one.

Hyper-V 1.0, released with the Windows Server 2008 64-bit platform, was mocked by the entire IT community, but it was more of a prototype meant to crash. Hyper-V does not come with 32-bit (x86) Windows platforms, though incidentally it was released as an x86 platform in beta versions. The next version was Hyper-V 2.0, which came out with Windows Server 2008 R2. This also marked the end of 32-bit server OS releases from Microsoft. Windows Server 2008 R2 was only available on x64 (64-bit) platforms. The second release of Hyper-V was quite stable and with dynamic memory and feasibility of the Windows GUI. It was well received and adopted by the IT community. However, it lacked the scalability and prowess of VMware's ESX and ESXi servers. The primary use case was cost when setting up an economical but not workload-intensive infrastructure. Windows Server 2012 came out with the third release of Hyper-V. It almost bridged the gap between ESXi and Hyper-V and changed the scales of market shares in Microsoft's favor, though VMware is still the market leader for now. There were many new features and major enhancements introduced to the virtualization stack, and features such as virtual SAN were added, which reduced the dependency of VMs on the parent partition. Windows Server 2012 R2 did not come with a major release but with some improvements and innovations to the third release. However, before we discuss the features and technical requirements of Hyper-V 2012 R2, let's first cover the architecture of Hyper-V.

The Hyper-V architecture – under the hood

It's imperative to know the underlying components that make up the architecture of Hyper-V, and how they function in tandem. This not only helps in designing a framework, but more importantly assists in troubleshooting a scenario.

In one of the previous sections, we discussed what hypervisors are and also that they run either bare-metal or hosted. However, before we proceed further with the terms related to Hyper-V, let's check out what OS Protection rings or access modes are. Rings are protection boundaries enforced by the operating system via the CPU or processor access mode. In a standard OS architecture, there are four rings.

The innermost, **Ring 0**, runs just above the hardware, which is the OS kernel and has high privileged CPU access. **Ring 1** and **Ring 2** are device drivers, or privileged code. **Ring 3** is for user applications. On the Windows OS, there are just two rings: **Ring 0** for the kernel mode and **Ring 3** for the user mode processor access. Refer to the following diagram to understand this:

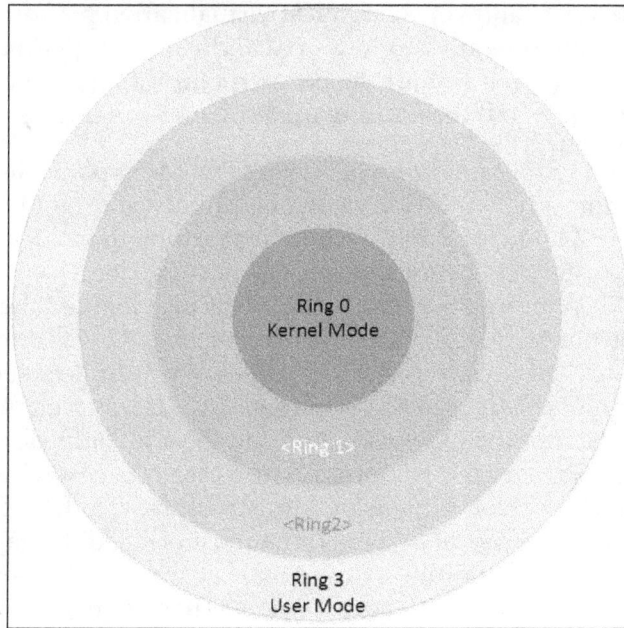

Figure 1-2: OS Protection Rings

Hyper-V is a Type-1 hypervisor. It runs directly on hardware, ensures allocation of compute and memory resources for virtual machines, and provides interfaces for administration and monitoring tools. It is installed as a Windows Server role on the host, and moves the host OS into the parent or root partition, which now holds the virtualization stack and becomes the management operating system for VM configuration and monitoring.

Since Hyper-V runs directly on hardware and handles CPU allocation tasks, it needs to run in Ring 0. However, this also indicates a possible conflict state with the OS kernel of both the parent partition and other VMs whose kernel modes are designed to run in Ring 0 only. To sort this, Intel and AMD facilitate hardware-assisted virtualization on their processors, which provide an additional privilege mode called the Ring-1 (minus 1), and Hyper-V (a Type 1 Hypervisor) slips into this ring. In other words, Hyper-V will run only on processors that support hardware-assisted virtualization. The following diagram depicts the architecture and various components that are the building blocks of the Hyper-V framework:

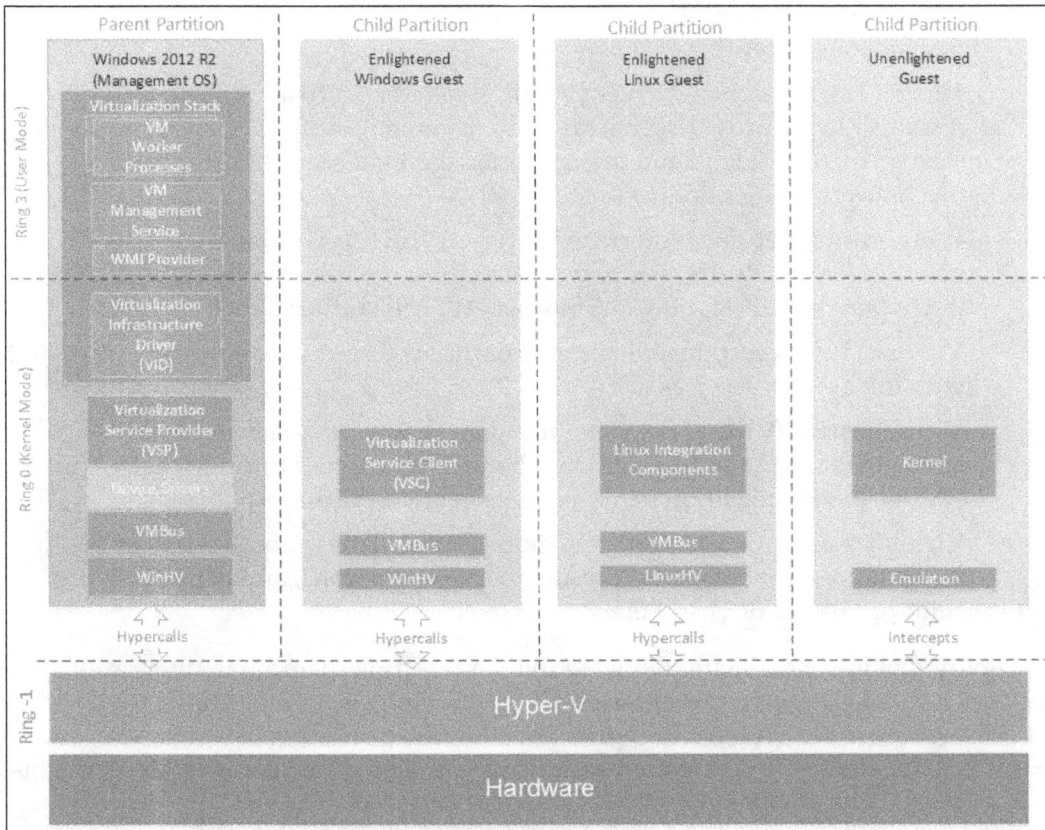

Figure 1-3: Hyper-V Architecture

Let's define some of the components that build up the framework:

- **Virtualization stack**: This is a collection of components that make up Hyper-V, namely the user interface, management services, virtual machine processes, providers, emulated devices, and so on.

- **Virtual Machine Management service (VMM Service)**: This service maintains the state of the virtual machines hosted in the child partitions, and controls the tasks that can be performed on a virtual machine based on its current state (for example, taking snapshots). When a virtual machine is booted up, the VMM Service creates a virtual machine worker process for it.

- **Virtual Machine Worker Process (VMWP)**: The VMM Service creates a VMWP (vmwp.exe) for every corresponding Hyper-V virtual machine, and manages the interaction between the parent partition and the virtual machines in the child partitions. The VMWP manages all VM operations, such as creating and configuring, snapshotting and restoring, running, pausing and resuming, and live migrating the associated virtual machine.

- **WMI Provider**: This allows VMMS to interface with virtual machines and management agents.

- **Virtual Infrastructure Driver (VID)**: Also referred to as VID, this is responsible for providing partition management services, virtual processor management services, and memory management services for virtual machines running in partitions.

- **Windows Hypervisor Interface Library (WinHv)**: This binary assists the operating system's drivers, parent partitions, or child partitions, to contact the hypervisor via standard Windows API calls rather than hyper-calls.

- **VMBus**: This is responsible for interpartition communication and is installed with integration services.

- **Virtualization/Virtual Service Providers (VSP)**: This resides in the management OS and provides synthetic device access through the VMBus to virtualization service clients in child partitions.

- **Virtualization/Virtual Service Clients (VSC)**: This is another one of the integration components that reside in child partitions, and communicates child partitions' device I/O requests over VMBus.

One entity that is not explicitly depicted in the preceding diagram is **Integration Services**, also referred to as **Integration Components**. It is a set of utilities and services — some of which have been mentioned in the preceding list — installed on the VMs to make them hypervisor aware or enlightened. This includes a hypervisor-aware kernel, Hyper-V-enlightened I/O, **virtual server client (VSC)** drivers, and so on. Integration services, along with driver support for a virtual device, provide these five services for VM management:

- **Operating system shutdown**: The service allows the management agents to perform a graceful shutdown of the VM.

- **Time synchronization**: The service allows a virtual machine to sync its system clock with the management operating system.

- **Data exchange**: The service allows the management operating system to detect information about the virtual machine, such as its guest OS version, FQDN, and so on.

- **Heartbeat**: The service allows Hyper-V to verify the health of the virtual machine, whether it's running or not.

- **Backup (volume snapshot)**: The service allows the management OS to perform a VSS-aware backup of the VM.

Here's a glimpse of the first Hyper-V setting for this title. The following screenshot shows the **Integration Services** section from a **Virtual Machine Settings** applet:

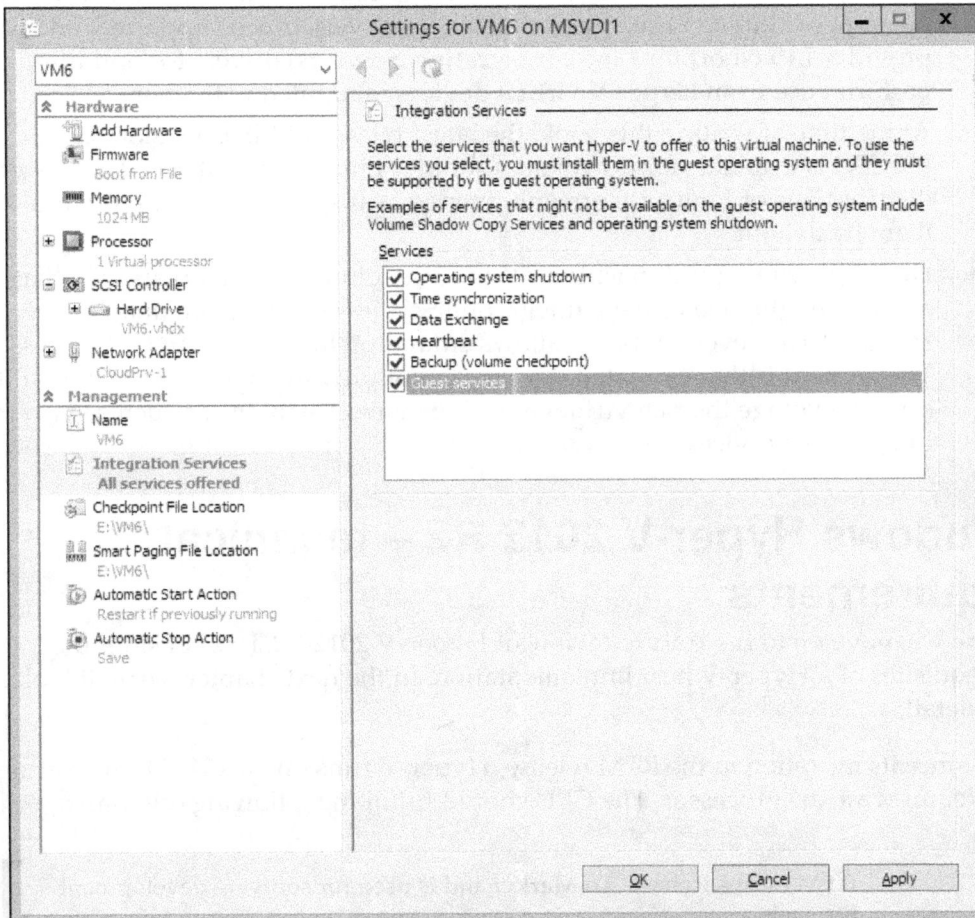

Figure 1-4: Integration Services

Hyper-V allows hosting of multiple guest operating systems in child partitions. Based on whether the VMs have IS installed, we can identify them as follows:

- **Enlightened Windows guest machines**: The Windows virtual machines that are Hyper-V aware are referred to as **enlightened**. They should either have latest Integration components built in by default (for example, a Windows Server 2012 R2 VM is considered enlightened if it is based on a Windows Server 2012 R2 host), or have the Integration Services installed on them. Integration components install VSCs, as stated earlier, and act as device drivers for virtual devices. VSCs communicate and transfer VM device requests to VSP via VMBus.

- **Enlightened non-Windows guest machines**: Beyond Windows, Microsoft supports multiple flavors of Linux (for example, RHEL, SUSE, and a few others), contrary to rumors spread by some communities that Hyper-V does not support Linux. Linux guest machines are very much supported, and MS provides **LIS** (short for **Linux Integration Services**) drivers for optimum performance from Hyper-V virtual devices integrated with them.

  At the time of writing this book, the latest release of LIS is version 3.5. The LIC ISO is available for download for older Linux distributions. The newer distributions of Linux are pre-enlightened as they have the LIS built into them by default.

- **Unenlightened guest machines**: Windows, Linux, or other platforms that are not enlightened or have Integration Services installed are unaware of Hyper-V. However, Hyper-V allows emulation for device and CPU access. The demerit is that emulated devices do not provide high performance and cannot leverage the rich virtual machine management infrastructure via Integration Services.

Windows Hyper-V 2012 R2 – technical requirements

Before we move on to the feature review of Hyper-V 2012 R2, let's consider the prerequisites of a Hyper-V host implementation. In the next chapter, we will look at it in detail.

Ever since its inception in the RTM release, Hyper-V runs on an x64 (64-bit) platform and requires an x64 processor. The CPU should fulfill the following criteria:

> **RTM** means **Release To Market** and is used for software development life cycle.

- **Hardware-assisted virtualization**: These processors include a virtualization option that provides an additional privilege mode below Ring 0 (Ring 1). Intel calls this feature Intel VT-x, and AMD brands it as AMD-V on their processors.

- **Hardware-enforced Data Execution Prevention (DEP)**: This feature is a security requirement from a Windows standpoint for preventing malicious code from being executed from the system memory locations. With DEP, the system memory locations are tagged as non-executable. The setting is enabled from BIOS. In Intel, the setting for DEP is called the **XD bit** (**Execute Disable bit**), and in the case of AMD, it is called the **NX bit** (**No Execute bit**). In Hyper-V, this setting is imperative, as it secures the VMBus to be used as a vulnerable connection to attack the host OS.

Windows Hyper-V 2012 R2 – what it brings to the table

Windows Server 2012 was released with a box full of goodies for admins and architects, but there was room for more. In the previous section, we took a brief look at the features that were rolled out with Windows Server 2012. R2 introduced very few but significant changes, as well as some noteworthy improvements to previously introduced features. In the last section of this chapter, there will be long list of features and gotchas from Hyper-V 2012 R2 compared to VMware's ESXi, but here let's look at the few important features for consideration:

- **Generation 2 virtual machines**: This has been one of the most talked-about inclusions in this release. In Hyper-V 2012 R2, there are two supported generations for virtual machines:
  - **Generation 1**: This still uses the old virtual hardware recipe available from previous Hyper-V releases, emulating the old Intel chipset.
  - **Generation 2**: This introduces a new set of virtual hardware, breaking the dependency on the older virtual hardware. It offers UEFI 2.0 firmware support and allows VM to boot off a SCSI virtual disk or DVD. It also adds the capability of PXE boot to a standard network adapter (doing away with legacy NIC). For now, four operating systems are supported on Generation 2 VMs: client OSes include Windows 8 and 8.1, and server OSes include Windows Server 2012 and 2012 R2.

- **Hyper-V replica**: The disaster recovery solution inside Hyper-V has finally included the change requested by many admins. Previously, administrators could create an offline copy of a VM on a second Hyper-V Server. If the first server failed, as a disaster recovery process, the replica would be brought online. With 2012 R2, it is possible to extend the replication ability to a third replica server, which will ensure further business continuity coverage. Earlier, the replica could only be configured via Hyper-V Manager, PowerShell, or WMI, but now the feature has been extended to Azure, and you need a VMM to push a replica to the cloud.

- **Automatic Virtual Machine Activation (AVMA)**: This feature saves a lot of activation overhead for admins when it comes to activating product keys on individual virtual machines. AVMA allows a VM to be installed on a licensed virtual server and activates the VM when it starts. The supported operating systems on VMs for AVMA are Windows Server 2012 R2 Essentials, Windows Server 2012 R2 Standard, and Windows Server 2012 R2 Datacenter. Windows Server 2012 R2 Datacenter is required on the Hyper-V host for this function. This feature has a few use cases:
    - Virtual machines in remote locations can be activated
    - Virtual machines with or without an Internet connection can be activated
    - Virtual machine licenses can be tracked from the Hyper-V Server without requiring any additional access rights or privileges to the virtual machines

- **Shared virtual disks**: With this exciting feature, admins may give iSCSI, pass-through, or even virtual SAN a miss. This feature, when added to a VHDX file, allows the file to be a shared storage for guest machine failover clustering.

- **Storage QoS**: This is an interesting addition, wherein the admin can specify minimum and maximum loads for IOPS per virtual disk so that the storage throughput stays under check.

- **Linux support**: Microsoft has put a lot of focus on building an OS independent virtual platform for hosting providers. Now, new Linux releases are Hyper-V aware, with Integration Services built in, and for older Linux platforms, MS has released LIS 3.5. This new IS allows a lot many feature additions for Linux VMs, which include dynamic memory, online VHD resize, and online backup (Azure Online Backup, SCDPM, or any other backup utility that supports backup of Hyper-V virtual machines).

Licensing – Windows Server 2012 / Windows Server 2012 R2

Microsoft made an aggressive move with licensing from Windows Server 2012 and maintained the same rhythm with Windows Server 2012 R2. They just came out with two primary editions: Standard and Datacenter. The word "Enterprise" was deprecated from the listing. The other two editions, namely "Essentials" and "Foundation" are a small business with almost no **VOSE (Virtual Operating System Environment)**. Our focus will be on primary editions only, since our agenda is virtualization.

> **POSE** stands for **Physical Operating System Environment**, wherein the running instance is on the physical server. **VOSE** indicates a virtual machine instance.

In principle, the "Standard" and "Enterprise" editions carry the same features as each other. However, the Enterprise version offers unlimited VOSE, and the Standard edition licenses only two virtual machine instances, or VOSE. For each edition, the license covers two processors or sockets (not cores). If the server has more than two processors, then for each edition, one additional license has to be purchased. An additional license purchase for the Standard edition can also provide for two more VOSEs as well as two processor sockets. Take a look at the the following table to understand this better:

Licensing examples	Datacenter licenses required	Standard licenses required
One 1-processor, non-virtualized server	1	1
One 4-processor, non-virtualized server	2	2
One 2-processor server with three virtual OSEs	1	2
One 2-processor server with 12 virtual OSEs	1	6

In the previous section, we looked at one of the new features, called **Automated Virtual Machine Activation (AVMA)**. If the host OS is Windows Server 2012 R2 Datacenter, then this feature can be utilized via the SLMGR AVMA key on the virtual machine in the same way as the KMS client key. The virtual machine can be deployed as a template. As stated earlier, this is only available for Windows Server 2012 R2 Server versions as VMs only.

> This section is not a licensing guide, but an effort to help learners understand the basics. For more information, always contact your Microsoft reseller or refer to http://www.microsoft.com/en-us/server-cloud/buy/pricing-licensing.aspx.

Hypervisors – let's compare again

It's a norm now; over the last couple of years, whenever there has been a discussion over the features of Hyper-V, experts and admins have pitted it against the other two leading competitors, though the focus used to be primarily on VMware. From being mocked at to becoming a serious competitor and now almost at par, the Hyper-V development team has pulled the reins strongly to catch up with VMware's ESXi. The community, which was once split in their opinion, is now adopting and becoming aware of both hypervisors, with experts from the other side honing their skills on Hyper-V. The rise of Hyper-V, in a way, can be attributed to VMware for their vision of server virtualization. The next notable contender in the list of hypervisors is Citrix's XenServer, which went fully open source last year, with its XS 6.2 release. There are similarities, yet there are differences between the products, both from the architecture and feature standpoints. Let's look at some of those striking features stacked together.

Architecture and scalability

The following table depicts the hypervisor's host attributes and configuration limits. These are considered as guidelines for setting up a virtual data center:

	Microsoft Windows Server 2012 R2 / System Center 2012 R2 Datacenter Edition	VMware vSphere 5.5 Enterprise Plus with operations management / vCenter Server 5.5	Citrix XenServer 6.2 Single Product Edition / XenCenter 6.2 management console
Hypervisor type and footprint	• Microkernel Hypervisor (Ring 1) with a footprint of 800 KB • Management (parent partition Ring 0 and 3) with a footprint of 5 GB, including drivers	• Monolithic Hypervisor, with drivers injected (Ring 1 and Ring 0) and a footprint of 155 MB • Management (vCenter Appliance Ring 3) with a footprint of 4 GB	• Microkernel Hypervisor (Ring -1) with a footprint of 10 MB • Management (Control Domain OS-Dom0/ Ring 0) with a footprint of at least 16 GB, including drivers. XenCenter (Ring 3) takes up a minimum of 100 MB disk space

	Microsoft Windows Server 2012 R2 / System Center 2012 R2 Datacenter Edition	VMware vSphere 5.5 Enterprise Plus with operations management / vCenter Server 5.5	Citrix XenServer 6.2 Single Product Edition / XenCenter 6.2 management console
Maximum memory (per host)	4 TB	4 TB	1 TB
Maximum number of processors (per host)	320 (logical)	320 (logical)	160 (logical)
Maximum number of active VMs / consolidation (per host)	1,024 VMs	512 VMs	450 VMs (Windows) 650 VMs (paravirtualized and Linux-based)
Maximum number of virtual CPUs (per VM)	64	64	16
Hot-adding virtual CPU to VM	Partial support by allowing alterations to virtual machine limits	Supported (limitations from VOSE and VMware FT)	Not supported
Maximum virtual RAM (per VM)	1 TB	1 TB	128 GB
Hot-adding virtual RAM to VM	Supported (via dynamic memory)	Supported	Not supported
Dynamic memory management	Supported (via dynamic memory)	Supported (via memory ballooning and transparent page sharing)	Supported (via dynamic memory control, or DMC)
Virtual NUMA support for VMs	Supported	Supported	Not supported
Maximum number of physical hosts per cluster	64 nodes	32 nodes	16 nodes
Maximum number of VMs per cluster	8,000 VMs	4,000 VMs	800 VMs

	Microsoft Windows Server 2012 R2 / System Center 2012 R2 Datacenter Edition	VMware vSphere 5.5 Enterprise Plus with operations management / vCenter Server 5.5	Citrix XenServer 6.2 Single Product Edition / XenCenter 6.2 management console
VM snapshots	Supported — support for 50 snapshots per VM	Supported — support for 32 snapshots per VM, (VMware, as best practice, recommends two to three snapshots.) If VMs are using an iSCSI initiator	Supported — support for one snapshot per VM
Bare-metal/ automated host deployment	Supported (System Center 2012 R2 Virtual Machine Manager)	Supported (VMware's auto-deploy and host profiles make it possible to perform bare-metal deployment of new hosts on a pre-existing cluster. However, it will not perform bare-metal deployment of new clusters.)	Supported (no integrated deployment application however possible via unattended installation over from a network repository)
GPU advancements	Supported via RemoteFX and VDI features in the RDS role	Supported via vDGA and vSGA features	Supported via HDX and vGPU (Kepler Architecture K1/K2) features
Boot from SAN	Supported via the iSCSI target server or third-party iSCSI / FC storage arrays	Supported via third-party iSCSI/FC storage arrays	Supported via third-party iSCSI / FC storage arrays
Boot from USB/Flash	Supported	Supported	Not supported

Supported guest operating systems

The following table shows comprehensively how each hypervisor supports various operating system platforms as virtualized workloads:

> For the most recent and complete list of supported operating systems, please refer to these links:
>
> **Microsoft**: Supported server and client guest operating systems on Hyper-V; http://technet.microsoft.com/library/hh831531.aspx
>
> **VMware**: A compatibility guide for guest operating systems supported on VMware vSphere; http://www.vmware.com/resources/compatibility
>
> **Citrix**: *XenServer 6.2.0 Virtual Machine User's Guide*; http://support.citrix.com/article/CTX137830

	Microsoft Windows Server 2012 R2 / System Center 2012 R2 Datacenter Edition	VMware vSphere 5.5 Enterprise Plus / vCenter Server 5.5 Standard Edition	Citrix XenServer 6.2 Single Product Edition / XenCenter 6.2
CentOS 5.5-5.6, 5.7-5.8, 5.9, 6.0-6.3, and 6.4 - 6.5	Supported	Supported	Supported
CentOS Desktop 5.5-5.6, 5.7-5.8, 5.9, 6.0-6.3, and 6.4 - 6.5	Supported	Supported	Supported
Oracle Linux 6.4 and 6.5 with UEK	Supported (Oracle certified)	Supported (Oracle has not certified any of its products to run on VMware)	Supported
Mac OS X 10.7.x and 10.8.x	Not supported	Supported	Not supported
Red Hat Enterprise Linux 5.5-5.6, 5.7-5.8, 5.9, 6.0-6.3, and 6.4 - 6.5	Supported	Supported	Supported
Red Hat Enterprise Linux Desktop 5.5-5.6, 5.7-5.8, 5.9, 6.0-6.3, and 6.4 - 6.5	Supported	Supported	Supported
SUSE Linux Enterprise Server 11 SP2 and SP3	Supported	Supported	Supported
SUSE Linux Enterprise Desktop 11 SP2 and SP3	Supported	Supported	Supported
OpenSUSE 12.3	Supported	Supported	Supported

	Microsoft Windows Server 2012 R2 / System Center 2012 R2 Datacenter Edition	VMware vSphere 5.5 Enterprise Plus / vCenter Server 5.5 Standard Edition	Citrix XenServer 6.2 Single Product Edition / XenCenter 6.2
Sun Solaris 10 and 11	Not supported	Supported (Oracle has not certified any of its products to run on VMware)	Not supported
Ubuntu 12.04, 12.10, 13.04, and 13.10	Supported	Supported	Supported
Ubuntu Desktop 12.04, 12.10, 13.04, and 13.10	Supported	Supported	Supported
Windows Server 2012 R2	Supported	Supported	Supported (with SP1)
Windows 8.1	Supported	Supported	Supported (with SP1)
Windows Server 2012	Supported	Supported	Supported
Windows 8	Supported	Supported	Supported
Windows Server 2008 R2 SP1	Supported	Supported	Supported
Windows Server 2008 R2	Supported	Supported	Supported
Windows 7 with SP1	Supported	Supported	Supported
Windows 7	Supported	Supported	Supported
Windows Server 2008 SP2	Supported	Supported	Supported
Windows Home Server 2011	Supported	Not supported	Supported
Windows Small Business Server 2011	Supported	Not supported	Supported

	Microsoft Windows Server 2012 R2 / System Center 2012 R2 Datacenter Edition	VMware vSphere 5.5 Enterprise Plus / vCenter Server 5.5 Standard Edition	Citrix XenServer 6.2 Single Product Edition / XenCenter 6.2
Windows Vista with SP2	Supported	Supported	Supported
Windows Server 2003 R2 SP2	Supported	Supported	Supported
Windows Server 2003 SP2	Supported	Supported	Supported
Windows XP with SP3	Supported	Supported	Supported
Windows XP x64 with SP2	Supported	Supported	Supported

Storage considerations

The following table depicts various storage-related features, from both the host and the VM perspective, promoted by each hypervisor platform:

	Microsoft Windows Server 2012 R2/ System Center 2012 R2 Datacenter Edition	VMware vSphere 5.5 Enterprise Plus / vCenter Server 5.5 Standard Edition	Citrix XenServer 6.2 Single Product Edition / XenCenter 6.2 Management Console
Maximum number of SCSI virtual disks per VM	256	60 (PVSCSI disks) and 120 (Virtual SATA disks)	16 (VDI via VBD)
Maximum size per virtual disk	64 TB (VHDX) and 2 TB (VHD)	62 TB	2 TB
4K Native (4K logical sector size) disk support	Supported	Not supported	Not supported
Boot VM from SCSI virtual disks	Supported (generation 2 VMs onwards)	Supported	Supported

	Microsoft Windows Server 2012 R2/ System Center 2012 R2 Datacenter Edition	VMware vSphere 5.5 Enterprise Plus / vCenter Server 5.5 Standard Edition	Citrix XenServer 6.2 Single Product Edition / XenCenter 6.2 Management Console
Hot-adding virtual SCSI (running VMs)	Supported	Supported	Supported
Hot-extending virtual SCSI (running VMs)	Supported	Supported (except 62 TB VMDKs)	Supported (via XenConvert)
Hot-shrink virtual SCSI (running VMs)	Supported	Not supported	Supported (via XenConvert)
Storage migration (running VMs)	Supported, with unlimited number of simultaneous live storage migrations. Provides flexibility to cap at a maximum limit that is appropriate as per for your datacenter limitations.	Supported, with two simultaneous storage vMotion operations per ESXi host. Alternatively, there can be eight simultaneous storage vMotion operations per data store. Also, the feature cannot be extended to VM Guest Clusters with MSCS	Supported, with three simultaneous storage Xenmotion with a cap of one snapshot per VM undergoing migration
Virtual FC to VMs	Supported (four Virtual FC NPIV ports per VM)	Supported (four virtual FC NPIV ports per VM). However, the feature cannot be extended to VM guest clusters with MSCS.	Not supported
Storage quality of service	Supported (storage QoS)	Supported (storage IO control)	Supported (I/O priority on virtual disks)
Flash-based read cache	Supported	Supported	Not supported

	Microsoft Windows Server 2012 R2/ System Center 2012 R2 Datacenter Edition	VMware vSphere 5.5 Enterprise Plus / vCenter Server 5.5 Standard Edition	Citrix XenServer 6.2 Single Product Edition / XenCenter 6.2 Management Console
Flash-based write-back cache	Supported — Storage Spaces	Supported — Virtual SAN	Not supported
Storage virtualization abilities	Supported — Storage Spaces	Supported — Virtual SAN	Not supported
Deduplication of shared storage hosting VMs	Supported (VDI workloads)	Not supported	Not supported

Networking considerations

This table mentions the networking features provided by each hypervisor model, which can help architects design their environments:

	Microsoft Windows Server 2012 R2 / System Center 2012 R2 Datacenter Edition	VMware vSphere 5.5 Enterprise Plus / vCenter Server 5.5 Standard Edition	Citrix XenServer 6.2 Single Product Edition / XenCenter 6.2 Management console
Distributed switch	Logical switch in System Center VMM 2012 R2	vDS (vNetwork distributed switch)	Open vSwitch (the distributed vSwitch is deprecated)
Extensible virtual switch	Supported. Extensions are offered by Cisco, Inmon, and 5nine	Replaceable, and not truly extensible	Supported via Open vSwitch
NIC teaming	Supported. Thirty-two NICs per team utilize dynamic load balancing	Supported. Thirty-two NICs per team utilize the Link Aggregation Group	Supported. Four NICs per bond utilize the Link Aggregation Group
PVLANs (private VLANs)	Supported	Supported	Supported

	Microsoft Windows Server 2012 R2 / System Center 2012 R2 Datacenter Edition	VMware vSphere 5.5 Enterprise Plus / vCenter Server 5.5 Standard Edition	Citrix XenServer 6.2 Single Product Edition / XenCenter 6.2 Management console
ARP spoofing security	Supported	Supported, via an additional paid add-on vCloud Network and security (vCNS) or vCloud suite	Supported
DHCP snooping security	Supported	Supported, via an additional paid add-on vCloud Network and security (vCNS) or vCloud suite	Not supported
Router Advertisement (RA) guard protection	Supported	Supported, via an additional paid add-on vCloud network and security (vCNS) or vCloud suite	Not supported
Virtual port ACLs	Built-in support for extended ACLs	Supported, via traffic filtering and marking policies in vSphere 5.5 vDS	Supported
Software-defined Networking (SDN) / network virtualization	Supported (the NVGRE protocol)	Supported, via an additional paid add-on VMware NSX	Supported, via paid add-on Cloud Platform SDN Controller and SDN plugins

Virtual machine management considerations

The final table depicts the high availability and mobility offerings by each hypervisor platform:

	Microsoft Windows Server 2012 R2/ System Center 2012 R2 Datacenter Editions	VMware vSphere 5.5 Enterprise Plus/ vCenter Server 5.5 Standard Editions	Citrix XenServer 6.2 Single Product Edition/ XenCenter 6.2 Management console
Live migration (running VMs)	Supported. There can be unlimited simultaneous live VM migrations, depending on the data center's capacity	Supported, but limited to four simultaneous vMotions for 1GbE and eight simultaneous vMotions for 10 GbE network adapters	Supported, but one at a time, and in a sequence
Live migration (running VMs without shared storage)	Supported	Supported	Supported
Live migration enabling compression of VM state	Supported	Not supported	Not supported
Live migration over RDMA network adapters	Supported	Not supported	Not supported
VM guest cluster (Windows Failover Clustering) live migration	Supported	Not Supported, as per the vSphere MSCS setup documentation	Not supported
Highly available (HA) VMs	Supported	Supported	Supported
Affinity rules for HA VMs	Supported	Supported	Not supported (workload balancing is a retired feature)
Orchestrated updating of hypervisor hosts.	The **Cluster-aware Updating (CAU)** role service	vSphere 5.5 Update Manager, with additional costs	XenCenter Management with additional license costs

	Microsoft Windows Server 2012 R2/ System Center 2012 R2 Datacenter Editions	VMware vSphere 5.5 Enterprise Plus/ vCenter Server 5.5 Standard Editions	Citrix XenServer 6.2 Single Product Edition/ XenCenter 6.2 Management console
Application monitoring and management for HA VMs	System Center 2012 R2 Operations Manager	VM Monitoring Service and vSphere App HA	Not supported
VM guest clustering (shared virtual hard disk)	Shared VHDX	Shared VMDK	Not supported (Shared VDI)
Maximum number of nodes in a VM guest cluster	64 VM nodes	5 VM nodes	Not supported
Fault-tolerant (Lockstep) VMs	Not supported. As per Microsoft, application availability can be well managed via highly available VMs and VM guest clustering, which is more economical and easier to manage. In the case of stringent requirements, fault-tolerant hardware solutions can be opted for	VMware FT	Not supported

This table lists a subset of feature considerations to bring to your attention how well the aforementioned products placed against are each other, with Hyper-V edging out VMware and Citrix in the race with its recent release. In later chapters, we will look at some of the these features closely.

Summary

This brings us to the end of the first chapter, so let's revisit what we have discussed so far. We saw how virtualization was first perceived and developed, and its evolution in recent times. It is now a building block of cloud computing. We also discussed different forms of virtualization based on resource layering. Thereafter, we looked at the characteristics and models of cloud computing.

In the section after that, we saw how well Windows 2012 was adopted, with the entire new arsenal it had to offer, from the OS and virtualization perspective. Windows 2012 R2 raised the bar further, with remarkable improvements to the original version.

We then took delved into the component architecture of Hyper-V, and discussed how the underlying entities communicate. This gave a little insight into OS protection rings and the place where the hypervisor (aka Hyper-V) gets stacked in the circles of trust (Ring 1). After that, we looked at the new features and improvements delivered with Windows Hyper-V 2012 R2, and how it is going to benefit modern data centers.

Further, we looked a bit into licensing considerations of Windows 2012 R2, from both operating system and Hyper-V standpoints. We closed the chapter with a showdown between Windows Hyper-V 2012 R2, VMware ESXi 5.5, and Citrix XenServer 6.2, and depicted the major areas of comparison. Now it is evident how well Hyper-V is placed in terms of its features and why it is gradually taking over market shares.

In the next chapter, we will delve further into the technical side of things, discussing how to identify virtualization needs and how to plan, design, and deploy Hyper-V in an environment.

2
Planning and Deploying Microsoft Hyper-V

In a review of Windows Server Hyper-V 2012 R2, we have seen so far what runs under the hood. It's time to turn the ignition on and give this masterpiece a test run. Hyper-V has become quite popular and has been adopted as a virtualization platform by many major organizations. Not only that, it is also rocking the charts in India and a few other countries already. Microsoft has delivered the promised stability and resilience of the product and kept it quite economical for all segments.

Now before you get excited and get set to adopt Hyper-V, you must realize the use case. This question should have an affirmative response: does your environment workload support virtualization? The next step is to identify your requirements, prepare the design plans, and work on a road map. After the design plans, deployment and implementation needs to be worked out, entailing all the hardware and software complexities of setting up and configuring the hosts adeptly. All of these phases require attention to details and efforts until you are finally ready with the deliverables.

In this chapter, you will learn about:

- Virtualization goals
- Design considerations
- Installing and configuring a Hyper-V role
- Hyper-V management

Virtualization goals

In the initial chapter, we saw the significance of virtualization in the present IT world. We also discussed the benefits and flexibility the Hyper-V platform offers in terms of resource utilization and management. However, all of these merits do not always justify Hyper-V being installed. There could be one or many predetermined reasons for adopting Hyper-V. These are use cases that contribute to the decision that Hyper-V is indeed a requirement for the enterprise, whether small, medium-sized, or large. The motives could vary from one enterprise to the other but they lay the foundation for the design details.

Let's look at a few scenarios under which firms prefer implementing virtualization.

The consolidation of server workloads

The prime facet of implementing server virtualization is to reduce the physical server count in the data center, which in turn has multifold merits. It brings down the hardware inventory and manageability costs. Thereby, it not only keeps the DC space under check and saves on the real estate cost, but also helps minimize electricity and cooling expenditure. One of the driving factors in adopting virtualization is reducing the carbon footprint (CO_2 emissions), to which many large enterprises are now willingly contributing.

Let's look at the two possible ways to move on from the physical data center to a virtual data center.

Building from the ground up

This is generally for smaller business start-ups or medium-sized enterprises looking for small deployments in remote locations. So it's not a full-fledged migration but a gradual adoption by building virtual servers in-house or at remote locations, thereby assessing the ROI and performance. The hosts can be standalone or highly available, depending on the business requirements and CAPEX the firms are interested in investing.

Physical-to-Virtual migration (P2V)

This process - the torchbearer for data center and server consolidation projects, often referred to just as P2V - was quite the buzzword in the last couple of years. As the abbreviation indicates, it serves to migrate physical server workloads to resilient virtual machines. The process also assists in converting servers hosting legacy applications and translating workloads to run successfully on VMs. After consolidation of legacy servers, the data center benefits quite a bit with respect to space and other expenditures by removing old and cumbersome legacy hardware.

Of course, there's a clause on whether the version of the legacy OS is still supported by Hyper-V. In the previous chapter, we looked at a long list of supported operating systems and also shared a TechNet page that stays updated with current information about the same. However, from Windows Server 2012 Hyper-V onward, Microsoft has stayed keen to extend the virtualization functionality to Linux and older Windows platforms. You may enable compatibility for old-generation Windows operating systems via new Hyper-V cmdlets and there are other workarounds as well, which we will discuss in the next chapter. The caveat is that even though Windows NT and 2000 platforms can be compatible, there's still no extended support for these platforms.

Microsoft had two offerings for P2V conversion, one being System Center 2012 SP1 Virtual Machine Manager and the second being Disk2vhd. However, this feature was deprecated in System Center 2012 R2. MS has plans to introduce it as a separate tool or include the feature in the next release of Microsoft Virtual Machine Converter (MVMC 3.0) during the fall of 2014. There is a workaround, however, and MS has recommended it for System Center enthusiasts. Let's look at the two options closely.

A System Center 2012 R2 P2V workaround

As per Microsoft GA, the 2012 R2 P2V workaround feature was pulled out of VMM 2012 R2 and is to be released as a separate tool. The reason stated is that P2V can be better managed and updated before the new releases instead of waiting for changes in the new releases. The tool still has tests underway and is awaiting release.

As a workaround, MS has advised to keep two parallel versions of VMM running: SP1 and R2. The former can be used under evaluation mode to perform P2V on the desired workloads, and post operation it can be seamlessly imported to a host managed by System Center 2012 R2 VMM. System Center 2012 R2 is beyond the scope of this book but there will be a few tips and tricks along the way.

Disk2vhd

Disk2vhd is another of those brilliant tools from the Sysinternals arsenal. The version available at the time of writing this is book is 2.01, which allows you to convert the local disk of your server/computer to VHD or VHDX. This can later be linked to a VM during creation. The end result is that you have a virtualized instance of your desired machine.

Hypervisor upgrade or migration

In the case of you having your workloads already virtualized with Windows Server 2008 R2 or Windows Server 2012 Hyper-V, the goal would be to raise the bar, upgrade to Windows Server 2012 R2, and avail yourself of the feature's benefits. There are upgrade paths for this, which we will look at later in this chapter.

If you already have virtualized workloads from other vendors (for example VMware) and you finally realize that Hyper-V has more to offer, then it is time to convert your VMware virtual machines to Hyper-V guest machines. There are quite a bunch of utilities and tools available for doing this, from both MS and some third-party vendors. Let's look at a few of them.

Microsoft Virtual Machine Converter

Version 2 for the **Microsoft Virtual Machine Converter** (**MVMC**) utility was launched when this book was being written. This is an excellent tool and can be used standalone, but it has native support for PowerShell, which enables the use of scripting and automation workflows and integration with System Center 2012 R2 Orchestrator. The tool is simple to use and can be invoked in two ways: by a GUI wizard or PowerShell cmdlets.

MVMC assists in migration of virtual machines from ESXi 5.5, 5.1, and 4.1, and converted VMs can be migrated to Hyper-V hosts or Azure. Moreover, it allows Linux VM conversions as well. It has the capability to convert VMware virtual disks to both VHD and VHDX.

> Note that Windows Azure has support for VHD only. VHDX is still not an option! This has been confirmed by technical architects in Azure IT camps and conferences. For more information and inter-conversion of the virtual disk format, refer to http://azure.microsoft.com/en-us/documentation/articles/virtual-machines-create-upload-vhd-windows-server/.

The tool comes with a handy guide and a `whitepaper` cmdlet which will assist you in planning your VM conversion seamlessly and accordingly.

System Center 2012 R2 Virtual Machine Manager

The MS flagship product in VMM 2012 R2 has a built-in feature for performing V2V operations on VMware guest machines and converting them to Hyper-V virtual machines. Although the P2V feature has been removed, the V2V feature still has its significance. VMM provides a wizard-driven interface for the operation, which makes it easier for the Hyper-V admin to walk through the process. However, it is limited when compared to MVMC, which allows support for PowerShell and integration with Orchestrator Automation Workflows, and helps achieve bulk operations in one phase.

Third-party vendors

The prowess of the Hyper-V is evident and vendors realize the same. They have released excellent utilities that allow the customer to perform V2V and provide additional capabilities other than the native MS tool. One such utility is the **Virtual Machine Migration Toolkit**, developed by Microsoft and Veeam. It is available only to MS Partners and MS Consulting Services.

> The following are some other known tools:
>
> - **5nine V2V Easy Converter**: http://www.5nine.com/
>   vmware-hyper-v-v2v-conversion.aspx
> - **StarWinds Converter**: https://www.
>   starwindsoftware.com/converter

These utilities are quite popular in the IT community, as they claim to convert even older Windows platforms that are not supported by MVMC. Also, some of them allow two-way V2V processes.

Business continuity – disaster recovery and contingency planning

A **business continuity plan** or **BCP** is an important decision facet for any organization. The objective is to sustain the organization's processes and operations in the event of any major disruption—which could be a catastrophe or a data-center-wide power outage—during and post the disruption. Organizations are adopting virtualization solutions along with high-end storage replication solutions to this measure. Hyper-V is a one-stop solution for both the disaster recovery and contingency planning perspectives.

Hyper-V Replica is an effective disaster recovery feature built into Hyper-V. It ensures that if, for any reason, the primary site/data center/facility cannot be accessed or is down due to an unforeseen circumstance, the offline copy (or copies) of the virtual workloads can be brought online on an alternate or recovery site. This feature, when enabled, replicates the VMs to a secondary server at a predefined replication frequency, starting at as low as 30 seconds. Another feature added in Windows Server 2012 R2 was increasing the number of recovery points from 16 to 24 which gives you wider coverage. Also, now you can have a tertiary site apart from second recovery site. We will discuss Hyper-V Replica in a dedicated chapter.

Microsoft took DRP to the cloud with GA's announcement of the **Windows Azure Hyper-V Recovery Manager (HRM)** service at the onset of last year. It is now referred to as **Azure Site Recovery**. The service is hosted and managed via Azure, but it seamlessly orchestrates and manages replication of workloads between the primary site and secondary site (local or Azure). The concept is hybrid, as it utilizes off-premise features to manage and orchestrate on-premise private clouds hosted in System Center 2012 SP1 and R2 Virtual Machine Manager.

From the contingency standpoint, Hyper-V ensures high availability when hosting VMs on Windows Failover Cluster nodes. The hosted VMs can be migrated under different factors among the nodes via live migration or quick migration. Hyper-V also incorporates storage migration, which allows VM storage files to be moved from the primary physical storage to the secondary storage or network share.

Finally, an extensive but simplified backup strategy needs to be worked on. Hyper-V has native support for VSS in its Integration Services. A good backup solution, which could be Data Protection Manager 2012 R2 or a third-party solution, can ensure backup of VMs along with the virtualization host and recovery of the same in times of exigency.

Cloud ready!

And we are here now! Enterprises have realized the benefits of virtualizing their server workloads and moving on to the next stage, which would be automation and seamless management via the concept of the cloud. The adoption could be any one of these three: private, public, or hybrid, as realized by the requirement analysis. Microsoft has more experience on the public cloud than most of its competitors, and its offerings on both the private cloud (the System Center suite) and public cloud (Azure, StorSimple, HRM, and so on) are based on customer feedback and feature requests. Each deployment delivery offers a complete solution, covering self-service, orchestration, automation, monitoring, and management.

A virtual desktop infrastructure

Another scenario is when an enterprise wishes to deploy a **Virtual Desktop Infrastructure (VDI)** as a remote desktop access solution. Microsoft used to promote RDS or Terminal Services as a remote desktop solution, but with the release of Windows Server 2008 R2, they have expanded remote desktop access to VDI as well. VDI is an excellent means of providing desktop mobility, where users can change locations and still be able to access their desktop environment, thus giving them the ability to work from anywhere and yet keeping the environment secure at the same time. Hyper-V forms the backbone for this scenario as well.

Design considerations

Now we are aware of the general reasons that enterprises implement virtualization. However, it's not a flag-off and then administrators would implement Hyper-V. There are certain important factors and principles that need to be considered further, for which a requirements' report is drafted. This is followed up by an environment assessment. Thereafter, the design plan is documented and implemented. Let's look at the design principles and then we will see how the solution accelerators and design guides for virtualization can help us assess and conclude the design plans:

- **Availability**: Availability is measured by defined factors to ensure that a solution is redundant and resilient. The objective is to determine how much availability is desired from the solution and how much RTO/RPO is to be sustained. The requirements differ greatly among organizations. For a small organization, the requirement would suffice with a single virtualization host with adequate storage and no high availability. On the contrary, for a large enterprise with a mission-critical application as a virtual workload, the availability should be more than 99 percent. They would employ almost everything from the technology arsenal, starting off with a tiered storage, failover clustering on nodes with high-throughput NICs (LACP teaming), live migration and shared nothing live migration, and finally the Hyper-V Replica configured at a DR site. If we look at the preceding aspects, it's evident that the architect will ensure that there is no single point of failure.

- **Performance**: Virtualization is all about effective abstraction and resource sharing, but not at the expense of declining performance. Any organization, whether small, medium, or large, would never approve a design where performance is given a back seat. This factor receives more attention by architects and can affect the CAPEX quite often. Consider employing blades, rack servers, network switches, or high-IOPS/low-latency storage solutions. All the entities are noted carefully, even if they are not stated in the design requirements.

- **Management**: This is meant to ensure that the solution is properly managed and imbibed in the pre-existing Windows ecosystem. Hyper-V integration with a Windows environment is seamless. However, operability has to be considered, not to mention keeping future expansion in mind and ensuring that the design is scalable. As stated earlier, the Microsoft System Center suite provides extensive management and monitoring abilities from the OS and virtualization perspectives. Hyper-V Manager is an inbuilt console on the parent partition that allows effective control of Hyper-V hosts.

- **Security**: It is imperative to ensure that all the security best practices and measures are followed when conceiving a design. Security policies and changes can easily be applied to Hyper-V as it is fundamentally Windows. Major settings include patching, access delegation, firewalling, antivirus, backup, physical security, and disaster recovery (DR) sites. One more aspect would be to opt for Server Core mode of Windows Server 2012 R2 instead of a full installation, which is beneficial on many accounts, namely a small footprint, a lesser attack surface, and so on.

The four aforementioned principles serve as the basic principles for preparing a design plan. However, the concept can be converted into a more complex form if virtualization is included at every layer and the resources and CAPEX are effectively utilized.

So far, you have understood the objectives of adopting virtualization and considered design principles. The next stage is to determine the functional requirements of the organization and gather necessary information around it; thereafter, perform an assessment of the environment to understand how to take things forward. Microsoft provides documentation and tools, referred to as solution accelerators, that assist admins and architects in assessing and designing effective Hyper-V solutions and several other Microsoft solutions.

Solution accelerators

Solution accelerators (SA) are resources provided by Microsoft to assist IT experts in planning and delivering end-to-end solutions and addressing operations and management challenges. These resources were developed by Microsoft experts and partners based on testing and fieldwork. Many Microsoft customers have also contributed to the progress of these resources. Solution accelerators range from guidance documentation providing best practices and frameworks on technology services and products, to toolkits and automation utilities for assistance in infrastructure development. The list is long, but here are the most popular ones:

- **Microsoft Assessment and Planning Toolkit (MAP)**: MAP is an agentless assessment utility used to provide readiness reports for deployments and migrations
- **Microsoft Deployment Toolkit (MDT)**: MDT is a collection of tools meant for ensuring systematic desktop and server deployments
- **Security Compliance Manager (SCM)**: SCM is used to ensure **Desired Configuration Management (DCM)** as per Microsoft security guidance and industry best practices
- **Infrastructure Planning and Design Guide (IPD)**: IPD is a huge collection of guides that provide best practices and suggestions to plan and design infrastructure for MS products
- **Microsoft Operations Framework (MOF)**: MOF provides a framework and guidance for IT life cycle management

Solution accelerators are handy resources utilized by admins and architects alike to ensure successful IT management. The simplified directions and steps in the documentation do not require you to be very experienced in designing. However, sufficient knowledge of working with and supporting the product is expected.

For Hyper-V planning and implementation, two SAs should suffice, namely IPD (Windows Server Virtualization) and the Microsoft Assessment and Planning (MAP) toolkit. Let's review them.

> *Microsoft Virtualization Solution Accelerators* can be downloaded from https://technet.microsoft.com/en-us/solutionaccelerators/cc197910.aspx.
> The page has connecting links to other SAs as well.

IPD – Windows Server virtualization

Before we tread forward and look at the merits offered by this guide, it's good to be know that the IPD posted on TechNet is an old one and does not document the latest Windows hypervisor platform. At the same time, the principles and best practices recommended still hold weight.

The IPD guide offers step-by-step instructions and a solid strategy for setting up an appropriately sized solution. This is worth a read!

Microsoft Assessment and Planning (MAP) Toolkit

As stated earlier, MAP is an agentless environment assessment utility used to gather readiness data for server and desktop deployments; desktop virtualization, VDI, and Hyper-V deployments and migrations; and other enterprise application reports. For Hyper-V, the focus is on the following:

- **Server consolidation with Hyper-V**: This encompasses the Windows server inventory, VMware ESX/ESXi discovery, and Microsoft workload discovery

- **Private cloud fast track**: This is a further analysis of server consolidation and the verdict on the P2V approach

To plan further with MAP, you will need to perform the following actions:

1. Discover inventory servers and computers (virtualization hosts and virtual machines).

2. Collect performance sample data of the discovered machine over a defined duration.

3. Determine the physical machines that can be consolidated and the number of hosts required to host them.

4. Set up hardware configurations for Hyper-V hosts and storage.

An extensive guide to the tool would be beyond the scope of the book. However, the following are a few screenshots depicting the inventory collection and performance data sampling procedure so as to illustrate the usage and help you with the know-how:

1. Launch the MAP utility and select the **Server Virtualization** track, as shown here:

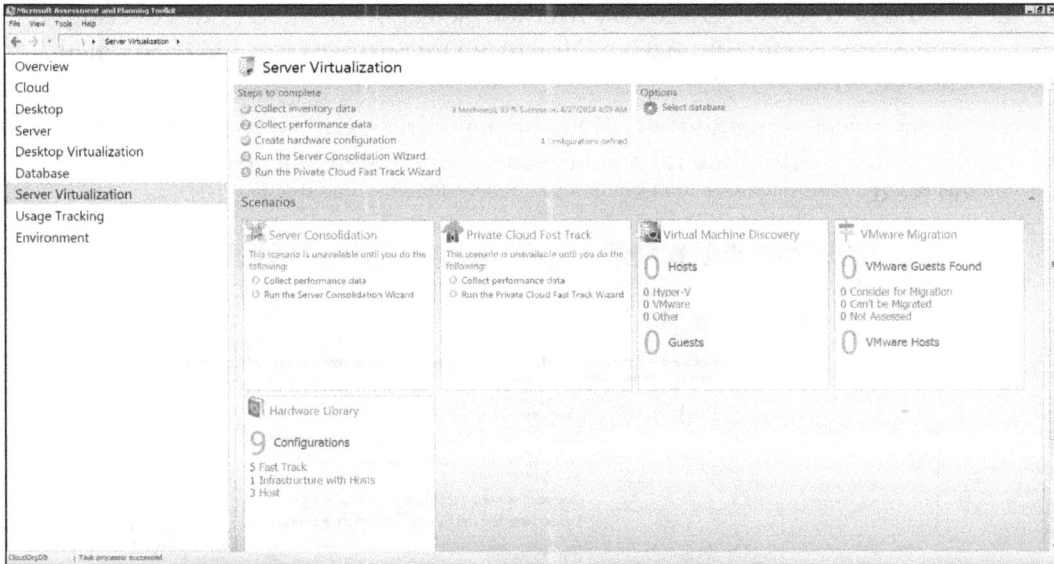

Figure 2-1: MAP – Server Virtualization Track

2. Select **Collect inventory data**. It opens **Inventory and Assessment Wizard**, as displayed in *figure 2-2*.

3. In the **Inventory Scenarios** screen, select the relevant options with respect to the OS platforms and hosted applications. Click on **Next**.

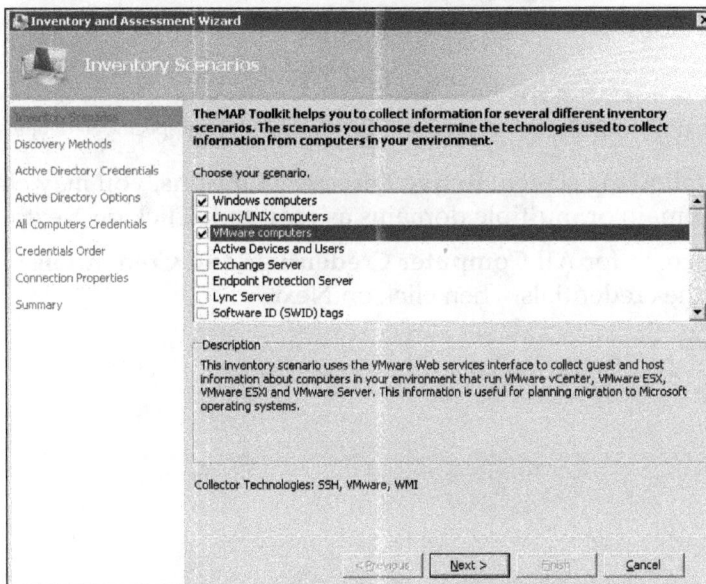

Figure 2-2: MAP – Collect Inventory Data

4. On the next screen, **Discovery Method**, select the method of discovering computers, preferably **Active Directory Domain Services (ADDS)**. Then click on **Next**.

5. As the selected method is ADDS, the next screen will be **Active Directory Credentials**. Enter the relevant details, as indicated in *figure 2-3*, and click on **Next**.

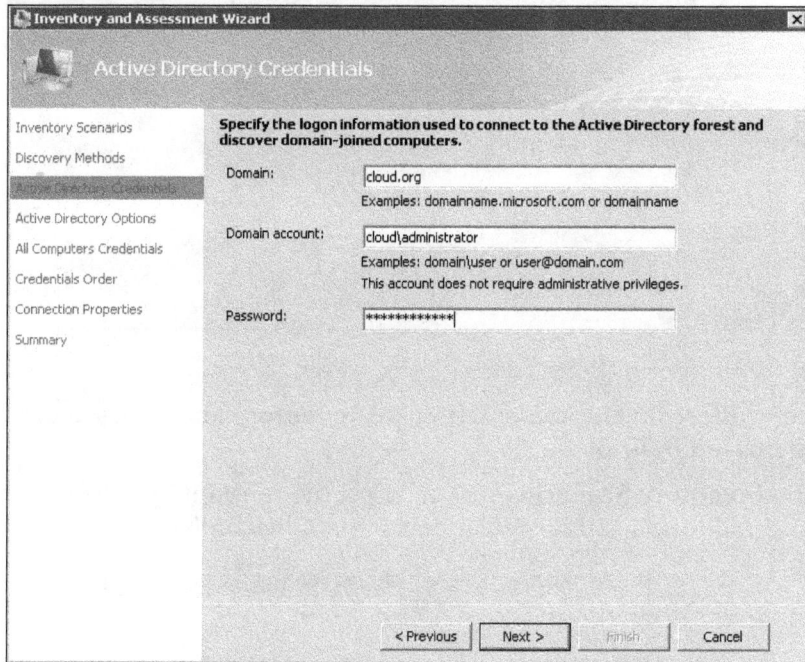

Figure 2-3: MAP – Collect Inventory Data queries AD via specific credentials

6. On the following screen, **Active Directory Options**, you may choose a single domain or multiple domains as required. Click on **Next**.

7. On the screen for **All Computer Credentials and Credentials Order**, update the credentials. Then click on **Next**.

8. On the **Summary** page, click on **Finish**.

9. Once the wizard completes, it presents you with a **Data Collection** dashboard, as shown in *figure 2-4*:

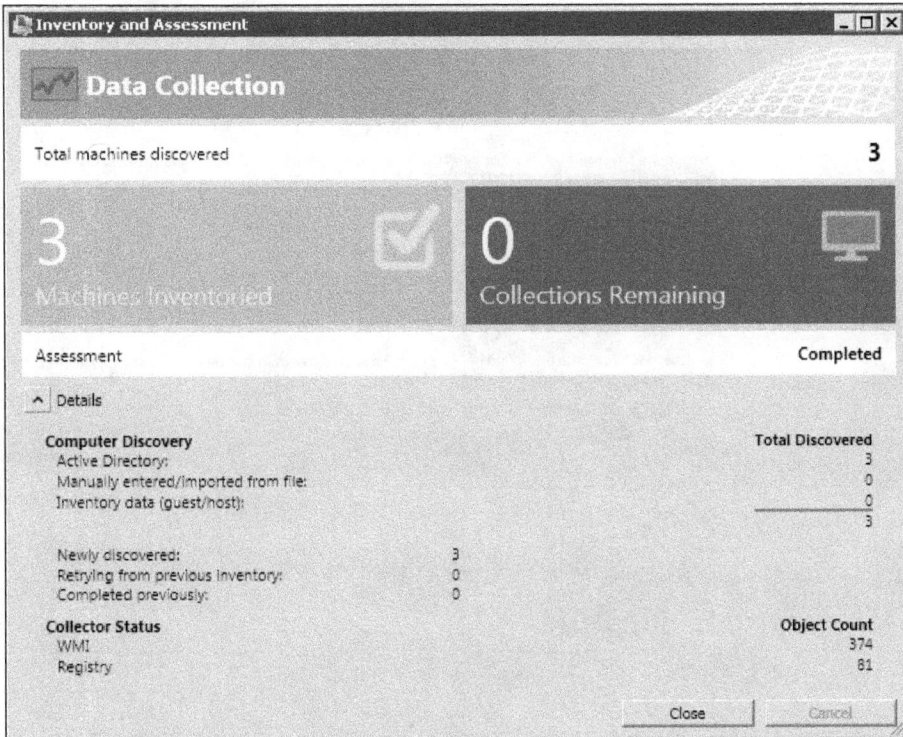

Figure 2-4: MAP – Machine Collection and Inventory Dashboard

Once you have discovered the computers, you may initiate a performance data capture against the selected discovered computers. To invoke the wizard shown in *figure 2-5*, select **Collect Performance Data** on the **Server Virtualization** track page.

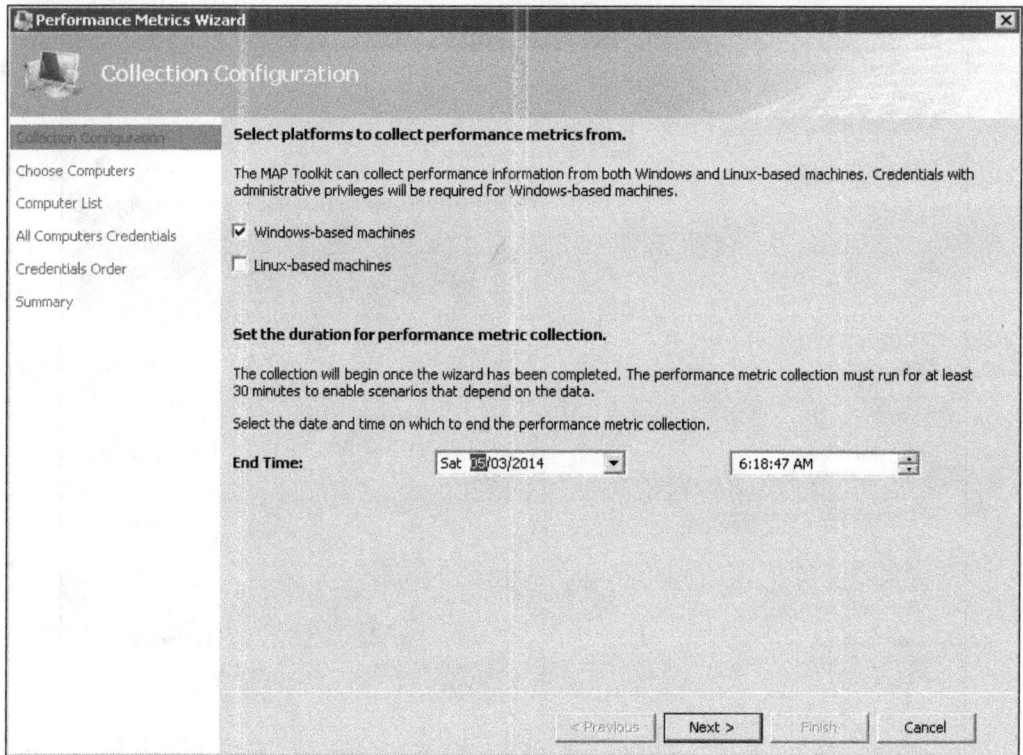

Figure 2-5: MAP – Performance Data Collection

Installing and configuring Hyper-V role

After all the design considerations and brainstorming, we are ready to roll out our new Hyper-V host. In this section, we will look at both building a fresh Windows Server Hyper-V 2012 R2 host and options for upgrading the older Hyper-V hosts. The process requires reviewing technical requirements for Hyper-V, which we looked at briefly in *Chapter 1, Introducing Release 2.0*. We will consider the Hyper-V checklist before installing the Hyper-V role. It is imperative to understand and follow the road map because if any aspect is missed, the admins have to backtrack and understand what the missed points are. Also, we will look at the differences between a full and a Server Core installation and their configuration.

Installing a new Hyper-V host

We will first look at the process of building a fresh Windows Server 2012 R2 Hyper-V host. The installation is quite similar to a standard Windows installation and the groundwork done prior to it. Let's look at the prerequisites before proceeding with the hypervisor installation.

Hardware prerequisites

The hardware prerequisites must be reviewed and confirmed before proceeding with the Hyper-V deployment. This is indispensable because unless the underlying platform supports and is certified to run Windows Server 2012 R2, the deployment will eventually fail. Any hardware or software has to clear stringent testing at Microsoft's labs to be certified to load and run Hyper-V and be maintained as a workload. At the *Windows Server Catalog* website (http://www.windowsservercatalog.com/), you may check whether your server or mission-critical application meets the conditions to be certified for the Windows Server 2012 R2 logo. Let's look at the underlying hardware requirements and their recommended configuration from a Hyper-V standpoint.

Processor requirements

Windows has progressed and migrated from 32-bit addressing to an x64 (64-bit) platform in the last decade. It was until Windows Server 2008 that Microsoft released both versions, x86 (32-bit) and x64. With Windows Server 2008 R2, Microsoft has discontinued x86 releases for server operating systems. Since its inception in the Windows Server 2008 RTM release, Hyper-V runs on an x64 (64-bit) platform and requires an x64 processor. However, as we discussed in *Chapter 1*, *Introducing Release 2.0*, the hypervisor (Hyper-V) brings a change to OS privilege levels, and adds another mode (Ring 1) under the Kernel.

Also keeping licensing and better performance for low-latency applications in mind, it is recommended to opt for processors with multiple cores. A **core** is a single physical processor unit and hyper-threading enabled. Each core is divided into one or two logical processors. Windows Server 2012 and R2 have native support for up to 320 logical processors, thereby allowing scaling up of workloads.

Another interesting feature is **Second-level Address Translation (SLAT)**. The requirement for this performance enhancement is optional for Windows Server Hyper-V 2012 R2, but is mandatory for Windows 8 Client Hyper-V. The guest physical memory is a subset of the host virtual memory. In an ideal situation, there are two stages of page address translation: one at the guest physical memory, and one at the host virtual memory. This feature reduces the additional lookup and treats a guest physical lookup as a host virtual lookup, thereby reducing processor and memory overhead considerably.

Let's look at the two primary processor vendors' CPU offerings from a virtualization perspective:

- **Intel processors**:
  - x64 processor architecture support
  - Intel VT-x for hardware-assisted virtualization support
  - The Execute Disable bit (XD bit) for hardware-enforced **Data Execution Prevention (DEP)** support
  - **Extended Page Tables (EPT)** for **Second-level Address Translation (SLAT)** support

- **AMD processors**:
  - x64 processor architecture support
  - AMD-V for hardware-assisted virtualization support
  - The No Execute bit (NX bit) for hardware-enforced **Data Execution Prevention (DEP)** support
  - **Rapid Virtualization Indexing (RVI)** or **Nested Page Tables (NPT)** for SLAT support

To identify the preceding information and logical-physical processor mapping, you may use another handy utility from Sysinternals, called `Coreinfo.exe`. The following screenshot shows what is seen when identifying whether the installed processor supports SLAT or not. As is apparent from this screenshot, the utility should be invoked when the hypervisor is not running on the host:

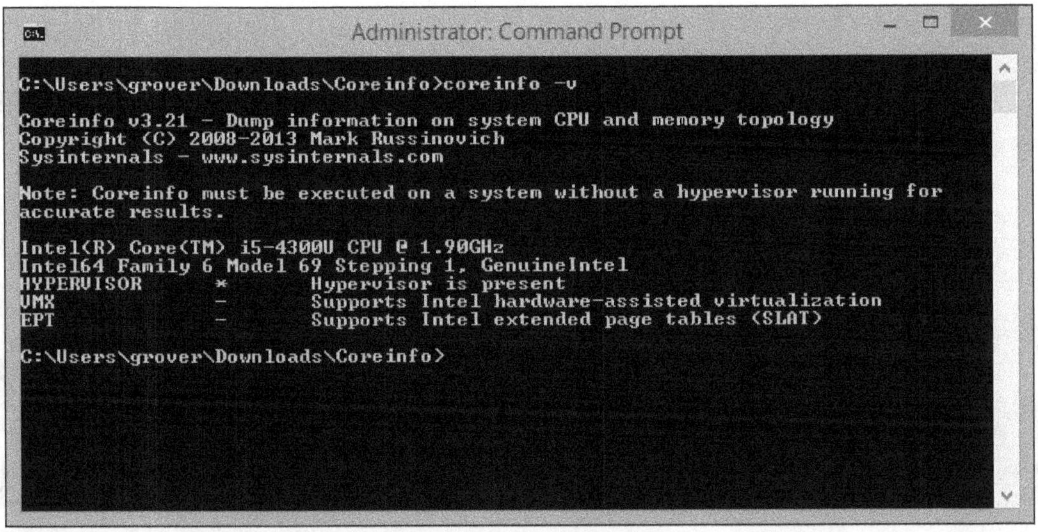

```
Administrator: Command Prompt                         _  □  ×

C:\Users\grover\Downloads\Coreinfo>coreinfo -v

Coreinfo v3.21 - Dump information on system CPU and memory topology
Copyright (C) 2008-2013 Mark Russinovich
Sysinternals - www.sysinternals.com

Note: Coreinfo must be executed on a system without a hypervisor running for
accurate results.

Intel(R) Core(TM) i5-4300U CPU @ 1.90GHz
Intel64 Family 6 Model 69 Stepping 1, GenuineIntel
HYPERVISOR      *       Hypervisor is present
VMX             -       Supports Intel hardware-assisted virtualization
EPT             -       Supports Intel extended page tables (SLAT)

C:\Users\grover\Downloads\Coreinfo>
```

Figure 2-6: Coreinfo utility

Memory requirements

RAM is one of the crucial resources that ought to be considered properly if you are
planning a high VM density on the Hyper-V host. Hyper-V is now equipped with
excellent memory management techniques like its closest competitor. Dynamic
memory has improved in Windows Server 2012 and takes care of startup RAM
limitations with the minimum memory setting, which enables Hyper-V to reclaim
the unused RAM that has been assigned to virtual machines. Along with this,
Windows Server 2012 also introduced **smart paging**, which assists in VM restart
operations. Minimum memory helps increase VM density but puts a pressure on
RAM availability. A VM startup or restart operation requires additional RAM. Under
normal running, a VM would have lesser RAM committed to it than its startup RAM.
A restart operation would require additional RAM. In a situation where there's no
physical RAM available to address this request, Hyper-V utilizes smart paging.
Dynamic memory and smart paging are used effectively with VDI.

To minimize the impact of smart paging on performance, Hyper-V uses it only when all of the following occur:

- The virtual machine is being restarted
- No physical memory is available
- No memory can be reclaimed from other virtual machines that are running on the host

Hyper-V smart paging is not used when:

- A virtual machine is being started from an off state (instead of a restart)
- Oversubscribing of memory for a running virtual machine would result
- A virtual machine is failing over in Hyper-V clusters

Memory management techniques assist in effective VM consolidation and memory utilization but we must always consider the option of scaling up the workloads. Windows Server 2012 allows a maximum size of 4 TB RAM, which provides enough room for expansion. Consider the trade-offs between performance and amount of RAM, and plan your CAPEX accordingly for a better ROI.

Network requirements

The networking aspect has received quite a lot of improvements in both releases of Windows Server 2012. Prior to Windows Server 2012, the customer had to depend on the hardware vendor for a load balancing NIC teaming solution. Designing a solution ended up in a complex affair, with cables making it uneconomical and inflexible. To add to the woes, during those days, Microsoft didn't even support NIC teaming. In the past, designing a granular, networked approach for the Windows Server 2008 R2 failover cluster was a cumbersome job, with one for each function, cluster traffic, live migration, management, and backup.

Microsoft has introduced NIC teaming from Windows Server 2012 onwards. The emergence of converged networking has simplified setting up networks, regardless of blade or rack servers. The former gives you more flexibility and control over setting up networks. To keep matters simple even in designing a cluster network, you may keep all the networks on the same **Converged Network Adapter (CNA)**, with only a single cable for both the storage and the network. You may keep the networking design a bit complex by following the segregation principle of retaining separate networks for different functions. We will cover more on this in later chapters.

Storage requirements

When it comes to considering design options for storage, you may be spoilt for choices such as local, DAS over SAS cable, iSCSI and FC. Hyper-V can utilize all the storage options available for Windows Server, and with the addition of SMB 3.0 to the shopping list, it becomes difficult to make the right choice. The deciding factor is to identify the workloads and their dependence on storage performance. Before selecting the storage, consider the IOPS, latency, and throughput depending on the workload hosted on the host.

For a higher **Input/Output Per Second (IOPS)**, you have to consider more read/write heads in your SAN and select the drives with higher RPM. A better but expensive alternative would be SSD or flash storage. In extensive designs, work on storage tiering, which keeps both costs and performance under check.

Software prerequisites

After deliberations on hardware requirements, let's proceed to the software bit and discuss the operating system and hypervisor. In *Chapter 1, Introducing Release 2.0*, we discussed that Microsoft has taken on licensing with an aggressive approach and ruled out the Enterprise edition from the Windows stable. So, as per the new licensing strategy, Windows Server 2012 and Windows Server 2012 R2 are available in two options:

- Standard Edition; x64 and two VOSE
- Datacenter Edition; x64 and unlimited VOSE

Fundamentally, there are no technical differences between the two primary editions as both possess the same technical features. The only difference is in the number of **Virtual Operating System Environment (VOSE)** or virtual instances they can host. This makes the Datacenter Edition the ideal choice for an organization if they are looking at enterprise-wide virtualization. Of course, you can extend the VOSE licensing for the Standard Edition by purchasing an additional license, as discussed in the previous chapter.

There's also a free Hyper-V Server 2012 R2 Edition offered by Microsoft. This product, in spite of being free, has all the features that would enable you to place it in high-performance scenarios. It is, in fact, a Server Core edition with the Hyper-V role along with supporting components and features such as failover clustering, a Windows driver model, and of course a minimal footprint. More than just a free trial software, organizations opting for server consolidation where no new Windows Server licenses would be required or hosting Linux guest machines or even VDI, should prefer the free edition. It does not limit you with the number of virtual machines (VOSE) on the host.

> The Hyper-V 2012 R2 free edition can be downloaded from https://www.microsoft.com/en-us/evalcenter/evaluate-windows-server-2012-r2.

Windows Server installation modes

A Windows installation gives you two installation modes, namely **server with a GUI (full installation)** and **Server Core installation**. The former is the standard Windows graphical user interface OS platform and Server Core in a command-line installation. The Server Core has a much smaller footprint, and is the recommended OS of choice for Hyper-V deployments due to three major benefits: it acquires less disk pace, there is a lesser attack surface, and there are less servicing requirements.

Server Core can be used on any major infrastructure roles apart from Hyper-V, unlike the free Hyper-V Server, which is a Server Core offering strictly with Hyper-V abilities only. Server Core has a footprint that is 4 GB less than a full installation, and does not have Server Manager or MMC for management purposes. It can be managed locally by PowerShell cmdlets or remotely from other servers via Server Manager, RSAT, and PowerShell. Also, from Windows Server 2012 onwards, you can easily switch between a server with a GUI and the Server Core mode.

There's another mode in Windows Server 2012 for installation, called the **Minimal Server Interface (MSI)** or MiniShell. It can be called a trade-off between full and Server Core modes. The MSI can be referred to as a scaled-down GUI mode, with features such as Internet Explorer 10, Windows Explorer, the start screen, and the desktop not installed. The MMC, Server Manager, and some control panel applets still make it convenient to manage like a full installation. This mode is not available as a default installation option, but is configured via Server Manager or PowerShell. The MSI has a 300 MB lesser footprint size than a full installation. Let's look at the prime dissimilarities among the modes, as shown in this table:

	Server with a GUI	**Minimal Server Interface**	**Server Core**
Footprint	Around 10 GB	300 MB less than full installation	4 GB less than full installation
Server Manager	Yes	Yes	No
Windows Explorer / desktop experience	Yes	No	No
MMC	Yes	Yes	No
PowerShell	Yes	Yes	Yes

System requirements

We have considered the resource requirements for Hyper-V from a solution's perspective. Let's now look at the minimum system requirements, as published on TechNet and Microsoft Support, to have a vanilla Windows Server Hyper-V 2012 R2 boot up and run. Of course, folks would want more from Hyper-V than to just start up and stay on. Refer to the following table for Windows Server 2012 R2 system requirements:

Resources	Minimum requirements
Processor	1.4 GHz / x64
Memory	512 MB (preferably 2 GB)
Disk space	32 GB (a few GB extra, keeping the page file math in mind)
Page file	System-managed
Keyboard/mouse	Preferred
DVD drive	Preferred
Super VGA	Preferred

Hyper-V installation best practices

To ensure that everything falls in place as planned, it's always good to have a defined checklist of best practices rolled out prior to the implementation. The following is a list of gotchas and suggestions that you should follow while deploying your Hyper-V hosts:

- **BIOS/firmware**: Ensure that the BIOS/firmware of your blade or rack servers and devices is updated to the latest version.

- **Host OS**: Preference should be given to Server Core or the Minimal Server Interface, knowing their benefits — being lighter and having a lesser attack surface. However, you may start off with a server with a GUI, as it's easier to manage and configure. Once you have the desired configuration, it can be seamlessly switched to the other two modes. It can also be considered a learning curve. By the time you really get comfortable with Server Core, you may use the old-school Windows GUI.

- **Drivers**: The same rule applies here. Install the latest version of the required drivers.

- **Windows update**: Keep your Hyper-V host up to date with the latest Windows and Hyper-V hotfixes. If the host (or hosts) is clustered, ensure that the cluster hotfixes are checked and applied accordingly:

  - *Hyper-V: Update list for Windows Server 2012 R2:*
    `http://social.technet.microsoft.com/wiki/contents/articles/20885.hyper-v-update-list-for-windows-server-2012-r2.aspx`

  - *Recommended hotfixes and updates for Windows Server 2012 R2-based failover clusters:*
    `http://support.microsoft.com/kb/2920151`

  - *Hyper-V: Update list for Windows Server 2012:*
    `http://social.technet.microsoft.com/wiki/contents/articles/15576.hyper-v-update-list-for-windows-server-2012.aspx`

  - *Recommended hotfixes and updates for Windows Server 2012-based failover clusters*: `http://support.microsoft.com/kb/2784261`

- **NIC / Networks / NIC teaming**: Install and configure the network cards, and set up NIC teaming as deemed important by your design.

- **MPIO**: Install the multipath I/O feature, if required.

- **Page file**: The page file should be set to `System Managed` as per the Hyper-V product group, as stated in the MS support article:

  How to determine the appropriate page file size for 64-bit versions of Windows:
  `http://support.microsoft.com/kb/2860880`

- **Host name and domain**: Modify the host/computer name and join it to the domain. This applies to cluster deployments and is recommended for independent hosts.

- **Failover clustering**: Install the feature if it is deemed as required as per the design and update as stated previously.

- **Roles**: Install the Hyper-V role and enable Remote Desktop for management.

- **Antivirus**: Install and configure the antivirus software on the host, and exclude the necessary Hyper-V locations. Go to `http://social.technet.microsoft.com/wiki/contents/articles/2179.hyper-v-anti-virus-exclusions-for-hyper-v-hosts.aspx` to see the list of locations.

- **Agents**: Finally, you may install and enable the System Center agents for management, backup, the forefront, and so on.

The preceding suggestions can be followed at will and even if you have any bare-metal deployment enabled, the aforementioned points can still prove helpful.

Setting up Windows Server 2012 R2

After all the virtualization realization, identification of goals, requirements analysis, planning and designing, and considering the suggestions for implementation, it is time to install the Windows Server 2012 R2 platform and implement Hyper-V. The process of the Windows setup is standard and straightforward, and you get to select from two options: server with a GUI or Server Core. The recommended and preferred mode is Server Core, or Minimal Server Interface. However, to keep the discussion simple, we will start off with a GUI, and later show the process of conversion from one mode to the other and vice versa:

1. Boot a Windows Server 2012 R2 product DVD or USB flash drive with the Windows setup files, like this:

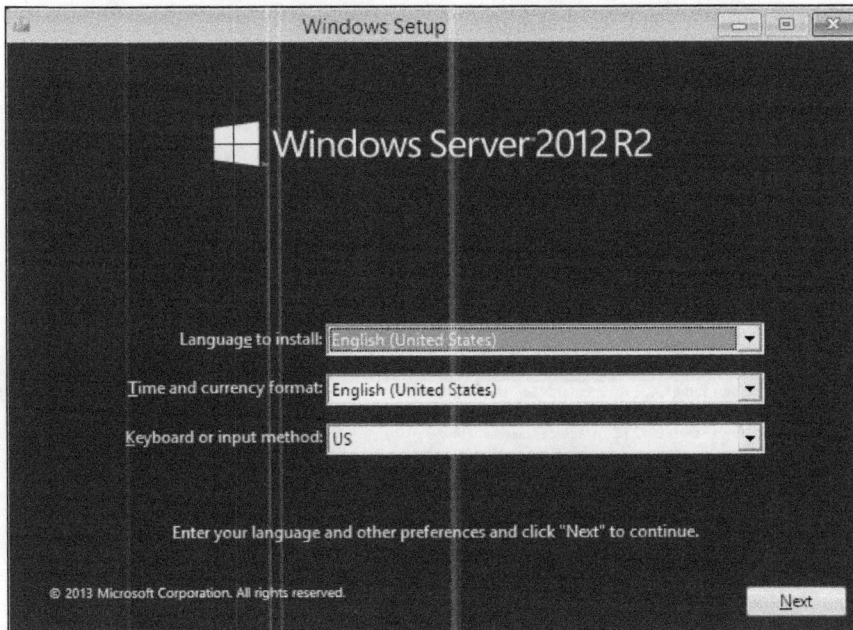

Figure 2-7: Windows Setup

2. On the Windows Server 2012 R2 setup screen (*figure 2-7*), click on **Next**. Then, as shown in the following screenshot, click on **Install now**:

Figure 2-8: Windows Setup

3. On the operating system selection screen, we have two decisions to make: the OS edition and the OS installation mode. Select the server with a GUI option, as discussed earlier.

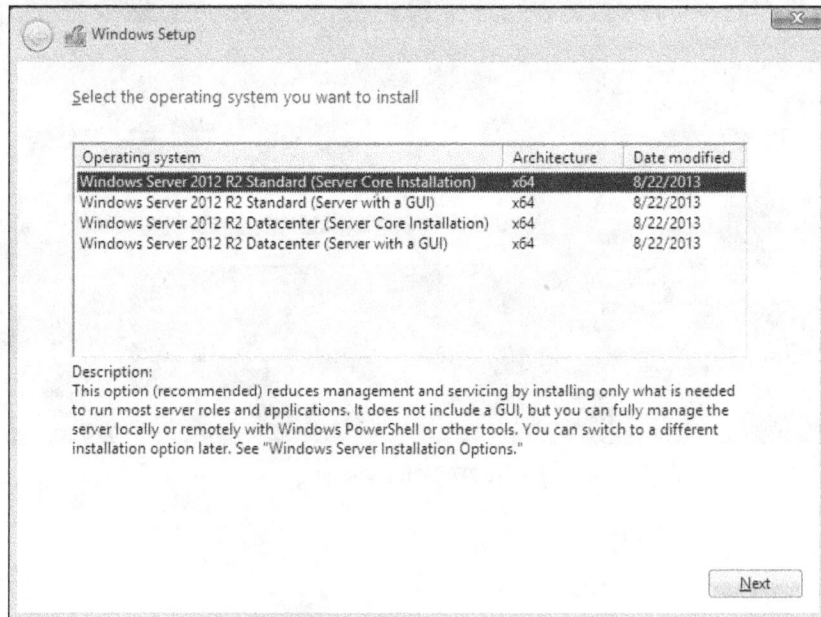

Figure 2-9: Windows Installation Modes

4. Follow the process of Windows installation and make the date and time settings.

Once your Windows installation has completed successfully, follow the best practices as stated earlier, beginning with driver installation and going ahead with the rest of the steps. Once the Windows Server 2012 R2 host is ready, we can proceed with Hyper-V or any other role setup. Post the basic configuration, you may convert the full installation to a Minimal Server Interface or Server Core, and vice versa. You may follow the process once you have configured Hyper-V on your server as well.

Installing Hyper-V role

Hyper-V is not an operating system installation option and is not enabled by default. Unless you were deploying free Hyper-V 2012 R2, you need to install it as other roles of Windows. We can install roles by three methods: Server Manager, Windows PowerShell cmdlets, and `DISM.exe`.

Server Manager

Server Manager is the **Graphical Management Interface** for the Windows Server platform. It's a quite intuitive and simplified way of managing server configuration and adding roles and features to it as per the requirement. Introduced in Windows Server 2008, it reminds you of the initial configuration tasks screen of Windows 2003.

Server Manager is a very convenient way of installing server roles and features, and is informative for any dependent features or management tools to be installed along with the role.

The following is the process, with screenshots for a better illustration:

1. Select **Add roles and features** from **Dashboard** or the **Manage** menu in the top-right corner. This opens the **Before you Begin** screen. Click on **Next**.

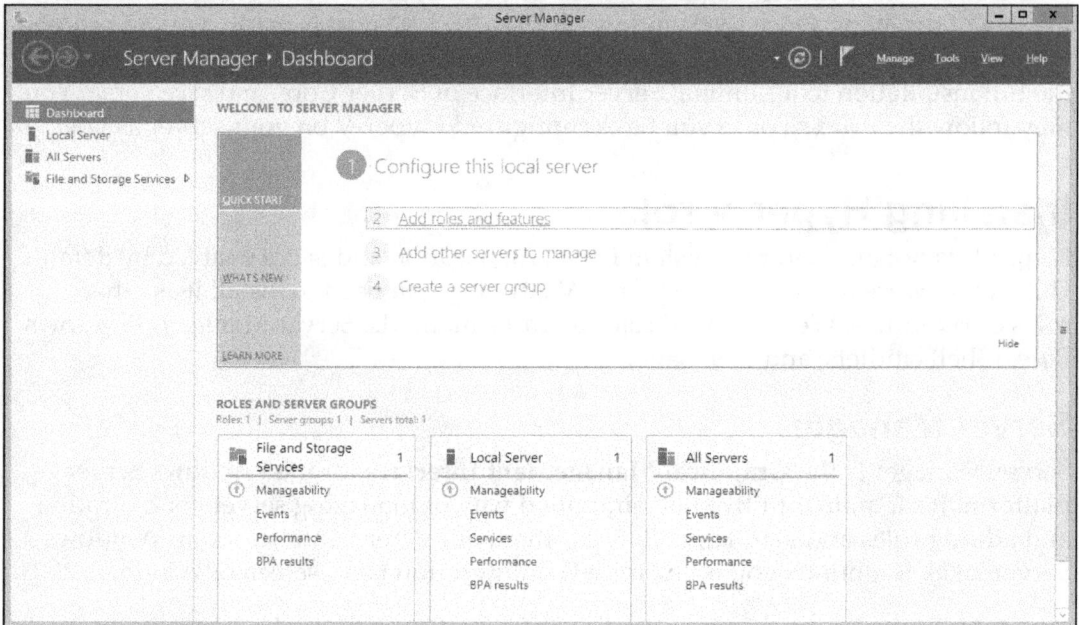

Figure 2-10: Server Manager – Add roles and features

2. Select **Role-based or featured-based installation**, as shown in *figure 2-11*, and click on **Next**:

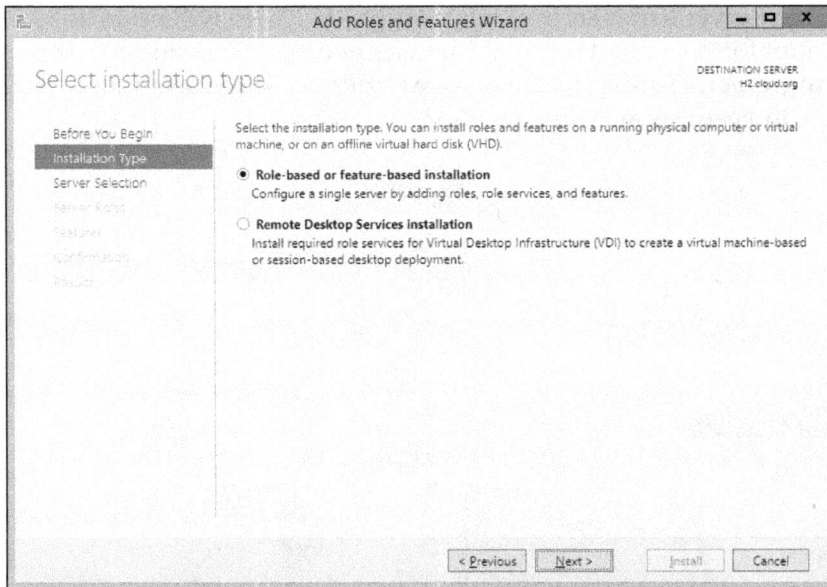

Figure 2-11: Role-based or feature-based installation

3. Select the destination server from the **Server Selection** screen, where you intend to install the Hyper-V role. This can be the local server or any server imported in the all servers pool. Click on **Next**.

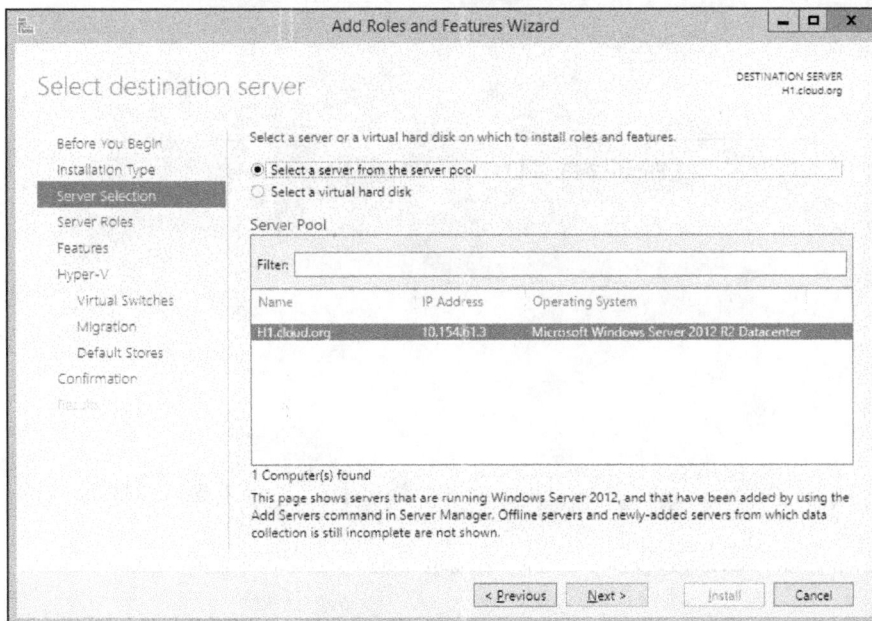

Figure 2-12: Server Selection

4. On the **Server Roles** screen, select **Hyper-V**. There will be an automatic prompt for selecting **Hyper-V Management Tools**, including **Hyper-V GUI Management Tools** and **Hyper-V Module for Windows PowerShell**. Click on **Add Features** and then on **Next**.

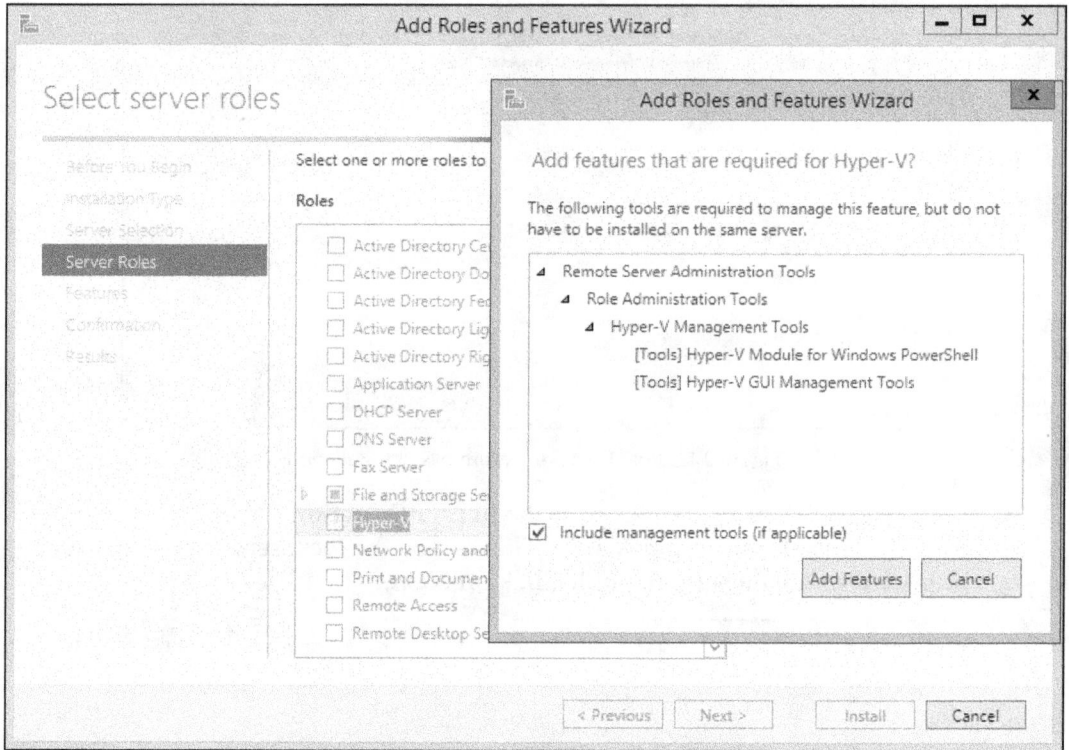

Figure 2-13: Add Hyper-V Management Tools

5. The next page is the default options screen for Hyper-V. The first is
   Create Virtual Switches. You can select now or configure it after the role
   installation. We will discuss how to modify the default options in the later
   section of this chapter.

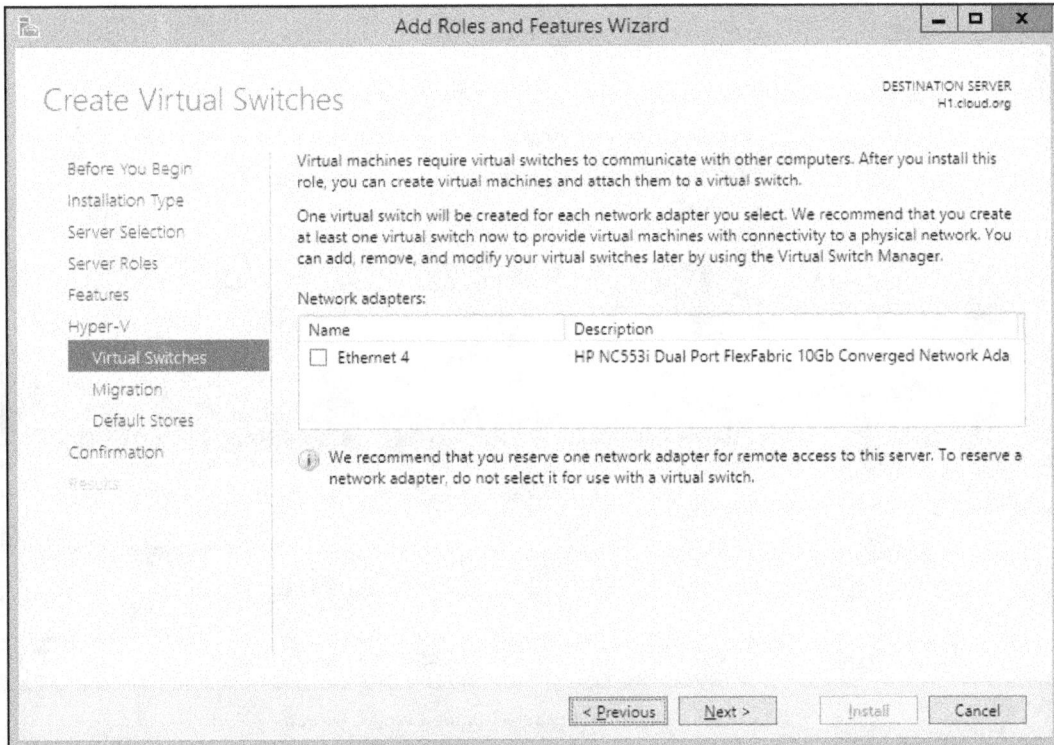

Figure 2-14: Default Options – Virtual Switch

6. **Virtual Machine Migration** is the next page for host defaults. The advice is the same as for the previous screen.

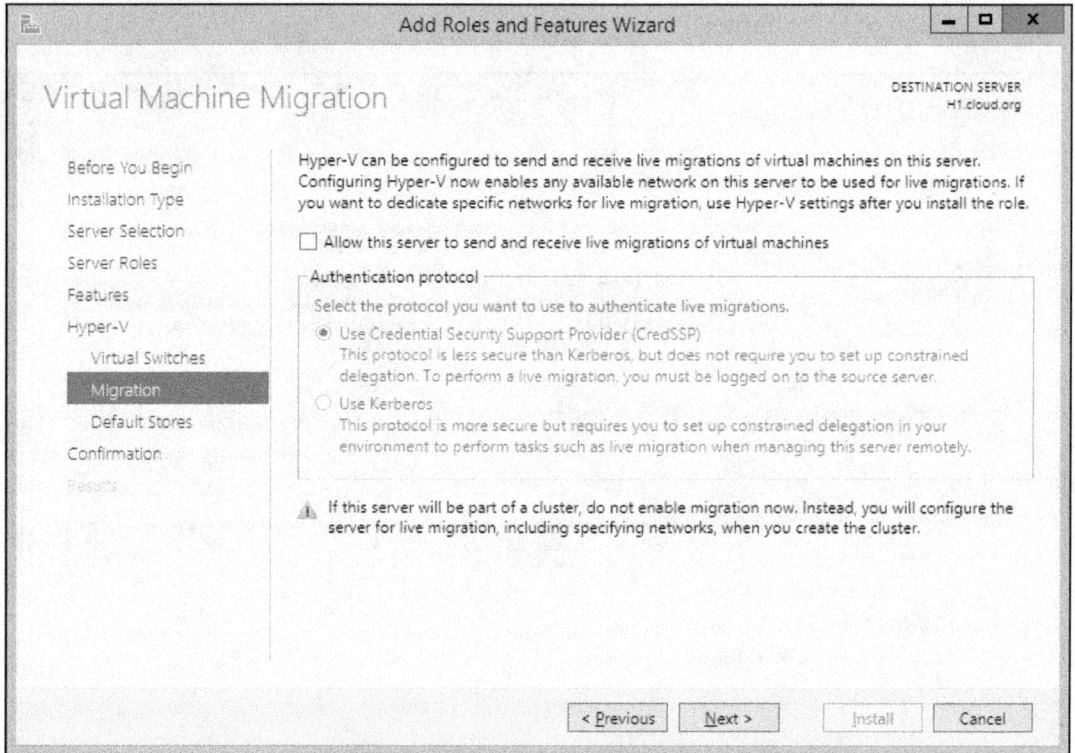

Figure 2-15: Default Options – Enable Live Migration

7. The next host default page is for **Default Stores**. You may customize the default to your desired drive or LUN, or configure it after the installation of Hyper-V.

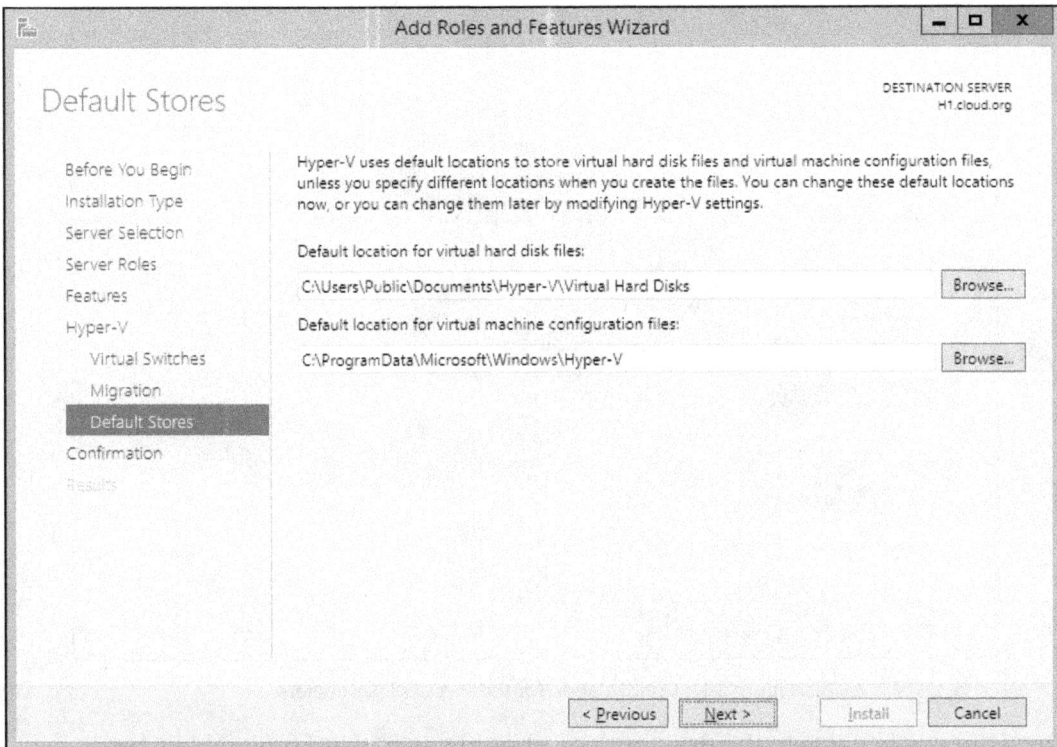

Figure 2-16: Default Stores for Hyper-V host

8. The last screen shows the confirmation of installation selections. Acknowledge and select **Restart the destination server automatically if required**. Then click on **Install**. The server reboots post installation.

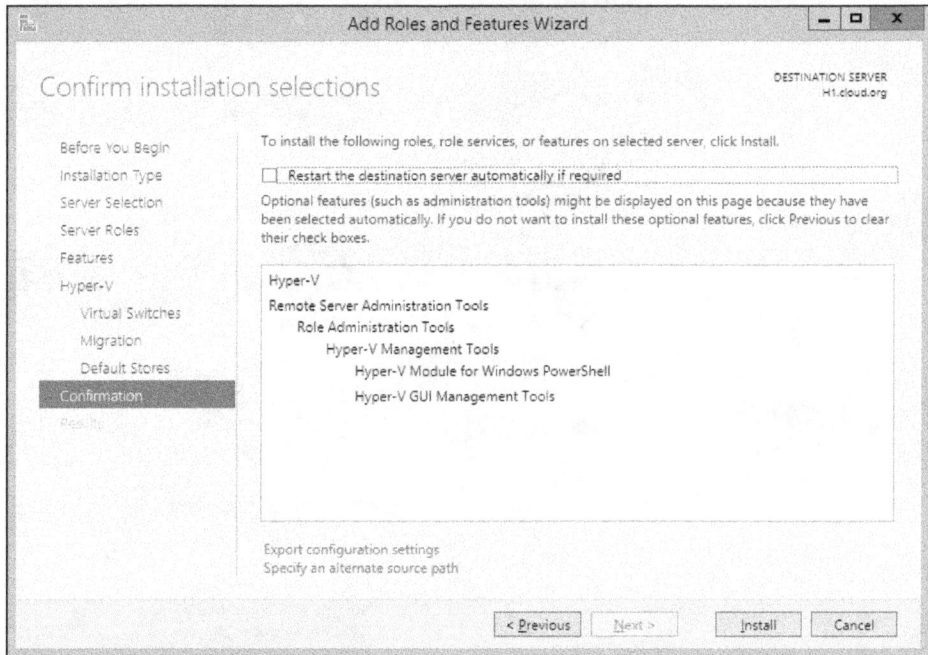

Figure 2-17: Confirmation for the specified parameters

Once the server boots to the desktop, you should verify that Hyper-V has been installed successfully. The GUI way is to look up the dashboard in the Server Manager. It's a telltale of sorts.

PowerShell

If you have been associated with the Windows world, you should know by now the power of PowerShell and the ease it lends to automation and deployment. If not, let's start right here. PowerShell comes in handy in all flavors of Windows installation modes—GUI, minimal, and core—alike.

The following cmdlets will help you achieve the same goal that we discussed previously. Note that PowerShell will require elevated privileges for role or feature installation:

- **Install Hyper-V**: This cmdlet installs Hyper-V along with two sets of management tools as also shown in the Server Manager demo:

```
Install-WindowsFeature Hyper-V -IncludeAllSubFeature -
IncludeManagementTools -Restart
```

- **Verify Hyper-V installation**: This cmdlet lets you check whether the role and associated features are installed successfully or not:

```
Get-WindowsFeature Hyper-V*
```

```
PS C:\Windows\system32> Get-WindowsFeature Hyper-V*

Display Name                                          Name               Install State
------------                                          ----               -------------
[X] Hyper-V                                           Hyper-V                Installed
        [X] Hyper-V GUI Management Tools              Hyper-V-Tools          Installed
        [X] Hyper-V Module for Windows PowerShell     Hyper-V-PowerShell     Installed
```

Figure 2-18: Using PowerShell to verify Hyper-V Installation

Prior to the installation of any role or feature, you may perform a Whatif analysis by appending a switch at the end of the cmdlet. The following screenshot shows this:

```
PS C:\Windows\system32> Install-WindowsFeature Hyper-V -IncludeManagementTools -IncludeAllSubFeature -Restart -Whatif
What if: Continue with installation?
What if: Performing installation for "[Hyper-V] Hyper-V".
What if: Performing installation for "[Remote Server Administration Tools] Hyper-V Module for Windows PowerShell".
What if: Performing installation for "[Remote Server Administration Tools] Hyper-V Management Tools".
What if: Performing installation for "[Remote Server Administration Tools] Role Administration Tools".
What if: Performing installation for "[Remote Server Administration Tools] Remote Server Administration Tools".
What if: Performing installation for "[Remote Server Administration Tools] Hyper-V GUI Management Tools".
What if: The target server may need to be restarted after the installation completes.

Success Restart Needed Exit Code    Feature Result
------- -------------- ---------    --------------
True    Maybe          Success      {Hyper-V, Hyper-V Module for Windows Power...
```

Figure 2-19: Using PowerShell to install a Hyper-V role and along with its management tools

Apart from these two methods, you may also install Hyper-V via the Windows image servicing tool **DISM.exe** (short for **Deployment Image Servicing and Management**):

```
dism.exe /Online /Enable-Feature:Microsoft-Hyper-V /All
```

Best Practices Analyzer

Best Practices Analyzer (BPA) is an excellent utility built into Windows Server2012 and Windows Server 2012 R2, and it is also present in Windows Server 2008 R2. This tool assists IT admins and architects in verifying that a role is installed and implemented as per the MS guidelines. The tool can be launched from the Server Manager or via Windows PowerShell cmdlets to perform a scan on an installed role (or roles) on the Windows Server.

The BPA scan measures a role's compliance on eight different strategic parameters, and the results are published on three standard severity levels: error, warning, and information

> For more information about this tool, you may refer to the *Run Best Practices Analyzer Scans and Manage Scan Results* TechNet page at http://technet.microsoft.com/en-us/library/hh831400.aspx.

The following are a few illustrations of the BPA scan and its end results for the Hyper-V role:

1. In the Server Manager, add the relevant servers to the dashboard. They get segregated easily as per their installed roles.

2. Select **Hyper-V** in the left pane, and scroll down to the **Best Practices Analyzer** frame.

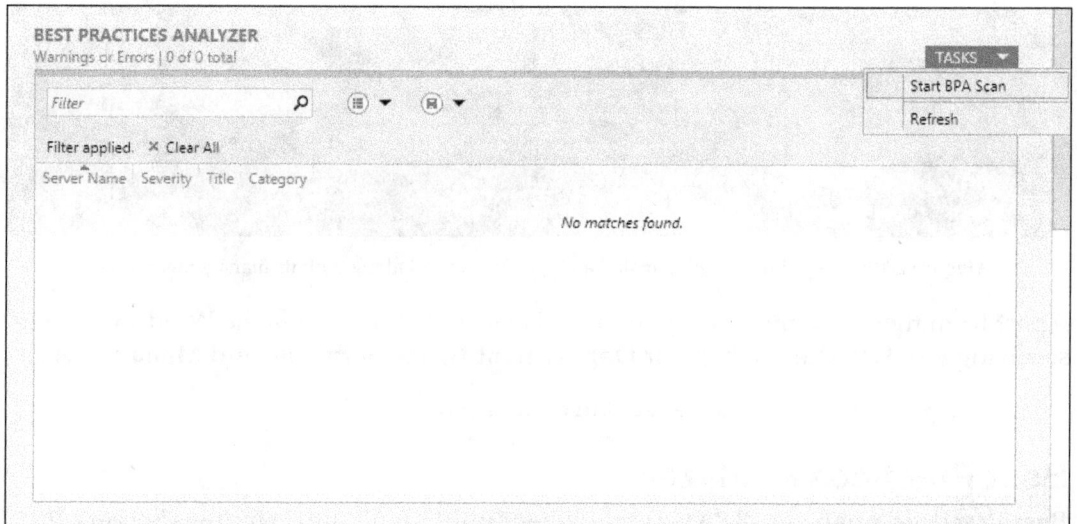

Figure 2-20: Invoke BPA Scan

3. On the right side, under the **TASKS** menu, click on **Start BPA Scan**. Look at *figure 2-20*:

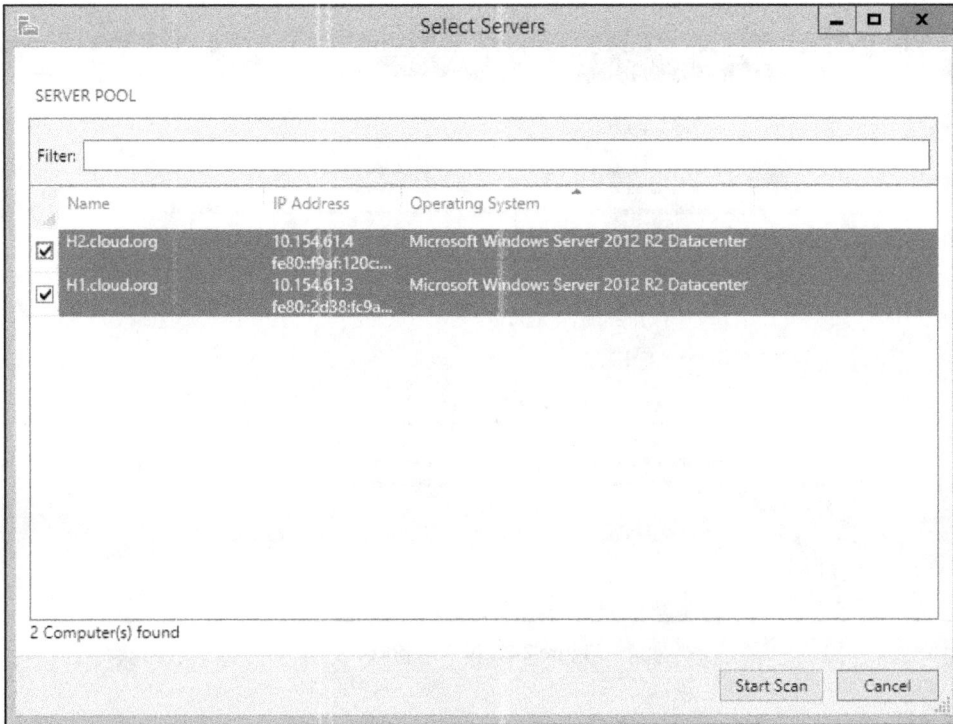

Figure 2-21: Select Servers from the pool

4. It prompts a box to select the server to run the scan against, so select the specific servers and click on **Start Scan**.

5. Once the scan completes, the report with errors and warnings is displayed in the BPA frame.

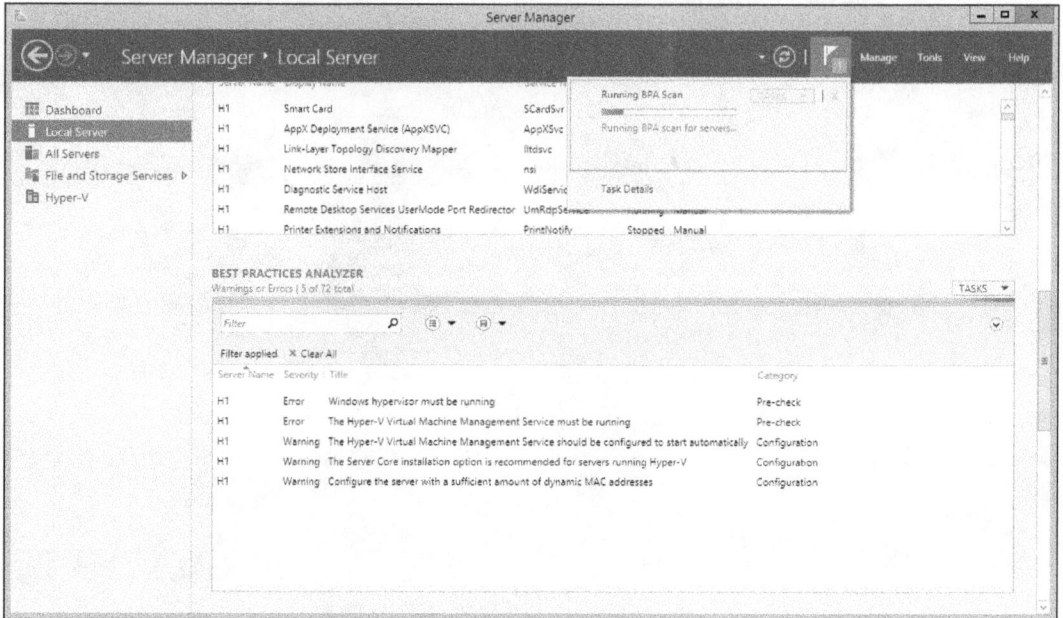

Figure 2-22: BPA Report

Configuring Hyper-V roles

Now we move on to customizing and configuring our new Hyper-V host. The convenient way to start off is by invoking the Hyper-V Manager console. The console can be accessed in several ways:

- **Server Manager | Tools | Hyper-V Manager**
- **Control Panel | Administrative Tools | Hyper-V Manager**
- **Start | virtmgmt.msc (Microsoft Management Console snap-in)**

Let's take a good look at the interface, as this could be the first time most of you are looking at it. It is divided into three panes:

- **Hyper-V Manager host pane**: Here, the local host and other imported hosts are listed
- **Virtual machines pane**: This lists all the VMs hosted on the Hyper-V selected on the first pane
- **Actions pane**: This enlists all the actions as per the selected entity, which could be a Hyper-V host or a virtual machine

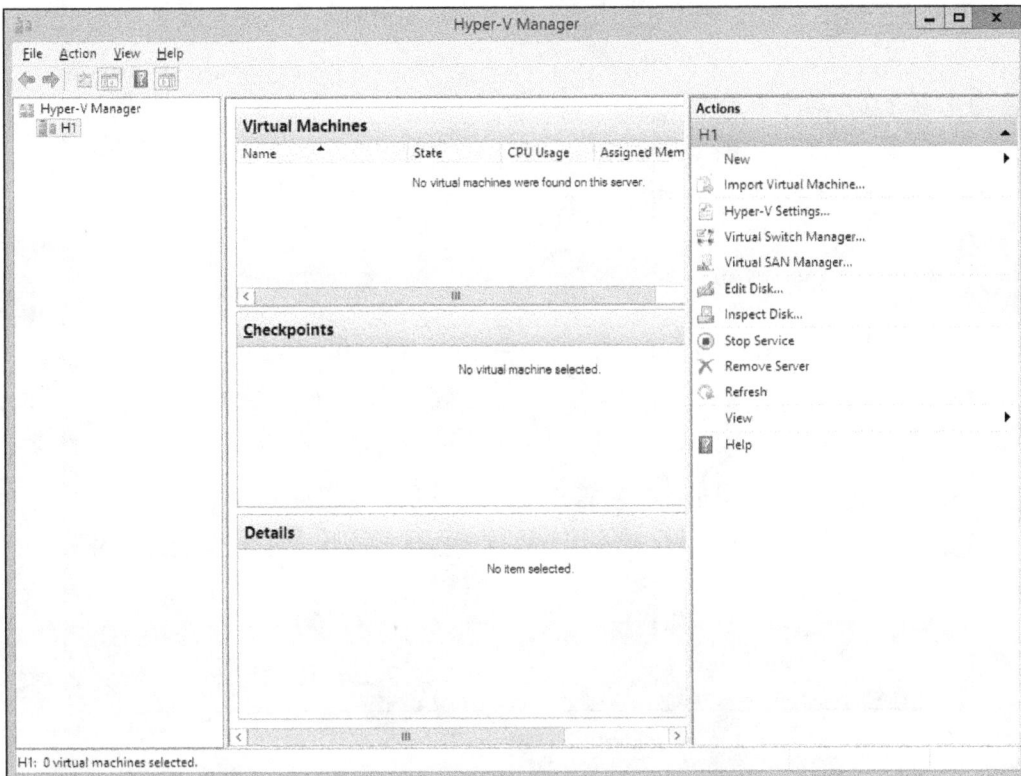

Figure 2-23: Hyper-V Manager – launch Hyper-V settings from the Actions pane

To set things in motion, we first need to modify the basic settings of a Hyper-V host. Select the host on the first pane, and from the **Actions** pane, select **Hyper-V Settings...**. This opens the Hyper-V settings applet for the Hyper-V host. It depicts all the primary options and attributes configured to the default state as per the initial Hyper-V installation.

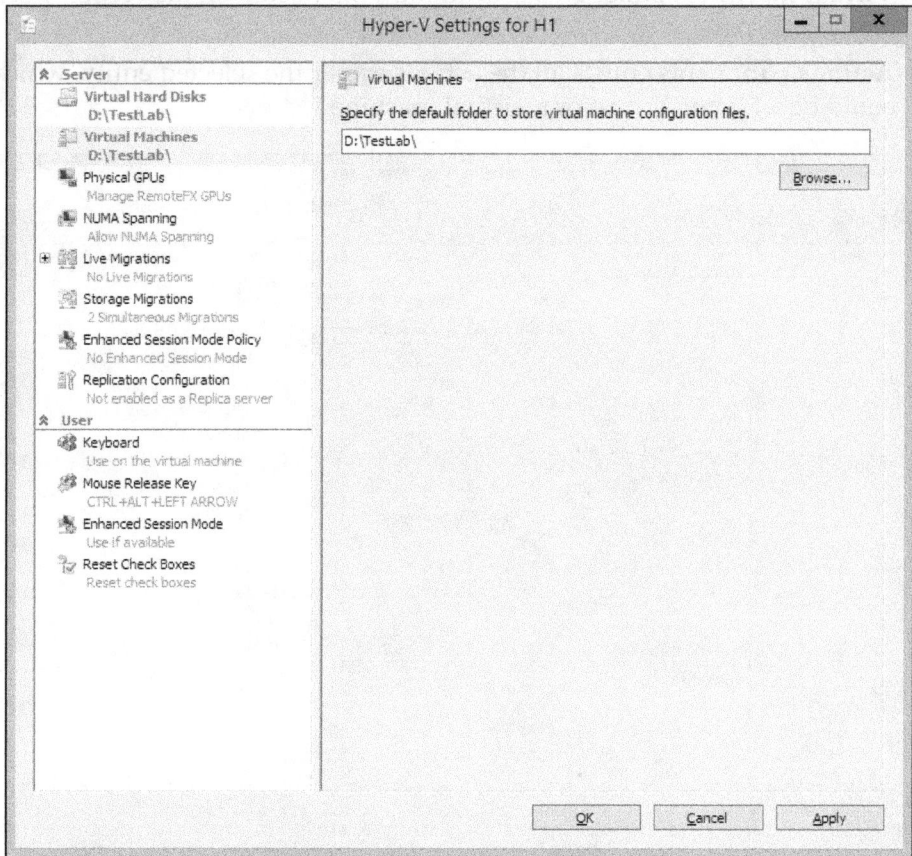

Figure 2-24: Hyper-V Settings

We will now consider each option; you will understand the significance of each option and what values can be assigned to these variables:

- **Default Stores**: If you recollect, this was the one of the screens seen when you were installing Hyper-V via the Server Manager. This allows you to set the location of the virtual hard disks and virtual machines (VM configuration files). The default location is as follows:

  - **Virtual Hard Disks**: `C:\Users\Public\Documents\Hyper-V\ Virtual Hard Disks`

○   **Virtual Machines**: `C:\ProgramData\Microsoft\Windows\Hyper-V`

It's advisable and recommended to modify the location to another drive or LUN that does not host OS files. The following is cmdlet for performing the aforementioned task:

```
Set-VMHost -VirtualMachinePath "D:\TestLab" -
VirtualHardDiskPath "D:\TestLab"
```

- **Physical GPUs**: This setting is required if you have a Remote Desktop virtualization host role installed for VDI deployment. **GPU** is the acronym of **Graphics Processing Unit**, and it is used to render high-end desktop experiences and 3D functions. In an ideal situation, graphical operations are CPU intensive and handed over to GPU. This helps in accelerated computing of resource-heavy and graphics-oriented applications. In Hyper-V, this setting is utilized to power RemoteFX, which renders real-desktop-like experiences on virtual desktops.

- **NUMA Spanning**: **Non-Uniform Memory Architecture (NUMA)** is a memory design concept that retains processor calls to the local memory rather than the non-local memory and delivers faster computing. This also assists in increasing VM density and can provide a VM with more memory, if required. However, this feature has a downside; it may affect overall performance. The following cmdlet is used to disable the feature. Swap the flag value to `$true` to enable it:

```
Set-VMHost -NumaSpanningEnabled $false
Restart-Service "Hyper-V Virtual Machine Management"
```

- **Live Migrations**: This is one of the most attractive features of virtualization. Live migration allows to migrate the running state of a VM from one Hyper-V host to another without losing the availability of the VM. Previously, it required the hosts to be clustered and maintain a shared storage. However, with the release of Windows Server 2012, the dependency has been removed and this is now referred to as **shared nothing live migration**. The setup requires configuring networks for live migration and opting for the relevant authentication protocol. We will see more on this in *Chapter 6, Planning a Virtual Machine's High Availability and Mobility*.

- **Storage Migrations**: This is another of the attractive features. It is used to migrate the virtual machine configuration files and storage without affecting the uptime. Under the settings, you can configure the number of simultaneous storage migrations that can be performed. This will be discussed in more detail in later chapters.

- **Enhanced Session Mode Policy**: This is an innovative attribute added in Windows Server Hyper-V 2012 R2. It allows redirection of resources in a VMconnect session to a guest machine. The behavior that is inherent to Remote Desktop has now been included in Hyper-V. The enhanced session mode is an RDP session that takes place via the VMBus, and a network connection is not a prerequisite anymore. It has some interesting use cases, including troubleshooting, moving data, printing to a local printer, and so on. You can either enable the feature through Hyper-V settings or use the following cmdlet:

```
Set-VMHost -EnableEnhancedSessionMode $true
```

- **Replication Configuration**: This is the disaster recovery feature which we discussed earlier as well. This feature is not enabled by default, and the configuration page allows you to enable and customize the authentication and port settings. In the later section of the page, you have to select **Allow replication from any authenticated server** and specify the VHD/VHDX storage location on the replica server. We will be discussing more on this feature in *Chapter 8, Hyper-V Replica*.

After configuring the Hyper-V settings for a host, we need to create virtual networks via the **Virtual Switch Manager**. Hosted on a hypervisor, virtual machines need to be provided with a communication channel to connect with other machines, virtual or physical, or other network components. Hyper-V provides a virtual switch, a software-based layer 2 network device, to serve the purpose. There are three kinds of virtual switches:

- **External**: This virtual switch binds to a physical network adapter or a NIC team, and allows the VMs to connect to the external physical network.

- **Internal**: This virtual switch creates a connection between the virtualization host and VMs hosted on it, and retains them on the same network.

- **Private**: The connection in this remains among the virtual machines as a private network to them, and is not even extended to the Hyper-V host. This may be considered for network isolation, but it limits the connection within the host. There are other options if you wish to achieve network isolation, such as software-defined network virtualization or protected VLANs.

The preceding information helps you with the basic setup, but with Hyper-V networking there are more intricate subjects to look at from a switch and failover clustering standpoint. We will look at them in separate chapters later on.

Virtual SAN manager was introduced in Windows Server 2012, and solved the challenge of virtualizing servers with dependency on fibre channel storage. Hyper-V provides support for virtual fibre channel ports within virtual machines that allows to connect to FC storage in a similar way as a physical machine would. There are basic prerequisites to make this barely function, however, such as FC HBAs (fibre channel host bus adapter) and NPIV-enabled SAN. There are some restrictions as well. This is beyond the scope of this chapter, but we will discuss more on this later.

There are more items under the actions pane but they are confined to virtual machine settings and minor troubleshooting steps, which we will discuss in the next chapter.

Switching between Windows installation modes

So far, we have configured a basic Hyper-V host and in the later chapters of this book we will look at a more complex approach from the availability and security standpoints. As we discussed earlier, the preferred approach to hosting Hyper-V is on the Server Core or, maybe, the Minimal Server Interface installation due to their known merits. You have installed Windows Server in a server with GUI mode, and now you may convert it into the other two modes. You may take this to task after configuring the Hyper-V role via the aforementioned GUI methods, or push off from the Server Core via PowerShell directly.

GUI

The GUI approach is simple, and is actioned via the Server Manager:

1. Go to **Server Manager | Local Server | Remove Roles and Features**, as shown here:

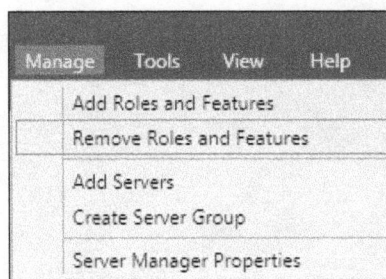

Figure 2-25: Server Manager – Remove Roles and Features

2. In the wizard, keep clicking on **Next** until you reach the **Features** page. Then go to **Features | User Interfaces and Infrastructure**, like this:

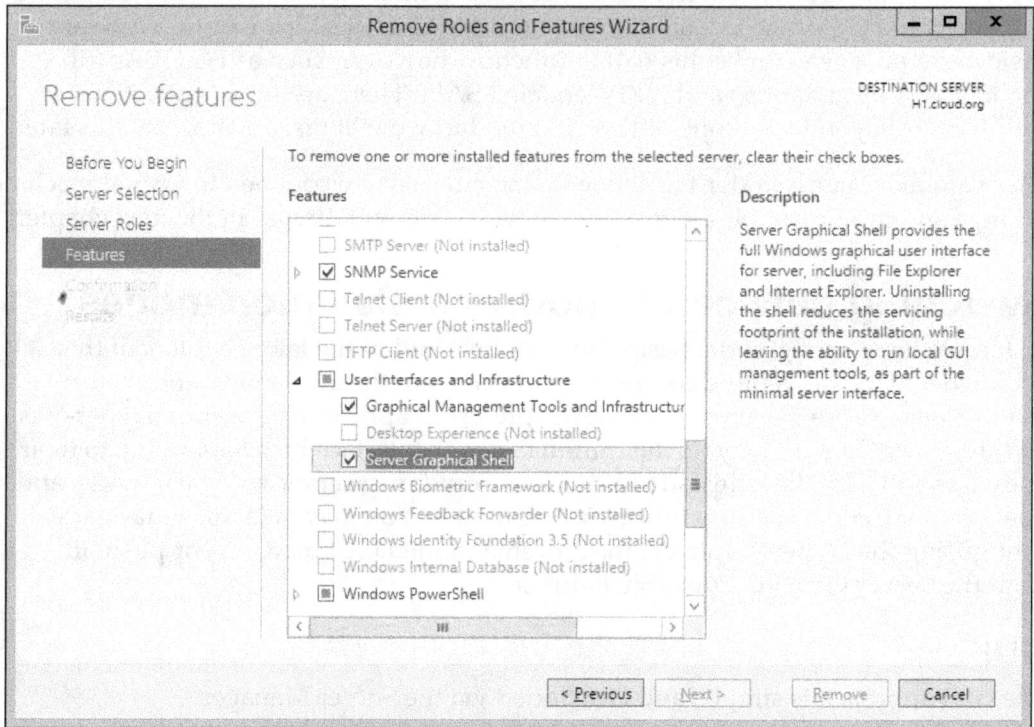

Figure 2-26: Server Manager – Remove Server Graphical Shell

3. To boot to the Minimal Server Interface, uncheck the **server graphical shell** subfeature and click on **Remove**.

Features | User Interfaces and Infrastructure | Server Graphical Shell

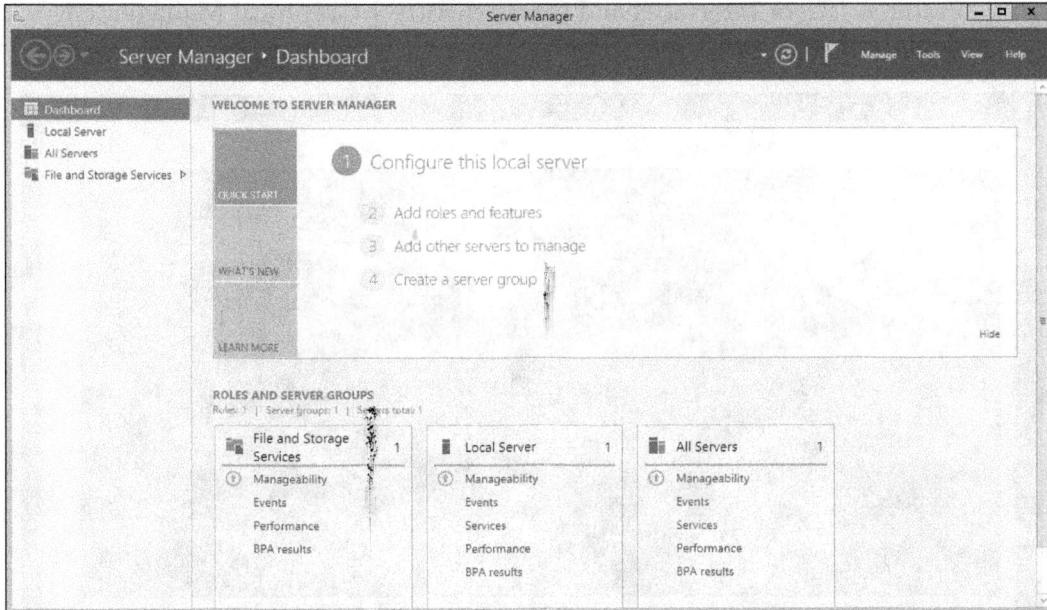

Figure 2-27: Minimal Server Interface (Server Manager and other Control Panel Applets without the Windows Shell)

4. To boot to Server Core, uncheck the **Server Graphical Shell** and **Graphical Management Tools and Infrastructure** subfeatures, and click on **Remove**.

Features | User Interfaces and Infrastructure | Server Graphical Shell

Features | User Interfaces and Infrastructure | Graphical Management Tools and Infrastructure

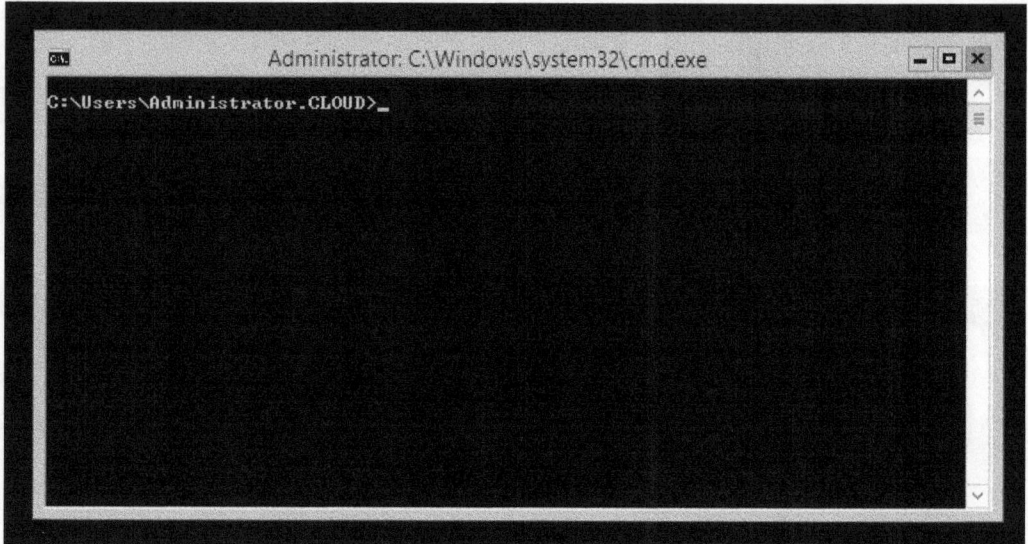

Figure 2-28: Server Core Primary Interface

PowerShell

The process is even simpler if you get used to the super command line from Microsoft–PowerShell. Uninstall the Server-GUI-Shell (**Server Graphical Shell**) feature for the Minimal Server Interface. The following is an excerpt of a whatif analysis of the uninstall call:

```
Uninstall-WindowsFeature Server-GUI-Shell -Whatif

What if: Continue with removal?

What if: Performing uninstallation for "[User Interfaces and
Infrastructure] Server Graphical Shell".

What if: The target server may need to be restarted after the removal
completes.
```

```
Success Restart Needed Exit Code      Feature Result
------- -------------- ---------      --------------
True    Maybe          Success        {Server Graphical Shell}
```

Uninstall both the `Server-GUI-Shell` (**Server Graphical Shell**) and `Server-GUI-Mgmt-Infra` (**Graphical Management Tools and Infrastructure**) features for Server Core. The following is an excerpt. You remove the features one by one or in a single command separated by a comma:

```
Uninstall-WindowsFeature Server-GUI-Mgmt-Infra -Whatif
```

What if: Continue with removal?

What if: Performing uninstallation for "[User Interfaces and Infrastructure] Graphical Management Tools and Infrastructure".

What if: Performing uninstallation for "[Remote Server Administration Tools] SNMP Tools".

What if: Performing uninstallation for "[Remote Server Administration Tools] Feature Administration Tools".

What if: Performing uninstallation for "[Remote Server Administration Tools] Remote Server Administration Tools".

What if: Performing uninstallation for "[User Interfaces and Infrastructure] Server Graphical Shell".

What if: Performing uninstallation for "[User Interfaces and Infrastructure] User Interfaces and Infrastructure".

What if: Performing uninstallation for "[Windows PowerShell] Windows PowerShell ISE".

What if: The target server may need to be restarted after the removal completes.

```
Success Restart Needed Exit Code      Feature Result
------- -------------- ---------      --------------
True    Maybe          Success        {Graphical Management Tools and
Infrastruc...
```

If you wish to revert to full installation mode from Server Core, then you will have to rely on PowerShell only. You just have to reinstall these two features: **Server Graphical Shell** and `Server-GUI-Mgmt-Infra` (**Graphical Management Tools and Infrastructure**). Look at the diagram for a better understanding:

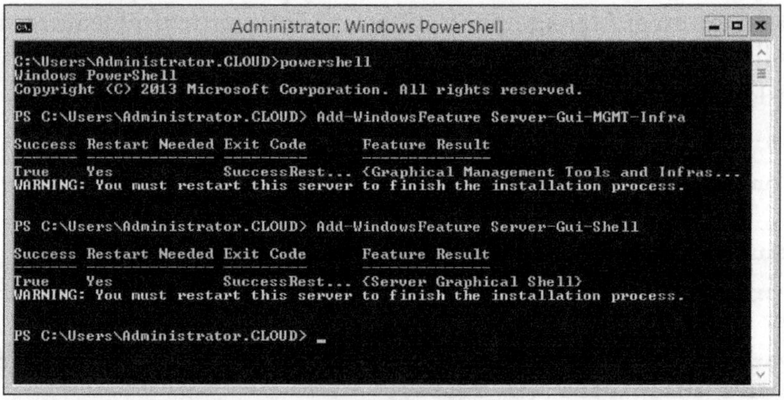

Figure 2-29: Server Core

If you wish to continue with Server Core and prefer the command-line-driven interface over the GUI, then the server configuration tool (referred to as `sconfig`) in Server Core should be of great assistance. Invoke the tool from Command Prompt, and you will get the following interface. The tool allows you to update or modify the domain/workgroup membership, change the hostname, perform remote management, and so on.

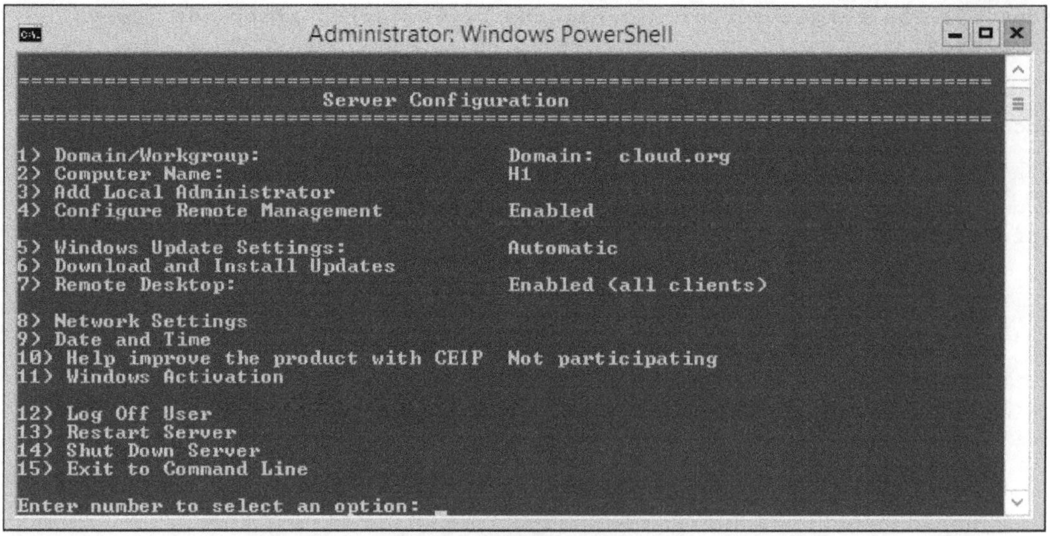

Figure 2-30: Server Core

Upgrading Hyper-V hosts

By now, you know most of the Hyper-V features that Windows Server 2012 and Windows Server 2012 R2 bring to the table. If you already have an older Hyper-V setup in your data center, then you should definitely plan to upgrade to Windows Server 2012 R2. However, for this, there are always two opinions. The first is to follow the in-place upgrade options as per the MS guidelines. The other is to migrate to the newer platform. Both the options have their pros and cons and experienced consultants recommend that you opt for migration rather than in-place upgrades. However, with some key features removed permanently from Windows Server 2012 R2, which were deprecated but still existed until Windows Server 2012, migration to the former is not a straightforward option anymore for older platforms.

The following links give you important information about upgrading to Windows Server 2012 R2 and migrating server roles to the same platform:

Windows Server Installation, Upgrade, and Migration:

```
http://technet.microsoft.com/en-us/windowsserver/dn458795
```

Migration guides:

```
http://technet.microsoft.com/en-US/windowsserver/jj554790.aspx
```

Migration guides e-book:

```
http://social.technet.microsoft.com/wiki/contents/articles/11608.e-
book-gallery-for-microsoft-technologies.aspx#MigrateRoles
```

There is no Hyper-V guide for migration from Windows Server 2008 R2 to Windows Server 2012 R2. So, if you are not using a cluster migration wizard or a third-party tool, you will need to double-hop (migrate twice) the VMs, first from Windows Server 2008 R2 to Windows Server 2012 and then to Windows Server 2012 R2. Let's look at the various methods of migrating from older and legacy Hyper-V platforms to Windows Server 2012 R2.

In-place upgrade (migration)

In-place upgrade is a seemingly convenient option wherein you upgrade to the same hardware. It's preferred for upgrading single Hyper-V hosts by many. However, there are certain prerequisites and gotchas you need to consider before loading the ISO or the DVD drive. You need to consider whether the installed roles, applications, and features are supported on the newer platform, not to mention whether the underlying hardware is certified to run Windows Server 2012 R2. Hyper-V adopters are normally at two separate stages — Windows Server 2008 R2 or Windows Server 2012 — which also points to the need to consider the licensing aspect.

The prerequisites also require ensuring a full server backup of the Hyper-V host with guest machines via Windows Server backup or any other Hyper-V and VSS-aware backup solution. Once the preceding conditions have been met, the process of upgrading is similar to the installation of Windows:

1. Log on to the Hyper-V host with the local administrator credentials.

2. Insert the DVD media or attach the ISO image via Remote Server Management (for example, HP iLO, Dell DRAC, and so on), and invoke `Setup.exe`.

3. Enter the product key, select the Windows installation mode, and accept the license terms.

4. Select the upgrade option. It runs a compatibility check and generates a report for further remedy, if required.

5. Install the Windows update and reboot.

6. Update the Integration Services on the guest machines.

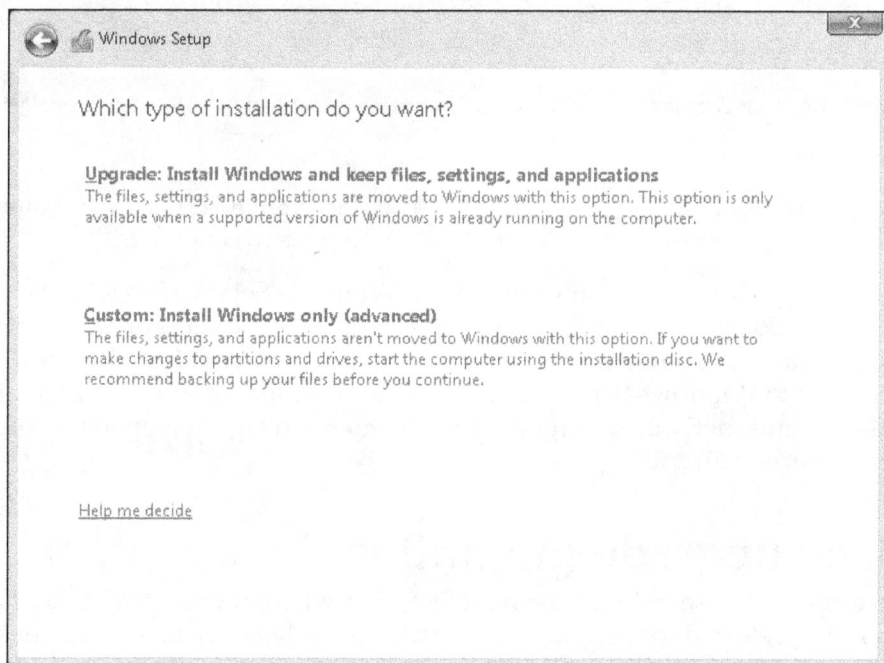

Figure 2-31: In-place migration

> For installation and upgrade options, consider seeing the *Upgrade Options for Windows Server 2012 R2* page at http://technet.microsoft.com/en-us/library/dn303416.aspx.

Cross-version live migration

Cross-version live migration is a really interesting feature with Windows Server 2012 R2. It allows virtual machines on the SMB 3.0 share to be live-migrated from a Windows Server 2012 Hyper-V host to a Windows Server 2012 R2 Hyper-V host without any downtime. It requires configuring both the hosts in a similar way and enabling live migration. This feature has not been extended to Windows Server 2008 R2. More information can be found in the guides listed previously.

Clustered Hyper-V role migration

The preceding two methods come in handy for standalone hosts. However, for Hyper-V failover clusters, you need to work out a migration strategy. The strategy differs for Windows Server 2008 R2 and Windows Server 2012.

For Windows Server 2012 hosts and clusters, cross-version live migration is a convenient migration option, or else you may use the cluster migration wizard. The latter can be used for Windows Server 2008 R2.

VM export and import

The most frequently used option for testing or performing production movements of virtual machines is export and import of virtual machines. If you are exporting VMs from Windows Server 2012 to Windows Server 2012 R2, they go through after a validation check. However, you will not be able to import a VM exported from a Windows Server 2008 R2 Hyper-V host. This is due to the feature, namespace for version 1.0 of WMI and WMI root\virtualization namespace v1 (in Hyper-V), have been removed permanently from Windows Server 2012 R2. The feature was deprecated in Windows Server 2012 but not removed. Hence, you could still import a VM from a Windows Server 2008 R2 Hyper-V host. Windows Server 2012 and Windows Server 2012 R2 use WMI namespace v2.

> *Features Removed or Deprecated in Windows Server 2012 R2*: http://technet.microsoft.com/en-us/library/dn303411.aspx

For now, you will need to export the VM from the Windows Server 2008 R2 Hyper-V host, import it to the Windows Server 2012 Hyper-V host, and then import it to the Windows Server 2012 R2 host.

There's an interesting workaround, well unsupported, that bypasses exporting of the virtual machine. On the Windows Server 2008 R2 Hyper-V host, first turn off the VM and then stop the **Hyper-V Virtual Machine Management Service (vmms.exe)**. Copy the VM folder to a Windows Server 2012 R2 host, and via the **Import Virtual Machine Wizard**, load the same machine. It works!

Hyper-V management

We are in the penultimate section of this chapter. Here, we will look at the options used to manage Hyper-V hosts and cluster nodes. In the entire chapter, we have already discussed and demonstrated two utilities. Let's look at the entire set Microsoft has to offer:

- **Hyper-V Manager**: The Hyper-V Manager console becomes the first choice and at times the ideal choice for Hyper-V management. It has the intuitive MMC interface, and you can do pretty much everything with Hyper-V through this console. Hyper-V Manager is available as an install feature for Windows Server 2012 and 2012 R2. If you wish to manage Hyper-V hosts from your workstation or client machine, you can download **Remote Server Administration Tools (RSAT)**. RSAT aids IT admins in monitoring various server roles and features from their respective client machines. For more information on RSAT downloads, refer to `http://social.technet.microsoft.com/wiki/contents/articles/2202.remote-server-administration-tools-rsat-for-windows-client-and-windows-server-dsforum2wiki.aspx`.

- **Windows PowerShell**: PowerShell is a scripting language and command-line shell that provides an automation framework based on cmdlets. cmdlets (pronounced as "commandlets") are lightweight commands based on the .NET framework's classes, and are instantiated and handled by the Windows PowerShell runtime. Developers can customize and write their cmdlets as per the requirement.

  Since its first release, Windows PowerShell has evolved comprehensively. Microsoft has handed more control over to Windows via PowerShell in versions 3.0 and 4.0, released with Windows Server 2012 and Windows Server 2012 R2 respectively. The cmdlet construct is defined as a verb-noun pair, which makes it convenient to remember and correlate to the attribute or role.

However, practice is required to first learn the language and hone the skills to utilize this wonderful tool to prepare automation scripts. Let's start off with some basic cmdlets. These will help you discover and work with other role- or feature-based cmdlets.

The `$PSVersiontable` parameter gives you the current version of PowerShell, the `BuildVersion` parameter gives compatibility with older versions of PowerShell (1.0, 2.0, and 3.0), and so on. You may start off with the `Get-Command` cmdlet. When used with module names, verb or noun parameters, or wildcard characters, it gives you the entire list of cmdlets associated with that module or object. If you need more information about a particular cmdlet, use the `Get-Help` cmdlet for that cmdlet:

```
Get-Command -Module <Module name>
Get-Command -Verb Start
Get-Command -Noun Service
Get-Help <Verb-Noun>
Get-Help <Start-Service>
```

Here's an interesting cmdlet that will give you the total count of available cmdlets on a Windows installation. You may launch it at different instances to identify the differences in the number of cmdlets between the default installations of Windows and after the import of any module:

```
Get-Module -ListAvailable | Import-Module ; Get-Command -co
cmdlet | measure
```

The preceding constructs should be used to identify the Hyper-V module's aspects as well. We will see more of the PowerShell action in the next chapters.

- **Failover cluster manager**: Failover clustering was a feature of Enterprise and above editions until Windows Server 2008 R2. With Windows Server 2012, aggressive licensing Microsoft has introduced all the Enterprise-level features to Standard Edition as well. Failover cluster is a feature, not a role, and is used to enhance applications' or roles' functionality by making them highly available. Failover clustering is also used alongside Hyper-V to ensure that the Hyper-V hosts are highly available and account for live migration and quick migration of VMs. As discussed earlier, Windows Server 2012 R2 provides shared nothing live migration, which removes the dependency of shared storage for live migration. Nonetheless, clustered Hyper-V hosts are still an indispensable component of every virtualized data center.

  Failover clustering provides an MMC-based console, which can be used similarly to the Hyper-V manager. It is used extensively when managing clustered Hyper-V hosts.

- **System Center 2012 / 2012 R2 Virtual Machine Manager (VMM)**: The VMM is one of the components of the System Center suite that enables architects to build a private cloud with Hyper-V. It is a powerful tool that goes beyond just Hyper-V management, empowers network and storage management, and extends support to VMware and XenServer virtualization hosts. System Center is beyond the scope of this book, but we will be looking at a few tips and tricks concerning it along the way.

Summary

This brings us to the end of the second chapter, and it's time to review what you learned. We reviewed the aspects and scenarios that encourage enterprises to adopt Hyper-V virtualization, primarily server consolidation and BCM. Organizations are also adopting Microsoft VDI as a Remote Desktop solution and looking at public cloud offerings in Windows Azure. Enterprises that have already adopted VMware virtualization are considering migrating to Hyper-V for all the known reasons.

In the next section, we discussed the design principles and parameters that should be considered before laying down a virtualization road map. Microsoft offers assessment tools, product design and deployment documentation, referred to as solution accelerators. These assist the customer in Hyper-V deployment to a great extent. We reviewed the **Infrastructure Planning and Design Guide** (IPD) and the Microsoft Assessment and Planning (MAP) Toolkit, and saw their merits.

Then we moved on to the installation routine for Windows Server 2012 R2 and the Hyper-V role, and their associated hardware and software prerequisites. We discussed the various Windows installation options and how to switch between full, minimal, and core modes. We also looked at the upgrade and migration rules from older Windows Server platforms to Windows Server 2012.

Finally, we looked at various means to manage Hyper-V standalone and clustered hosts via consoles and the command line. Consoles included Hyper-V Manager and the failover cluster manager, which are inherently Windows-based tools. Another one is System Center Virtual Machine Manager, which does a lot more than just Hyper-V management. We also brushed Windows PowerShell and saw how remarkable this command line can be from a Windows management perspective.

Let's gear up for the next chapter now, where we will look at the various types of virtual machines and how to deploy and manage them smartly.

3
Deploying Virtual Machines

Now that we know how to deploy Hyper-V hosts and manage them accordingly, it's time to learn how to deploy workloads on the hosts. Before we do let's revisit the definition of a virtual machine from *Chapter 1, Introducing Release 2.0*.

> *A virtual machine is an emulation of a physical computer, and it runs as an isolated operating system container (partition), serving as a physical machine.*

The objective of creating virtual machines is to host more than one guest machine on a physical machine (host) thereby effectively allocating its resources amongst the VMs as per their specified hardware profile. As discussed in the previous chapter, after the performance sampling of the server workloads, it is determined which machines can be consolidated and hosted on Hyper-V hosts. We can either create the VMs or convert the server workloads to VMs as deemed suitable per the design and migration strategy. The methods to create or convert VM are either console driven or command driven.

Windows Server 2012 R2 also came out with the next generation of Hyper-V virtual machines, referred to as Generation 2 VM. The new feature uses **Unified Extensible Firmware Interface (UEFI)** boot architecture, instead of the old school Hyper-V BIOS. However, the support for Generation 2 VM is limited to most recent Windows and some Linux platforms only.

In this chapter, you will learn about:

- Hyper-V Generation 2 virtual machines
- Virtual machine creation and conversion
- Virtual machine settings and configuration
- Virtual machine capacity considerations

Virtual machine – Generation 1 versus Generation 2

A virtual machine workload can be created in two possible ways. You can either create a new VM and set up, or convert a previously active physical server to a virtual machine. Apart from this, in the following section we will also see how to convert a VMware guest machine to a Hyper-V VM.

However, before we get into the thick of the things, let's first look at the new generation virtual machine offering in Windows Server 2012 R2. Until the previous release of the Windows Server Hyper-V platform, virtual machines used to depend on emulation of old chipsets and devices. These virtual machines are now referred to as Generation 1. With the release of Windows Server Hyper-V 2012 R2, Microsoft released Generation 2 virtual machines, which promised to remove the limitations of the older version. The new version introduces kernel enlightenments and removes the dependency on BIOS. The Generation 2 VMs boot off UEFI instead of standard BIOS, which enables booting off SCSI devices and removes the dependency of booting from the legacy network card, allowing you to boot off the synthetic network card. Generation 2 will form the basis of the future releases of Hyper-V which is yet to see some development and some features have not been included due to some underlying dependencies. Let's review some aspects of Generation 2 virtual machines and in the follow-up sections we will delve into the enhancements and differences from the previous generation as the chapter progresses:

- UEFI boot.
- No legacy devices, e.g. floppy drives, IDE controllers or legacy network card.
- No pass-through optical devices (CD/DVD). OS installation from ISO or network (PXE) boot is promoted.
- Only supports VHDX, and no support for VHD format of virtual hard disk.
- No support for 32-bit operating systems or operating systems prior to Windows 8/2012.
- Faster boot times than Generation 1 VMs.
- Allows for online expansion of boot disk and hot-add of CD/DVD drives to VMs.
- Does not include the support for RemoteFX for now, due to PCI dependency. However, it will be employed in future releases.

New virtual machine setup

A new virtual machine can be created on a standalone Hyper-V host or on a Hyper-V failover cluster. When you create a new VM, you are preparing a hardware profile for the expected workload; thereafter you will follow the normal staged process of installing the operating system, followed by installing the relevant roles, features, and applications, and linking it to your corporate, production, or test network. There are two ways you can create a VM, by invoking the **New Virtual Machine Wizard** or PowerShell cmdlets.

Setup via the New Virtual Machine Wizard

The GUI wizard presents an easy way to set up a new VM and gives a description for each setting on pages that appear during the setup. The **New Virtual Machine Wizard** can be invoked from either the Hyper-V Manager or the failover cluster manager depending on whether the failover cluster feature is enabled and the host is clustered or not. Let's do a quick recap from *Chapter 2, Planning and Deploying Microsoft Hyper-V*, where we discussed the Hyper-V Manager console and its three panes, and what you could achieve from the items in various panes. The **Actions** pane, the third pane, presents you with options that can be performed on the Hyper-V host. Select **New**, then in the menu select **Virtual Machine**. This launches the **New Virtual Machine Wizard**. From the failover cluster manager you can create a highly available (HA) VM via the same wizard, as discussed in the previous chapter. To launch the wizard, under **Cluster Name** select **Roles**, **Virtual Machines** in the **Actions** pane for failover cluster manager, and invoke a new virtual machine. Thereafter, select the node on which you load the HA VM, and this launches the wizard again. We have a dedicated chapter on failover clustering for Hyper-V later on where we will discuss this at length.

Let's walk through the various screens and explain the pages as they are.

The first page is a generic one and explains the purpose of the wizard and virtual machine. *Figure 3-1* depicts the illustration:

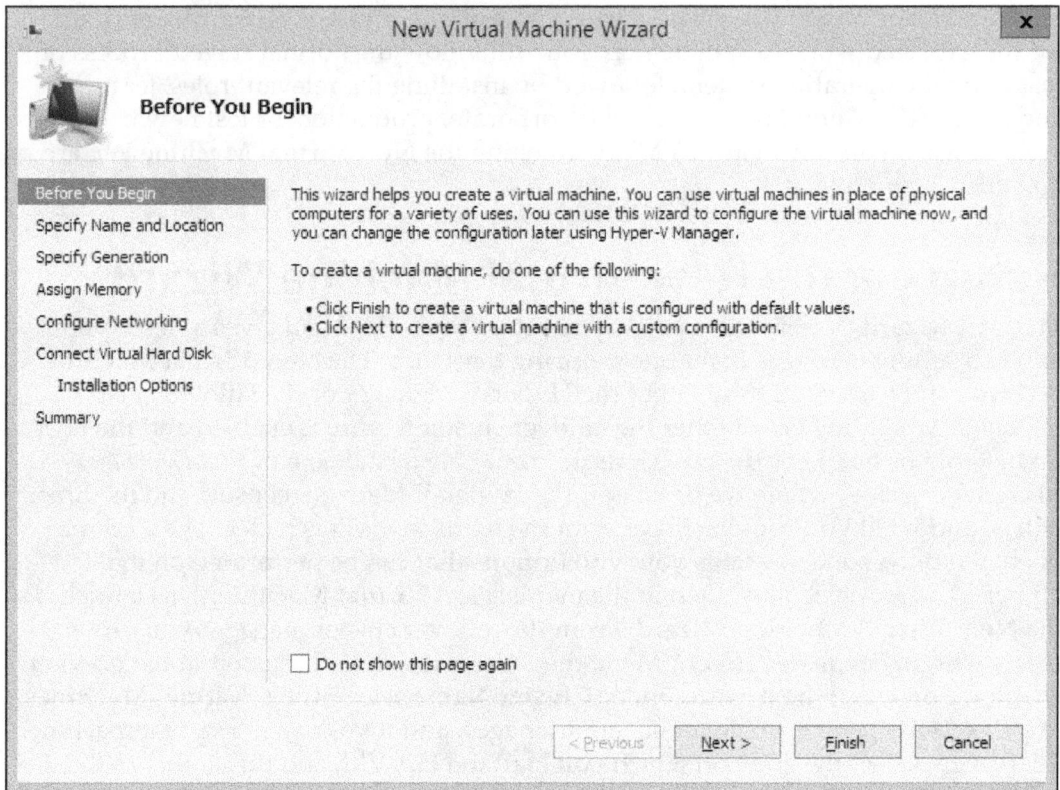

Figure 3-1: New Virtual Machine Wizard – Before You Begin

On the second page you specify the name and location of the VM configuration files. If you can recollect from the previous chapter, the default stores page from Hyper-V roles installation and the Hyper-V settings applet. This page allows you to stick to the default location or specify a different location other than the default. The storage location could be local, DAS or iSCSI/FC LUN depending on your design strategy.

Figure 3-2 shows the screen snapshot of the second page:

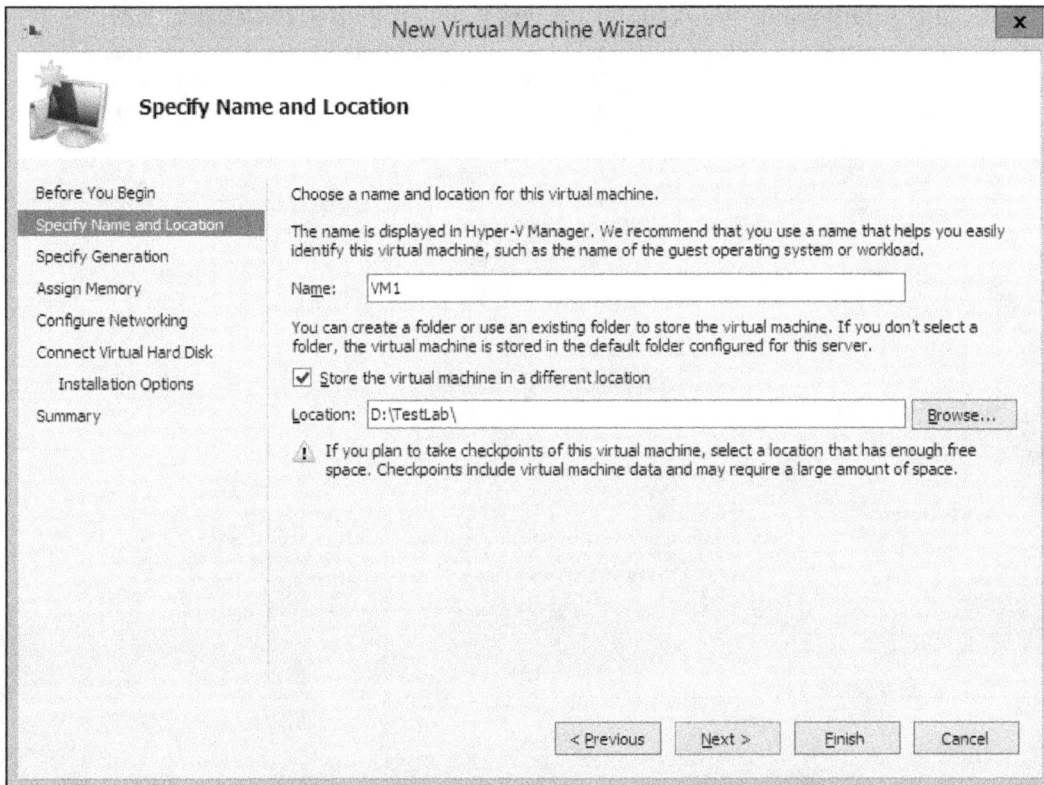

Figure 3-2: New Virtual Machine Wizard – Specify Name and Location

The next would be the page everyone should be keen on the post release of Windows Server 2012 R2. On this page you select the generation of VM you wish to create on your Hyper-V host. We have two options: Generation 1 and Generation 2. As the name implies, the former is an old-school virtual machine that uses an Intel emulated chipset and legacy network adapter for PXE boot. The latter, Generation 2, offers more and delivers what was being demanded of Hyper-V for quite some time, SCSI boot and a few more caveats. However, more on this in a later section of this chapter. As an architect/admin you are given the two choices, however if you opt for the Gen-2, the VOSE should be running the latest Windows platforms only. *Figure 3-3* illustrates the view clearly.

Another important condition is that once you have created a VM as per your required generation model, you will not be able to switch between generations. Microsoft has not made a provision for this yet, however there are migration strategies available which require manual intervention during the process. The process is beyond the scope of the book.

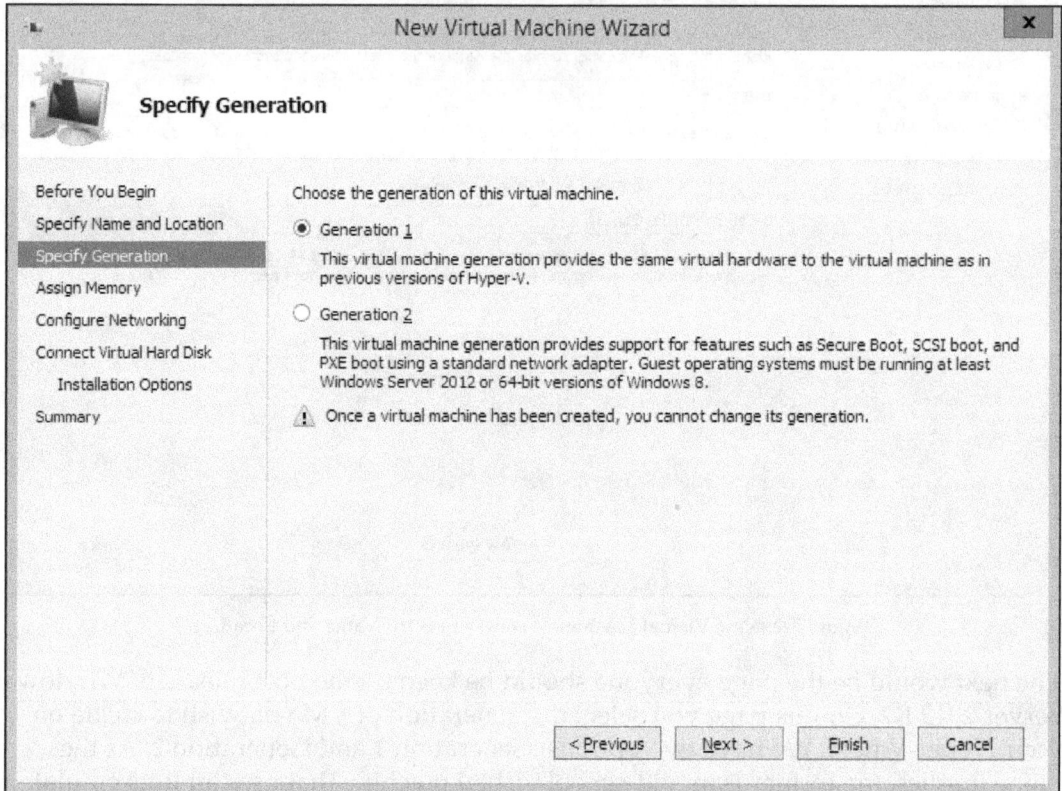

Figure 3-3: New Virtual Machine Wizard – Specify Generation

The next page is about the memory capacity you decide to assign to your virtualized workload. This will be a careful decision, as determining the application workload capacity further assigns the RAM. The memory specified here is referred to as startup RAM. On the page you will also see a checkbox **Use Dynamic Memory for the virtual machine**. *Figure 3-4* indicates the purpose. This was an intuitive memory management feature introduced with SP1 of Windows 2008 R2, which allowed for ballooning up or down of the assigned RAM to a virtual machine. This greatly benefits in increasing the VM density on a Hyper-V setup, however the way it functions some application workloads does not support the dynamic memory feature. We will cover this in the next section.

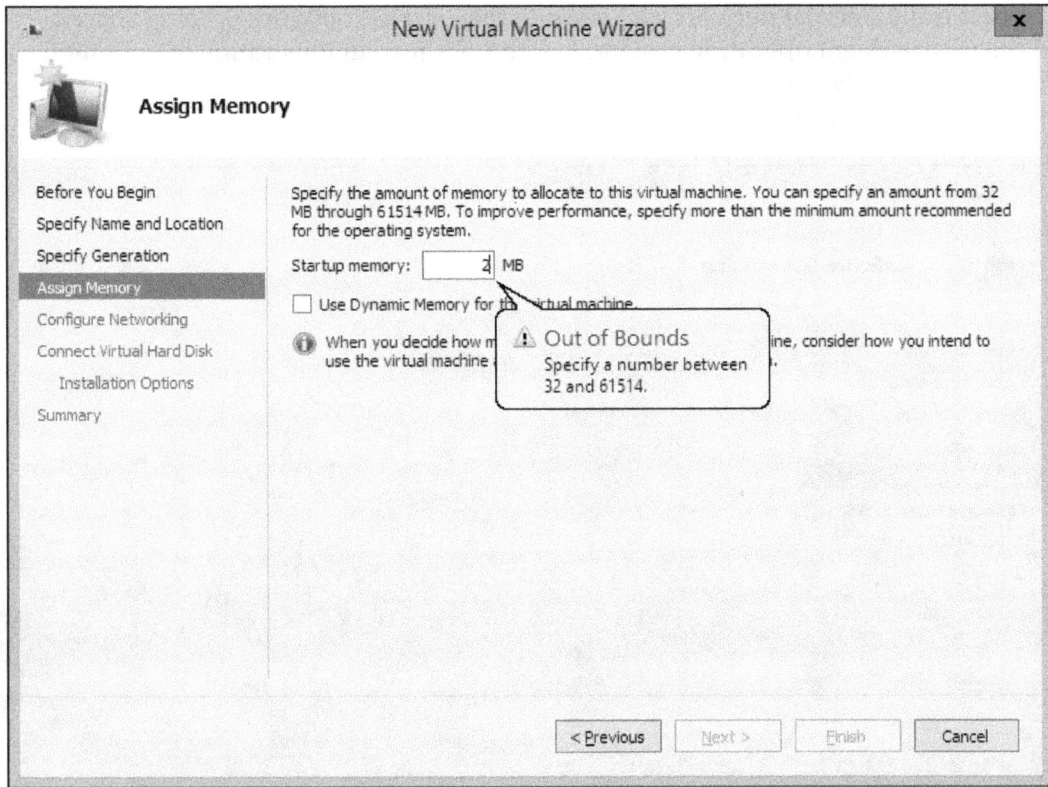

Figure 3-4 New Virtual Machine Wizard – Assign Memory

In the **Configure Networking** screen, you need to give this new virtual machine a network presence. This page provides you with a dropdown menu that gives you the virtual networks linked to the virtual switches you would have created, as discussed in the previous chapter external, internal, and private.

You can create multiples of either of the network options and, to maintain sanity, Hyper-V allows you to give a name to each of the switches. It also depicts them as vEthernet in the **Network Connections** window for the management operating systems. This allows the administrator to identify the virtual networks in the dropdown windows in the virtual machine settings and also differentiate from physical NIC cards on the management operating system. However, there will only be two conditions out of four when you see the vEthernet network card in the management operating system.

The first is the internal network and second, the external network is being shared by the management operating system. *Figure 3-5* is just an illustration of assigning a virtual network. However, we will look at the various parameters and components of virtual networks in the next chapter.

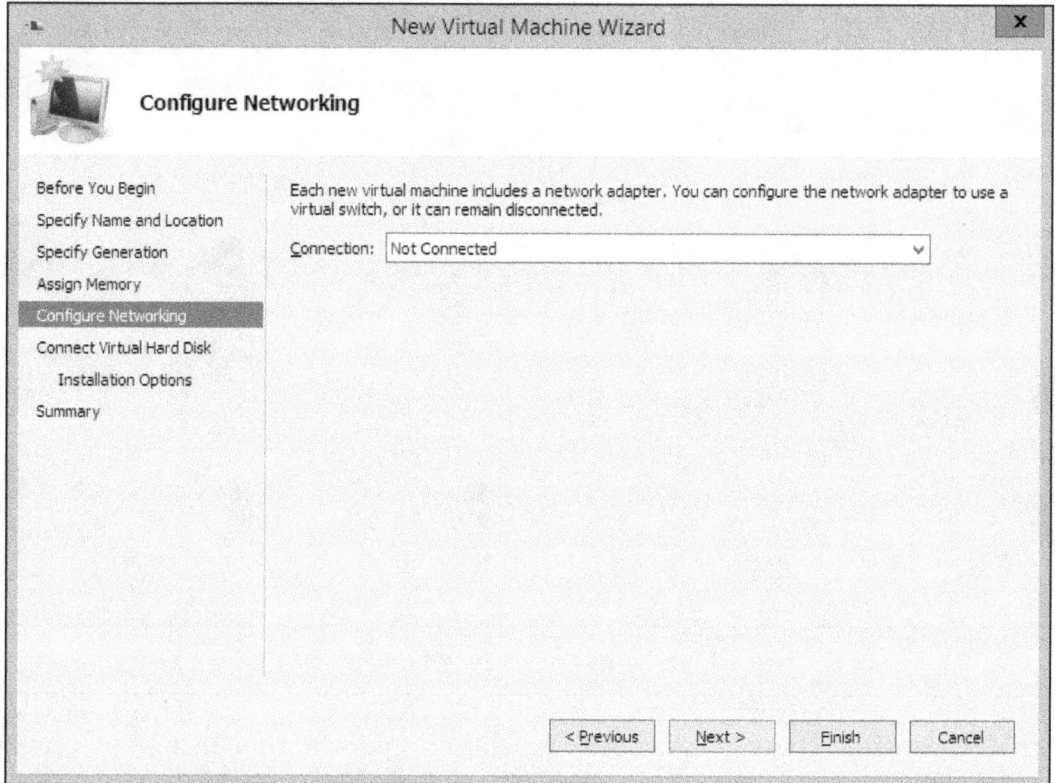

Figure 3-5: New Virtual Machine Wizard – Configure Networking

After the network selection we fall back again on the second of the default stores. On this page you select the location for storing the virtual hard disks for your virtual machine. If you look at the illustration in *figure 3-6*, you will see three options for setting up the virtual storage for VM:

- **Create a virtual hard disk**: This option allows you to create a dynamically expanding VHDX for your VM on the fly when you are creating a hardware profile for your VM via the wizard. In the location, you will see the default store location for this Hyper-V host as set in the Hyper-V settings of the host. You may very well modify it to store it on a secondary local disk or on a LUN or a CSV volume in a clustered environment.

CSV or **Cluster Shared Volume** is the cluster file system that I set up on available shared storage in clustered nodes. A LUN marked as CSV will be installed as a mount point on the `%systemdrive%` (not necessarily the `C:`) under the folder `ClusterStorage`. For keeping things simple, we will refer to the location as `C:\ClusterStorage`.

- Also, there are two more kinds of virtual hard disks – fixed-size and differencing. You do not see them as an option here and will have to convert a previously created dynamically expanding disk or create the desired virtual hard disk separately. Another point is that you do not see an option to create VHD by default method, only VHDX.

- **Use an existing virtual hard disk**: This option allows you to link a previously created VHD or VHDX to the new VM. This option has multiple facets as it can link to `sysprepped` VHD, which could be used a gold virtual disk or a Disk2vhd converted disk.

- **Attach a virtual hard disk later**: Here you create a virtual machine configuration, its hardware profile, and save it. You may thereafter create a customized virtual hard disk and link to this VM (e.g. fixed-size or differencing VHD), which you could not do under the default options or as stated to link a gold VHD or P2V converted VHD.

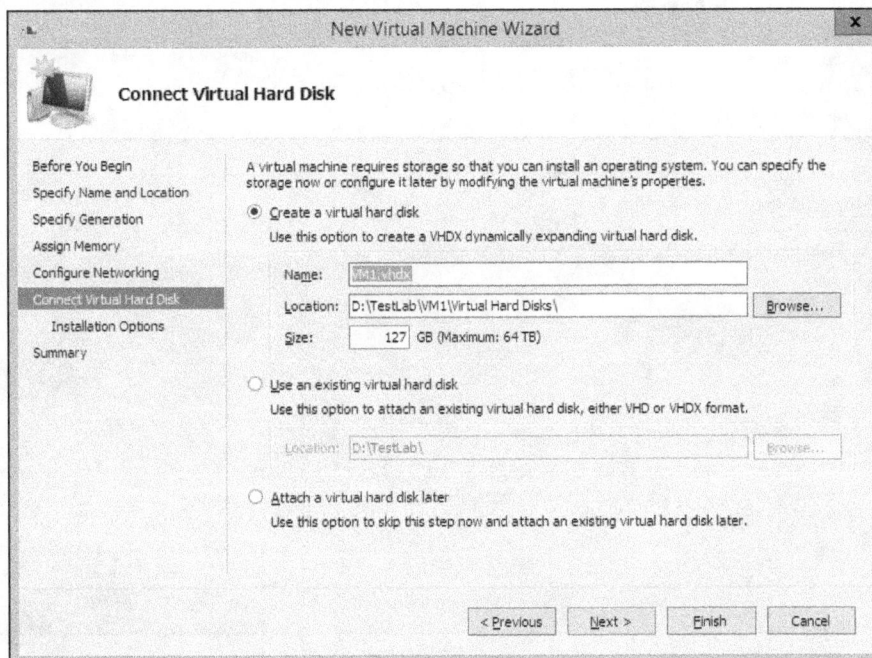

Figure 3-6: New Virtual Machine Wizard – Connect Virtual Hard Disk

On the penultimate page, you get to select the **how you wish to install the Operating System** option, if you have created or linked a blank virtual hard disk. Here again we have four options as you can see in *figure 3-7*:

- **Install an operating system later**: This option is self-explanatory.

- **Install an operating system from a bootable CD/DVD-ROM**: Here you have two sub options, wherein you may choose to link the physical optical drive of the Hyper-V host for the installation media or link a stored OS installation media ISO.

- **Install an operating system from a bootable floppy disk**: This one is the same as previous, although it allows you to link a virtual floppy disk image instead. In case someone is nostalgic about floppy drives!

- **Install an operating system from a network-based installation server**: This one is used for deploying Windows on the virtual machine and requires a legacy network adapter for PXE boot. Generation 1 machines do not PXE boot with synthetic network adapters. The feature was added in Generation 2 VMs, which allows the VM PXE boot with synthetic network adapters.

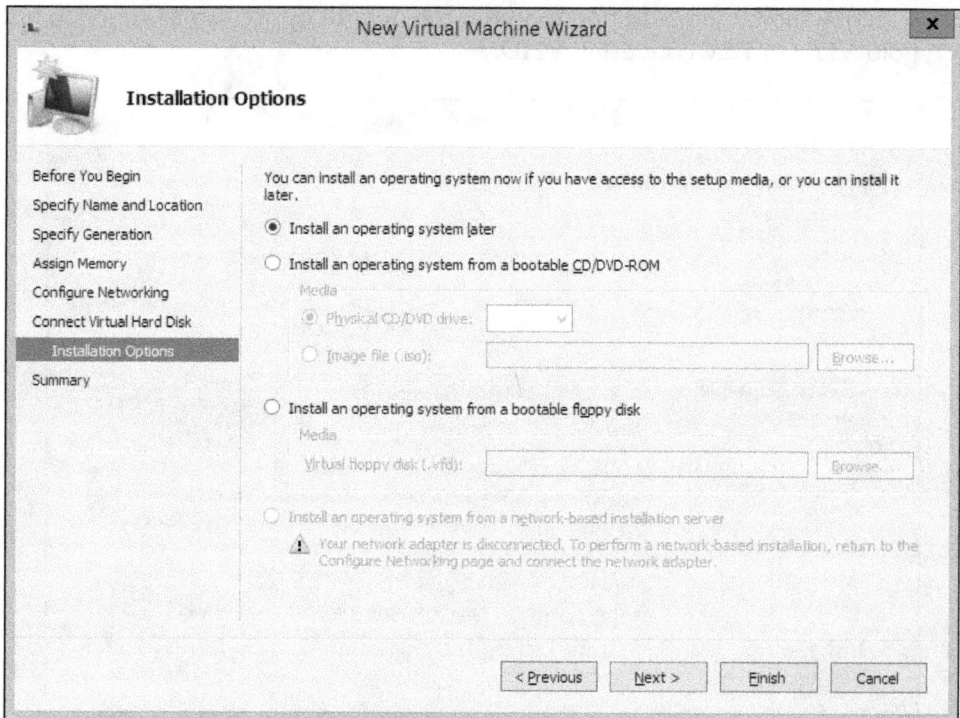

Figure 3-7: New Virtual Machine Wizard – Installation Options

This brings us to the final screen, which displays the summary of your selected options as you can see in *figure 3-8*. Once you click on the **Finish** button, you will see the new virtual machine created in your Hyper-V Manager console (or failover cluster console). The process is pretty straightforward and if you wish to upgrade the hardware profile or modify some aspects of the VM you may open the VM settings by right-clicking the VM name in the console and select **settings**.

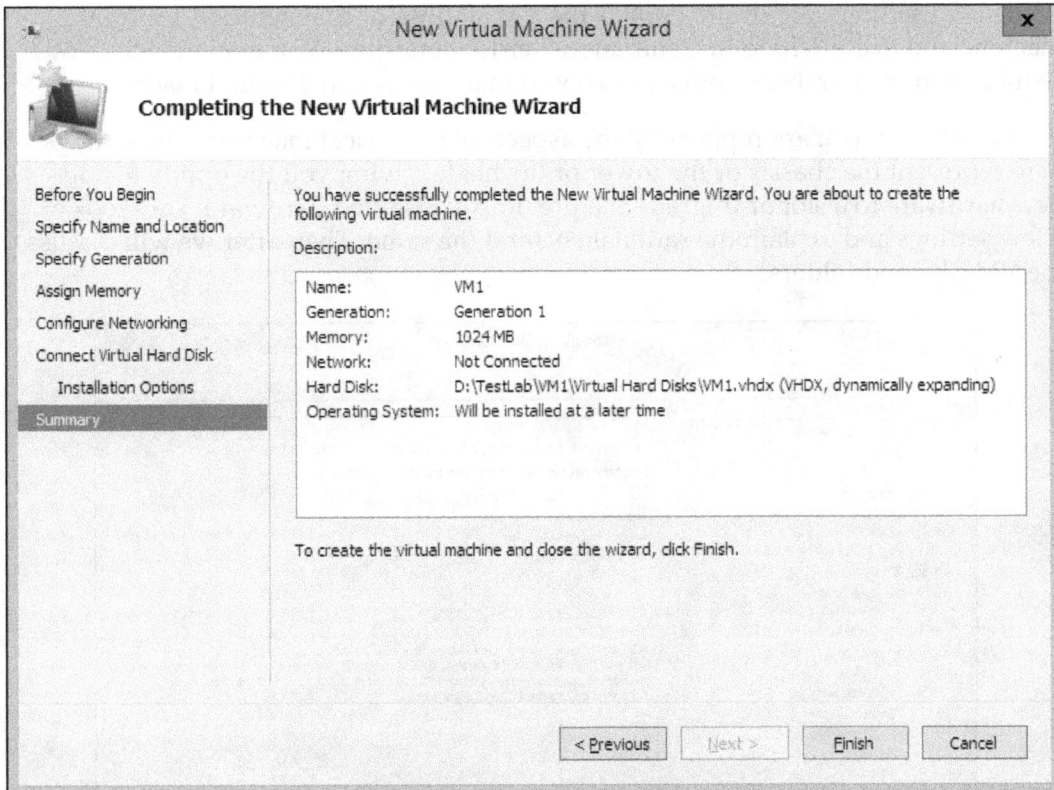

Figure 3-8: New Virtual Machine Wizard – Summary

Understanding and configuring virtual machine settings

It is now time to dig deeper into the Hyper-V Manager console and see what else the GUI mode has to show you unambiguously. As per the wizard, we could either follow the default options or tweak them a bit to build a VM or else create VM configuration and customize it later on. To access this, open up the Hyper-V Manager and in the middle pane for virtual machines, right-click the name of the virtual machine and select **Settings**.

This launches the VM settings applet. In the top-left corner, you will be able to see the name of the VM which is a dropdown menu as well. If you drop down the menu, you can see all the VMs hosted on the Hyper-V host and you can switch between the settings of the VM easily from within the applet.

In the lower-left pane, you can see the hardware profile for the selected virtual machine. Selecting each hardware aspect gives you the option to customize predefined settings. *Figure 3-9* depicts the VM settings of a Generation 1 virtual machine and *figure 3-10* for a Generation 2 virtual machine. You may note the reduction in the number of devices exposed in a Generation 2 virtual machine.

If you compare, you are replicating the aspects of a physical machine. The settings here represent the chassis or the tower or the blade, giving you the option to add new hardware to a slot or upgrade the previously installed hardware. Let's look at a few settings and explain the rationale behind the same. Thereafter we will discuss the VM files and folders.

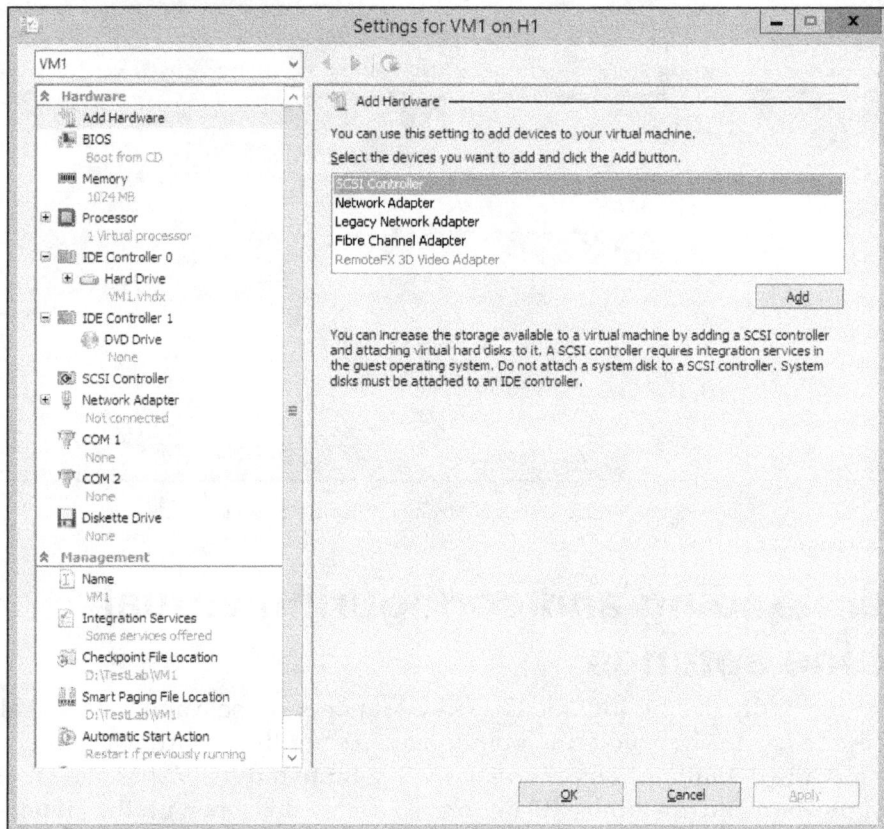

Figure 3-9: Virtual Machine Settings – Generation 1 VM

Add Hardware

This subsection allows you to add virtual adapters for additional computing and storage connectivity. In Generation 1, you may add SCSI controllers, network adapters, legacy network adapters, fiber channel adapters, and RemoteFX 3D video adapters. On the contrary, three out of five options are present for the Generation 2 VM. As stated earlier, the legacy network adapter and RemoteFX adapter are not included. You can make out the purpose of SCSI controllers and network adapters, however the fiber channel adapter is a little new to the scene and was introduced with Windows Server Hyper-V 2012. It allows you to expose an FC LUN directly to the virtual machine. You will learn more about the virtual fiber channel adapter in *Chapter 5, Storage Ergonomics*.

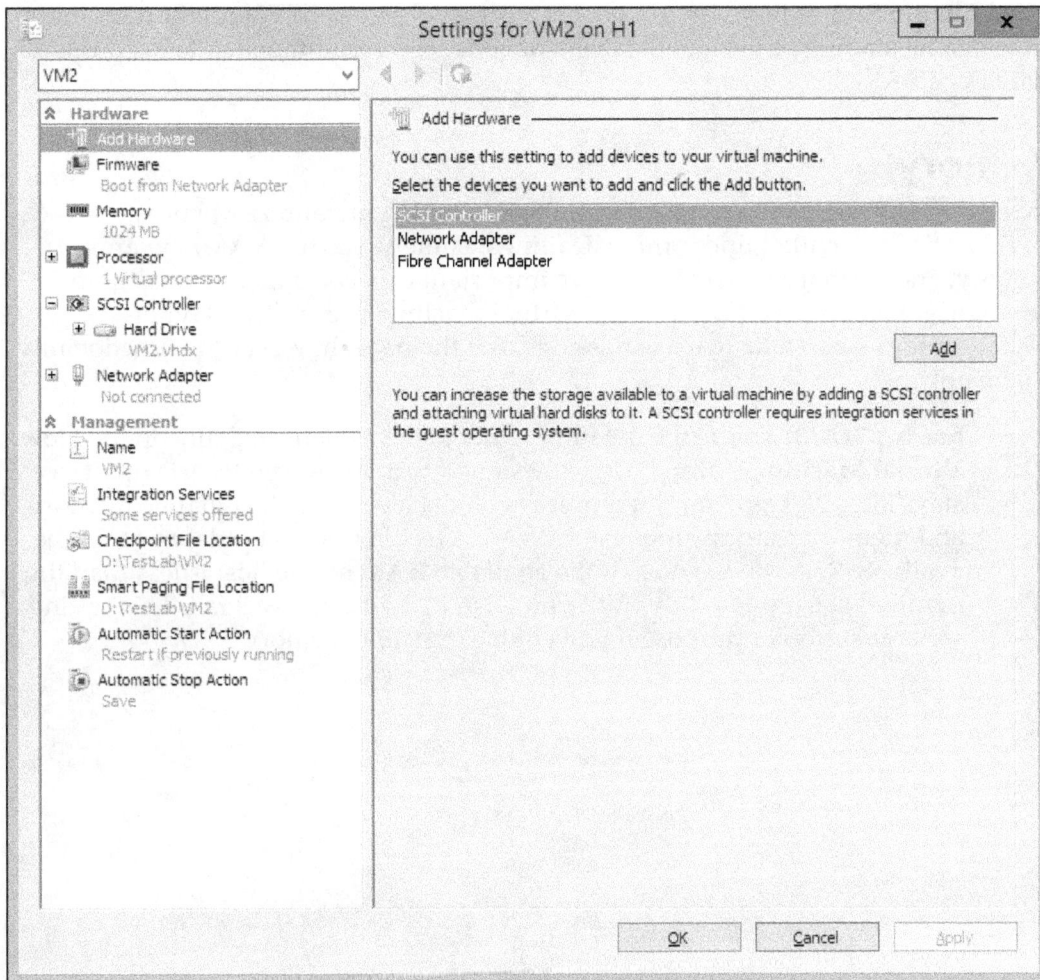

Figure 3-10: Virtual Machine Settings – Generation 2 VM

BIOS versus Firmware

This is the crucial and major difference between both generations. Generation 1 is based on standard Hyper-V BIOS and Generation 2 on **Unified Extensible Firmware Interface (UEFI)**. UEFI provides you with a standard firmware interface that is more secure and ensures faster booting and recovery from hibernation than BIOS. It has been intended to replace BIOS and provides legacy BIOS support.

If you compare the boot options in both generation VMs under the BIOS/firmware section, they display the typical boot order though with two notable differences. First the UEFI boot order, as indicated earlier, does not list floppy or legacy network or CD/DVD drive as boot devices and shows only network adapter and SCSI based VHDX as boot options. Secondly there is a checkbox in Generation 2 VM settings called **Enable Secure Boot**. Secure boot is a protocol as per UEFI specification that prevents the loading of unsigned drivers or code. It is recommended to keep this option enabled.

Memory

This section gives you the same look and feel in both generations. Memory configuration is divided under three headings, namely: startup RAM, dynamic memory, and memory weight. These are important aspects to memory assignment and management from a Hyper-V and virtual machine perspective. Hyper-V loyalists will realize static RAM is missing from the page, however the functionality is here only:

- **Startup RAM**: This is the default memory size, which we define in the **New Virtual Machine Wizard**. This is assigned to a VM when it starts up. It stays allocated as committed unless you decide to enable dynamic memory and memory sharing amongst the VMs. The allotment also depends on the available RAM on the host. If the available RAM on the host is less than the required startup RAM of a VM you wish to boot up, it will fail. This setting serves a different purpose if you enable dynamic memory.

- **Dynamic Memory**: The setting can be enabled via the wizard or the VM settings page. The current screen has a checkbox **Enable Dynamic Memory** to set the feature on for the VM. It has three attributes: minimum RAM, maximum RAM, and memory buffer. Once the feature is enabled, the allotted RAM to VM is not just confined to assigned RAM as per the startup RAM. Startup RAM size is allotted for the VM to boot up and start the roles and services. Thereafter the VM RAM allocation fluctuates, it is incremented or balloon-reduced as per the memory pressure on the VM, again based on roles and applications installed. The memory assignment varies depending on the minimum RAM and maximum RAM settings:

    ◦ **Minimum RAM**: Minimum RAM, as the name indicates, is the bottom limit for RAM that a VM can stay on, in a unused idle state, with a negligible memory pressure from installed apps and roles. When enabled, it is the same as the startup RAM, however, based on the memory utilization behavior you may modify the value as deemed suitable. You can also alter but only decrease the minimum RAM setting even while the virtual machine is running.

    ◦ **Maximum RAM**: This setting is the roof limit set for memory utilization for the particular VM. As the memory pressure or requirement is raised, additional memory from the startup RAM gets automatically allotted to the VM. This setting can also be altered without shutting down the VM, however it can be increased from the current value. Interestingly the default value present there is 1 TB, however regardless of the value set here the maximum memory cannot be more than the available physical RAM installed on the Hyper-V host. The maximum value should be set after performance tracking and realizing the capacity requirement of the installed role or application.

    ◦ **Memory Buffer**: Buffer accounts for supplementary memory to a VM enabled for dynamic memory. When you enable the dynamic memory feature for a VM, you also enable a default 20 percent additional memory to the assigned memory. For example if you have assigned 1 GB of RAM to a VM, as per the default value, 20 percent extra is appended to the original allotment, which makes it 200 MB of file cache. This is a failsafe mechanism in lieu of dynamic memory delay. You may lower or raise the percentage depending on the workload behavior. For example, certain applications are resource hungry and will commit as much memory as is assigned to them, so set a lower value or a workload requires a quick commit and release of memory before dynamic memory can respond.

- **Memory Weight**: This should remind the Hyper-V loyalists of the memory priority setting in the previous Hyper-V platform. The memory weight feature gives you a slider that lets you fix the priority for memory provisioning amongst VMs on a Hyper-V host. The slider lets you specify the priority as low or high, which lowers or raises a VM's stake on the shared RAM on the Hyper-V host. A high setting for a VM gives it more leverage for memory availability in case of a contention on the host. Avoid modifying the setting unless the VM is hosting a more critical role than the parallel installed VMs.

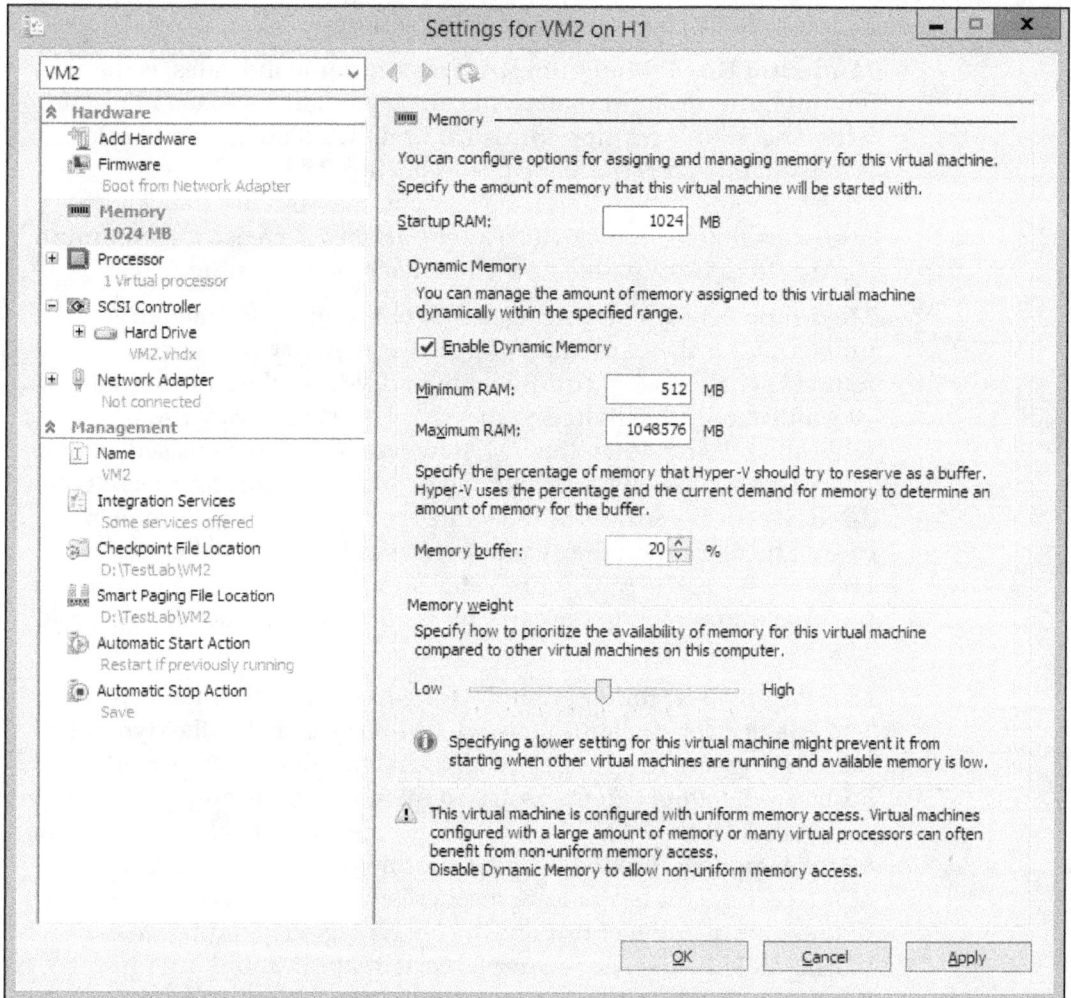

Figure 3-11: Virtual Machine Settings – Memory

Processor

This attribute is again similarly maintained for both generations of virtual machines. You may customize a VM's number of virtual CPUs and their CPU sharing preferences from this section. This page has two further subsections: compatibility and NUMA. You can view them by expanding the processor property.

The primary setting under this section is the number of virtual processors for a given VM. The maximum number of virtual processors or CPUs that can be assigned to any VM is 64. The former figure is the highest possible bracket; however the actual figure is dependent on the number of logical processors available on the physical host. The number of virtual CPUs cannot exceed the number of logical processors on the Hyper-V host. The logical processor count would depend on whether you enabled Hyper-threading in BIOS or not. Enabling Hyper-threading doubles the number of logical processors (virtual cores) with almost a significant improvement in performance allowing simultaneous execution of threads and improvised sharing of CPU resources. Now let's look how, inside Hyper-V, the CPU resources can be effectively managed.

Resource Control

Under this section, you should be able to tweak and prioritize the processor utilization for a specific VM. There are three subsets to resource control management. However, it is preferable to let Hyper-V manage the same, unless you have a virtual workload that has a demanding processor utilization predefined:

- **Virtual Machine Reserve (percentage)**: This value lets you reserve a share of logical processor(s) addressing the VM. The figure is updated in percentage value and regardless of the number of cores specified, the percentage value is per core (logical processor). For example, if you have specified 10 percent here and 12 virtual CPUs before, then this machine is allocated 10 percent of utilization across 12 logical processors feeding this VM. The next field, **Percent of total system resources**, gets calculated and filled automatically. It's a little math that translates this reservation and gives a generic reservation against total numbers of cores in percentage value. For let's say 10 percent on each core with 12 virtual CPUs assigned on a server with 24 logical cores, the value would be around 5 percent.

- **Virtual Machine Limit (percentage)**: This value contrasts with the previous setting. Unlike the previous one where you reserve a minimal allocation, here you limit the processor utilization per virtual CPU to not go beyond the specified value. **Percent of total system resources** field gets updated automatically as per the total logical processor count.

- **Relative Weight**: This value allows you to set a processor utilization preference giving *weightage* to specific machines. By default, all the VMs have a value 100 set. This keeps the allocation standard for the existing VMs on a host unless you decide to specify a relative weight to machines to allow for more PCU time in case of contention. The value range you can set here is 0 to 10,000.

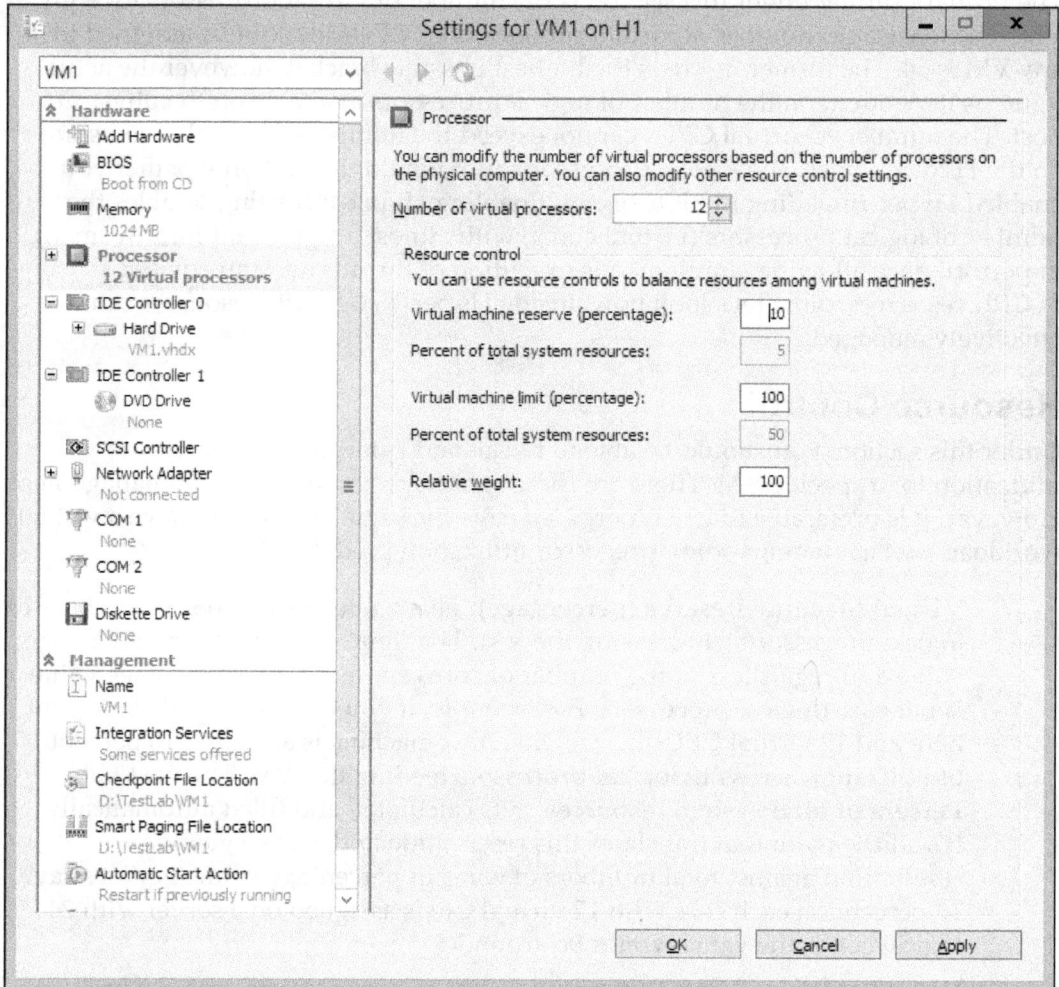

Figure 3-12: Virtual Machine Settings – Processor

Compatibility

The compatibility feature can be enabled by striking off the checkbox disabled by default. This setting is used to enable the live migration (shared storage or shared nothing) capability of a running VM on hosts with different processors within the same CPU family and manufacturer. As realized, you cannot enable live migration between Intel and AMD CPUs, however we can restrict the live migration between the different releases of processors of each manufacturer respectively. This definitely helps architects in enhancing an ongoing setup of older hosts with newer hosts, however the trade-off comes with a downside. The setting enabled does not allow the VMs to use the abilities of the processors completely but confines them only to a limited attribute set.

NUMA

NUMA stands for **Non-Uniform Memory Access** and is quite a popular processor architecture design. Let's get a little insight about this terminology. The ability to add more processing power to hosts (320 logical processors and 4 TB RAM) and thereafter VMs (64 virtual CPUs and 1 TB RAM) has definitely helped the scalability clause, however with the current number of logical processors supported by Hyper-V not all the logical CPUs have faster uniform access to all the linked RAM. The simple end result is division into NUMA nodes, which is a union of a certain number of logical cores and having direct connections to certain memory banks. This design assists in reducing memory contention.

Hyper-V supports NUMA, also for Linux workloads now, and allows virtual NUMA for virtual machines alongside the hardware NUMA topology of the host. The Hyper-V host attempts to assign memory to a loaded VM from the local NUMA node, if the requirement is on the rise and cannot be satisfied by the local node, then a remote NUMA node is looked up for memory allocation. This activity is called **NUMA spanning**. The local node access is always faster than the remote node! If you can recollect from the previous chapter, we enable the setting from Hyper-V settings of the host. The setting is enabled by default and allows you to utilize the dynamic memory ability to span multiple NUMA nodes. However, this setup may affect the overall performance of NUMA-aware workloads.

To configure virtual NUMA, the first prerequisite is to disable dynamic memory. The virtualization v2 namespace is Windows Server 2012 R2, and does not automatically turn on/off the virtual NUMA with disabling or enabling of dynamic memory. The features have to be separately configured. You may customize the virtual NUMA node from NUMA subsection under the processor applet of the VM setting.

If you have a large VM supporting NUMA workloads, the ideal way would be to disable the NUMA spanning and migrate the VM to host with the smallest NUMA node. Then from the VM setting, invoke the **Use Hardware Topology** button, which aligns the virtual NUMA as per the physical NUMA of the host. This can be universally adjusted with other hosts with larger NUMA nodes, not to mention if you have such a setup.

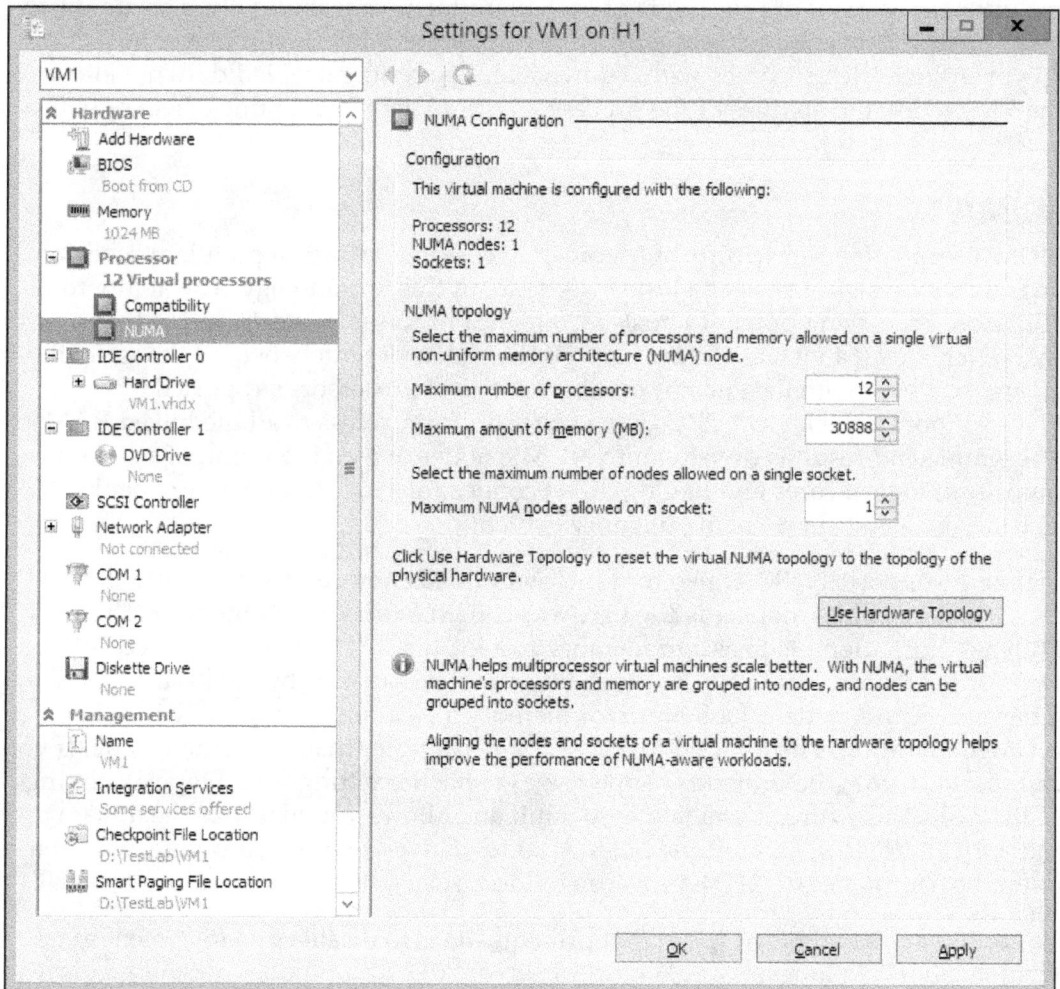

Figure 3-13: Virtual Machine Settings – Processor NUMA

IDE and SCSI Controllers

The next section is about virtual storage and storage controllers for virtual machines. The notable difference between the two generations of VMs is the absence of IDE controllers in Gen 2 VM and the capability introduced to allow the VM to boot from a virtual hard disk hooked up to a virtual SCSI controller, thereby removing the dependency on the virtual IDE controller.

In Gen1 VM there are two IDE controllers with two slot locations, each to which you may add a VHD/VHDX or a virtual DVD drive or a pass-through disk. The latter is a raw LUN presented to the Hyper-V host, however it can be used by a VM. The LUN should be set to offline state in the disk management. Once set to offline state, it would be visible in the dropdown menu for the physical hard disk. Interestingly you can use the pass-through LUN as a boot device.

SCSI controllers are present for both generations of VMs, however you may not be able to add a virtual DVD drive in Gen1 VMs. You can add up to four virtual SCSI controllers with each controller offering, until 64 slot locations have been used or opted to connect to 64 virtual disk files.

There are various operations you may perform on virtual hard disks on this screen, for example, create new VHD/VHDX, convert between types, and inspect the type. There is a dedicated chapter on storage on Hyper-V where most of the aspects discussed here will be covered in detail.

Advanced Features

Every virtual hard disk has a subsection that includes the advancements introduced with Windows Server Hyper-V 2012 and 2012 R2. From here you may enable **storage Quality of Service (QoS) management** for any installed virtual hard disk (VHD or VHDX) and sharing of virtual disks (applicable only with VHDX).

- **Storage QoS** – This feature is optional and put to good use if tracking tenant VM storage utilization is in the IOPS count of 8 KB. The setting is set on the lines of capacity management, wherein you plan what virtual workload you want to host on the VM, its demand and impact on virtual storage, and thereby storage. There are two parameters you can set under this head, minimum IOPS and maximum IOPS.
    - **Minimum**: This setting is not a minimum IOPS assurance but more of an alarm that gets triggered and notifies if the IOPS figure goes below the specified limit.
    - **Maximum**: This is the upper limit cap for storage utilization that you plan to allow for the hosted virtual workload. The VM would not be allowed to go beyond the IOPS specified here.

- **Virtual Hard Disk Sharing** – This is a very interesting feature that has been expected for quite some time. As the name indicates you may now share a VHDX on a SCSI controller among two or more VMs, and use it to share storage for failover clustering on Windows guest machines. Though it would be obvious in the applet, just a mention that VHDs and VHDX on IDE controllers don't pass for this feature.

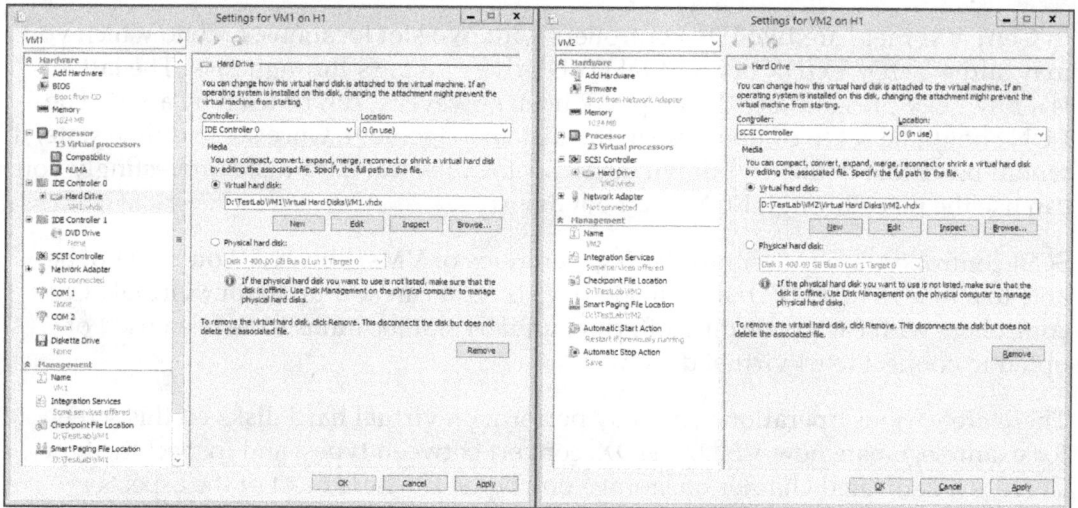

Figure 3-14: Gen-1 and Gen-2 Virtual Machine Settings – IDE/SCSI Controllers

Network Adapter

This section takes you to the next stage of preparing a network communications framework for virtual machines. We talked about creating virtual switches in the previous chapter, going forward from there you add virtual network adapters to connect to the respective virtual network (vSwitch) earlier planned and created. Until Windows Server Hyper 2012, you would see the presence of two kinds of network adapters, namely the legacy network adapter and synthetic network adapter, however Gen2 VMs in 2012 R2 removes the dependency on older chipset emulation and deprecates the legacy network adapter completely. The legacy network adapter is a prerequisite if you are planning to do a PXE boot and OS deployment in Gen1 VMs. Both virtual hardwares are added by the **Add Hardware** option under VM **settings**, thereafter each can be configured and customized accordingly. The hardware can be removed by invoking the **Remove** button control at the bottom of the primary screen. We will look at some of settings briefly, as most of it will be covered in the next chapter:

- **Virtual Switch**: This allows you to link a network adapter to a previously created vSwitch regardless of its type being external, internal, or private. Once you have made the mentioned selection, you may enable VLAN identification and specify the identifier tag (VLAN ID). These settings are similar in both adapters.

- **Bandwidth Management**: This setting is for enabling network QoS on the synthetic network adapters, and is not available for the legacy one. The setting like the storage QoS has an upper and lower limit by giving you options to configure maximum and minimum bandwidth.

- **Hardware Acceleration**: This section is focused on improving the hardware throughput and allows you to set up traffic offloading to the physical NIC. There is more on this aspect in the later chapter.

Advanced Features

This has an interesting set of aspects that you may like to implement if there's the requirement for it:

- **MAC address**: A Hyper-V host associates dynamic MAC addresses to virtual NIC of VMs from a predefined pool that can be verified and customized from the virtual switch manager for the Hyper-V host. The figure is generated dynamically and is unique. Otherwise, you may also configure a valid static MAC address for the VM as per the range. There might be a preference for a static MAC because certain apps bind to MAC and if the VM is configured for live migration the VM would be assigned a new MAC address. Just under this, there is a checkbox **Enable MAC address spoofing**. Enabling MAC spoofing (less secure) has some merits though, which includes enabling VMs to receive broadcasted unicast packets when used alongside promiscuous mode. It allows you to analyze network traffic. Also, this enables the port to send and receive packets from any MAC address thereby assisting the layer 2 virtual switch in building the forwarding table. You may also need the setting enabled for the network load balancing service.

- **DHCP guard**: This can be used to prevent accidental DHCP lease assignment from rogue or unauthorized DHCP servers, set up on virtual machines. Inadvertently an administrator may set up DHCP in the network segment that they should not and end up leasing out leases, and at times breaking networking communication of the respective virtual machines. This setting prevents the DHCP server from answering the client lease requests.

- **Router guard**: Similar to the preceding item, this is again a security enhancement setting. When enabled, this restricts the VM if configured for routing services to forward routing advertisements and redirect messages on the network to which the particular synthetic network adapter is hooked to.

- **Port mirroring**: This setting is from a diagnostic perspective and used to perform network traffic analysis of a particular machine by mirroring its network port on the diagnostic virtual machine. This is done under a situation wherein you can't install diagnostic tools on the desired VM, however since you mirror the port you get the mirrored traffic for analysis on the diagnostic machine.

  The setting is pretty straightforward. Set **Mirroring mode** to Source on the problem VM, and **Destination mode** on the diagnostic machine.

- **NIC teaming**: This is from a virtual machine perspective only and not related to management host NIC teaming. When enabled, this allows the particular synthetic adapter to be part of a NIC team inside the guest operating system.

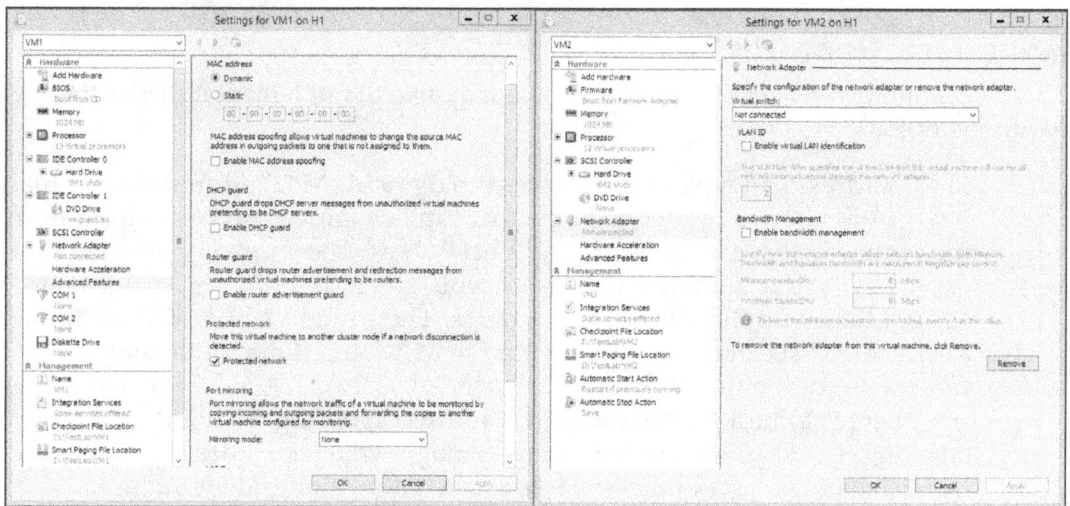

Figure 3-15: Gen-1 and Gen-2 Virtual Machine Settings – Network Adapter

COM Ports and Virtual Floppy Drive

These two emulated devices are no longer available in Generation 2 VMs. VFD have been deprecated, however you many still get back COM ports via PowerShell for live debugging if required.

Management Settings

Until now we have seen hardware settings for a virtual machine and learnt how to add, configure, and to certain extent customize it via the GUI. In the same applet, you could see management settings on the left pane after the hardware settings. There are quite a few attributes which are imperative for you to know and understand their significance. However, before we proceed in the deciphering them, let's see what makes up a virtual machine and how and where it is stored.

Virtual Machine Files

The first attribute under the **Management** settings is the **Name** attribute. This is the first attribute you assign to a VM when you are creating it. This also becomes the label of the VM in the Hyper-V VM pane and elsewhere. Now, you may keep it the same as the hostname of the Windows or Linux guest you install, or chose to make it different. Thereafter you add the configuration and create the virtual hard drive. The following files get created as an end result and some get created later on by respective VM maintenance operations.

- **GUID XML**: This file stores the configuration and virtual hardware specs of the virtual machine and is located under the **Default stores** location that we have discussed previously. It retains the ID/GUID of the virtual machine as the name.

- **BIN**: This is the placeholder for the memory of the virtual machine or VM snapshot.

- **VSV**: This is the file that holds the saved state of devices configured for the virtual machine.

- **VHD/VHDX**: These are the two varieties of virtual hard disk files that you can create for the virtual machines. They can be converted from one form to the other.

- **AVHD/AVHDX**: These are checkpoints of virtual hard drives and there is one created for each virtual hard disk.

- **EXP**: This file gets generated when you are exporting a Generation 1 virtual machine, and will retain the virtual machine ID or GUID as its name. Gen 2 VMs have XML files as exported configuration files.

- **Smart Paging**: These files are generated when Hyper-V invokes smart paging for VMs.

Integration Services

We covered this in the first chapter when we observed the Hyper-V architecture. The components are installed on the guest machines to make them Hyper-V aware and perform operations not requiring management OS intervention. Let's reiterate the old ones and also look at a new inclusion in the Windows 2012 R2:

- **Operating system shutdown**: The service allows the management agents to invoke a graceful shutdown of the VM.

- **Time synchronization**: The service allows the virtual machine to sync its system clock with the management operating system.

- **Data exchange**: The service allows the management OS to detect information about the virtual machine, like its guest OS version, FQDN, and so on.

- **Heartbeat**: The service allows Hyper-V to verify the health of the virtual machine and determine if the VM is a running state or not.

- **Backup (volume snapshot)**: The service allows the management OS to perform a VSS backup of the VM and its apps if they are VSS aware and supported by Hyper-V.

- **Guest services**: The service was introduced in Windows 2012 R2 and has really caught attention. Unlike the other services, this is not enabled by default and you will have to voluntarily enable it. The service allows you to copy files to VMs, in other words use simple copy-paste operations between VM console and the management operating system console, over VMbus regardless of their network presence.

Checkpoint (snapshot) File

The terminology snapshot has been rechristened as checkpoint from Windows Server 2012 R2 onwards (imported from the virtual machine manager naming convention). The base fundamental is the same though as it has been since its inception. Checkpoint or snapshots present system restore points for a virtual machine to a particular point in time, to which you could return or revert after making changes to the same. For example, you save a checkpoint on 1 January for a VM and over the next few days you make changes to the VM, wherein you install apps or drivers or even upgrade it. On the 5th, if you realize the setup is not stable, you may apply the checkpoint from the 1st; all the committed changes would be reverted to the state of the VM on the 1st. On the contrary, if you wish to retain the changes permanently, you may merge the checkpoint.

In Hyper-V you can create a maximum of 50 checkpoints. In every such operation you create a child virtual hard disk called an **advanced virtual hard disk** or **AVHD/ AVHDX** to parent VHD or VHDX respectively. Each child is linked to its immediate parent. Let's say you create the first checkpoint, thereby one VHD followed with AVHD. Thereafter you felt the need to create another checkpoint which generated the second AVHD, which would be child to first AVHD, and so the genealogy goes on. This a seemingly convenient option to undo some unwanted changes and would remind you of a system restore from good old Windows XP days, however the under-the-hood function works differently. With multiple AVHDs created there's notable performance degradation seen with the VM given the fact there's dataset to be accessed which is spread across multiple AVHDs then a read operation issued on all virtual disk files. Also, snapshot/checkpoint is not a recommended way to retain system state or perform backups, as your installed workloads and applications may not be snapshot aware. One classic example would be the USN rollback concern on **domain controllers** (DC) hosted as guest machines. A snapshot restore resulted in hampering active directory replication for the DC with no easy remedy, just a forceful demotion. This was until Windows Server 2012 Hyper-V, which now ensures healthy virtualized domain controllers via the attribute VM Generation-ID. More discussion on this would be beyond the scope of this book.

> For more information on the Active Directory Domain Services Virtualization, please refer to the following page:
>
> https://technet.microsoft.com/en-us/library/
> hh831734.aspx

Another feature upgrade is that Windows 2012 allows live-merge of checkpoints (snapshots), which means you would not need to shut down the VMs to perform a checkpoint merger, unlike its predecessor in Windows 2008 R2. When you right-click a checkpoint you get a few options such as whether to apply, rename, or export the checkpoint. There are two more options: **Delete** and **Delete Checkpoint Subtree**, which means they perform a live merger of current checkpoint or checkpoint hierarchy respectively without the need to shutdown the VM.

The checkpoint/snapshot file location is generally under **Default Stores** unless you customize the location. The AVHD file would be created under the same directory as the parent VHD, however you can alter the location of the snapshots directory, which is typically in the primary folder for the virtual machine name.

Smart Paging

The smart paging feature was introduced with Windows Server 2012 to address the concern of memory depletion on a Hyper-V host when configured with dynamic memory to gain high VM density. Earlier we discussed how dynamic memory is based around three values, namely minimum RAM, startup RAM, and maximum RAM. Using these settings, installed RAM on the Hyper-V host was effectively distributed on the virtual machines based on the fundamental that all VMs would not utilize the committed RAM entirely at all times. The unused RAM would be ballooned out of the VM and returned to the host to be shared further to other requesting VMs.

However, there may be situations where demand for memory by virtual machines may be more than the installed memory on the host. For example, an unexpected reboot of the host is performed and all the VMs are set to start automatically. As per their dynamic memory configuration, all would present a demand of startup RAM and the sum would be more than the sum of their minimum RAM and installed RAM on the host. Another situation may be when a set of VMs are restarted together and it will present the same situation. Of course, the situations are partially hypothetical but cannot be ruled out. To address the situation, demand for memory is more than available on the Hyper-V host, the feature smart paging kicks in. Smart paging creates a file in the virtual machine folder, similar to the checkpoint location, which acts as a memory substitute. This is only for a short duration and as the host boots or recovers, the alternative is no longer required. From a design perspective, to address the slower access speeds of hard drive, as an alternative, SSD drives could be used for this purpose.

Automatic Start Action

These are predefined proactive actions that you should decide and select for your virtual machine in the event of the reboot of your Hyper-V host or if it just boots up. These are the following three options:

- **Nothing**: The action means no action, and the VM would not be booted up.

- **Automatically start if it was running when the service stopped**: This option is the default selection. The action is based on the state of the virtual machine, if it was running when the host was shutdown, then automatically start upon reboot of the host.

- **Always start this virtual machine automatically**: Select this option if you need to keep the virtual machine running regardless of its original state, and it will be started whenever the host is booted up.

There is another option you need to address if you are selecting your virtual machines to startup automatically, **Automatic start delay**. The startup delay is specified in seconds which delays the start of the virtual machines, hence they don't compete for the resources and result in a contention situation.

Automatic Stop Action

This covers the situation in reverse to the previous one and focuses on actions to change the state of the virtual machine in case if the Hyper-V host is shutdown or rebooted:

- **Save the virtual machine**: This option is selected by default and in the event of the shutdown of the host, the VM's device state is saved in a VSV file in the virtual machine folder along with a BIN file that amounts to the size of the memory assigned to the virtual machine thereafter retains slightly enough space to dump the state of the memory. It's similar to hibernating a physical machine. If you restart the VM, it would read the state from the VSV and BIN files respectively and load the guest machine at the same state it was saved.

- **Turn off the virtual machine**: This option is preferably used to power down machines in a similar way you turn off physical machines by pushing the power button.

- **Shut down the guest operating system**: This option is self-explanatory and if enabled it gracefully shuts down the virtual machine via Integration Services when the host is set to shutdown. This has been recommended under circumstances when administrators do not wish to retain the BIN files and save on storage space.

Setup via Windows PowerShell

If you wish to skip all the clicks and options and prefer to set up the VMs in one go, PowerShell is your answer. You may eventually learn to perform large deployments with the help of this scripting platform. In this section you will learn to achieve the same end result as you would have with the wizard and the GUI in the previous section but with the help of PowerShell. The objective of keeping this section separate from the previous was to ensure that first you got the knowhow of the basic features, then revisited them with PowerShell to look at more granular settings.

1. Let's begin by creating a new virtual machine. For example, here we will create a new VM and name it VM5; thereafter define its default stores and assign them to a previously created virtual switch named CLoudExt1:

```
New-VM -Name VM5 -Path "D:\TestLab" -Generation 2 -
SwitchName
CloudExt1
```

2. Now let's customize the primary hardware and management settings, specifying processor and dynamic memory settings.

```
Set-VM -Name VM5 -ProcessorCount 2 -DynamicMemory -
MemoryStartupBytes 1024MB -MemoryMinimumBytes 512MB -
MemoryMaximumBytes 2048MB -AutomaticStartAction
StartIfRunning -AutomaticStopAction ShutDown -
SmartPagingFilePath "D:\TestLab\VM5\SmartPaging"
```

3. Now customize the processor compatibility, virtual machine reserve, and limit.

```
Set-VMProcessor -VMname VM5 -
CompatibilityForMigrationEnabled $True -Reserve 50 -Maximum
100
```

4. You may set the processor compatibility for older Windows platforms as well allowing you the flexibility of hosting older machines.

```
Set-VMProcessor -VMname VM1 -
CompatibilityForOlderOperatingSystemsEnabled $true
```

5. Next you should create and attach a virtual hard disk and attach an ISO file to a virtual DVD drive to install an operating system, if deploying a fresh install.

```
New-VHD -Dynamic -SizeBytes 40GB -Path
"D:\TestLab\VM5\Virtual Hard Disks\VM5.vhdx"
Add-VMHardDiskDrive -VMName VM5 -Path
"D:\TestLab\VM5\Virtual Hard Disks\VM5.vhdx"
Add-VMDvdDrive -VMName VM5 -Path
"C:\en_windows_server_2012_x64_dvd_915478.iso"
```

6. You may choose to enable new network features on the synthetic network adapter:

```
Set-VMNetworkAdapter -VMName VM5 -DynamicMacAddress -
DhcpGuard On -RouterGuard On -AllowTeaming On -
PortMirroring None
```

7. For booting the new virtual machine, use the following cmdlet:

```
Start-VM -Name VM5
```

8. To capture a checkpoint for the new virtual machine to ensure you can revert to this state:

```
Checkpoint-VM VM5 -SnapshotName "Base Install"
Get-VMSnapshot -VMname VM5
```

Operating system installation

In this chapter so far, you have learnt how to setup a virtual machine. It is time to put it to the use for which you have built it for and install some software. The next thing you will be installing is an operating system on this virtual machine. In the first chapter, we looked at the supported list of operating systems for Windows Server Hyper-V 2012 R2. The list may go stale anytime; however, the shared URL alongside it would be constantly updated by Microsoft as they expand their list to include or exclude certain operating systems.

Before you begin installing an OS you need to understand its prerequisites for hardware requirements and follow-up configuration of virtual hardware, also verify if the OS is enlightened (comes with latest version of integration components) or you need to download the latest integration components or services for it. Thereafter the process of installation of an operating system is no different to the way you would accomplish it on a physical machine.

The process will require the OS optical media or ISO file:

1. Ensure the BIOS/firmware (UEFI) is set to boot from CD/DVD.
2. Under **Hardware** options, from virtual machine settings set the DVD drive to `Image File` and select the OS ISO media. Alternatively, you may capture the optical drive of the Hyper-V host as well by toggling the physical CD/DVD drive option.

    PowerShell cmdlet:

    ```
    Set-VMDvdDrive -VMName VM2 -ControllerNumber 0 -
    ControllerLocation 1 -Path
    C:\en_windows_server_2012_x64_dvd_915478.iso
    ```

3. From the Hyper-V Manager, right-click the virtual machine and select **Start**.

    Powershell cmdlet:

    ```
    Start-VM -Name VM2
    ```

4. From the Hyper-V Manager, right-click the virtual machine and select **Connect**. There is no PowerShell cmdlet defined for this, however you can either create a new function or use `vmconnect`. (e.g. `vmconnect hostname vmname`).
5. Once you get the VMconnect console, it allows you to emulate keyboard and mouse captures and you may install the OS seamlessly.

You may also choose to install OS over the network through PXE boot on the legacy network adapter for Gen 1 or synthetic NIC for Gen 2 VMs.

It is imperative that you follow up the OS installation with an Integration Services install update. From the VM connection window, click on the **Action** menu and in the dropdown select **Insert Integration Services Setup Disk**. It will prompt you to run the setup. Using PowerShell you can do the following:

```
Set-VMDvdDrive -VMName VM2 -ControllerNumber 0 -ControllerLocation
1 -Path VMGuest.iso
```

This is applicable for Windows, however if you are deploying Linux you will need to download the **Integration Components** (**IC**) ISO file. The directions to apply the IC are specified in the DPF file, which can be downloaded along with ISO.

Virtual machine conversion

Now you know how to set up and build a new guest machine and understand the various settings from a virtual hardware and management perspective. This helps if you are building everything from the ground up and planning accordingly as per your new requirements. However, environments hosting physical servers with critical roles, that may be running legacy operating systems or applications or building the same roles from scratch on a virtual machine, would not be a feasible idea. However, they will still like to consolidate and reduce their physical server count for reasons we have discussed multiple times so far. The process is called **P2V** or **physical to virtual conversion**. The physical workloads can be converted using System Center 2012 SP1 **Virtual Machine Manager** (**VMM**) as the feature has been deprecated in System Center 2012 R2 Virtual Machine Manager. There is also another Microsoft tool called Disk2vhd which is not as robust as the previous one, but assists in easily converting hard drives of the physical machines into VHD/VHDX, which can be later attached to a virtual machine configuration. Once that is done, all you need is to boot the VM up and you would have a virtual instance of the physical machine you wanted to consolidate.

Another situation could be when you have a virtualization solution in place, let's say VMware, and you wish to employ Hyper-V now. All you need to do is convert the VMware virtual machine to the Hyper-V virtual machine and the process is called **V2V** or **virtual to virtual conversion**. Microsoft has a powerful tool called **Microsoft Virtual Machine Converter** (**MVMC**) which can be used to perform the task. The V2V operation can also be performed by VMM as well, however in the following sections we will focus on the workings of the free tools.

> At the time of writing this chapter, MVMC 3.0 was yet to be released and MVMC 2.0 has been used in the following examples. MVMC 3.0 supports P2V as well.

P2V via Disk2vhd

The **Disk2vhd** tool is another free utility from Sysinternals (now with Microsoft) and can be downloaded from TechNet. The tool is a downloadable executive and does not need to be installed. You only need to invoke the tool and follow the screens. If you wish to avoid GUI there's a provision to use it as a command line which comes in handy for converting large sets. Let's walkthrough the Disk2vhd screens to see how it achieves the conversion and what considerations you would need to make before going ahead with the process:

1. Download the executive on the physical machine whose hard drive you wish to convert. For illustration refer to the system information of a physical machine in *figure 3-16*, prior to conversion:

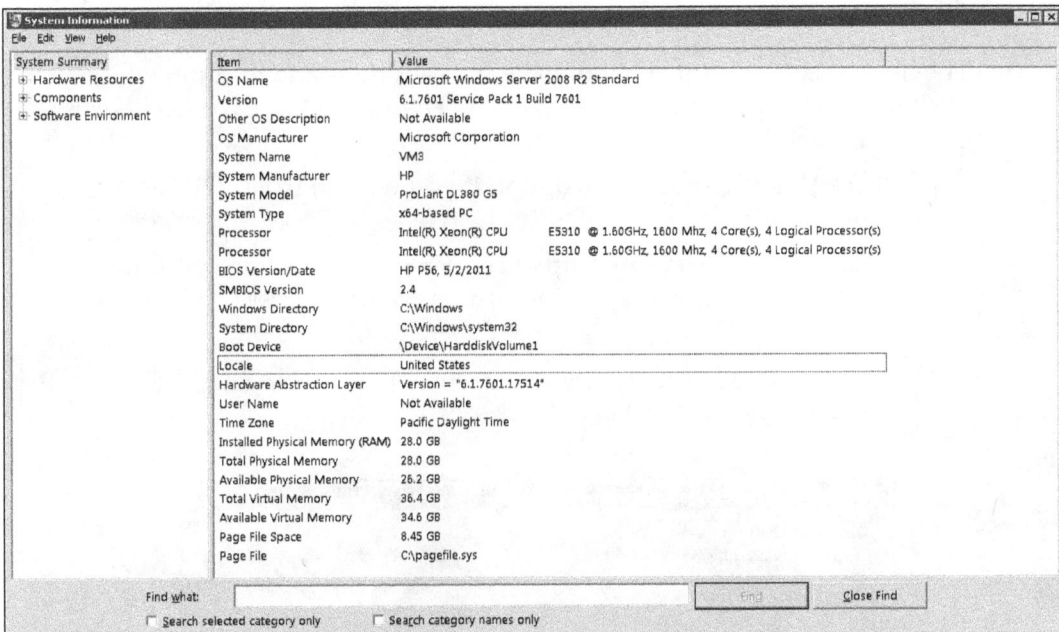

Figure 3-16: System Information (before conversion)

2. Invoking the .exe would present you with the standard license agreement. Click on **Agree**.

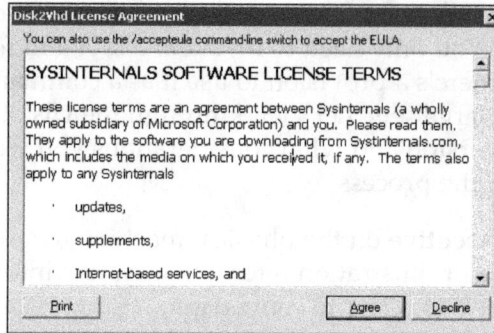

Figure 3-17: Sysinternals License Agreement

3. The next screen prompts you to make the selections and location where you wish to save the converted VHD/VHDX. The screen has two checkboxes enabled by default:

    °   Use VHDX (disable this option if you wish to have VHD as an output).

    °   Use **Volume Shadow Copy** (The **VSS** allows you to continue using the system while conversion process is in progress.

Please note that Disk2vhd will not convert drives greater than 128 GB in size.

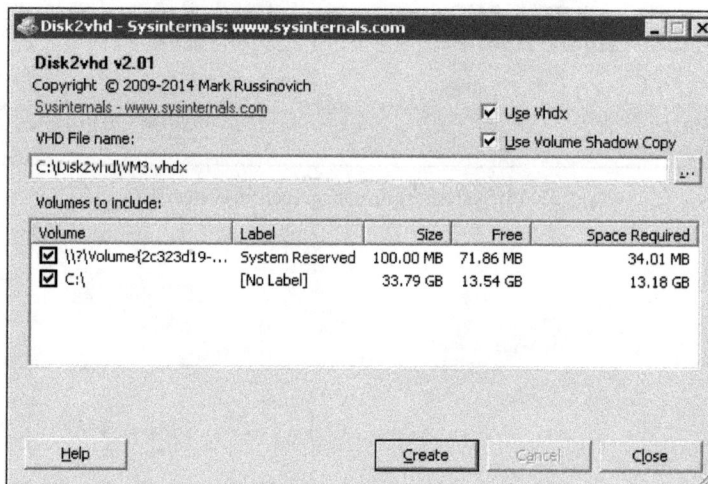

Figure 3-18: Virtual Drive Information

4. In the field for VHD file name you specify the location where the virtual hard drive should be saved post conversion. In the following shared snapshot, you could see the system reserved volume along with the `C:` drive. Ensure you check this one for conversion of the `C:` as a boot drive otherwise the created VHD will not be bootable. Once you are sure of the updated information, click **Create**.

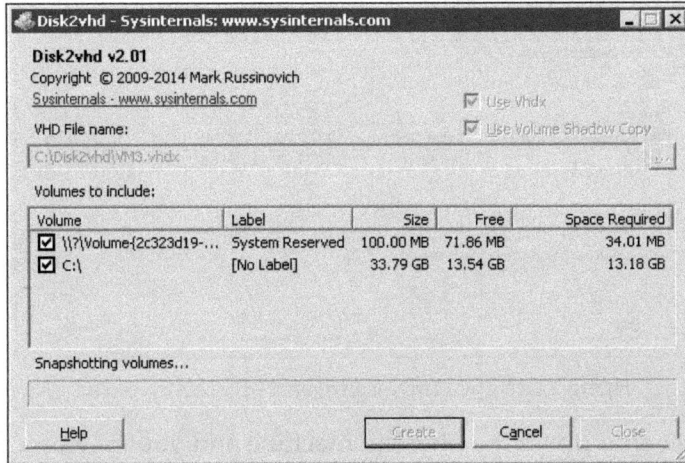

Figure 3-19: Virtual Drive Conversion – Snapshotting of Volumes

5. The conversion process initiates the snapshotting process and thereafter prepares the VHD/VHDX.

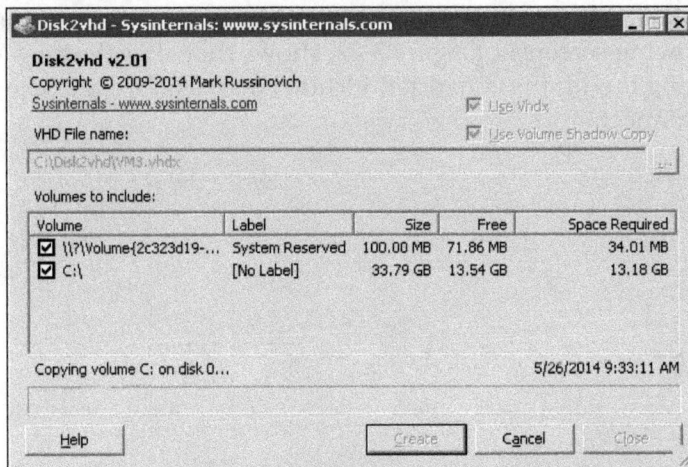

Figure 3-20: Virtual Drive Conversion – Creating Virtual Disk

6. Once the conversion process is successful and the virtual hard disk is exported to the preferred location, move the disk to the location from where you would link it to the placeholder virtual machine.

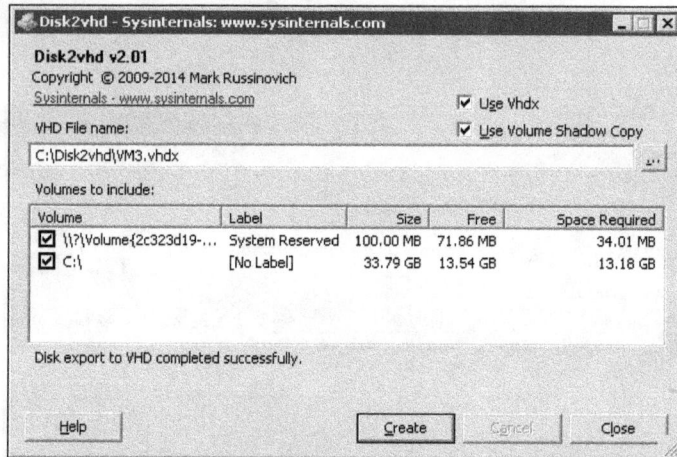

Figure 3-21: Virtual Drive Conversion – Process Successful

7. Thereafter shut down the physical machine and you may proceed with the creation of a new virtual machine using the Hyper-V Manager. Ensure the hardware configuration you specify when the wizard coincides with the specifications of the physical machine. At the screen for **Connect virtual hard disk** either select **Use an existing virtual hard disk** and state the location of the newly converted virtual disk or select the third option **Attach a virtual hard disk later** if you wish to do it later from the virtual machine settings. The following screenshot, *figure 3-22*, shows that after the new VM creation and linking it with the converted virtual hard disk, we are able to connect via VMconnect.

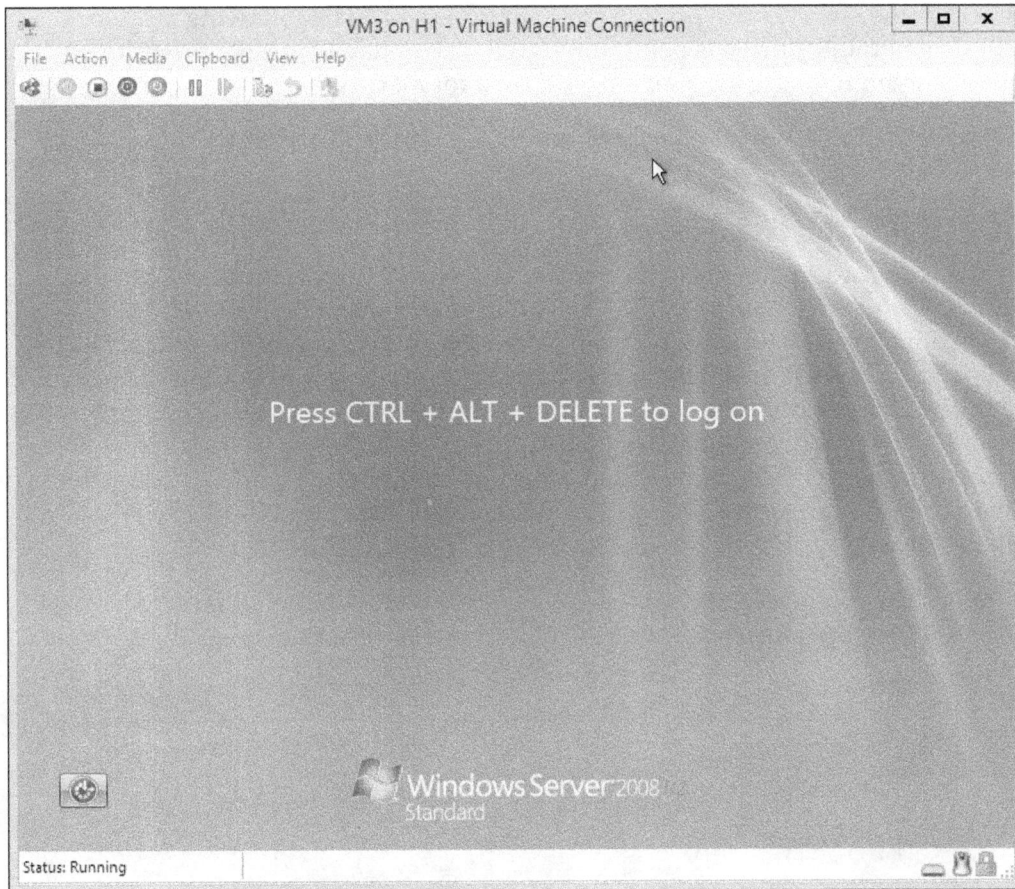

Figure 3-22: Hyper-V Virtual Machine with converted VHDX

> The Disk2vhd tool can be downloaded from here:
> `https://technet.microsoft.com/en-us/library/`
> `ee656415.aspx`

The command line for the executive is equally simple and you may use it as well:

```
disk2vhd [-h] <[drive: [drive:]...] | [*]> <vhdfile>
```

-h switch is used in case if you wish to convert a Windows XP or Windows 2003 for a virtual PC and thus it patches the converted VHD with the right **HAL** (**Hardware Abstraction Layer**).

The rest of the switches are pretty simple to figure out. The following is a quick example wherein C: drive is being converted. If you have multiple drives to be converted, you may use the * as the wild card for all drives.

```
disk2vhd C: C:\downloads\text.vhdx
```

V2V via MVMC (2.0)

The preceding was a quick insight into a supposed P2V. Let's now look at how to convert a virtual machine hosted on an ESXi 5.5 virtualization host. MVMC 2.0 is again a free download offering from Microsoft and is a quite efficient tool as it allows you to connect to either an ESX or vCenter server for migrating machines. The utility cannot only convert for an in-house Hyper-V host but also port convert machines to Azure. Unlike the previous utility, MVMC has to be installed, and for better performance it's recommended to be installed on the Hyper-V host, where you wish to host the converted VMs. Let's walk through the screens and see how MVMC achieves the end results:

1. When you invoke the MVMC, it prompts you with the initial screen that advises the purpose of the tool. Click **Next** to select the migration destination.

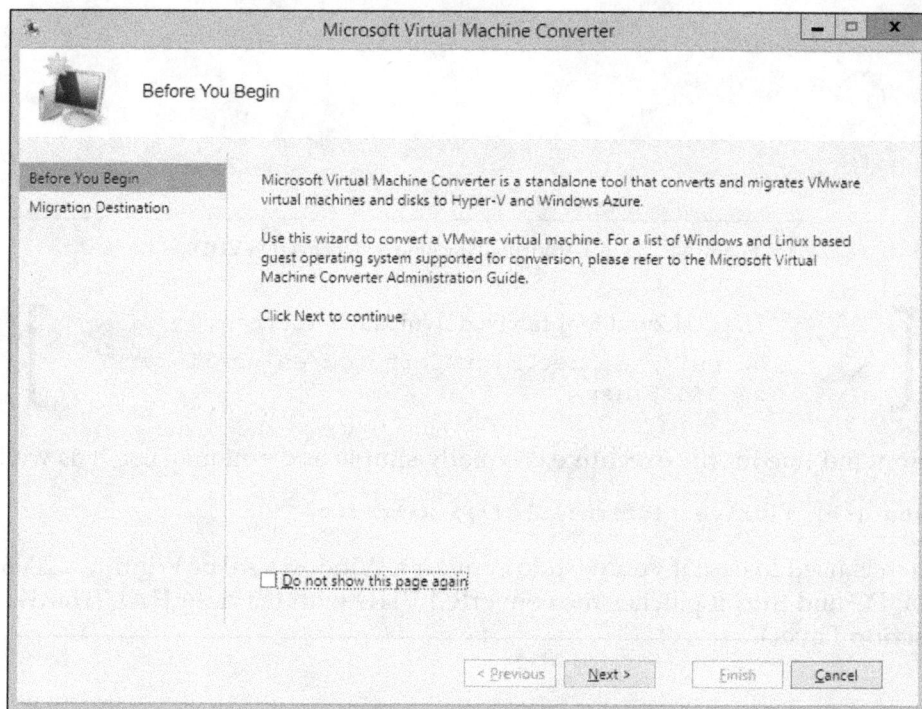

Figure 3-23: MVMC – Before You Begin

2. On the **Migration Destination** page, you need to decide whether to convert for the local virtual infrastructure or private cloud, or port the VM to Azure (yes, Azure!). MMC allows you to convert and load the VM to Azure public cloud.

In the following case, we are going to keep it simple and within the boundaries of this book and select Hyper-V. There are some prerequisites that you need to consider like enabling remote WMI access on the root namespace of the VMware source machine to administrators and also allowing access for Windows Management Instrumentation on the Windows Firewall. Click **Next**.

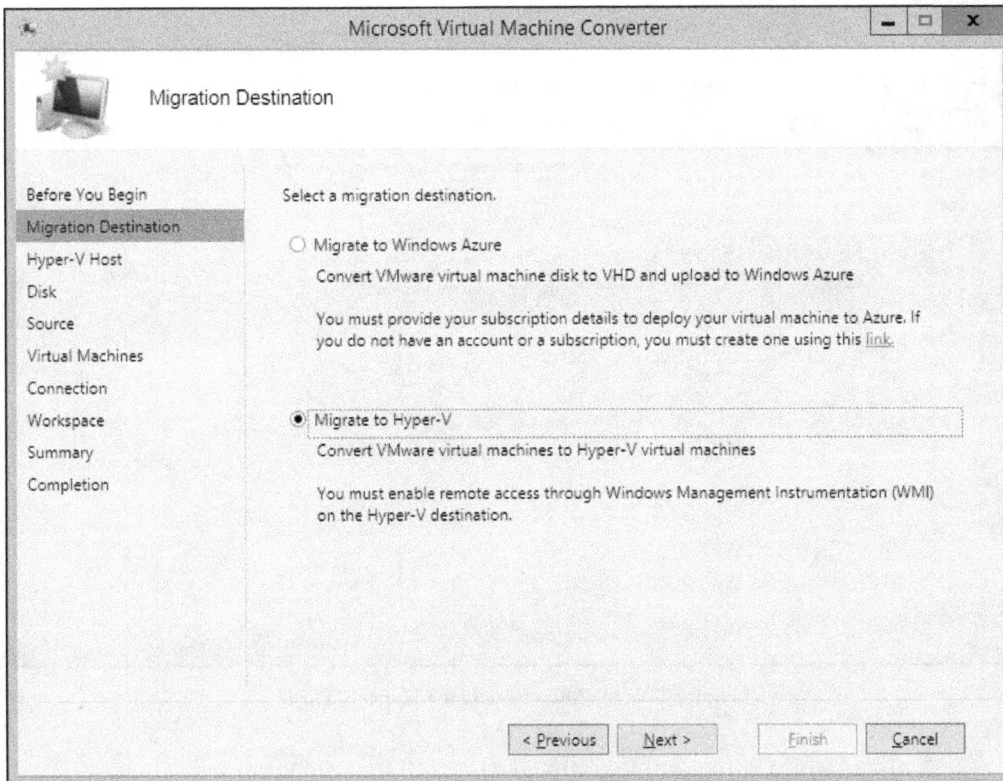

Figure 3-24: MVMC – Migration Destination

3. Since you have selected **Migration Destination** as Hyper-V, the next screen prompts you to specify the FQDN of the host or the IP address, along with the credentials with admin privileges and delegation the Hyper-V host. If you are logged on the Hyper-V host with domain admin credentials and MVMC is installed on the same server, you may just check **Use my Windows user account** for using the same credentials. Click **Next**:

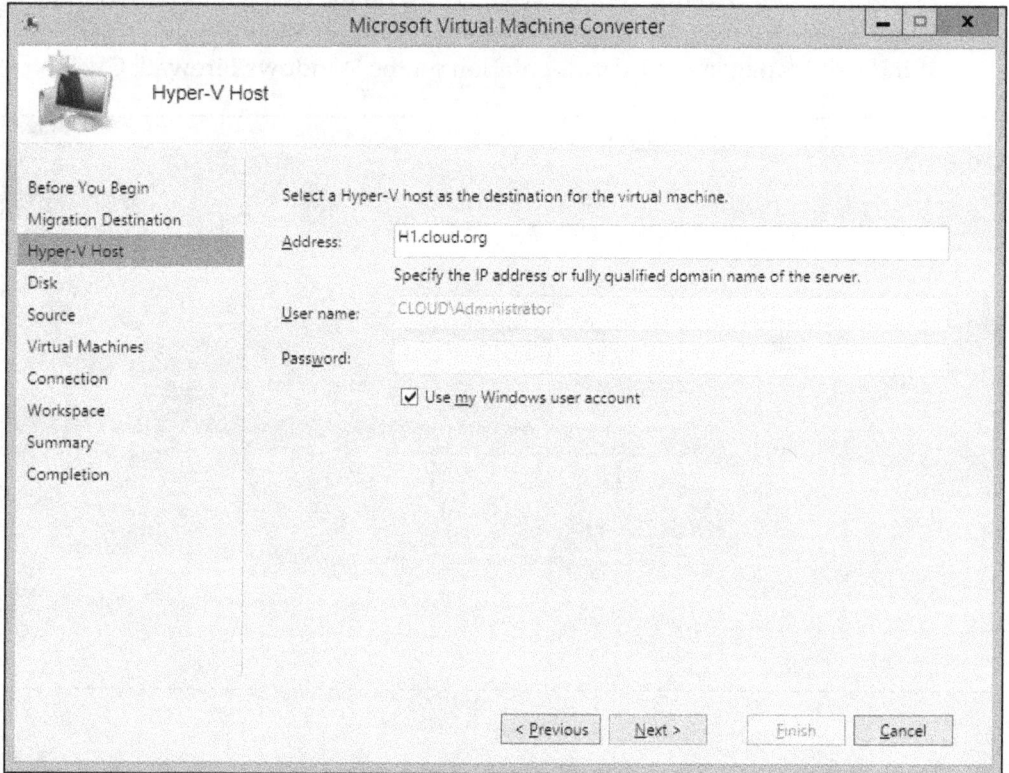

Figure 3-25: MVMC – Specify the Hyper-V Host

4. In the next screen, you need to make choices for your virtual hard disk type and the location where you wish to save it. In **Path** specify the location where you wish to save the VMDK converted VHD/VHDX files. Also, specify the type and format of virtual hard disk you wish to use. Click **Next**:

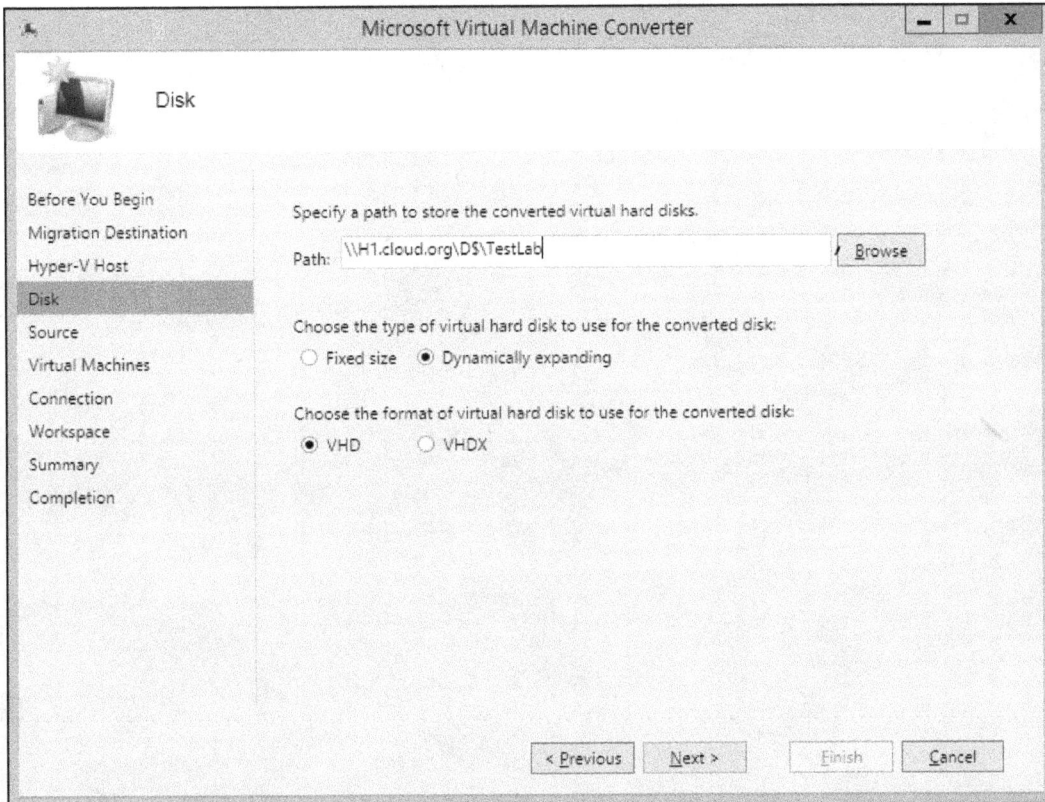

Figure 3-26: MVMC – Specify the Virtual Hard Disk Type, Format and Location

5. In the follow-up screen you are required to update the details of the source machine. The source machine could either be the ESXi host or the vCenter hooked to the ESXi hosts. Apart from that you would need to specify the credentials for the host so that MVMC can load and convert the VMs from that host impersonating the account. Click **Next**:

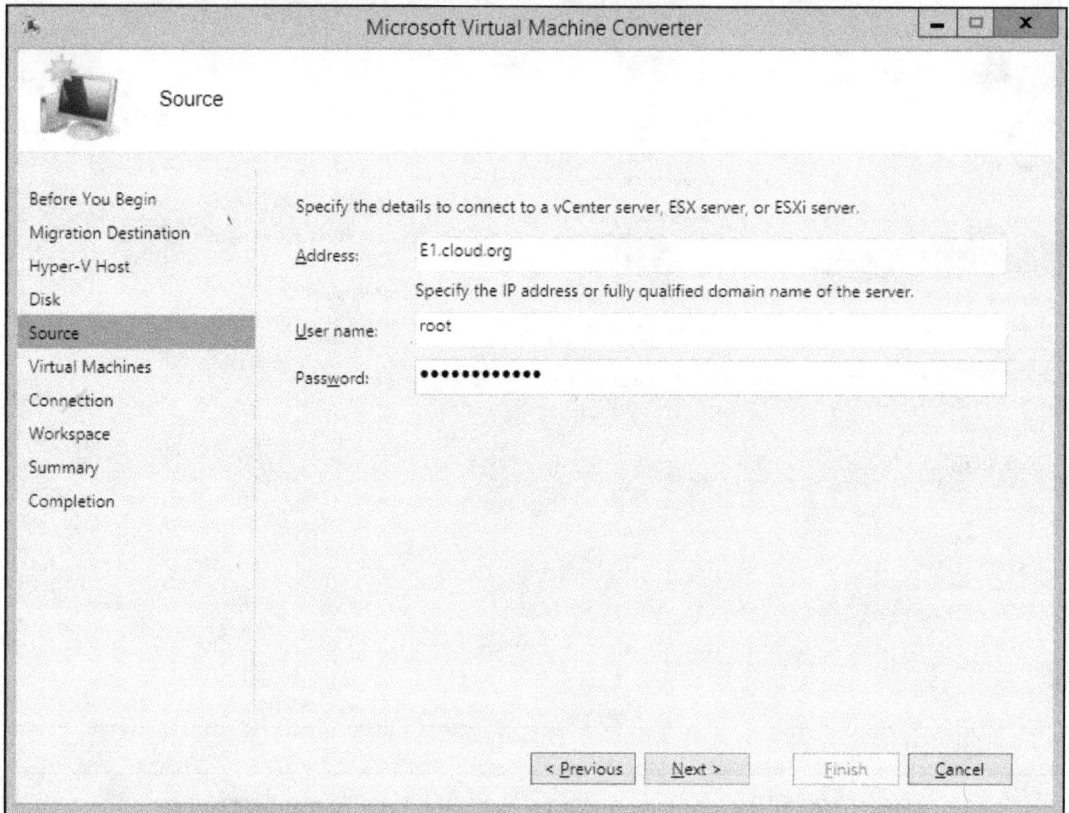

Figure 3-27: MVMC – Specify the ESXi Host or the vCenter Server

6. The next screen is pretty straightforward. All you need to do is select the VMware-based virtual machines identified by the MVMC on the ESXi host(s) that you need to convert. Click **Next**:

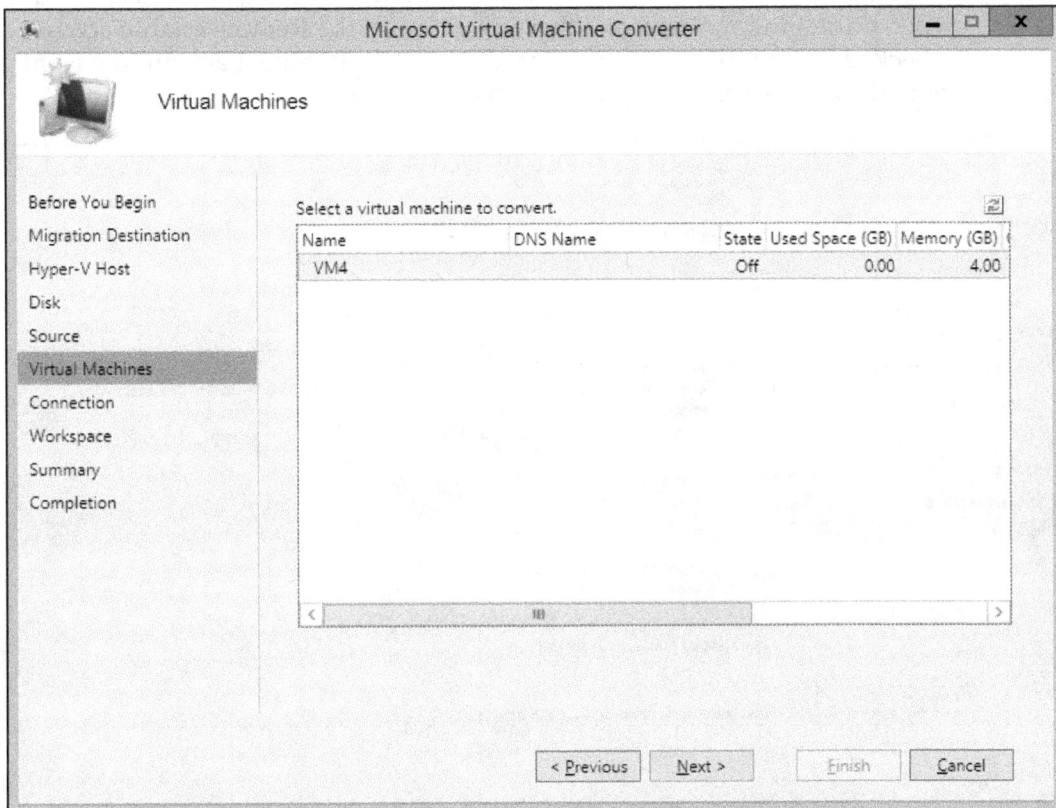

Figure 3-28: MVMC – Select the VMware Virtual Machines for Conversion

7. This screen talks about the prerequisites to take care of on the source virtual machines. First is the removal of VMware tools if you wish to convert the VM in the running state. It would be good to remove the VMware tools beforehand because post conversion you will need to purge them and install Hyper-V Integration Services either way. Ensure the **Remote enable access** is checked for the root namespace on the virtual machine. Last, put the right credentials in the required fields that have the admin privileges on the VM:

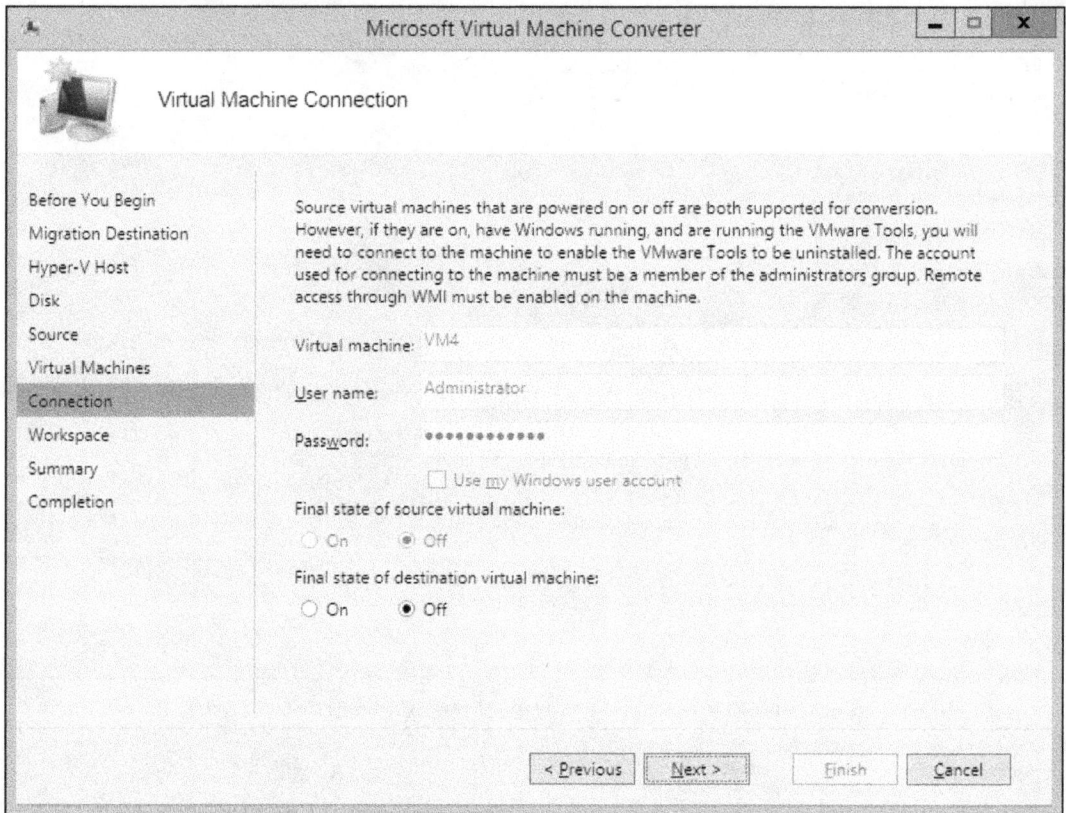

Figure 3-29: MVMC – VMware VM conversion prerequisites check

8. The next page is to specify the workspace location that you could relate with the staging area, where the converted virtual drives would be initially stored. It is imperative the storage location should have ample space, as less space may result in failed end results. Click **Next**:

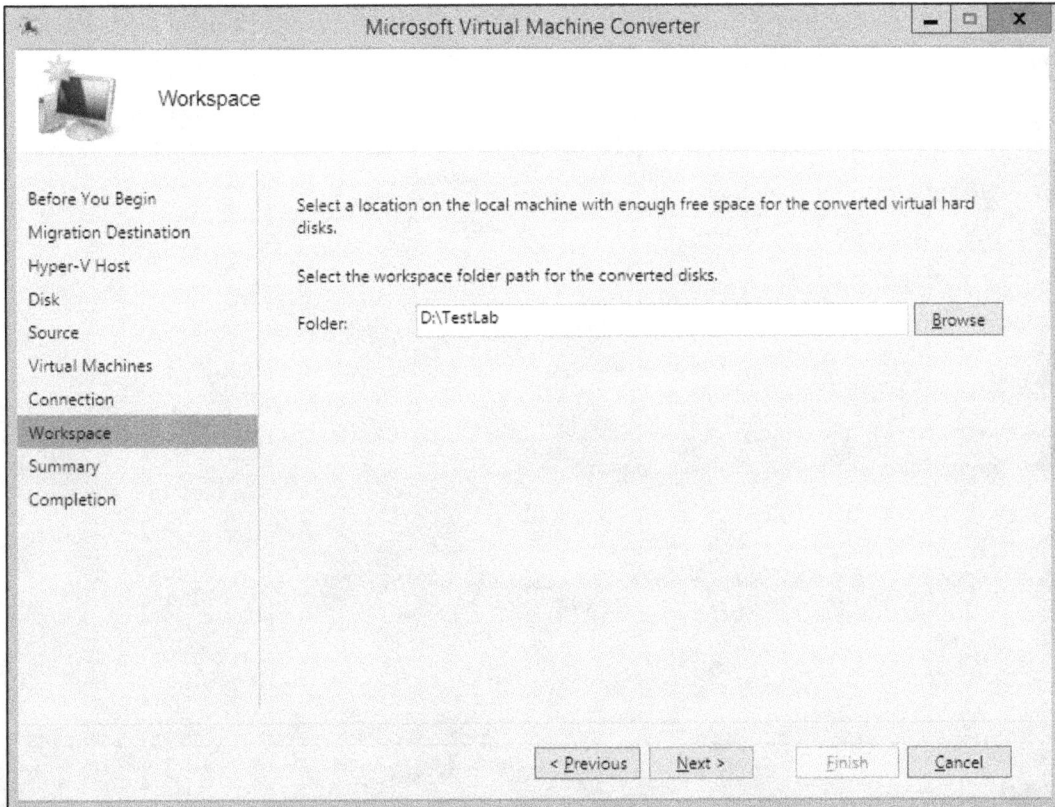

Figure 3-30: MVMC – Specify the Workspace location

9. On the **Summary** screen, verify the details of the expected conversion. Click **Next**.

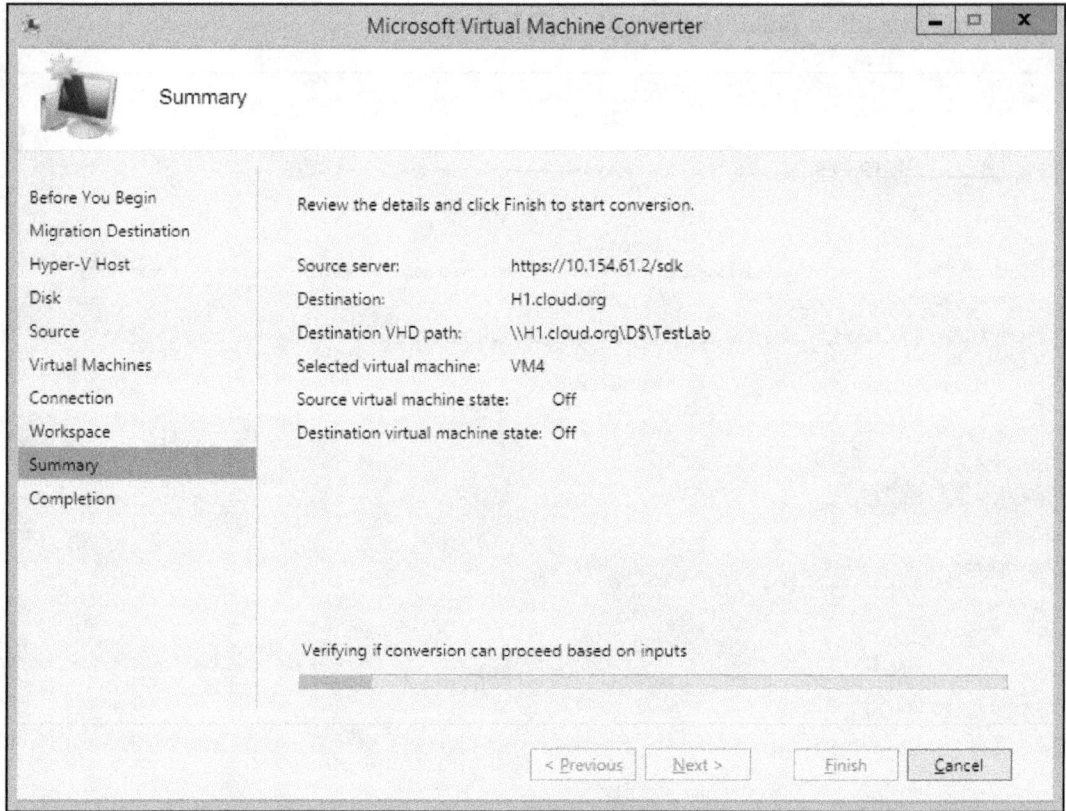

Figure 3-31: MVMC – Summary

10. Post summary, the MVMC gets activated and performs background tasks of validating, converting, analyzing, exporting disk, and finally provisioning the Hyper-V guest from the VMware guest machine.

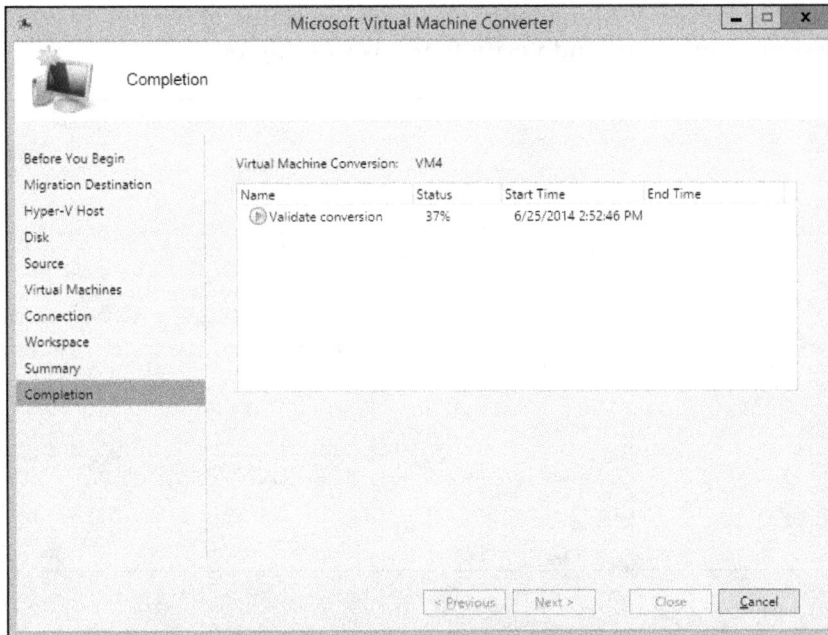

Figure 3-32: MVMC – Completion

11. Once the process is successful, click on **Close** to exit the MVMC wizard.

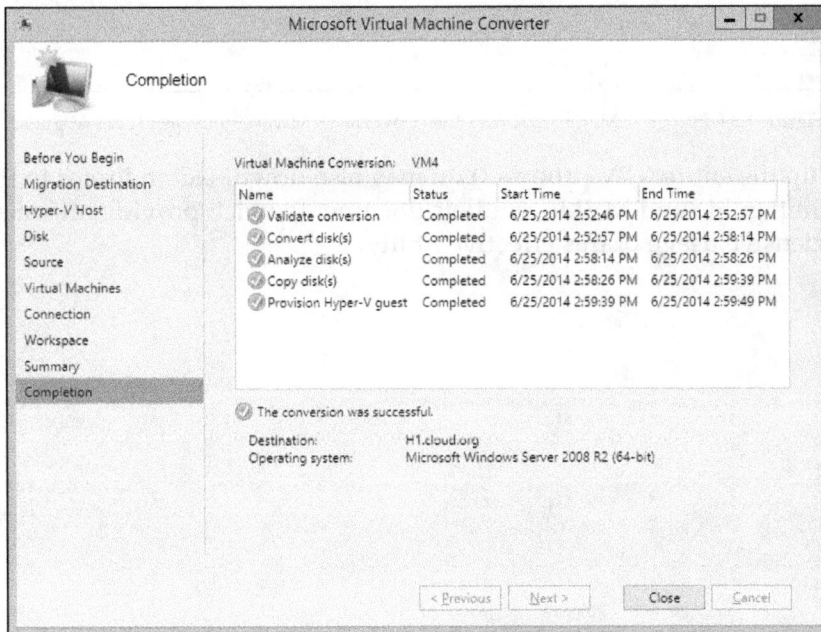

Figure 3-33: MVMC – Completion Successful

12. Open the Hyper-V Manager to check on the status of the newly converted guest machine. Start and verify that it is running perfectly.

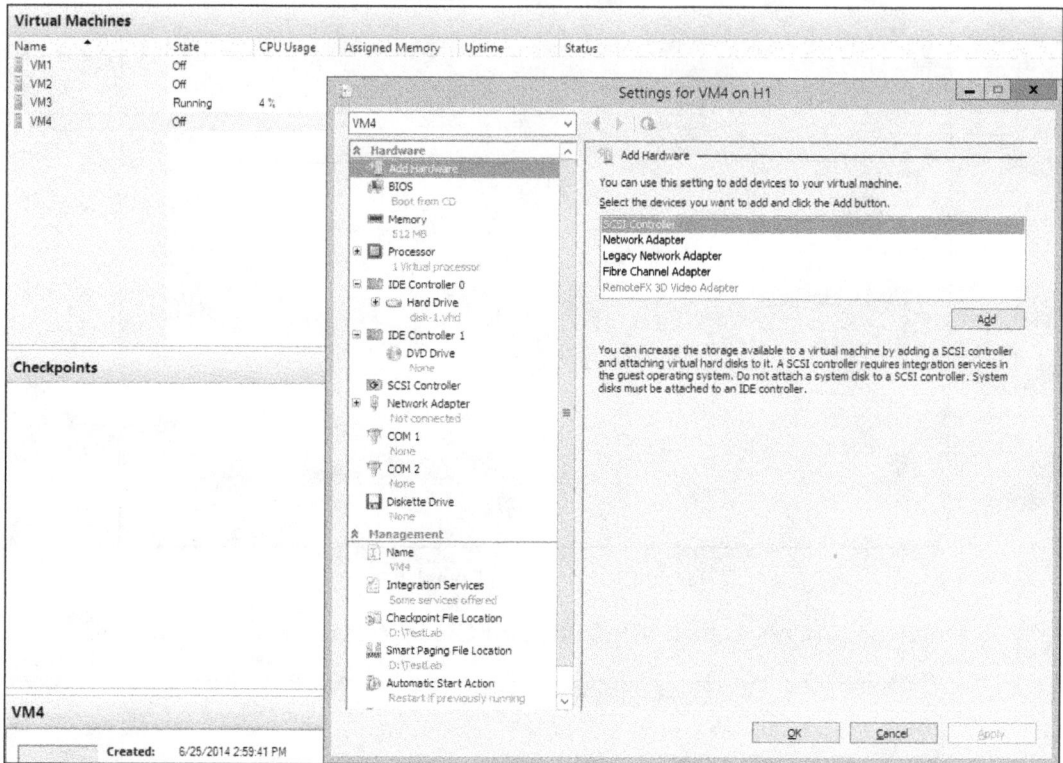

Figure 3-34: Hyper-V Manager shows the converted VMware guest as Hyper-V guest

This sums up the entire V2V process. You may also download and refer to the MVMC admin guide and MVMC cmdlets document, which provide information on more extensive usage of this effective utility.

The MVMC feature set can be extended and automated using another free toolkit from Microsoft called **Migration Automation Toolkit (MAT)**, which is a collection of PowerShell scripts to make your conversion tasks seamless.

The MVMC tool can be downloaded from:

```
https://www.microsoft.com/en-us/download/details.
aspx?id=42497
```

The MVMC admin guide can be downloaded from:

```
http://download.microsoft.com/download/9/1/E/91E9F42C-
3F1F-4AD9-92B7-8DD65DA3B0C2/Virtual%20Machine%20
Converter%20Administration%20Guide.doc
```

MAT can be downloaded from:

```
https://gallery.technet.microsoft.com/Migration-
Automation-c5842c98
```

Virtual machine capacity and design considerations

In this chapter so far, you have come to know different ways to set up virtual machines. Every technique is straightforward and with automation the methods will let you create virtual machines on the fly. It is quite evident now that setting up virtual machines is not a daunting task; it's the planning that requires a great deal of homework and thought. In the second chapter you saw how the Microsoft Assessment and Planning (MAP) Toolkit helped you assess an environment and identify which servers should be used as Hyper-V hosts or decommissioned, as well as what would be the total expected virtual workload if you plan to consolidate them. That does help in planning the capacity of the Hyper-V hosts. In the next stage, you will consider designing virtual machines and plan their capacity from the application perspective which they would be hosting. Planning a virtual machine for an application is almost the same as planning it for a physical machine. You would need to know the resource requirements of the application. It can be identified by collecting samples of resource utilization for the app via the performance monitor (**Perfmon**). Virtualization allows you to mix different workloads, which may not perform well together if resources are shared. For example, Sharepoint recommends 100 percent virtual machine reserve to avoid sharing of logical processors. In addition to the former, you would also need to verify that the application is supported on a virtualization platform and thereafter Hyper-V. From an application perspective, the software vendors would provide you with the latest documentation, support statements, and best practices.

Next, you target the performance tuning of the virtual machine and follow the best practices on the rest of the VM set. The tuning measures may differ from one VM to other depending on their virtual workload. Nevertheless, implement the basic ones, for example keep the Integration Services up-to-date, reduce background activities on idle VMs which help reduce futile CPU cycles, remove devices which are not in use like CD/DVD drives, COM ports, and so on. For more insight into performance tuning, please refer to the following link:

Performance Tuning for Hyper-V Servers:

http://msdn.microsoft.com/en-us/library/windows/hardware/dn567657.aspx

All the facts discussed here attribute to better design principles when planning a virtual machine.

Summary

This is the last section of the third chapter and we will conclude with a little review of what has been discussed so far. We started off with an introduction to the Generation 2 virtual machine, which is one of the strong features of the Windows Server Hyper-V 2012 R2. We also depicted that it differentiates from its predecessor in the Generation 1 virtual machine. Thereafter we learnt how to create new virtual machines via both **New Virtual Machine Wizard** and PowerShell.

We then looked at virtual hardware through virtual machine settings and also discussed how to customize to meet your needs. We also looked at management settings, which included Integration Services, smart paging, checkpoint, and automatic start and stop actions. These settings can be effectively reviewed and modified via PowerShell as well.

In the following section we discussed how to perform operating system installation and install or upgrade Integration Services (components).

We then proceeded toward another method of VM creation, which is consolidation and conversion. We reviewed two utilities Disk2vhd and MVMC 2.0 which assist in converting physical and virtual machines respectively.

Finally, we looked at best practices for identifying capacity requirements for applications to be installed on virtual machines and what measures should be taken to design them and how to tune them for an optimized performance.

In the next chapter we delve a little away from virtual machine terminologies and focus on Hyper-V networking details, looking closely at advancements introduced with Windows Hyper-V 2012 R2.

4
Hyper-V Networking

The real world of physical servers is connected. You are now skilled in replicating the real world and creating your own virtual machine world. In this chapter, you will learn how to connect the entities in the virtual world and link them with the real world as well. With a more technical description, we will discuss the networking components that enable communication among virtual machines on the same host or other hosts, and other entities on the physical network.

Windows Server 2012 introduced some major improvements and advancements in the operating system and Hyper-V networking attributes, and Windows Server 2012 R2 raised the bar a bit more. The older virtual network, which was sometimes referred to as a virtual switch, was succeeded by the **Hyper-V Extensible Switch**, referred to as a **Hyper-V Virtual Switch**. This runs as a layer 2 Ethernet switch in the Management OS. The new virtual switch is feature loaded, and helps with traffic offloading and load balancing effectively.

Also released with Windows 2012 is the NIC teaming feature, which Microsoft finally decided to create and support. It was a greatly awaited feature in the Windows arsenal. Also, there's a lot of focus on network virtualization from Microsoft.

In this chapter, we will cover the following topics:

- An overview of the Extensible Virtual Switch and the types of networks it can create
- Windows NIC teaming overview
- Insights into other new networking features

The Hyper-V Extensible Virtual Switch

Virtual networking has been one of the most crucial aspects of Hyper-V. The same has evolved quite a bit from the first release of Hyper-V. The Hyper-V Extensible Switch replaces and adds upon the features of the older virtual network. In the Hyper-V architecture, the virtual switch sits in the parent partition of the management host and provides the network path to the respective child partitions over the VMBus. The diagram had a simpler outlook until Hyper-V 2.0 and Windows 2008 R2 Sp1. The new Extensible Virtual Switch adds extensions as layers to the structure, presenting a greater level of functionality and monitoring, and ensuring control over workload isolation and network security. The Extensible Switch was released as a feature packed with Windows 2012, allowing end users to benefit from the network virtualization concept, implemented as **Hyper-V Network Virtualization** (**HNV**). End users may use the virtual switch as is or link third-party-vendor-provided extensions to it for additional functionalities.

Before we go deeper and discuss the niche terms, let's start with the basic functions and entities the Hyper-V Extensible Switch provides. Once you develop an understanding, thereafter, we will look at more features that can be added to the networking abilities of a virtual machine and host alike.

A virtual switch – the basic definition and differentiation

A network switch is a device that connects machines to a computer network and allows connectivity between them. A virtual switch does more or less the same job, and is the first piece in the **Software-defined Networking** (**SDN**) concept. A virtual switch ensures a communication framework between virtual machines loaded on the Hyper-V hosts. In the earlier two chapters, we came across this term when configuring virtual machines network adapters, while creating a new VM or customizing it from the VM settings applet, and when we discussed virtual switch manager while configuring a Hyper-V host.

A virtual network adapter, legacy or synthetic, is the network interface controller for the Operating System Environment (OSE) installed on a VM that allows it connect to the assigned computer network. As stated earlier, the network is provided by the virtual switch, which resides in the parent partition, and the connectivity to it is provided over the VSC, VMBus, and VSP channel. You can install a virtual network adapter on a Hyper-V host as well. Of course, there's a design requirement, which we will discuss in the following section. Microsoft veterans should be able to relate the virtual network adapter on the Hyper-V host to the famous Microsoft Loopback Adapter.

The latter was a prerequisite when installing an application (more often RDBMS) that had a dependency on the presence of a network adapter on the Windows OSE and the Type-2 hypervisor offering from Microsoft called **Virtual Server**. The purpose of a virtual NIC on a Hyper-V host, however, is more from a membership- or management-only approach.

Private Network

The simplest approach to virtual networking can be customized to serve a greater purpose. Also referred to as a **private virtual switch**, the virtual device creates an isolated and secure network for the virtual machines that connect to it. The members of this network can communicate with each other only, and cannot be contacted by other machines, or even by the management host over the network. The available way to obtain access would be via VMConnect.

Private network creates a limitation when you have set the VMs for live migration. The virtual switch is confined until the original host and members cannot communicate with virtual machines on another host, even if the private virtual switch has the same name on both the hosts. The end result would be failed networking between VMs if all of them are not migrated together.

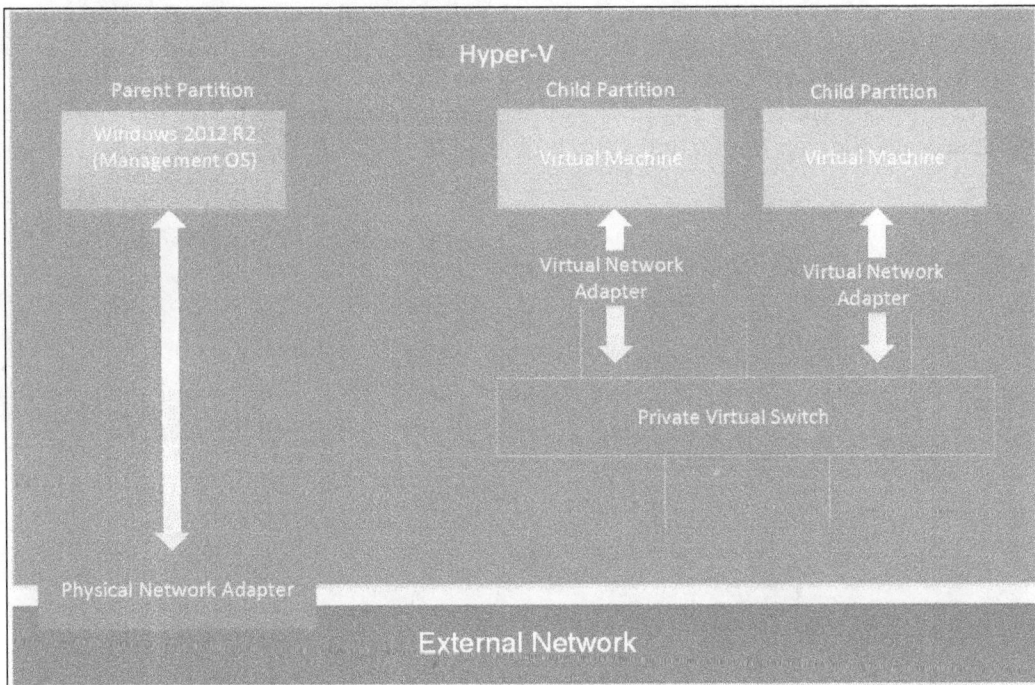

Figure 4-1: Private Virtual Switch

The design approach can be followed for the purposes of setting up a testing environment or building a secure nested environment. In theory, the number of private virtual switches you can create is unlimited. However, their limiting figure will be governed by the available resources.

Internal Network

The **internal virtual switch** is a bit different from the previous one. The virtual switch creates private network of virtual machines, and also ensures the membership of the Hyper-V host with the network. It installs a virtual NIC on the management host (or the parent partition), and the NIC adds the host as a member to this network. The equation is the same as that of the private virtual switch. However, since the host has access to this network, it is termed as internal network.

The limitations and benefits are almost the same, except for the fact you can access the services on the virtual network from the host, and vice versa. The VMs can access the host over the same network. One apparent demerit could be the assignment of networking parameters (IP, DNS, gateway, and so on). If not planned and assigned properly, the host network traffic may be affected due to conflicts in networking parameters (for example, DNS or gateway).

Similar to the private switch, internal virtual switches can be as many as a host can allow. For each internal network, there is a vEthernet virtual NIC installed on the Hyper-V host. In the network connections of the Hyper-V host, the name of the network interface shows up as vEthernet (the name of the switch). You may also enable access mode on the virtual switch by enabling VLAN tagging (VLAN ID).

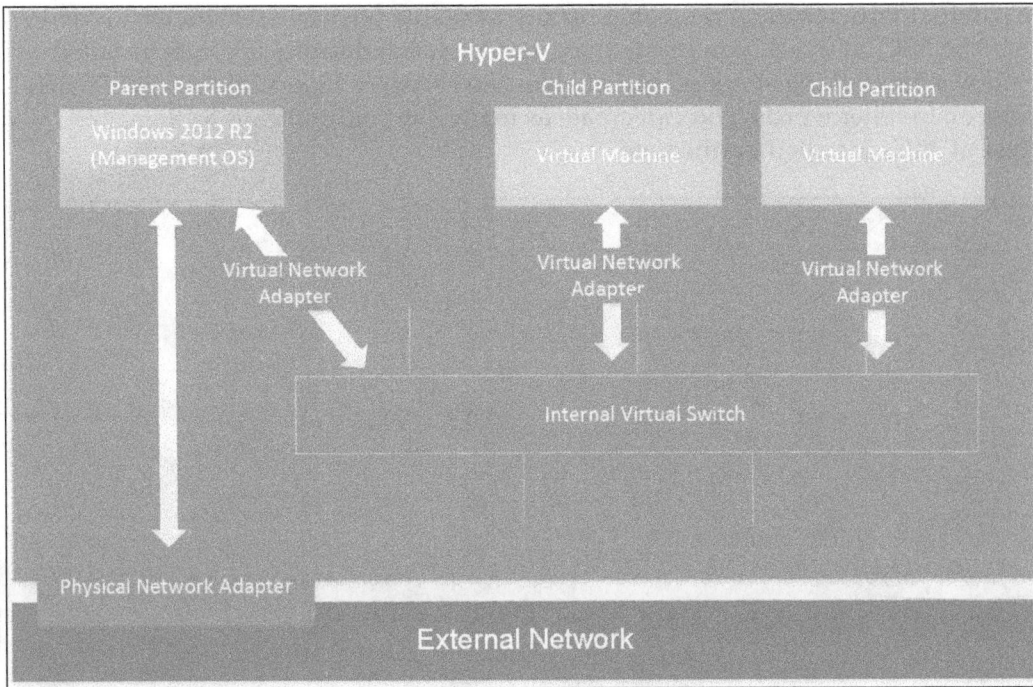

Figure 4-2: Internal Virtual Switch

External Network

External network is the most used of the lot. As the name indicates, the virtual switch links the virtual machines to external computer network or LAN. The switch forms the layer 2 device between the external physical network and the network adapters of the virtual machines. Once the networking path is set up, the VMs will have a normal presence on the physical network, like any other physical computer, and have uniquely assigned IP and MAC addresses.

An external virtual switch is created on any available physical NIC on the Hyper-V host. The NIC on which you create the external switch disables all of its installed Windows networking services, and enables the Hyper-V Extensible Virtual Switch Protocol. In other words, you can create as many external switches as there are physical NICs installed on the host.

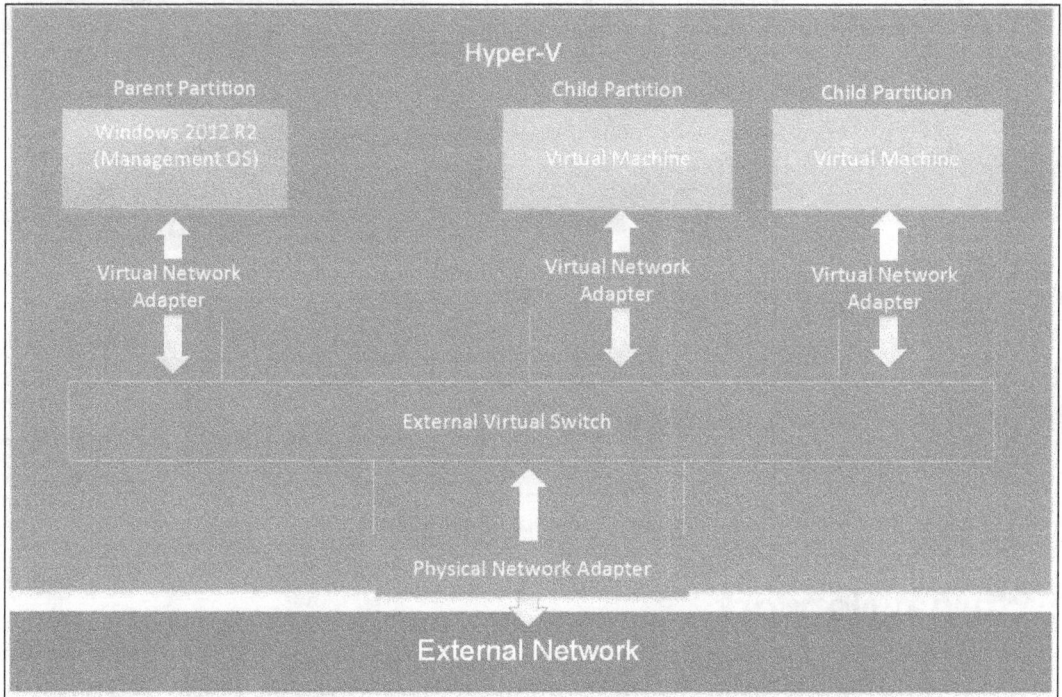

Figure 4-3: External Virtual Switch

Let's consider a scenario where you have two physical NICs on an independent Hyper-V host. You decide to use one for normal networking operations for the host, and on the other, you load the extensible virtual switch. The NIC used for normal operation will not interfere or conflict with the virtual NICs hooked up to the external switch created on the secondary NIC of the host, and they can very well be on the same subnet and communicate like any two physical machines on the network.

As with an internal switch, you may choose to include the management host on the external switch. It depends on your design flexibility and resilience. If you have a limited number of physical NICs on the host, or let's say just one NIC, you may allow the host (parent partition) to share the virtual switch like the virtual machines (child partitions). The visible changes will be similar to the internal virtual switch, wherein a vEthernet (name of the switch) virtual NIC will be installed under the network connections of the host, and will have all the standard network parameters (IP, DNS, gateway, and so on) specified like a physical NIC, which are imperative from a network presence perspective. You may choose to modify the networking services and protocols on the virtual NIC if required.

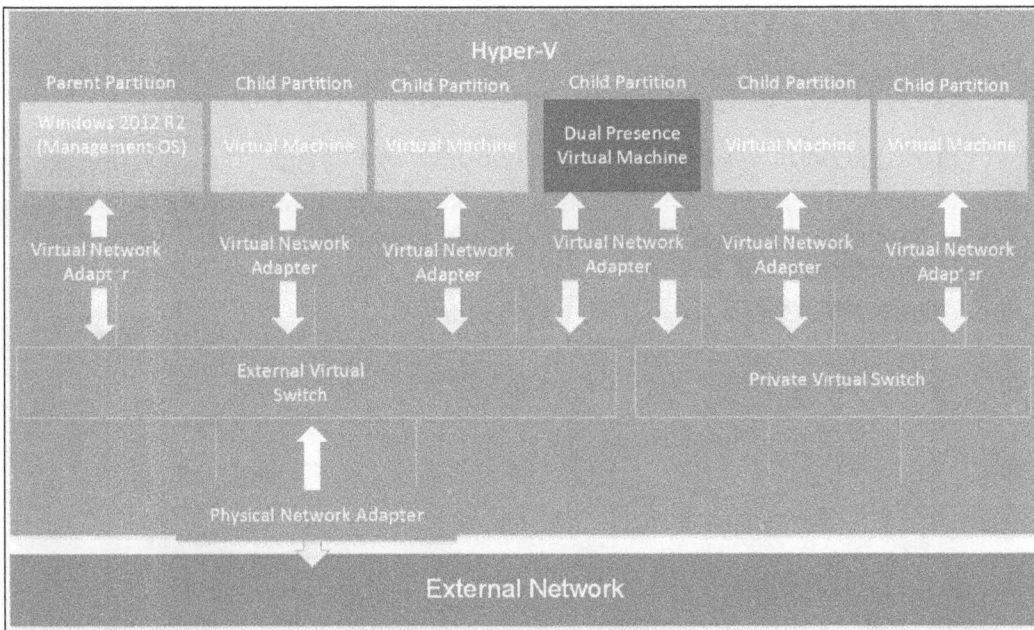

Figure 4-4: Dual Network Presence

From a secured isolation perspective, on a private switch, you may enable external network access if you are keeping a VM with dual network presence. Configure a VM with two virtual NICs, one linked to private network and the other to external network. Enable RRAS or RAS (DirectAccess), depending on your choice of the operating system, on the virtual machine that allows Network Address Translation (NAT), or a specific routing path.

Switch setup and configuration of associated parameters

With a fair understanding of virtual switches, let's proceed to understand the process of creating a switch. The fundamental steps remain the same for each of the three switches. However, they differ in the follow-up configuration. The procedure can be followed via both the Hyper-V Manager console as well as PowerShell. The latter can be utilized in all Windows installation options, namely a server with a GUI, server core, and free Hyper-V as well.

Switch setup via Hyper-V Manager

The process is simple and straightforward, given that you should be familiar with the Hyper-V Manager console by now. The steps are listed as follows:

1. From the **Actions** pane, invoke **Virtual Switch Manager**.

2. In the applet screen on left pane, select **New virtual network switch**, and from the right pane for **Create virtual switch**, select the type of switch: **External**, **Internal**, or **Private**.

3. Click on the **Create Virtual Switch** button.

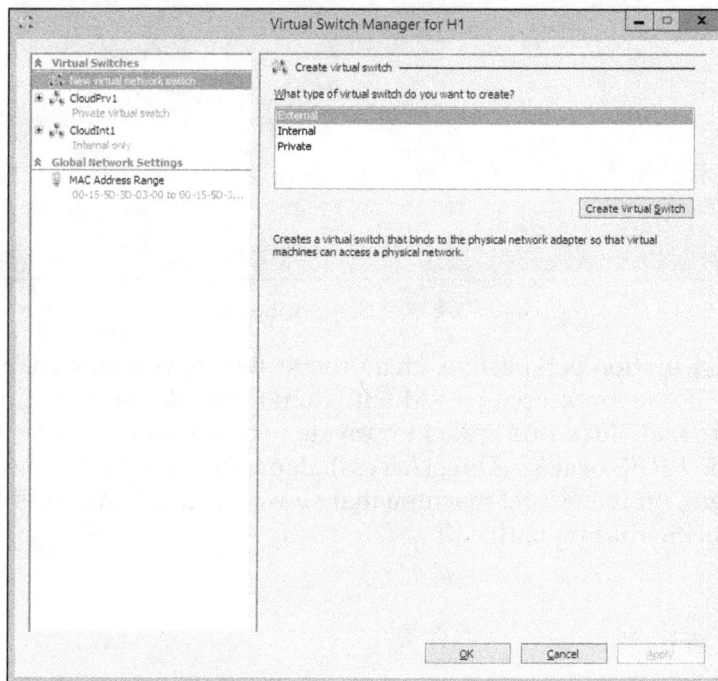

Figure 4-5: Create Virtual Switch

4. In the left pane, you can now see that a new virtual switch has been created.

5. Select **New virtual network switch** and review the properties on the right pane. You can update the name and type of the switch later on as well, and modify the other properties we have discussed so far:

   ° **External switch**: Under this, you will have the following options to enable or customize:

   Allow management operating system to share this network adapter: The use case, reason, and effect on the management host has been discussed in the previous section.

   Single Root Input Output Virtualization (SR-IOV): This is an exciting feature that allows virtual machines to bypass the VMBus and have separate access to the network adapter via the virtual function. We will discuss more on this in the next section.

   Enable virtual LAN identification for the management operating system (VLAN ID): This is meant for VLAN tagging of the parent partition, similar to VLAN tagging of the child partition. It is preferably used when the Management OS is sharing its network connection via an external virtual switch.

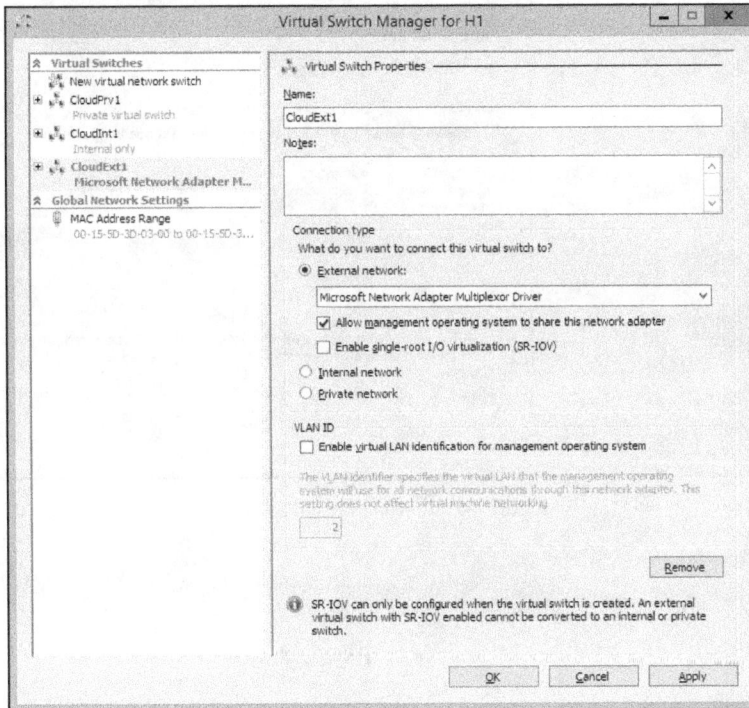

Figure 4-6: External Virtual Switch

○ **Internal switch**: Under this, there's only one additional option. However, as stated earlier, internal network is just another private network that is shared with the Management operating system.

Enable virtual LAN identification for the management operating system (VLAN ID): This is meant for VLAN tagging of the parent partition, as discussed previously.

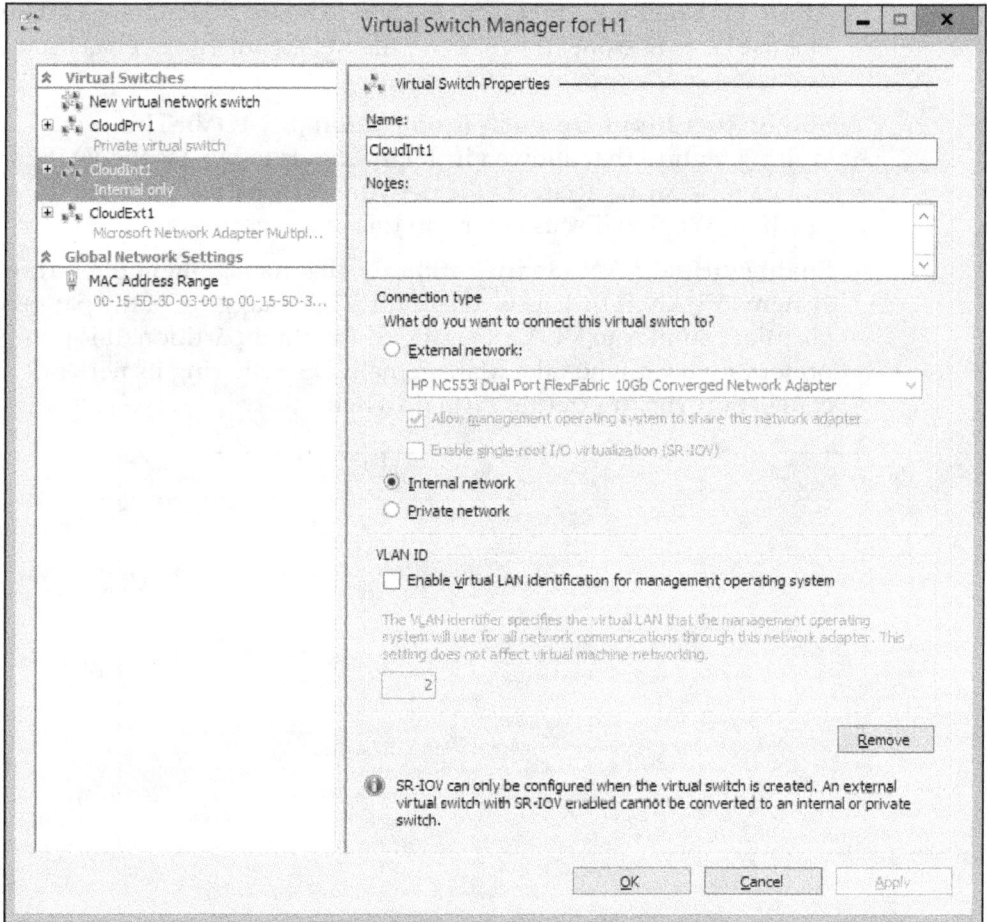

Figure 4-7: Internal Virtual Switch

- ° **Private switch**: This is a vanilla base for virtual machines only, and none of the previous two options exist for this setup.

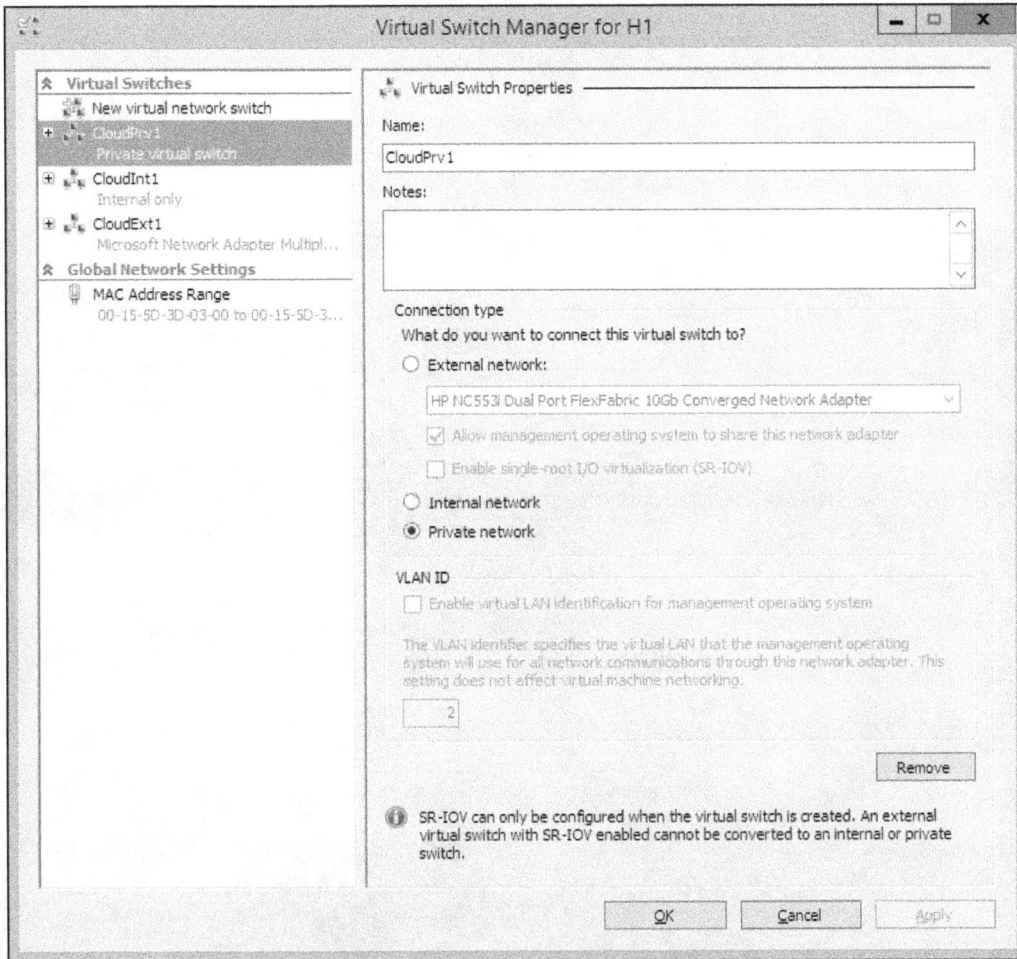

Figure 4-8: Private Virtual Switch

6. Click on **OK**. Your new switch will be created as shown in the screenshots.

MAC address range

In the **Virtual Switch Manager** applet, if you look up the left pane, you will see that there's a small section called **Global Network Settings**. The only option listed there is **MAC Address Range**. The range is randomly generated for each Hyper-V host. If you closely monitor and manage the networking in your environment or perform some testing, you may update the manual figure in these fields.

The specified range is the MAC pool from where the virtual network adapters of the VMs get their MAC dynamically assigned. You might recollect that we discussed this in the previous chapter.

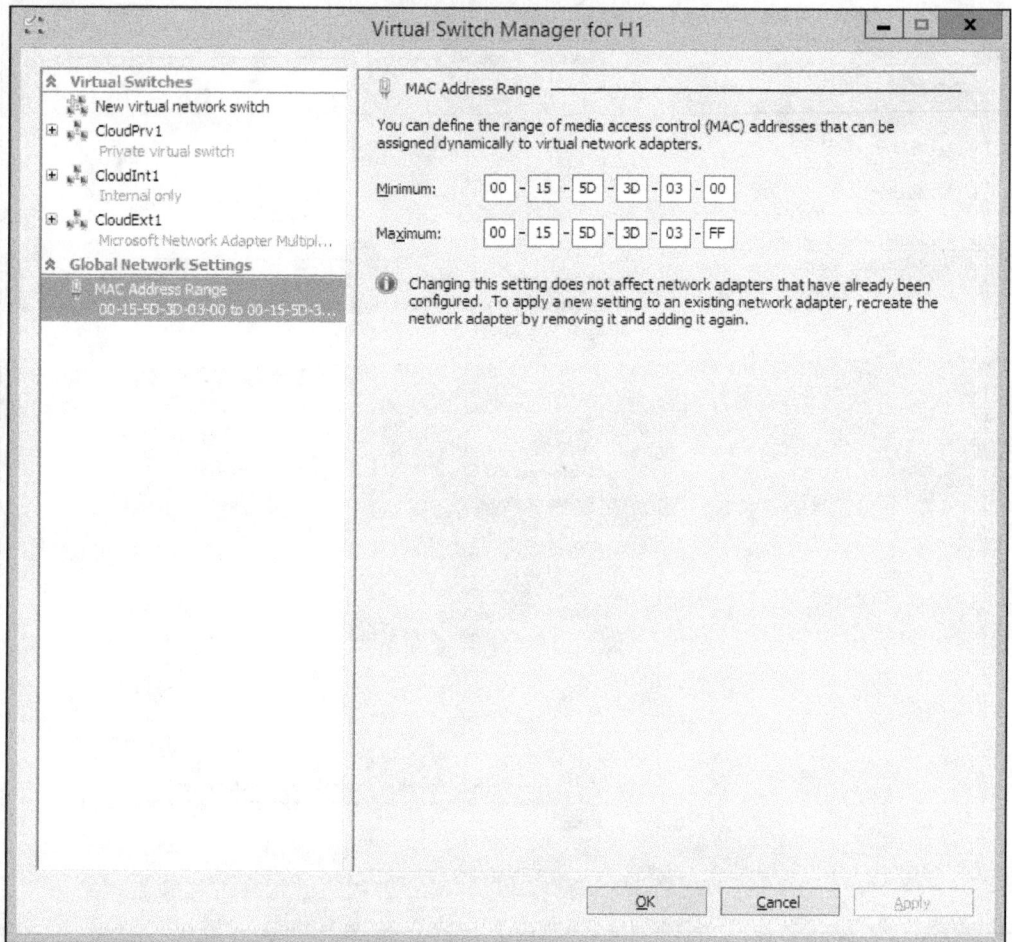

Figure 4-9: MAC Address Range

Switch setup via PowerShell

Now is the time to take the course of the command line or cmdlets. PowerShell equips you with all the options with the help of which you can create and control the virtual networking effectively:

1. First, let's create a new virtual switch for external network allowing Management OS and SR-IOV disabled:

   ```
   New-VMSwitch "CloudExt1" -NetAdapterName "Microsoft Network
   Adapter Multiplexor Driver" -AllowManagementOS 1 -EnableIov 0
   ```

2. Second, let's look at the option of creating internal or private network switch:

   ```
   New-VMSwitch "CloudInt1" -SwitchType  {Internal | Private}
   ```

3. Define the MAC address range for the local Hyper-v host. Ensure that the MAC address string is separated with a colon (:):

   ```
   Set-VMhost -MacAddressMaximum "00:15:5d:01:04:ff" -
   MacAddressMinimum "00:15:5d:01:04:00"
   ```

The configuration of additional features and enhancements

The Windows Server 2012 release was advertised as a cloud OS, with a major focus on network virtualization and SDN. We may not be able to discuss all the aspects here, but we will discuss the building blocks of the technology. First of all, we will look at the extensible feature set of the new Hyper-V switch, and thereafter look at hardware-oriented feature enhancements.

Virtual switch extensions

This will be one of the most interesting facts you will learn about Hyper-V, but before we start discussing Hyper-V Switch Extensions, let's understand the bigger picture into which this piece fits.

Hyper-V Network Virtualization (HNV) in Windows Server 2012 and R2 provides readiness for the Software-defined Networking (SDN) concept, and allows cloud providers to host multitenant virtualization environments. You have seen with server virtualization that you can decouple the OSE from the physical hardware and run it as a virtual machine, along with others, on a single physical server. The platform is transparent to the OSE, and it continues to run as it would on physical hardware. Thus, multiple Hyper-V hosts owned by a firm make up a separate physical network environment. Network virtualization applies the same concept of server virtualization to network environments, where each physical network is converted into a virtual network. It is then hosted alongside, and yet isolated from, other virtual networks in a single common physical network environment.

HNV allows customers to retain their internal IP addresses when migrated to the cloud, and runs the environment in seclusion from other environments. This happens without any conflict, even if the other hosted customer environments have a similar subnet and IP addresses. Each VM in each environment has two IP addresses: one local to its inherent topology, which is referred to as the **Customer Address** (**CA**), and the second from the cloud provider, referred to as the **Provider Address** (**PA**) as per the cloud terminology.

HNV leverages **Network Virtualization for Generic Routing Encapsulation** (**NVGRE**) as the mechanism to virtualize and encapsulate CA in PA. As per the NVGRE packet format, the VM payload packet is encapsulated in another packet using PA, along with the source and destination IP addresses, and the virtual subnet ID of the VM. The virtual subnet ID helps in differentiating one VM from another VM in another virtual subnet, and delivers seamless traffic.

Figure 4-10: GRE Encapsulation

With a keen vision for network virtualization, Microsoft recreated the virtual switch in Windows Server 2012 Hyper-V, rather than building upon the older one. The virtual switch, apart from performing its layer 2 responsibilities, can be programmatically enhanced (using published Windows APIs) by adding extensions for monitoring, modifying, and forwarding traffic to the extensible ports. Unlike VMware, where the vSwitch is replaced, Hyper-V allows third-party developers to build extensions that are MS-certified filter drivers based on the **Network Driver Interface Specification** (**NDIS**) and **Windows Filtering Platform** (**WFP**).

The HNV fabric was placed below the virtual switch, and the extensions reviewing the traffic would only identify the CA as encapsulation. Decapsulation was happening at the HNV filter before it reached the virtual switch that hosted the extensions. Hence, the design did not permit the extensions to review or monitor packets addressed for the PA space.

In Windows Server 2012 R2, the HNV filter was exposed to the extensions and moved inside the virtual switch. This allowed extensions to see packets for both address spaces, CA and PA. If the packet is NVGRE-based, pass it on to the customer address space, and if it's a standard packet, bypass the HNV module and forward it to the provider address space. If a forwarding extension is implemented, based on the packet header, it may apply the policies and then forward the packet.

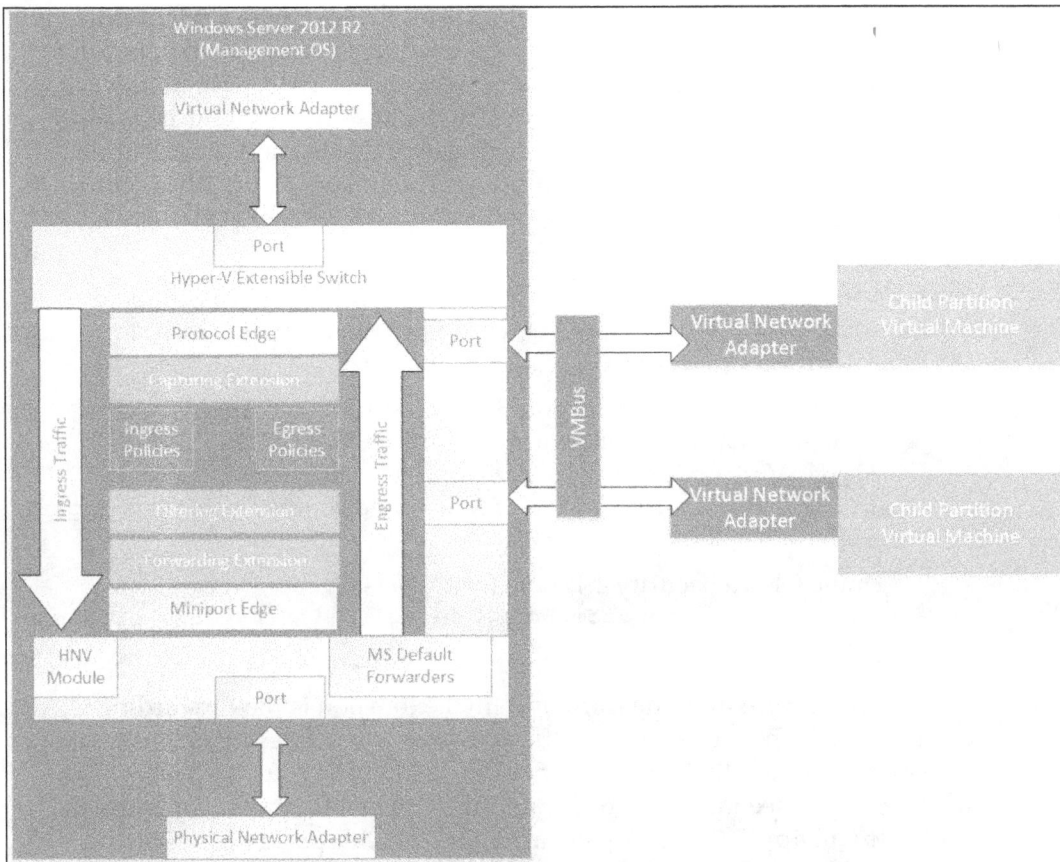

Figure 4-11: Windows Server 2012 R2 – Extensible Switch Extensions

Let's move ahead from the HNV logic to the traffic flow through the extensions. There are three types of extensions that can be installed in a Hyper-V Extensible Switch:

- **Capturing extension**: This is an NDIS-capture-based extension that monitors the ingress (inbound) and egress (outbound) traffic flowing through the virtual switch. It does not modify or alter the traffic or add the delivery address to out-of-band packets. This extension may report traffic conditions to monitoring applications.

  InMon provides the sFlow monitoring extension, which can be added to the virtual switch to enhance NDIS monitoring. For more information, refer to `http://www.inmon.com/technology/`.

- **Filtering extension**: This extension adds on to the capturing extension. Unlike the latter, it can not only monitor but also alter or generate packets and insert them into the virtual switch. It can also restrict packet delivery to destinations or drop packets. A filtering extension is the middle layer, and sees the inbound traffic before the capturing extension. It may apply filter rules as per the source port. It sees outbound traffic after the capturing extension, and applies the filtering policies as per the packet's source and destination port.

  This is a security-based extension and provides firewall-like functionality. 5nine provides solutions for large cloud deployments, which include WFP-based filtering Agentless Security Manager:

  - The Agentless Virtualization Security solution for the Windows server virtualization platform, featuring extensibility of a new Hyper-V virtual switch:
    `http://www.5nine.com/News/news-hyper-v-security-manager.aspx`

  - 5nine Cloud Security 4.1, new for Hyper-V:
    `http://www.5nine.com/5nine-security-for-hyper-v-product.aspx`

- **Forwarding extension**: The third and final extension is the forwarding extension, which can perform all the activities of the filtering extension as well as core packet forwarding as per the destination port. This extension is the first one to see incoming traffic and the last one to review the outbound traffic. It will apply the rules even after the NVGRE packet has been forwarded by the HNV module.

  There are two offerings for this powerful extension: one from Cisco, as Nexus 1000V, and the second from NEC, as ProgrammableFlow PF100:

  - Cisco Nexus 1000V switch for Microsoft Hyper-V:
    `http://www.cisco.com/c/en/us/products/switches/nexus-1000v-switch-microsoft-hyper-v/index.html`

  - NEC ProgrammableFlow PF100:
    `http://www.nec.com/en/global/prod/pflow/pf1000.html`

As a designing and planning routine, always refer to the white paper and documentation provided by the vendors for better and effective results. You can enable or disable the installed and inbox extensions from the Hyper-V Manager, if required. The applet also allows you to reorder the extension from the default tier pattern to your desired tier pattern.

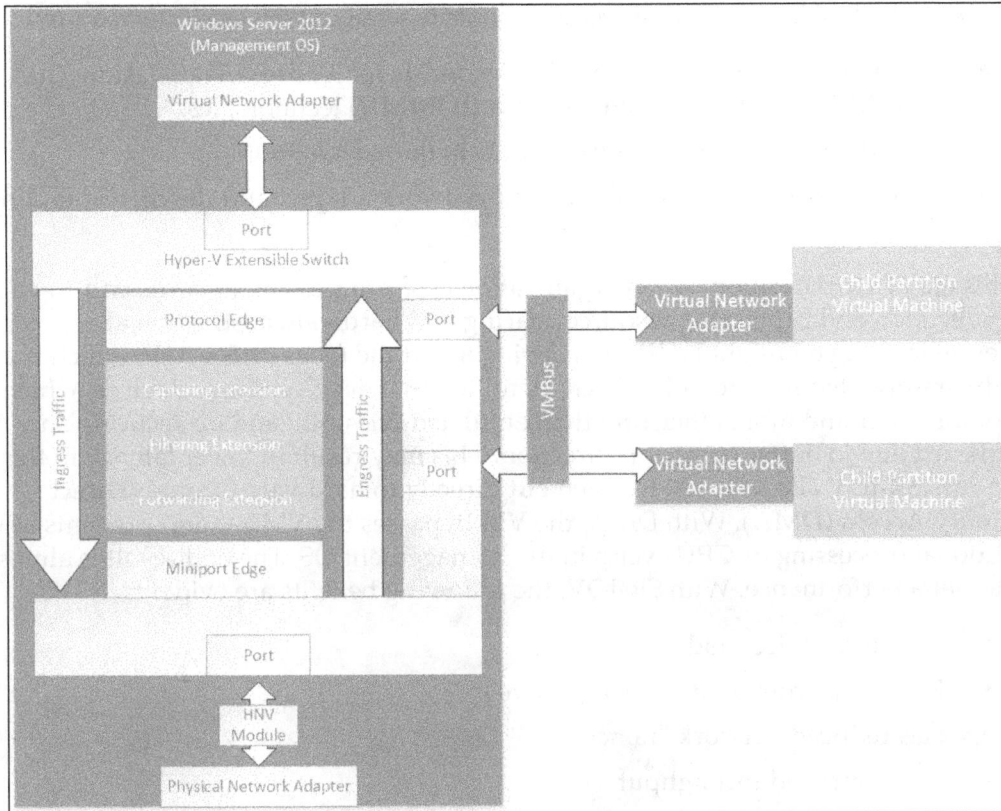

Figure 4-12: Windows Server 2012 – Extensible Switch Extensions

Hardware-supported features

Virtualization has been all about effective hardware abstraction and resource sharing. Windows Server Hyper-V 2012 and R2 have significant routines for delivering positive results. However, there may be situations where hardware features need to be aptly and directly utilized for a high-performance-driven requirement. Let's look at the features and enhancement brought forth in Windows Server 2012 and R2.

Single root input/output virtualization (SR-IOV)

The SR-IOV feature was discussed in the section where we discussed the creation of an external virtual switch. The SR-IOV interface is a specification introduced by the **PCI Special Interest Group (SIG)** and based on the PCI Express (PCIe). The interface allows bypassing of the software switch layer and lets the VM make function calls directly to the hardware. There are some notable merits when you enable this feature. However, there are prerequisites as well to get it to function.

Let's begin by looking at the basic requirements to avail ourselves of this feature:

- The processor should support the **Second-level Address Translation (SLAT)** and **I/O Memory Management Unit (IOMMU)** technologies.
- SR-IOV should be enabled from BIOS in the system ROM
- Ensure you have an SR-IOV-capable network adapter and the corresponding driver

In this era of virtualization, when organizations are progressing towards end-to-end virtualization and promoting resource sharing and hardware abstraction at different layers, you might be left wondering about the focus on SR-IOV, which is a hardware-oriented feature. It has been identified that even synthetic devices, which work far better and more efficiently than emulated ones, still end up securing an overheard due to buffer copy or redirection. This may result in lower latency in the long run. SR-IOV allows a VM to reach out directly to hardware through **Direct Memory Access (DMA)**. With DMA, the VM bypasses the VMBus and prevents any additional processing or CPU cycles in the Management OS. The end result is almost bare-metal performance. With SR-IOV, the following benefits are evident:

- A secure device model
- Is scalable from a future perspective
- Has reduced network latency
- Has improved throughput
- Has fewer CPU cycles and less resource utilization

It is imperative to understand what runs under the hood of IOV so as to help determine when you will need to enable this feature and how it affects any corresponding features. SR-IOV allows access to devices, the network adapter in this case, via PCIe hardware functions. There are two types of hardware functions:

- **Physical function (PF)**: This function is loaded in the Management OS, and promotes the SR-IOV capabilities of the device. They are normal PCIe functions, and are discovered and managed like a normal PCIe device.
- **Virtual function (VF)**: This is a lightweight PCIe function corresponding to the PF in the Management OS (parent partition). There could be around 256 VFs for a network adapter so, in other words, you can hook up 256 virtual NICs to a virtual switch enabled for SR-IOV. VFs consume less configuration space, given that their settings are drawn from the corresponding PF.

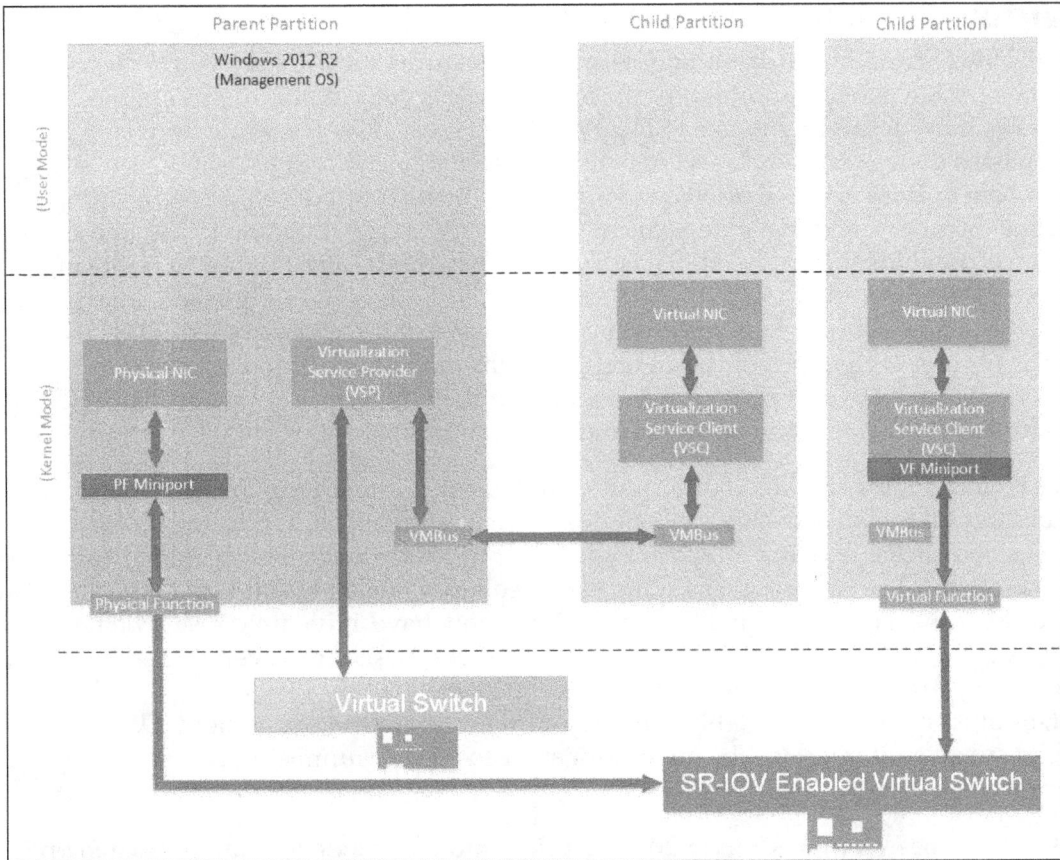

Figure 4-13: Packet Path for SR-IOV and Non-IOV

There are a few facts that you should consider before boarding this channel. You will not be able to use the NIC teaming feature (the most talked-about feature) on the SR-IOV adapter, as VFs bypass the networking stack in the parent partition. However, you can perform guest machine teaming. Also, QoS can't be used alongside SR-IOV. When you enable SR-IOV on an external virtual switch, you will realize the fact—which is stated there—that you can enable SR-IOV on the switch when it is being created, not later on.

Virtual Machine Queue (VMQ)

Let's look at another streamlining networking feature that will help you with your needs for low latency and high performance, unless your requirements are not as dire as they are when you need SR-IOV. Of course, SR-IOV has some drawbacks. It bypasses the virtual switch and networking stack in the parent partition. You will not benefit from NVGRE or NIC teaming at the host level, but setup NIC teaming inside of guests. **Receive-side Scaling** (**RSS**) and VMQ are not new terms, and have been around for some time. RSS has been used to enable the **Scalable Networking Pack** (**SNP**) since Windows 2003 SP2. VMQ, an RSS alteration for virtualization, has been there since Windows Server 2008 Hyper-V R2. The objective of these two features is to deliver performance and better throughput by utilizing hardware acceleration. Networking interruptions are handled by one CPU core or logical CPU. With RSS/VMQ, the load was distributed on multiple cores.

VMQ in Windows Server 2008 R2 mapped dedicated queues for virtual network adapters on the physical NIC. When traffic reaches the physical NIC meant for a specific virtual network adapter, they were put on its queue and delivered accordingly. The mapping was static to one core per queue, which was noted as a drawback, and in Windows Server 2012, we now have a dynamic VMQ. Being dynamic, DVMQ does work on a *first come first serve* basis. However, rather than assigning one queue per core, it monitors the queue load on a logical CPU and maps it, or other queues, to available cores as and when there's a requirement. Once the load subsides, it migrates the queues together to a lesser number of cores, thereby achieving effective CPU sharing.

So, what does Windows Server 2012 R2 bring into the scene? A bit more excitement! **vRSS**, or **Virtual Receive-side scaling**, is another feature set added to the previously present scale up feature. Hyper-V now allows you to create powerful virtual machines with up to 64 virtual CPUs. However, the limitation of addressing networking interrupts being handled by one logical CPU (here, one virtual CPU) is still there. vRSS brings the benefits of RSS inside of a virtual machine, allowing the networking load to be addressed by multiple virtual CPUs rather than just one.

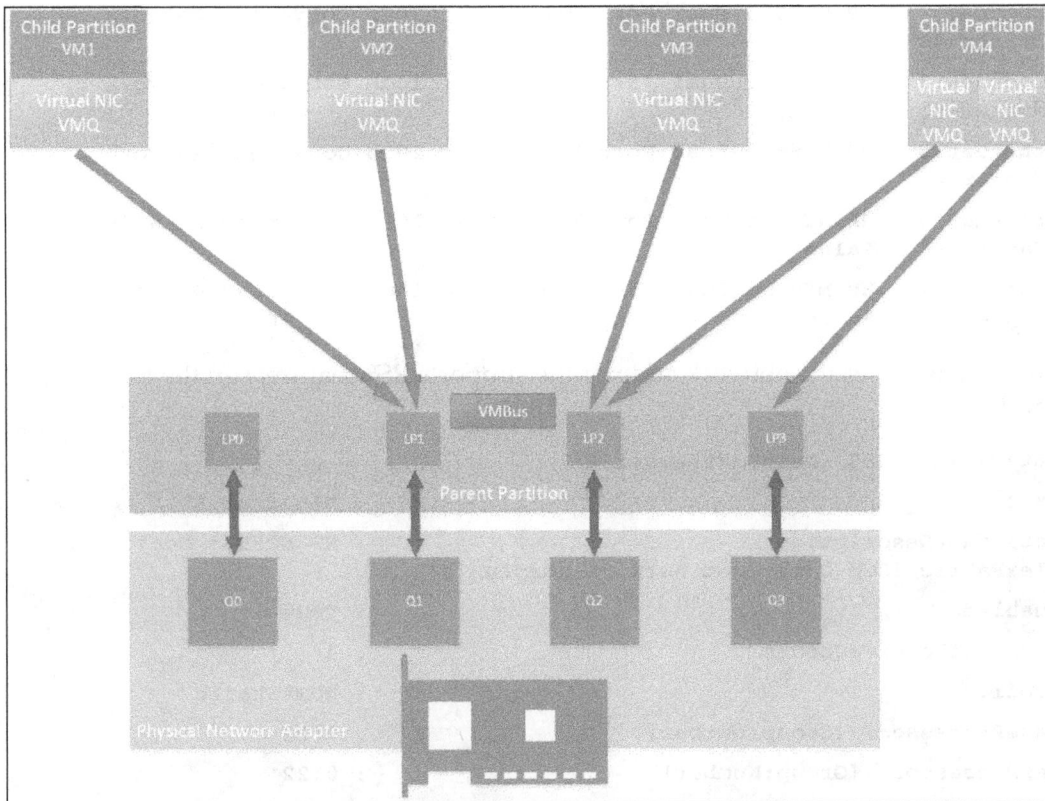

Figure 4-14: Dynamic VMQ

Here's some PowerShell delight. The following cmdlet will help you identify whether the network adapter supports VMQ or RSS. For VMQ, ensure that it is linked to a virtual switch, and then run the following cmdlet. The **Enabled** column depicts the status of the network adapter:

```
Get-NetadapterVMQ |ft Name, InterfaceDescription, Enabled,
BaseVmqProcessor,NumberOfReceiveQueues   -AutoSize


Name           InterfaceDescription          Enabled BaseVmqProcessor
NumberOfReceiveQueues

----           --------------------          ------- ----------------   ----------
----------

HClus1-Team2 Microsoft Network Adapter Multiplexor Driver #2 False 16

HClus1-Team1 Microsoft Network Adapter Multiplexor Driver True 60

Ethernet       HP NC553i Dual Port FlexFabric 10Gb Converged Network
Adapter        False                                30
```

```
Ethernet 2      HP NC553i Dual Port FlexFabric 10Gb Converged Network
Adapter #2      False                               30

Ethernet 3      HP NC553i Dual Port FlexFabric 10Gb Converged Network
Adapter #3      True                                30

Ethernet 5      HP NC553i Dual Port FlexFabric 10Gb Converged Network
Adapter #5      True                                30

Ethernet 6      HP NC553i Dual Port FlexFabric 10Gb Converged Network
Adapter #6      False                               16

Ethernet 4      HP NC553i Dual Port FlexFabric 10Gb Converged Network
Adapter #4      False                               16
```

To check whether the network adapter the supports RSS feature, run the following cmdlet:

```
Get-NetAdterRSS -Name "Ethernet 6"

Name                                                : Ethernet 6

InterfaceDescription                                : HP NC553i Dual Port
FlexFabric 10Gb Converged Network Adapter #6

Enabled                                             : True

NumberOfReceiveQueues                               : 4

Profile                                             : NUMAStatic

BaseProcessor: [Group:Number]                       : 0:0

MaxProcessor: [Group:Number]                        : 0:22

MaxProcessors                                       : 12

RssProcessorArray: [Group:Number/NUMA Distance] : 0:0/0   0:2/0   0:4/0
0:6/0   0:8/0   0:10/0   0:12/0   0:14/0

                                                      0:16/0   0:18/0
0:20/0   0:22/0

IndirectionTable: [Group:Number]                    : 0:0     0:12    0:2
0:14    0:0     0:12    0:2     0:14

                                                      0:0     0:12    0:2
0:14    0:0     0:12    0:2     0:14

                                                      0:0     0:12    0:2
0:14    0:0     0:12    0:2     0:14

                                                      0:0     0:12    0:2
0:14    0:0     0:12    0:2     0:14

                                                      0:0     0:12    0:2
0:14    0:0     0:12    0:2     0:14

                                                      0:0     0:12    0:2
0:14    0:0     0:12    0:2     0:14

                                                      0:0     0:12    0:2
0:14    0:0     0:12    0:2     0:14
```

					0:0	0:12	0:2
0:14	0:0	0:12	0:2	0:14			
					0:0	0:12	0:2
0:14	0:0	0:12	0:2	0:14			
					0:0	0:12	0:2
0:14	0:0	0:12	0:2	0:14			
					0:0	0:12	0:2
0:14	0:0	0:12	0:2	0:14			
					0:0	0:12	0:2
0:14	0:0	0:12	0:2	0:14			
					0:0	0:12	0:2
0:14	0:0	0:12	0:2	0:14			
					0:0	0:12	0:2
0:14	0:0	0:12	0:2	0:14			
					0:0	0:12	0:2
0:14	0:0	0:12	0:2	0:14			
					0:0	0:12	0:2
0:14	0:0	0:12	0:2	0:14			

IPsec offloading

IPsec is a cryptographic methodology implemented over **Internet Protocol (IP)** networks to protect communications. IPsec provides data integrity, peer authentication, and encryption abilities, and ensures data security over the wire. However, the crypto-algorithms are a bit compute-intensive on the OSE. Bear in mind that on a Hyper-V host, there will be multiple VOSE running, and enabling IPsec will bump up the CPU cycles. IPsec offloading comes to the rescue by moving the compute load to the network adapter.

There are prerequisites for this feature, both on the hardware and software sides. The network adapter must be capable enough and should have the supporting driver installed. IPsec offloading is enabled by default when you create a new virtual machine, unless you don't wish to keep it. In that case, it can be disabled.

You may toggle with the idea of enabling or disabling this feature from the virtual machine settings loading hardware acceleration under **Network Adapter**. Also, you can restrict the number of **Security Associations (SA)** to be offloaded. Every supporting network adapter will have an upper limit, for which you can confirm from the documentation provided by the hardware vendor.

Here's something for the folks who are focused on the command lines-- here are the cmdlets for PowerShell. If you set the SA value to `0`, this disables IPsec offloading on the virtual machine:

```
Set-VMNetworkAdapter -VMName VM5 -
IPsecOffloadMaximumSecurityAssociation <0-4096>
```

Windows Server 2012 R2 NIC teaming

NIC teaming was a long desired feature so far, which Microsoft neither provided built-in, nor supported when offered by hardware vendors. They finally introduced the long-awaited ability in Windows 2012, and it was received well by customers. From a solution perspective, you no longer need to depend on any hardware vendor's offering it, as MS provides this feature inherently. Also referred to as **Load Balancing and Failover** (**LBFO**), the feature is primarily used for Hyper-V hosts and Windows Servers, but can be used in virtual machines as well. As per the Microsoft directive, a maximum of 32 NICs can be used as NIC team members on a host, though only two for a virtual machine.

There are two evident use cases for employing NIC teaming:

- **Aggregation of the NIC bandwidth**: Bandwidth or link aggregation allows distribution of traffic on multiple NICs. It does not add up the bandwidth, but load balances the traffic generated by the roles or VMs over two or more network paths, as offered by the contributing NICs.

- **Failover to maintain network connectivity**: This is the active-passive concept, wherein one link stays active over a network path. In the event of a failure in that route, which could be due to a switch failure, a link down, or any other unexpected situation, the other passive link takes over and ensures network connectivity. This is imperative for critical roles and services that cannot allow unplanned downtime.

The Windows Server 2012 and R2 NIC teaming solution allows the use of any NIC type in a team formation. Not only that, you may also use NIC models from different vendors. The condition for this is that the hardware device should have passed MS certification and the **Windows Hardware Quality Labs** (**WHQL**) test for Windows 2012/R2. The same can be verified from the hardware compatibility list on the *Windows Server Catalog* website (`www.windowsservercatalog.com`).

Windows NIC teaming is inclined towards the host, rather than the virtual machines. Unless you are using external switches over SR-IOV adapters, teaming is futile and disastrous for VMs. This makes way for the only condition that allows you to utilize NIC teaming on VMs. Let's look at the fundamentals and algorithms briefly before you learn how to create a new NIC team.

The NIC teaming architecture

The underlying design of a NIC team is almost a standardized affair, as almost all vendors follow the same pattern. The participating components, which are physical NICs and are more than one, form the team. They are presented as virtual NICs, also referred to as tNICs or team interfaces, to the end consumer, which may be a Windows or a Hyper-V host. The team interfaces contribute to the inbound and outbound traffic logic and, depending on your VLAN configuration, you can have either one or more tNICs defined.

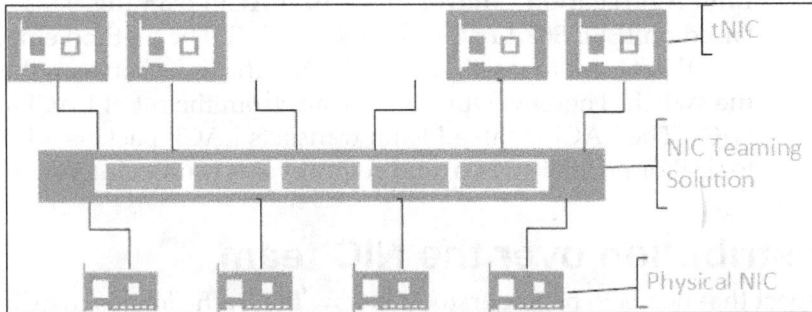

Figure 4-15: NIC Teaming Solution

The NIC teaming configuration

It is imperative to understand the configuration parameters for NIC teaming before you implement it. The design decision should be finalized after considering the workload you are planning to set up on your Hyper-V host and the LAN switching environment.

Teaming Mode

The teaming mode is decided as per the switch environment, and based on the same, it is determined whether to keep the teaming dependent on the linking switch or not. There are primarily two teaming modes, which we will discuss now:

- **Switch independent**: This is the default selection when you are creating a NIC team. The setup does not require participation of the switch or switches connected to the host. The teaming mode functions as a load sharing group of NICs in the wake of the fact that they might all be connected to the same or multiple switches. However, the switch (or switches) plays no role in the unit. At any point of time, all the NICs are active and divide the load among themselves. You may choose to keep one team member on standby in this mode. If any of the active members fails, the standby NIC takes over and keeps the load balancing intact.

- **Switch dependent**: This is the second selection, and as the name indicates, the LAN switch plays a major role in the teaming abilities of the host. In this configuration, all the NICs are connected to ports from the same LAN switch. There is further differentiation under this approach:

    ○ **Static teaming**: Also referred to as generic teaming, this format is based on IEEE 802.3ad draft v1. This requires manual configuration at both the host and switch ends, and due care should be taken when working on the setup, as a mistake will result in an erroneous setup.

    ○ **Link Aggregation Control Protocol (LACP) teaming**: This format is based on IEEE 802.1ax developed by IEEE. The method employs the LACP protocol to intelligently identify the links between the host and the switch. Thereby, work out a team from the set of LACP-enabled NICs. The LACP-enabled team transacts LACP packets with the peer logical or normal switch, and requires less human intervention.

Load distribution over the NIC team

The next aspect that needs to be understood is how the traffic load is distributed between the participants in the NIC team. There are standard algorithms defined for this purpose, which should be used as per your requirements. Although there were originally two of them, Windows Server 2012 R2 added one more algorithm to the list:

- **Address hash**: This used to be the default algorithm with Windows Server 2012. It is a very intuitive method, wherein a hash is generated based on the address of the outgoing packets and then allocated to a specific adapter, thereby utilizing its complete bandwidth. This is a rational load balancing approach. There are three approaches to this form:

    ○ **Source and destination MAC addresses**: When the traffic is not IP-address-based.

    ○ **Source and destination IP addresses**: This is also referred to as two-tuple hashing.

    ○ **Source and destination TCP/UDP ports and source and destination IP addresses**: This is also referred to as four-tuple hashing. This form provides the most granular distribution of traffic stress, which is well balanced between the members.

- **Hyper-V port**: This is the next choice, and is more suitable when you are using it with Hyper-V, as the name indicates. This kind of team should be created when you are going to link a virtual switch to Hyper-V hosts with a high VM density. Each VM, with its virtual NIC connected over a virtual switch to a NIC team, gets assigned to one physical NIC in the team only, both for ingress and egress loads.

  As we discussed earlier, all VMs have unique MAC addresses. Either the MAC or the port linked to the virtual switch forms the basis of load balancing. This is more appropriate if **VMQ** (short for **Virtual Machine Queue**) is used, as it binds the MAC of a virtual NIC to a physical NIC in the team. Thus, the traffic comes to the desired interface. If it were not for this logic, the traffic would hit all the interfaces in the team.

- **Dynamic**: This is the default algorithm selection in Windows Server 2012 R2. This method incorporates the best of the other two algorithms. For outgoing traffic, it utilizes four-tuple hashing based on TCP/UDP ports and IP addresses, and inbound traffic follows the same algorithm as used by the Hyper-V port.

  The outgoing traffic is balanced via flowlets, which are breaks in a TCP traffic flow. When the algorithm detects and determines the flow break, it rebalances the flow to the next team interface.

The NIC teaming setup

If you have understood the concepts and parameters and know what suits your design, setting up a NIC team will rather be straightforward. Going forward, let's learn the process to set up a basic NIC team with two members. As always, there are two possible ways to achieve the goal: the GUI and PowerShell.

Server Manager

The NIC team console can be invoked via exploring the Server Manager or via calling the LBFOadmin.exe executable over the command line. Let's see the steps:

1. Launch **Server Manager**. From the left pane, select **Local Server**.

2. In the right section, under the **PROPERTIES** part of the host server, look for **NIC Teaming**. The status will normally be **Disabled** unless it has been set to **Enabled**. Click on the hyperlink **Disabled** to launch the **NIC Teaming** console.

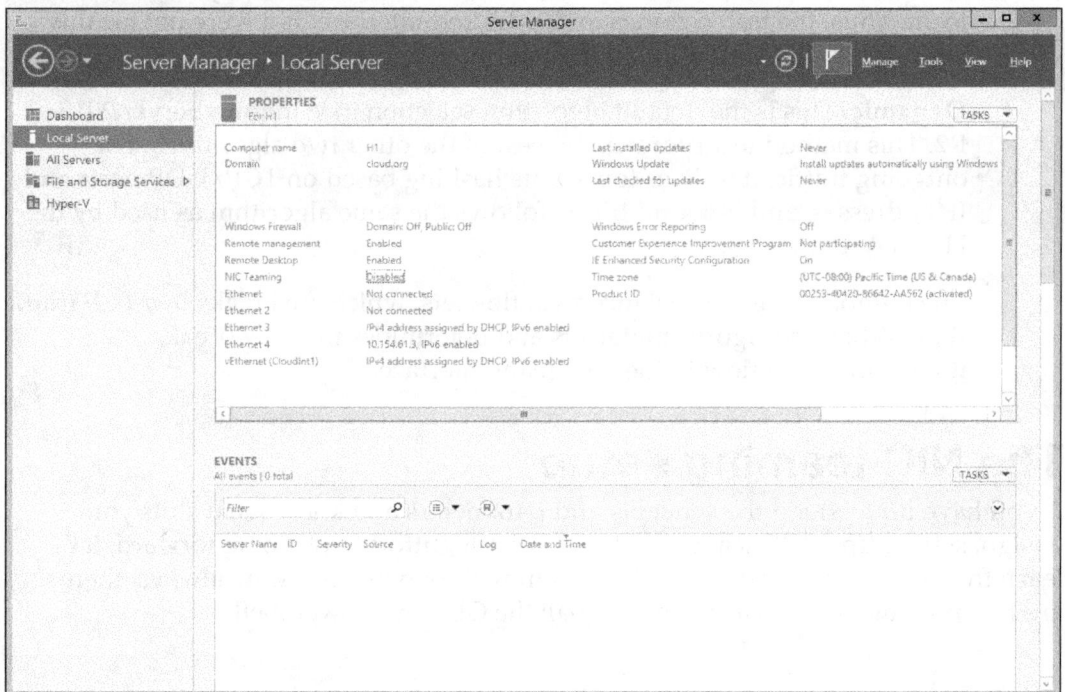

Figure 4-16: Enable NIC Teaming

3. The NIC teaming console is segregated into three segments, namely **SERVERS, TEAMS,** and **ADAPTERS AND INTERFACES.** The third one, **ADAPTERS AND INTERFACES,** shows the available NICs and teams, along with their state and speed. To create an NIC, select the **TASKS** dropdown from the second or third segment, and then select **New Team.** This invokes the **New team** applet.

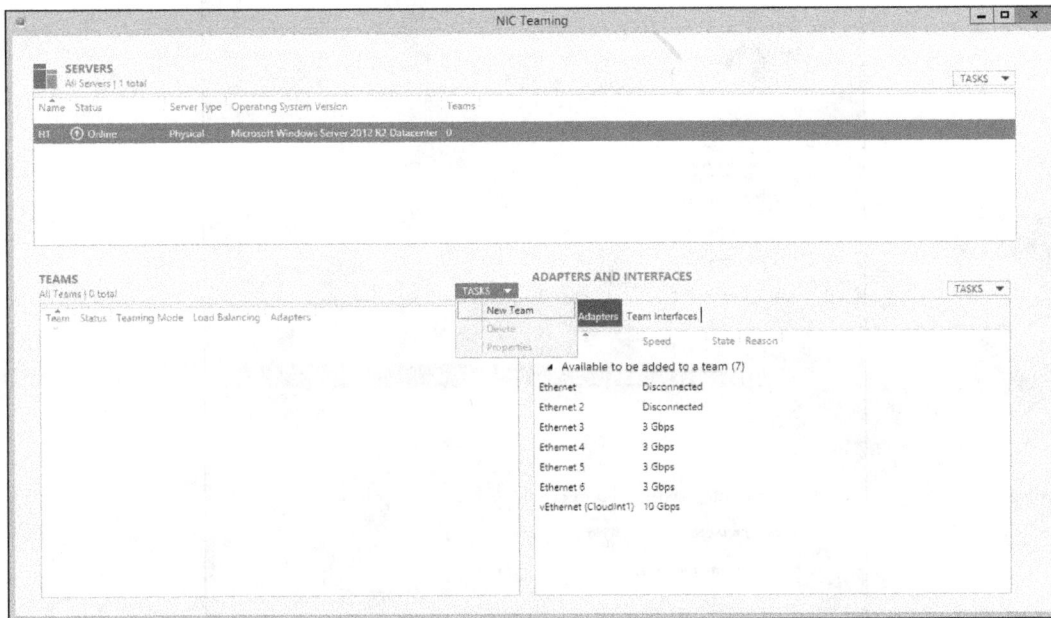

Figure 4-17: Setup New Team

4. In the **New team** applet, select the Ethernet NICs that you figured out should be members for a new team. Specify a logical name as per your followed naming conventions.

5. Expand **Additional properties** and, from the drop-down fields, select the relevant **Teaming mode**, **Load balancing mode**, and **Standby adapter** (if you are picking **Switch Independent**) as determined in your NIC teaming design.

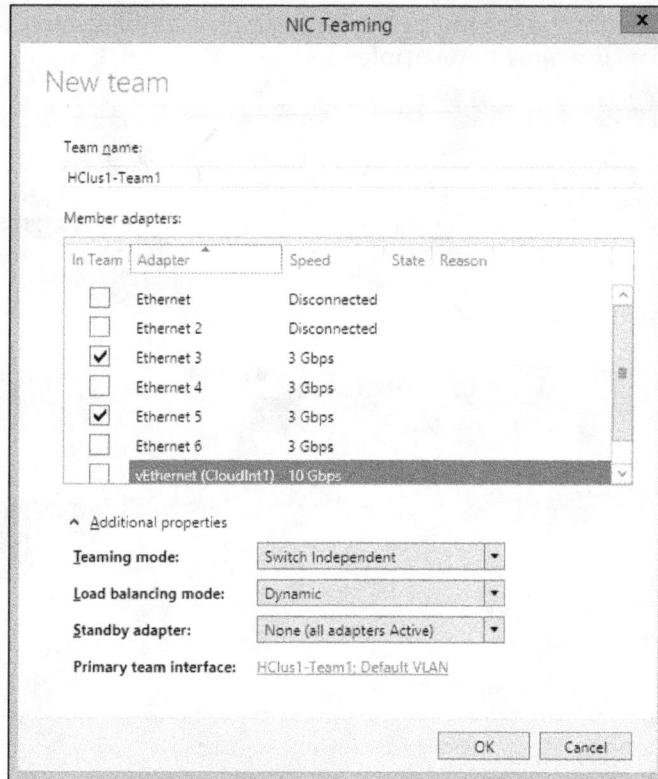

Figure 4-18: New Team Setup and Configuration

6. The last option in the list is **Primary team interface**. In the default state, it accepts traffic for VLAN segments, except those VLAN IDs that have been tagged on other teams on the same host.

7. Click on **OK**. The new team will reflect under **Teams Segment** in the NIC teaming console, and the NIC members will show up as members of the new team under **ADAPTERS AND INTERFACES**.

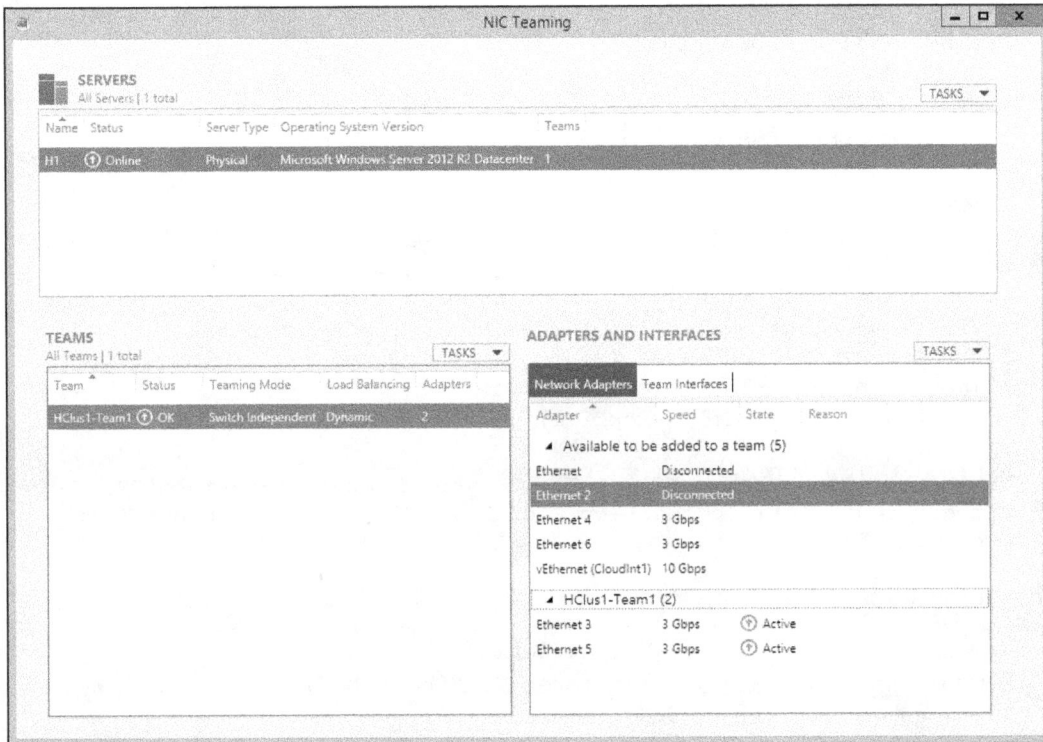

Figure 4-19: NIC Team – Post Setup

8. Under **Network Connections**, the new team adapter will show up with **Microsoft Network Adapter Multiplexor Driver** as a **Device Name**. The connection name will be under **Team Name** as you have assigned previously.

PowerShell

Alright! Now here's something for the folks who have an inclination towards the Windows Server 2012 R2 core and Hyper-V Server 2012 R2. PowerShell can help you achieve the preceding settings in a matter of a few key strokes. There are many interesting cmdlets that you will find handy, such as `New-NetLBFOteam`, `Add-NetLbfoTeamNIC`, `Set-NetLbfoTeamNIC`, and so on.

Let's look at the entire process of creating a new team via PowerShell, and follow the routine of discovering the cmdlet options as well. The previous one that we created was with the dynamic load balancing algorithm. However, via PowerShell, we go with Hyper-V port, the next suitable option for virtualization:

```
Get-Help New-NetLbfoTeam

NAME
     New-NetLbfoTeam

SYNTAX
     New-NetLbfoTeam [-Name] <string> [-TeamMembers]
<WildcardPattern[]> [[-TeamNicName] <string>] [[-TeamingMode]
<TeamingModes> {Static | SwitchIndependent | Lacp}]
     [[-LoadBalancingAlgorithm] <LBAlgos> {TransportPorts |
IPAddresses | MacAddresses | HyperVPort | Dynamic}] [-CimSession
<CimSession[]>] [-ThrottleLimit <int>]
     [-AsJob] [-WhatIf] [-Confirm]  [<CommonParameters>]


New-NetLbfoTeam -Name "HClus1-Team2" -TeamMembers "Ethernet 2",
"Ethernet 6" -TeamingMode Lacp -LoadBalancingAlgorithm HyperVPort
-Confirm:$false
```

The end result is as follows:

```
Name                      : HClus1-Team2
Members                   : {Ethernet 2, Ethernet 6}
TeamNics                  : HClus1-Team2
TeamingMode               : Lacp
LoadBalancingAlgorithm    : HyperVPort
Status                    : Up
```

Quality of Service

We discussed Quality of Service (QoS) briefly in the previous chapter. QoS is not an entirely new feature in Windows Server 2012 and R2. However, its implementation and use cases have been extended to Hyper-V, and beyond. You came across the bandwidth management QoS feature for virtual machines in the previous chapter. However, there are more interesting updates on this aspect.

QoS is put to use to implement effective network traffic management in an environment, and to ensure that applications and users get the most out of the available bandwidth. Windows Server 2012 implemented QoS in much more innovative ways than just bandwidth control and manipulation. Apart from traffic control and admission control, QoS is utilized for the following goals:

- Bandwidth management
- Implementing QoS on physical and virtual networks
- Protocol classification
- Priority-based flow control (PFC)

Now, before you learn about the preceding features, let's look at one very important installable feature from the Windows Server 2012 arsenal, called **Data Center Bridging (DCB)**. DCB is an IEEE-released standard that defines 802.3, the Ethernet interface that supports converged networking or fabric, allowing LAN and SAN traffic from a single entry-exit route. An improved NIC device, called **Converged Network Adapter (CNA)**, adds the capability of merging Ethernet along with offloaded storage traffic from iSCSI, RDMA over converged Ethernet and FCoE. On a Hyper-V cluster setup, there was always a need to segregate different roles on different network segments (including storage), hence there were separate network connections, but with a converged fabric. All of this could be efficiently offloaded on the virtual switch created on an NIC team of CNAs. QoS policies, along with DCB, provide excellent network performance.

Now let's discuss the preceding features of QoS, and see how they work together for a greater benefit of Windows as well as Hyper-V admins:

- **Bandwidth management**: Maximum bandwidth has been an old deliverable for QoS. Windows 2012 introduced minimum bandwidth. Yes, the same one that we looked at under the network adapter for virtual machine settings in *Chapter 3*, *Deploying Virtual Machines*. You can specify weight in percent for either or both of the values. QoS policies guarantee the percent value of the available bandwidth specified as the minimum bandwidth to the virtual machine, and at the same time, will not allow the VM to take up more throughput than specified in maximum bandwidth, even if the host doesn't have any asking bandwidth requirement.

  Minimum bandwidth and DCB are not recommended to be enabled together, as both perform the same task. NIC teaming works well with an upward throttle check in the maximum bandwidth. However, it is not able to trim the throughput as per the minimum bandwidth or hardware enforced minimum bandwidth (DCB).

- **Protocol classification**: It is imperative to understand what type of payload is being tracked and managed. Policy-based QoS has predefined filters for protocols and criteria for implementing the filter. Beyond bandwidth management, you can prioritize and create a windows profile for any traffic and apply QoS policies.

- **Implement QoS on physical and virtual networks**: Apart from a Hyper-V virtual network, QoS can be used to track and manage physical networks. Policy-based QoS has been formulated to address physical networks, and Hyper-V-based QoS is for what was discussed under protocol classification. Policy-based QoS enforces settings for **Extended QoS (eQoS)** via Group Policies to tag packets for the 802.1p value. If not AD joined, QoS can be forced via local policies. Through policy-based QoS you may be able to force a minimum bandwidth on a kind of traffic identified by a five-tuple check (source and destination IP addresses, source and destination port number, and the protocol in use).

- **Priority-based flow control (PFC)**: This is a standard defined under the DCB workgroup that supports merging traffic between lossless protocols, along with "lossy" protocol traffic, and yet delivers the payload successfully. This bypasses the networking stack, so the Software QoS packet scheduler will not deliver. Therefore, DCB should be used at both Ethernet ends. This feature works significantly well with NIC teaming as it works at the hardware level.

Summary

This goal of this chapter was to help you understand the Hyper-V networking framework, its attributes, and how it connects the physical machine and the virtual machine worlds. At the onset, we studied the new Hyper-V Extensible Virtual Switch, and saw how it was different from the virtual network offerings in the previous releases of Hyper-V. We began with the very basics of creating different kinds of switches, namely private, internal, and external. We explained the significance of each with respect to VMs. PowerShell is a quick alternative to GUI methods, and we also shared the steps of using the new command shell to create and customize virtual switches.

Thereafter, we looked at the new attributes of the Extensible Switch that earned it its name, and reviewed the extensions that can be imported and customized to provide very granular monitoring and tracking of traffic entering or leaving a virtual environment. A discussion on extensions cannot start or end without a clear understanding of network virtualization via NVGRE, and we also explained the nitty-gritty behind the procedure of encapsulation.

We then looked at other networking features and advancements introduced with Windows Server 2012 and R2, namely SR-IOV, VMQ/vRSS, and IPsec offloading. We also saw how, and in which situations, each one of them can be utilized.

Next, we looked at the innovative NIC teaming feature, and discussed at length the architecture, underlying work patterns, and use cases of NIC teaming. We closed the chapter with a short discussion on QoS and DCB, along with the converged fabric. We saw how they benefit in managing the network bandwidth and throughput of current physical and virtual networks.

In the next chapter, we will focus on the storage aspects of Windows Server 2012 R2 Hyper-V, and see what is new in the current release.

5
Storage Ergonomics

Here, we are discussing the last of the basics to get you equipped to create and manage a simple Hyper-V structure. No server environment, physical or virtual, is complete without a clear consideration and consensus over the underlying storage. In the course of this chapter, you will learn about the details of virtual storage, how to differentiate one from the other, and how to convert one to the other and vice versa.

We will also see how Windows Server 2012 R2 removes dependencies on raw device mappings by way of pass-through or iSCSI LUN, which were required for guest clustering. VHDX can now be shared and delivers better results than pass-through disks. There are more merits to VHDX than the former, as it allows you to extend the size even if the virtual machine is alive.

Previously, Windows Server 2012 added a very interesting facet for storage virtualization in Hyper-V when it introduced virtual SAN, which adds a virtual **host bus adapter (HBA)** capability to a virtual machine. This allows a VM to directly view the fibre channel SAN. This in turn allows FC LUN accessibility to VMs and provides you with one more alternative for shared storage for guest clustering.

Windows Server 2012 also introduced the ability to utilize the SMI-S capability, which was initially tested on System Center VMM 2012. Windows 2012 R2 carries the torch forward, with the addition of new capabilities. We will discuss this feature briefly in this chapter.

In this chapter, you will cover the following:

- Two types of virtual disks, namely VHD and VHDX
- Merits of using VHDX from Windows 2012 R2 onwards
- Virtual SAN storage
- Implementing guest clustering using shared VHDX
- Getting an insight into SMI-S

Virtual storage

A virtual machine is a replica of a physical machine in all rights and with respect to the building components, regardless of the fact that it is emulated, resembles, and delivers the same performance as a physical machine. Every computer ought to have storage for the OS or application loading. This condition applies to virtual machines as well. If VMs are serving as independent servers for roles such as domain controller or file server, where the server needs to maintain additional storage apart from the OS, the extended storage can be extended for domain user access without any performance degradation.

Virtual machines can benefit from multiple forms of storage, namely VHD/VHDX, which are file-based storage; iSCSI LUNs; pass-through LUNs, which are raw device mappings; and of late, virtual-fibre-channel-assigned LUNs. There have been enhancements to each of these, and all of these options have a straightforward implementation procedure. However, before you make a selection, you should identify the use case according to your design strategy and planned expenditure. In the following section, we will look at the storage choices more closely.

VHD and VHDX

In *Chapter 3, Deploying Virtual Machines*, we looked at the various virtual machine files, and briefly looked at the definition of the virtual hard disk files, namely VHD and VHDX. VHD is the old flag bearer for Microsoft virtualization ever since the days of virtual PC and virtual server. The same was enhanced and employed in early Hyper-V releases. However, as a file-based storage that gets mounted as a normal storage for a virtual machine, VHD had its limitations. VHDX, a new feature addition to Windows Server 2012, was built further upon the limitations of its predecessor and provides greater storage capacity, support for large sector disks, and better protection against corruption. In the current release of Windows Server 2012 R2, VHDX has been bundled with more ammo.

VHDX packed a volley of feature enhancements when it was initially launched, and with Windows Server 2012 R2, Microsoft only made it better. If we compare the older, friendlier version of VHD with VHDX, we can draw the following inferences:

- **Size factor**: VHD had an upper size limit of 2 TB, while VHDX gives you a humungous maximum capacity of 64 TB.

- **Large disk support**: With the storage industry progressing towards 4 KB sector disks from the 512 bytes sector, for applications that still may depend on the older sector format, there are two offerings from the disk alignment perspective: native 4 KB disk and 512e (or 512 byte emulation disks). The operating system, depending on whether it supports native 4 KB disk or not, will either write 4 KB chunks of data or inject 512 bytes of data into a 4 KB sector. The process of injecting 512 bytes into a 4 KB sector is called **RMW**, or **Read-Write-Modify**.

  VHDs are generically supported on 512e disks. Windows Server 2012 and R2 both support native 4 KB disks. However, the VHD driver has a limitation; it cannot open VHD files on physical 4 KB disks. This limitation is checked by enabling VHD to be aligned to 4 KB and RMW ready, but if you are migrating from the older Hyper-V platform, you will need to convert it accordingly.

  VHDX, on the other hand, is the "superkid". It can be used on all disk forms, namely 512, 512e, and the native 4 KB disk as well, without any RMW dependency.

- **Data corruption safety**: In the event of power outages or failures, the possibility of data corruption is reduced with VHDX. Metadata inside the VHDX is updated via a logging process that ensures that the allocations inside VHDX are committed successfully.

- **Offloaded data transfers (ODX)**: With Windows Server 2012 Hyper-V supporting this feature, data transfer and moving and sizing of virtual disks can be achieved at the drop of a hat, without host server intervention. The basic prerequisite for utilizing this feature is to host the virtual machines on ODX-capable hardware. Thereafter, Windows Server 2012 self-detects and enables the feature. Another important clause is that virtual disks (VHDX) should be attached to the SCSI, not IDE.

- **TRIM/UNMAP**: Termed by Microsoft in its documentation as "efficiency in representing data," this feature works in tandem with thin provisioning. It adds the ability to allow the underlying storage to reclaim space and maintain it optimally small.

- **Shared VHDX**: This is the most interesting feature in the collection released with Windows Server 2012 R2. It made guest clustering (failover clustering in virtual machines) in Hyper-V a lot simpler. With Windows Server 2012, you could set up a guest cluster using virtual fibre channel or iSCSI LUN. However, the downside was that the LUN was exposed to the user of the virtual machine.

  Shared VHDX proves to be the ideal shared storage. It gives you the benefit of storage abstraction, flexibility, and faster deployment of guest clusters, and it can be stored on an SMB share or a cluster-shared volume (CSV).

Now that we know the merits of using VHDX over VHD, it is important to realize that either of the formats can be converted into the other and can be used under various types of virtual disks, allowing users to decide a trade-off between performance and space utilization.

Virtual disk types

Beyond the two formats of virtual hard disks, let's talk about the different types of virtual hard disks and their utility as per the virtualization design. There are three types of virtual hard disks, namely dynamically expanding, fixed-size, and differencing virtual hard disks:

- **Dynamically expanding**: Also called a dynamic virtual hard disk, this is the default type. It gets created when you create a new VM or a new VHD/ VHDX. This is Hyper-V's take on thin provisioning. The VHD/VHDX file will start off from a small size and gradually grow up to the maximum defined size for the file as and when chunks of data get appended or created inside the **OSE** (short for **operating system environment**) hosted by the virtual disk.

  This disk type is quite beneficial, as it prevents storage overhead and utilizes as much as required, rather than committing the entire block. However, due to the nature of the virtual storage, as it spawns in size, the actual file gets written in fragments across the Hyper-V CSV or LUN (physical storage). Hence, it affects the performance of the disk I/O operations of the VM.

- **Fixed size**: As the name indicates, the virtual disk type commits the same block size on the physical storage as its defined size. In other words, if you have specified a fixed size 1 TB, it will create a 1 TB VHDX file in the storage. The creation of a fixed size takes a considerable amount of time, commits space on the underlying storage, and does allow SAN thin provisioning to reclaim it, somewhat like whitespaces in a database. The advantage of using this type is that it delivers amazing read performance and heavy workloads from SQL, and exchange can benefit from it.

- **Differencing**: This is the last of the lot, but quite handy as an option when it comes to quick deployment of virtual machines. This is by far an unsuitable option, unless employed for VMs with a short lifespan, namely pooled **VDI** (short for **Virtual Desktop Infrastructure**) or lab testing.

The idea behind the design is to have a generic **virtual operating system environment (VOSE)** in a shut down state at a shared location. The VHDX of the VOSE is used as a parent or root, and thereafter, multiple VMs can be spawned with differencing or child virtual disks that use the generalized OS from the parent and append changes or modifications to the child disk. So, the parent stays unaltered and serves as a generic image. It does not grow in size; on the contrary, the child disk keeps on growing as and when data is added to the particular VM.

Unless used for short-lived VMs, the long-running VMs could enter an outage state or may be performance-stricken soon due to the unpredictable growth pattern of a differencing disk. Hence, these should be avoided for server virtual machines without even a second thought.

Virtual disk operations

Now we will apply all of the knowledge gained about virtual hard disks, and check out what actions and customizations we can perform on them.

Creating virtual hard disks

This goal can be achieved in different ways, a few of which we have discussed in earlier chapters:

- You can create a new VHD when you are creating a new VM, using the **New Virtual Machine Wizard**. It picks up the VHDX as the default option.
- You can also launch the **New Virtual Hard Disk Wizard** from a virtual machine's settings.
- This can be achieved by PowerShell cmdlets as well:
  ```
  New-VHD
  ```

These three methods have been discussed in *Chapter 3, Deploying Virtual Machines*. Let's look at newer methods to do this.

You may employ the **Disk Management** snap-in to create a new VHD as well. The steps to create a VHD here are pretty simple:

1. In the **Disk Management** snap-in, select the **Action** menu and select **Create VHD**, like this:

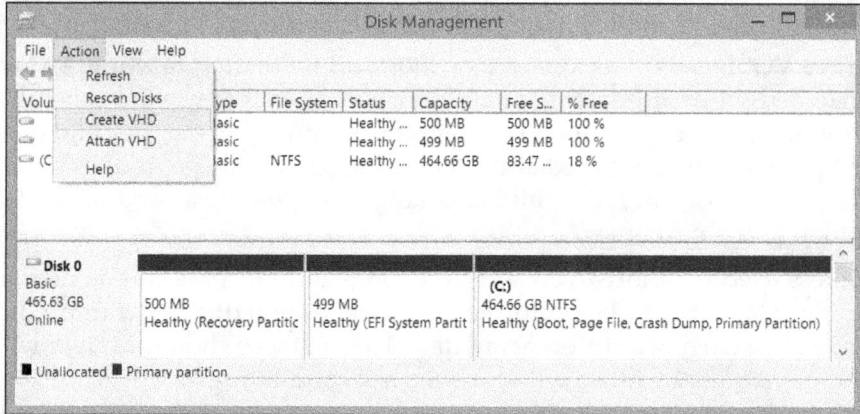

Figure 5-1: Disk Management – Create VHD

2. This opens the **Create and Attach Virtual Hard Disk** applet. Specify the location to save the VHD at, and fill in **Virtual hard disk format** and **Virtual hard disk type** as depicted here in *figure 5-2*:

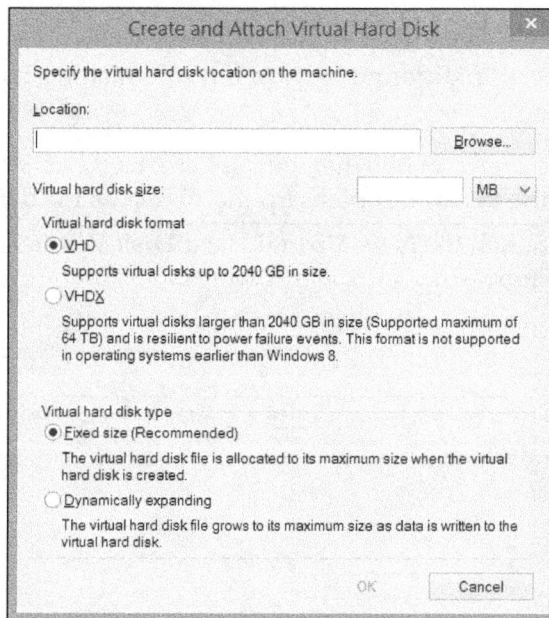

Figure 5-2: Disk Management – Create and Attach Virtual Hard Disk

The most obvious way to create a new VHD/VHDX for a VM is by launching **New Virtual Hard Disk Wizard** from the **Actions** pane in the Hyper-V Manager console. Click on **New** and then select the **Hard Disk** option. It will take you to the following set of screens:

1. On the **Before You Begin** screen, click on **Next**, as shown in this screenshot:

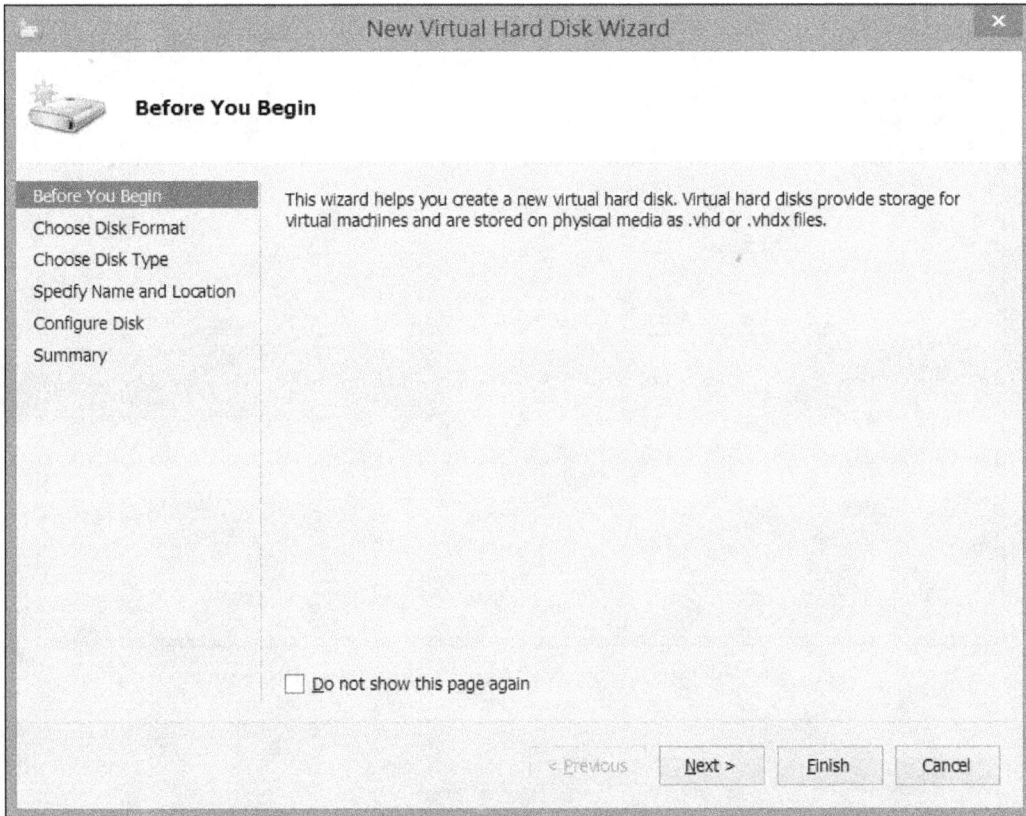

Figure 5-3: New Virtual Hard Disk Wizard – Create VHD

2. The next screen is **Choose Disk Format**, as shown in *figure 5-4*. Select the relevant virtual hard disk format, namely VHD or VHDX, and click on **Next**.

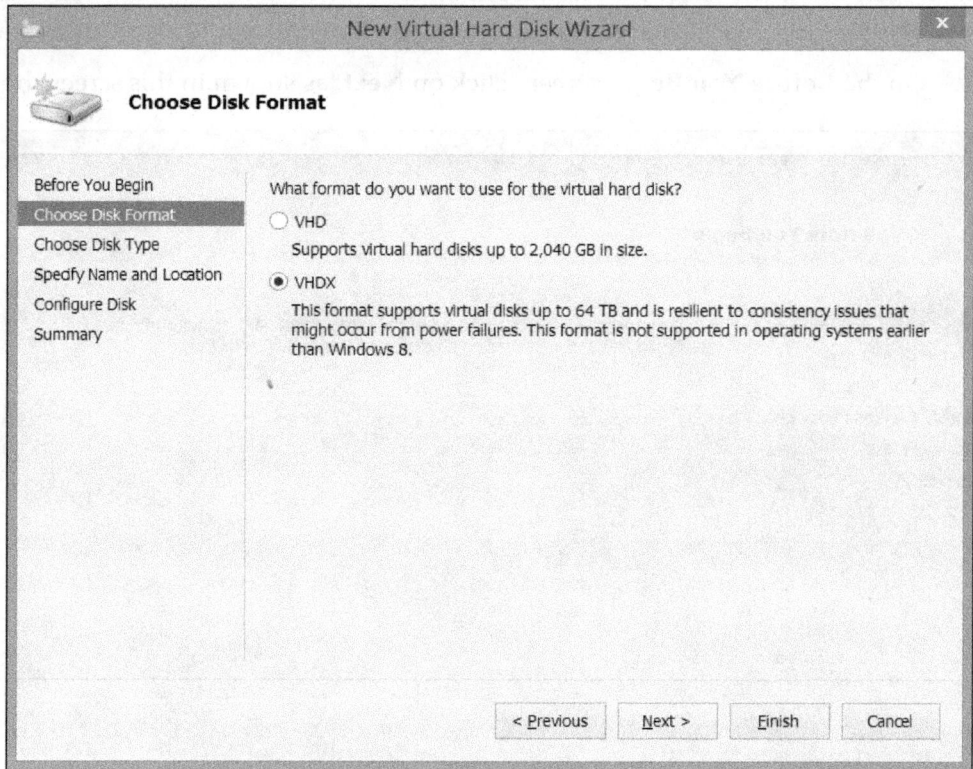

Figure 5-4: New Virtual Hard Disk Wizard – Virtual Hard Disk Format

3. In the screen for **Choose Disk Type**, select the relevant virtual hard disk type and click on **Next**, as shown in the following screenshot:

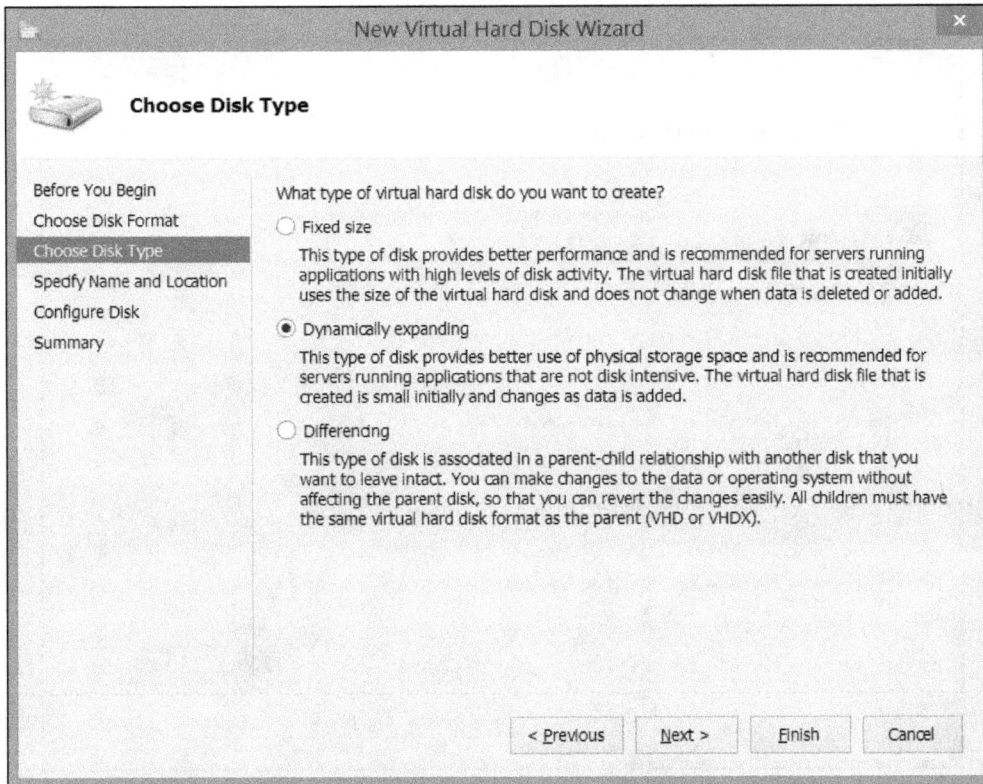

Figure 5-5: New Virtual Hard Disk Wizard– Virtual Hard Disk Type

4. The next screen, as shown in *figure 5-6*, is **Specify Name and Location**. Update the **Name** and **Location** fields to store the virtual hard disk and click on **Next**.

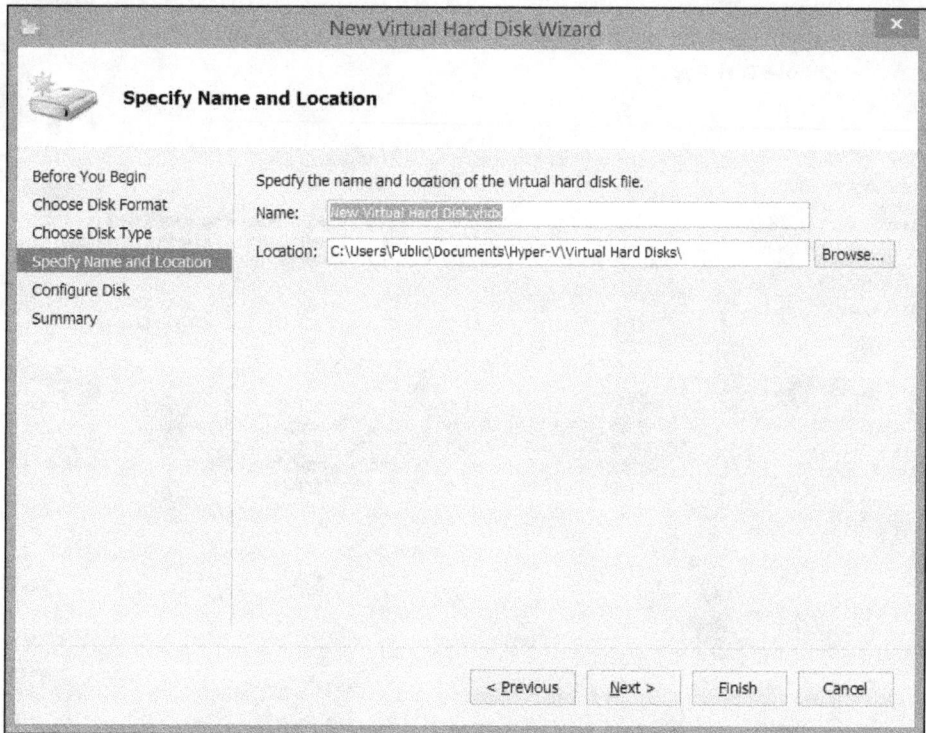

Figure 5-6: New Virtual Hard Disk Wizard – File Location

5. The **Configure Disk** screen, shown in *figure 5-7*, is an interesting one. If needs be, you can convert or copy the content of a physical storage (local, LUN, or something else) to the new virtual hard disk. Similarly, you can copy the content from an older VHD file to the Windows Server 2012 or R2 VHDX format. Then click on **Next**.

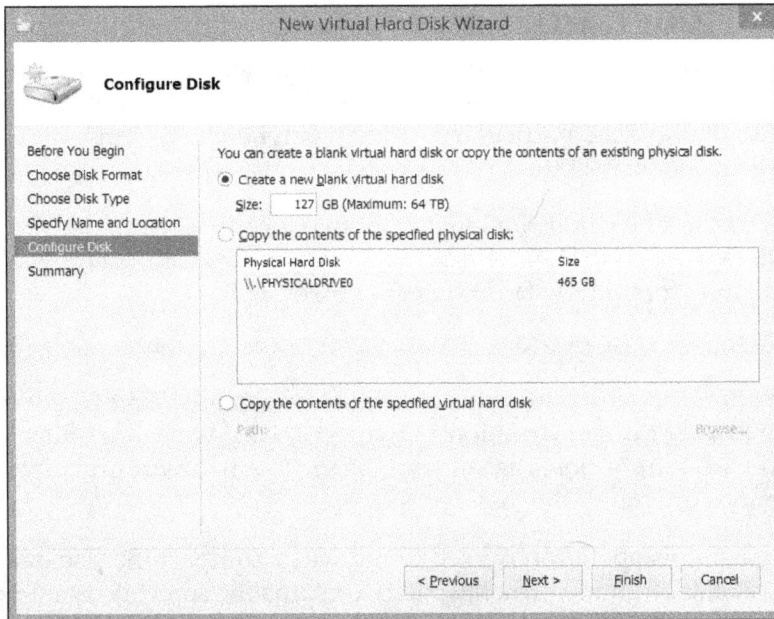

Figure 5-7: New Virtual Hard Disk Wizard – Configure Disk

6. On the **Summary** screen, as shown in the following screenshot, click on **Finish** to create the virtual hard disk:

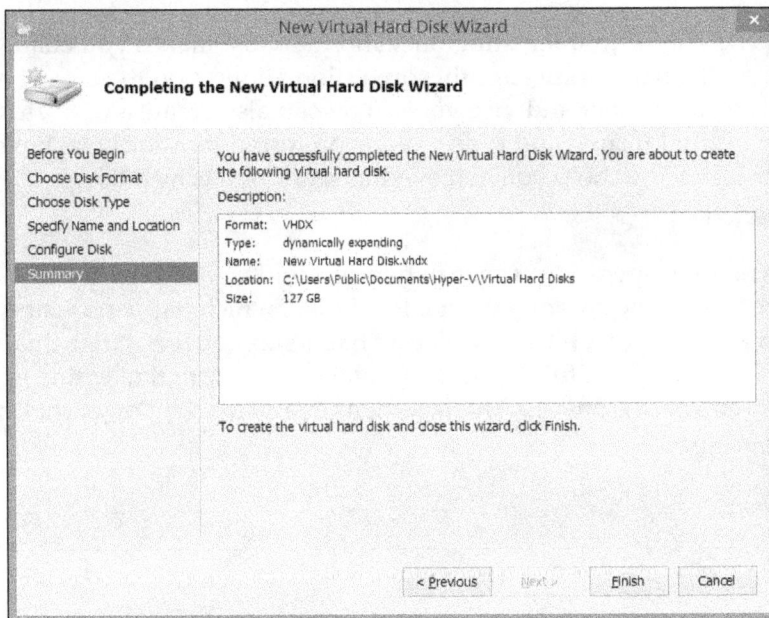

Figure 5-8: New Virtual Hard Disk Wizard – Summary

Editing virtual hard disks

There may be one or more reasons for you to feel the need to modify a previously created virtual hard disk to suit a purpose. There are many available options that you may put to use, given a particular virtual disk type. Before you edit a VHDX, it's a good practice to inspect the VHDX or VHD.

The **Inspect Disk** option can be invoked from two locations: from the VM settings under the IDE or SCSI controller, or from the **Actions** pane of the Hyper-V Manager console. Also, don't forget how to do this via PowerShell:

```
Get-VHD -Path "E:\Hyper-V\Virtual hard disks\1.vhdx"
```

You may now proceed with editing a virtual disk. Again, the **Edit Disk** option can be invoked in exactly the same fashion as **Inspect Disk**. When you edit a VHDX, you are presented with four options, as shown in *figure 5-9*. It may sound obvious, but not all the options are for all the disk types:

- **Compact**: This operation is used to reduce or compact the size of a virtual hard disk, though the preset capacity remains the same. A dynamic disk, or differencing disk, grows as data elements are added, though deletion of the content does not automatically reclaim the storage capacity. Hence, a manual compact operation becomes imperative reduce the file size. PowerShell cmdlet can also do this trick, as follows:

  ```
  Optimize-VHD
  ```

- **Convert**: This is an interesting one, and it almost makes you change your faith. As the name indicates, this operation allows you to convert one virtual disk type to another and vice versa. You can also create a new virtual disk of the desired format and type at your preferred location. The PowerShell construct used to help you achieve the same goal is as follows:

  ```
  Convert-VHD
  ```

- **Expand**: This operation comes in handy, similar to **Extend a LUN**. You end up increasing the size of a virtual hard disk, which happens visibly fast for a dynamic disk and a bit slower for its fixed-size cousins. After this action, you have to perform the follow-up action inside the virtual machine to increase the volume size from disk management. Now, for the PowerShell code:

  ```
  Resize-VHD
  ```

- **Merge**: This operation is disk-type-specific — differencing virtual disks. It allows two different actions. You can either merge the differencing disk with the original parent, or create a new merged VHD out of all the contributing VHDs, namely the parent and the child or the differencing disk. The latter is the preferred way of doing it, as in utmost probability, there would be more than differencing to a parent. The merge option can also be used to merge checkpoints or snapshots, which you might remember from *Chapter 3, Deploying Virtual Machines*. In PowerShell, the alternative the cmdlet is this:

```
Merge-VHD
```

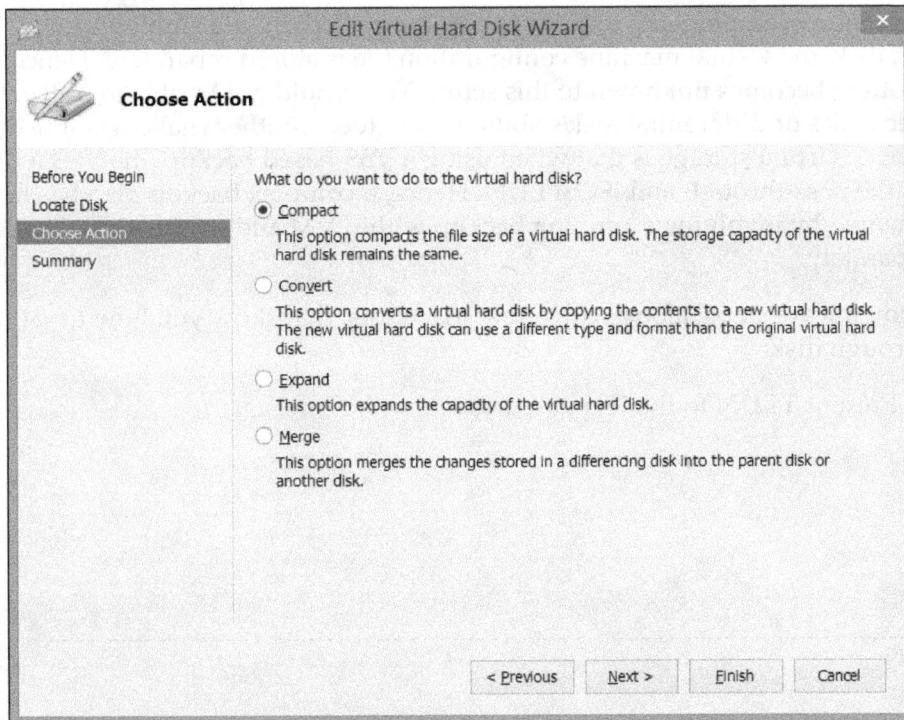

Figure 5-9: Edit Virtual Hard Disk Wizard – Choose Action

Pass-through disks

As the name indicates, these are physical LUNs or hard drives passed on from the Hyper-V hosts, and can be assigned to a virtual machine as a standard disk. A once popular method on older Hyper-V platforms, this allowed the VM to harness the full potential of the raw device bypassing the Hyper-V host filesystem and also not getting restricted by the 2 TB limit of VHDs. A lot has changed over the years, as Hyper-V has matured into a superior virtualization platform and introduced VHDX, which went past the size limitation. with Windows Server 2012 R2 can be used as a shared storage for Hyper-V guest clusters.

There are, however, demerits to this virtual storage. When you employ a pass-through disk, the virtual machine configuration file is stored separately. Hence, the snapshotting becomes unknown to this setup. You would not be able to utilize the dynamic disk's or differential disk's abilities here too. Another challenge of using this form of virtual storage is that when using a VSS-based backup, the VSS writer ignores the pass-through and iSCSI LUN. Hence, a complex backup plan has to be implemented by involving a running backup within VM and on the virtualization host separately.

The following are steps, along with a few snapshots, that show you how to set up a pass-through disk:

1. Present a LUN to the Hyper-V host.

2. Confirm the LUN in **Disk Management** and ensure that it stays in the **Offline State** and as Not Initialized.

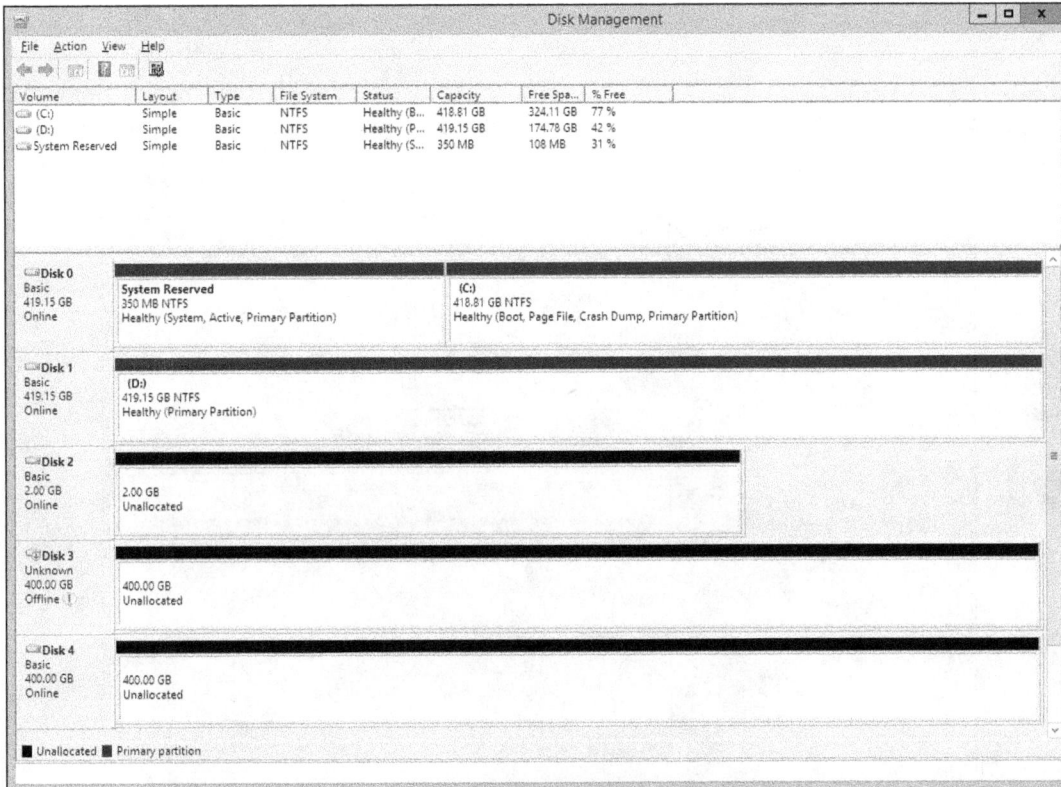

Figure 5-10: Hyper-V Host Disk Management

3. In Hyper-V Manager, right-click on the VM you wish to assign the pass-through to and select **Settings**.

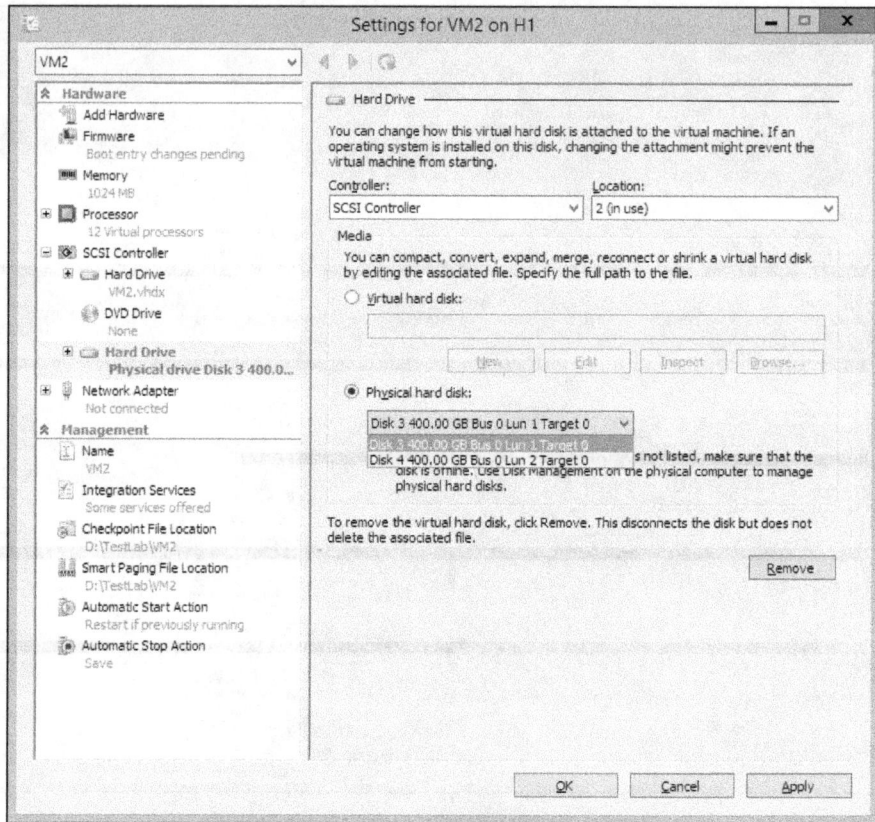

Figure 5-11: VM Settings – Pass-through disk placement

4. Select **SCSI Controller** (or **IDE** in the case of Gen-1 VM) and then select the **Physical hard disk** option, as shown in the preceding screenshot. In the drop-down menu, you will see the raw device or LUN you wish to assign. Select the appropriate option and click on **OK**.

5. Check **Disk Management** within the virtual machine to confirm that the disk has visibility.

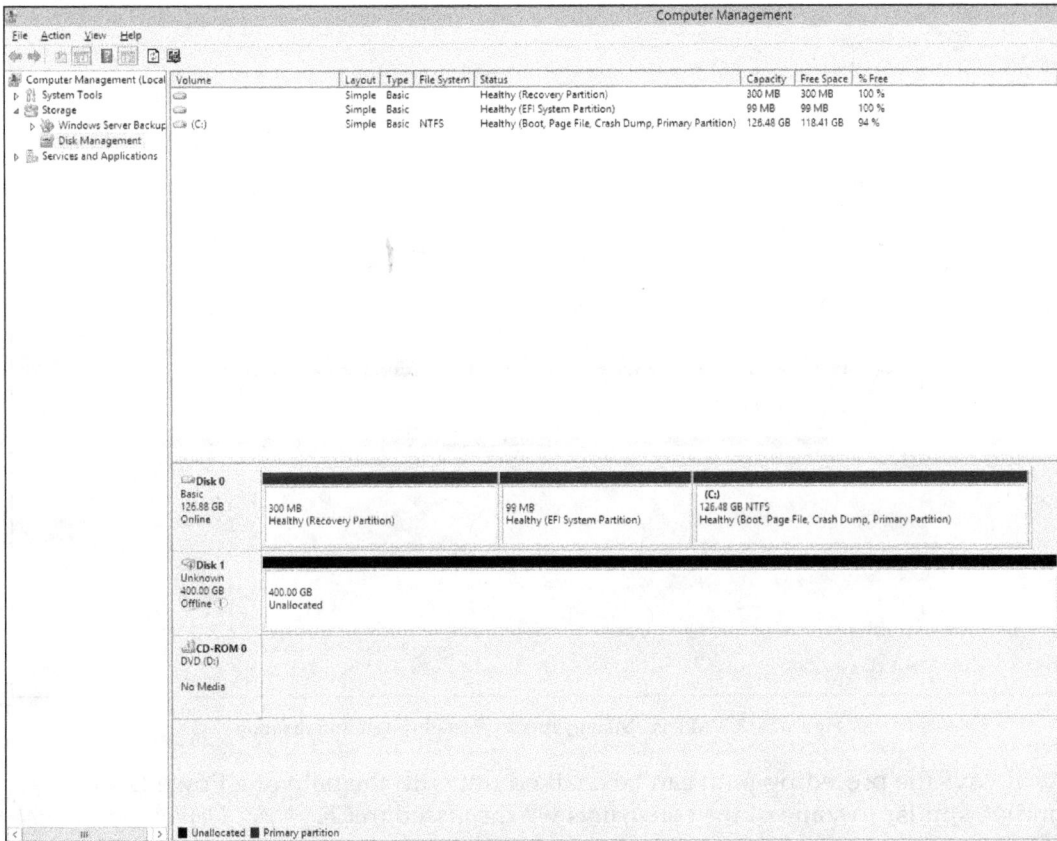

Figure 5-12: VM Disk Management – Pass-through Assignment

6. Bring it online and initialize.

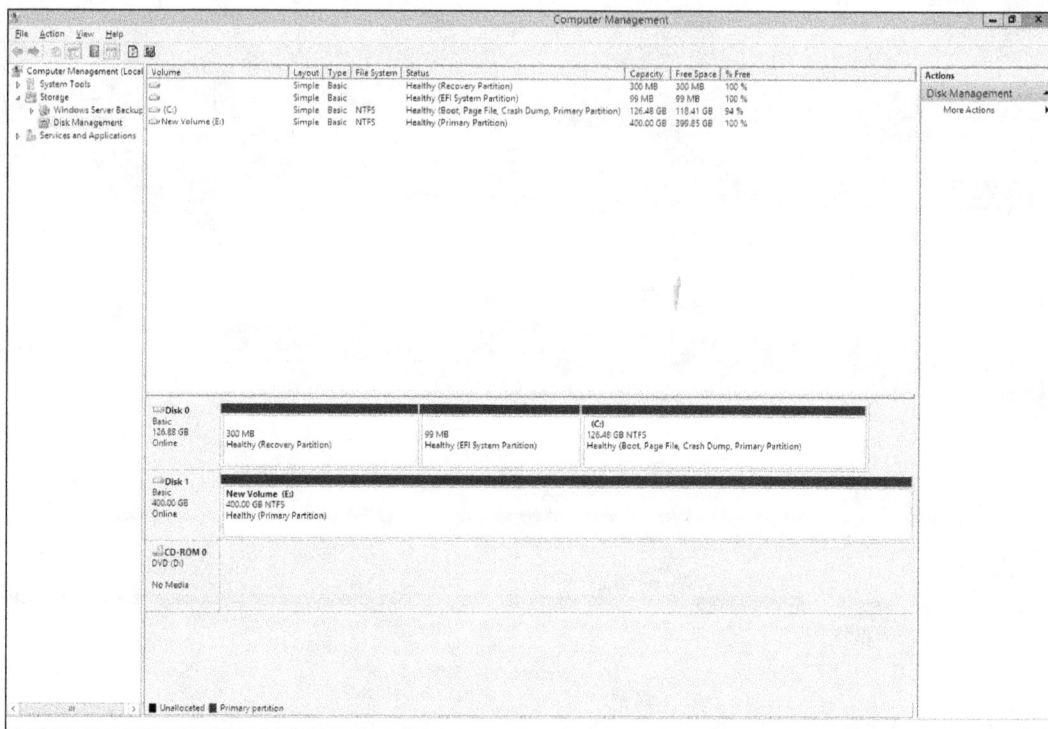

Figure 5-13: VM Disk Management – Pass-through Initialization

As always the preceding path can be chalked out with the help of a PowerShell cmdlet, similar to some of the constructs we discussed in *Chapter 3, Deploying Virtual Machines*:

```
Add-VMHardDiskDrive -VMName VM5 –ControllerType SCSI –
ControllerNumber 0 –ControllerLocation 2 –DiskNumber 3
```

Virtual fibre channel

Let's move on to the next big offering in Windows Server 2012 and R2 Hyper-V Server. There was pretty much a clamor for direct FC connectivity to virtual machines, as pass-through disks were supported only via iSCSI LUNs (with some major drawbacks not with FC). Also, needless to say, FC is faster. Enterprises with high-performance workloads relying on the FC SAN refrained from virtualizing or migrating to the cloud.

Windows Server 2012 introduced the virtual fibre channel SAN ability in Hyper-V, which extended the HBA (short for host bus adapter) abilities to a virtual machine, granting them a WWN (short for world wide node name) and allowing access to a fibre channel SAN over a virtual SAN. The fundamental principle behind the virtual SAN is the same as the Hyper-V virtual switch, wherein you create a virtual SAN that hooks up to the SAN fabric over the physical HBA of the Hyper-V host. The virtual machine has new synthetic hardware for the last piece. It is called a **virtual host bus adapter** or **vHBA**, which gets its own set of WWNs, namely WWNN (node name) and WWPN (port name). The WWN is to the FC protocol as MAC is to the Ethernet. Once the WWNs are identified at the fabric and the virtual SAN, the storage admins can set up zoning and present the LUN to the specific virtual machine.

The concept is straightforward, but there are prerequisites that you will need to ensure are in place before you can get down to the nitty-gritty of the setup:

- One or more Windows Server 2012 or R2 Hyper-V hosts.
- Hosts should have one or more FC HBAs with the latest drivers, and should support the virtual fibre channel and NPIV. NPIV may be disabled at the HBA level (refer to the vendor documentation prior to deployment). The same can be enabled using command-line utilities or GUI-based such as OneCommand manager, SANSurfer, and so on.
- NPIV should be enabled on the SAN fabric or actual ports.
- Storage arrays are transparent to NPIV, but they should support devices that present LUNs.
- Supported guest operating systems for virtual SAN are Windows 2008, Windows 2008 R2, Windows 2012, and Windows 2012 R2.
- The virtual fibre channel does not allow boot from SAN, unlike pass-through disks.

We are now done with the prerequisites! Now, let's look at two important aspects of SAN infrastructure, namely NPIV and MPIO.

N_Port ID virtualization (NPIV)

An ANSI T11 standard extension, this feature allows virtualization of the N_Port (WWPN) of an HBA, allowing multiple FC initiators to share a single HBA port. The concept is popular and is widely accepted and promoted by different vendors. Windows Server 2012 and R2 Hyper-V utilizes this feature to the best, wherein each virtual machine partaking in the virtual SAN gets assigned a unique WWPN and access to the SAN over a physical HBA spawning its own N_Port. Zoning follows next, wherein the fabric can have the zone directed to the VM WWPN. This attribute leads to a very small footprint, and thereby, easier management and operational and capital expenditure.

Multipath I/O (MPIO)

Multipath I/O or MPIO is a fault tolerance mechanism that is used to ensure consistent performance and connectivity from a server to the storage array by employing access over multiple physical paths, including HBAs, controllers, fabric, and so on. Windows Server 2012 and R2 Hyper-V extend the MPIO feature to the virtual machines over vHBA and virtual SAN, thereby ensuring continuous access to the FC paths. Microsoft also provides an MPIO framework, which assists in resolving HBA or path failure to the storage arrays. MPIO allows 32 alternate paths for redundancy and load balancing.

To ensure that the MPIO routines function as desired, the following offers some design guidance for the implementation:

- **MPIO on the Hyper-V host**: Install MPIO on the host that has multiple FC HBAs (more than one port) and ensure that multiple alternate paths to the LUNs are assigned to it.

- **MPIO on the virtual machine**: You can enable only four vHBAs for a virtual machine. If using more than one vHBA, it amounts to a requirement of redundancy and load balancing, which can be achieved by the Microsoft native MPIO and DSM. However, for VMs configured for live migration, to maintain consistent LUN access when migrated from one host to the other, it is recommended to install a vendor-specific **DSM** (short for **device-specific module**) on VMs.

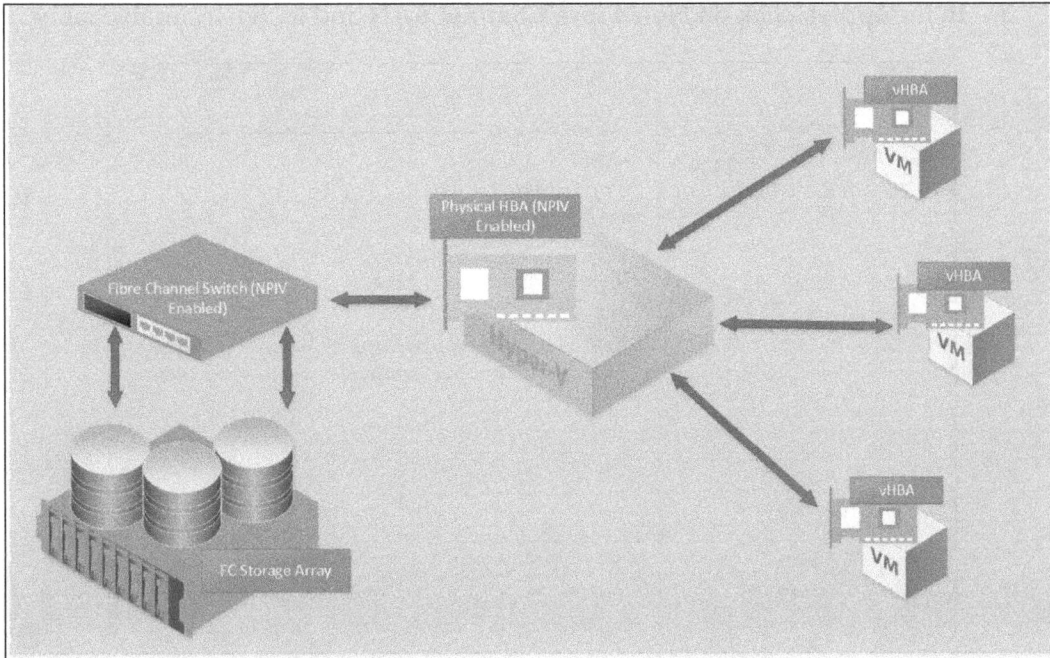

Figure 5-14: Virtual Fibre Channel SAN Architecture

Setting up the virtual SAN and the virtual fibre channel adapter

Well-versed with the prerequisites and guidance, let's move on with creation of the virtual SAN and the following synthetic equipment:

1. In the Hyper-V Manager console, invoke **Virtual SAN Manager** from the **Actions** pane.

2. In the applet, click on **New Fibre Channel SAN** and assign a suitable name.

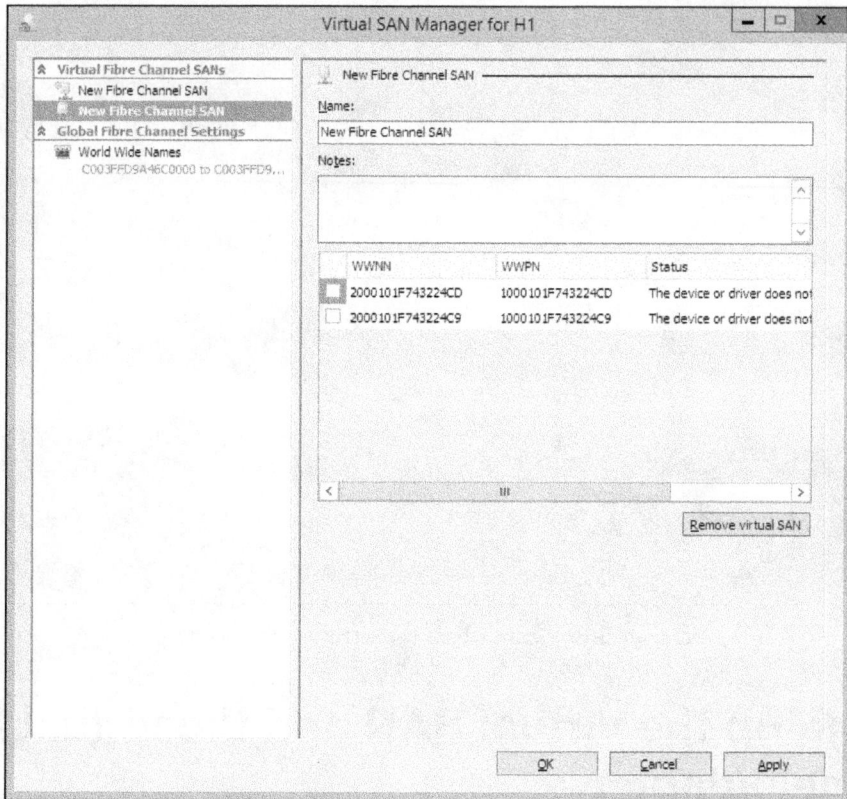

Figure 5-15: Virtual SAN Manager – New Fibre Channel SAN

3. From the list of available HBAs, select the appropriate ones and ensure that the status does not say **The device or driver does not support virtual Fibre Channel**. If it does, ensure that you are running the latest driver and the vendor supports virtual fibre channel. Next, check whether the NPIV is enabled on the HBA or not.

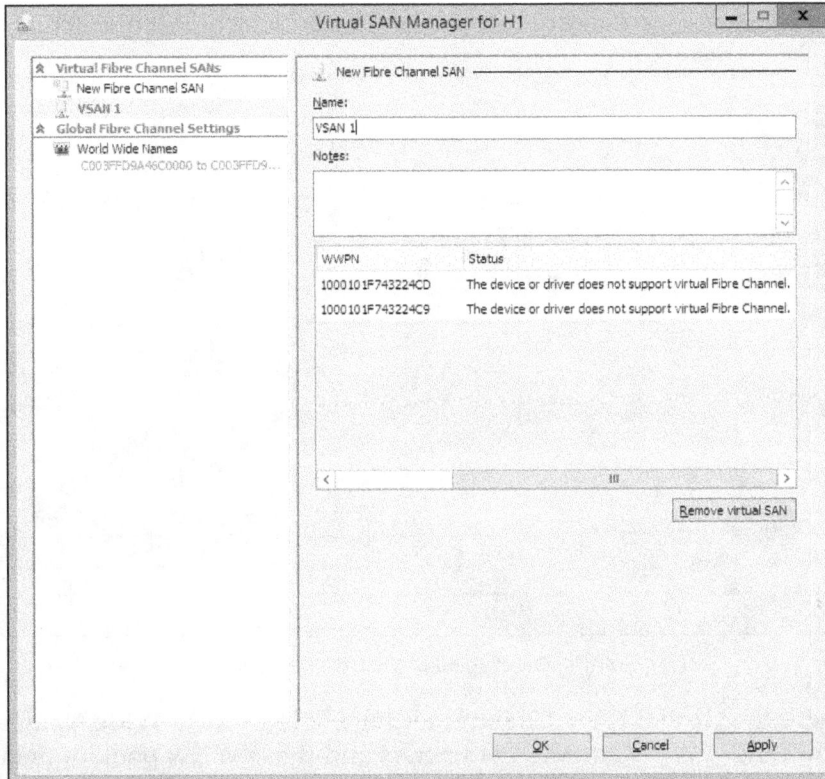

Figure 5-16: New Fibre Channel SAN – NPIV not enabled on HBA

4.   Enabling NPIV on the HBA or a driver update requires a reboot of the host.

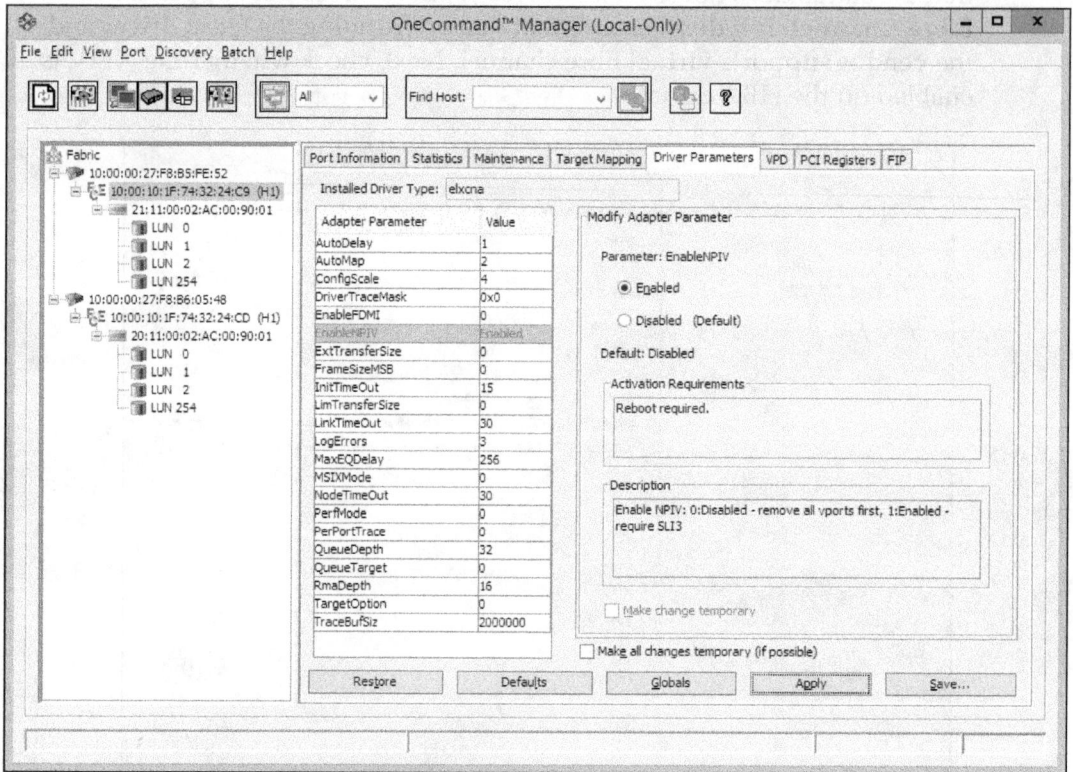

Figure 5-17: OneCommand Manager – EnableNPIV

5.   Under the **Global Fibre Channel** settings, select **World Wide Names**. This shows the WWPN address parameters and the WWNN pool for default assignment to Hyper-V ports.

6.   Click on **OK** to create the new virtual SAN.

7.   Identify the virtual machine you need to assign to the new virtual SAN.

8.   From the VM settings, select the **Add Hardware** option from the **Hardware** section and add a fibre channel adapter.

9.   Select the new fibre channel adapter and check out the properties screen on the right. Select the **Virtual SAN created**.

10. Under the **Virtual SAN**, you can see the port address assigned from the default pool of WWNNs and WWPNs under **Port addresses**. You may notice that there are two sets of addresses, namely **Address set A** and **Address set B**. Windows Server 2012 and R2 Hyper-V maintain the two sets of addresses to ensure continuous access to FC LUNs to the VM configured for live migration. The LUN path is handed off to the alternate set when the VM is migrated to the destination host from the source host, and reversed when it is migrated back.

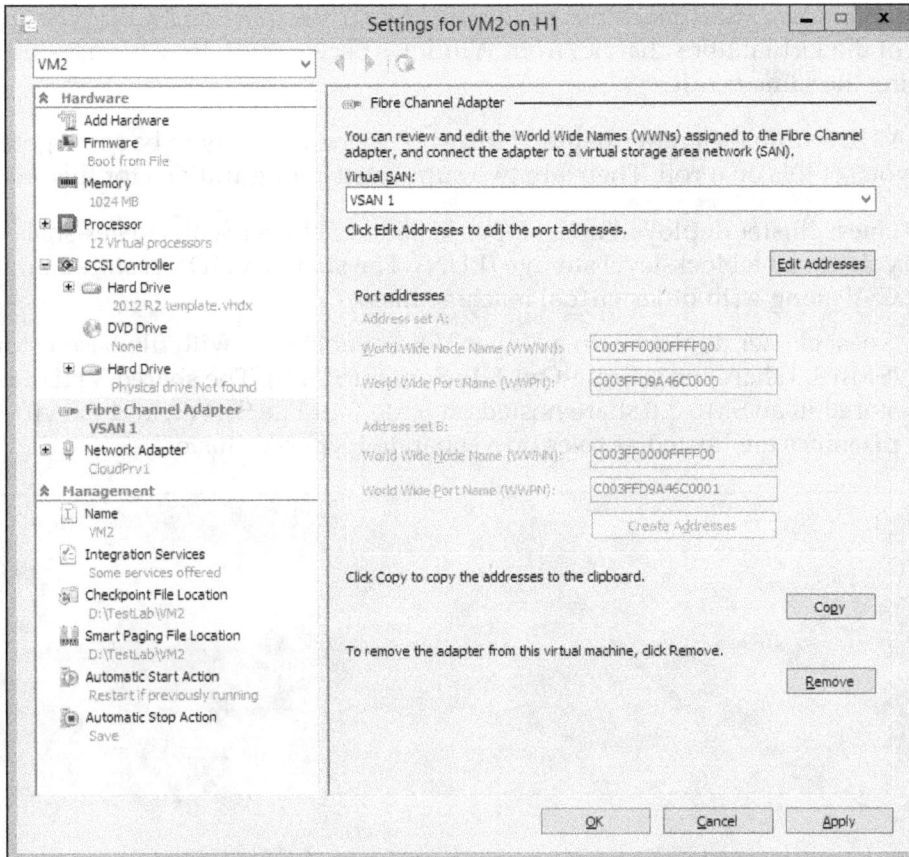

Figure 5-18: VM Settings – New Fibre Channel Adapter

Now, for the PowerShell coder's delight, here is the cmdlet construct that can achieve the preceding result:

```
Get-InitiatorPort
New-VMSan –Name VSAN1 –Note "Test Virtual SAN" –WorldWideNodeName
2000101F743224CD –WorldWidePortName 1000101F743224CD
```

Guest cluster setup using shared VHDX

Failover clustering is one of the most utilized features on Windows servers, and is used to provide high availability and fault tolerance to certain Windows-based roles and third-party applications. There's not much that is new about this Windows feature other than what it has already brought onto the table. It has proven to be path breaking, yet consistent. Windows failover clustering has been employed on physical servers and guest machines alike, using the same shared storage principle. Physical servers have always used the iSCSI, FC, and FCOE LUNs for this requirement, whereas Windows guest machines have relied by far the most on iSCSI. With the advent of the virtual fibre channel from Windows Server 2012, they have been delivering the same result.

Shared VHDX unfolds a new chapter. However, there are likely to be some gotchas before you set this on a roll. There are two supported configurations for this setup:

- Guest cluster deployed on a Hyper-V failover cluster with cluster-shared volume on a block-level storage (LUN). The shared VHDX is stored on the CSV along with other virtual machine files.

- Guest cluster deployed on a Hyper-V failover cluster with file-based storage (SMB 3.0 share) on a **Scale-Out File Server** (**SOFS**). The shared VHDX is stored in an SMB 3.0 share hosted on Scale-Out File Server, and the virtual machines are hosted as roles on a separate Hyper-V cluster.

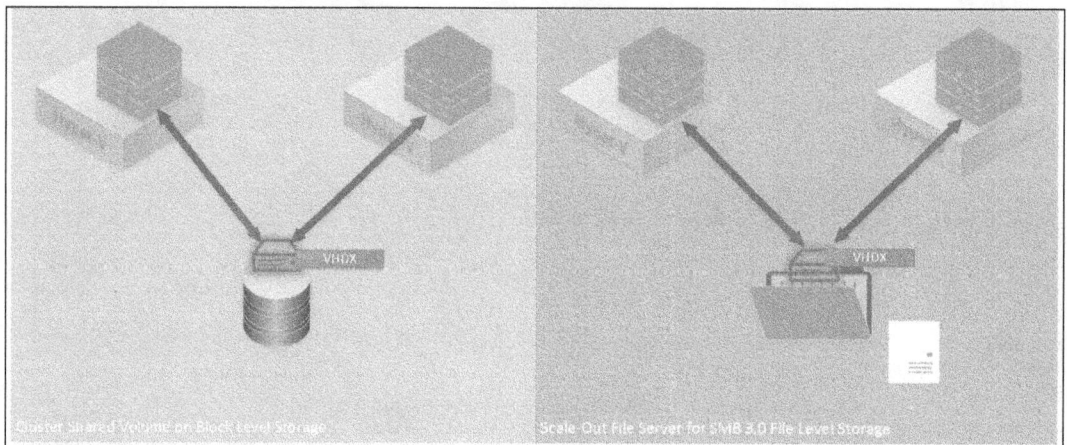

Figure 5-19: Guest Cluster Scenarios

> SOFS is a Microsoft solution for providing continuous file-level access for application servers. It is an active-active failover cluster role that hosts SMB 3.0 shares designed to store Hyper-V-related files and application servers (primarily SQL). It is not meant for end user shares.

We will be looking at the prerequisites and guidance to setting up a Hyper-V failover cluster in the next chapter, wherein you will also learn how to make a highly available virtual machine.

Now let's review the steps of converting a VHDX into a shared VHDX for guest clustering. You may initiate the process from the Hyper-V Manager or failover cluster manager:

1. First, create a new VHDX using **New Virtual Hard Disk Wizard**, as we discussed earlier in this chapter.

2. In the wizard, on the **Specify name** and **Location page**, you may do the following:
    ◦ In the name field, set the name appropriately as per your infrastructure naming convention.
    ◦ In the location field, depending on the configuration, you may pick and set the location accordingly. For example, for the first configuration, where the shared storage is a CSV disk, the path should be as follows:

    `C:\ClusterStorage\VolumeX`

    Here, `C:\` represents the system drive and `x` represents the desired CSV volume number.

    For the second configuration, where the shared storage is an SMB file share, specify the path like this:

    `\\ServerName\ShareName`

    Here, `ServerName` is the **Client Access Point (CAP)** for the Scale-Out File Server, and `ShareName` is the name of the SMB file share.

3. Once you have created the new VHDX, enable the flag for sharing the VHDX with the following steps:

    1. In the VM settings under **Hardware** section, under **SCSI Controller**, expand the virtual hard drive that you just created.
    2. Select **Advanced Features**.
    3. Check the box for **Enable virtual hard disk sharing**.

4. Click on **OK**.

5. Now link the VHDX to the second virtual machine and set up the guest clustering.

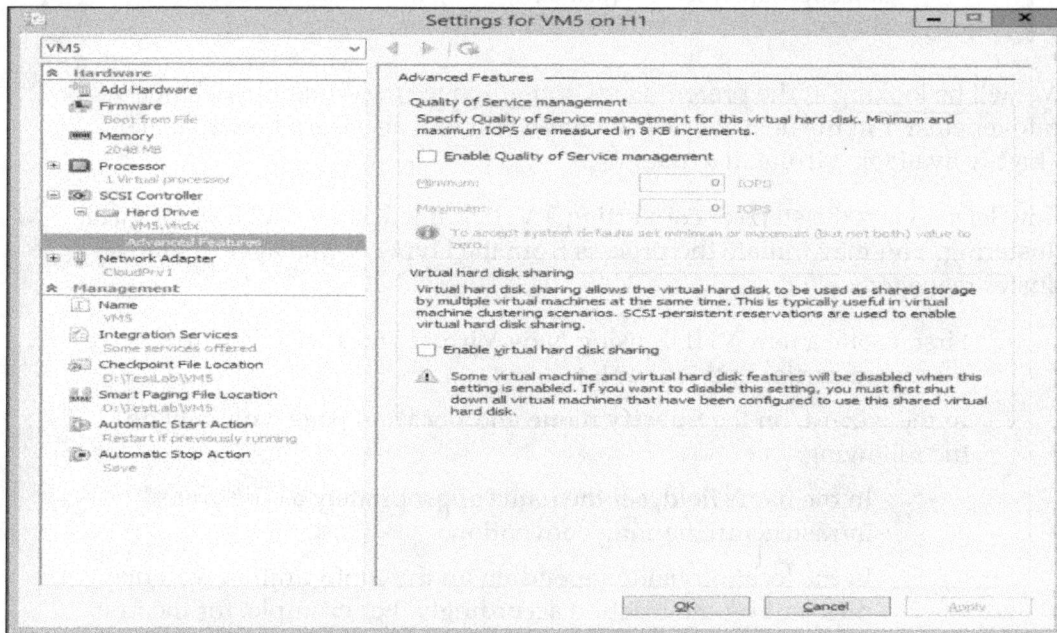

Figure 5-20: Shared VHDX

For PowerShell pleasure, the following cmdlets will perform the task that we just covered:

```
New-VHD -Path C:\ClusterStorage\Volume2\SharedDisk.VHDX -Fixed -
SizeBytes 50GB Add-VMHardDiskDrive -VMName VM5 -Path
C:\ClusterStorage\Volume2\SharedDisk.VHDX -ShareVirtualDisk
Add-VMHardDiskDrive -VMName VM6 -Path
C:\ClusterStorage\Volume2\SharedDisk.VHDX -ShareVirtualDisk
```

SMI-S

Storage Management Initiative Specification, better known as **SMI-S**, is a SNIA standard that facilitates the management of storage devices from multiple vendors in a storage area network. Microsoft is party to the SMI-S workgroups, and has worked in collaboration with many storage vendors to develop providers and extend the capabilities of storage discovery and provisioning to Microsoft applications and platforms.

SMI-S integration was first added in System Center Virtual Machine Manager 2012, and the later in Windows Server 2012. The suite continued with R2 (short for Release 2) of both the products.

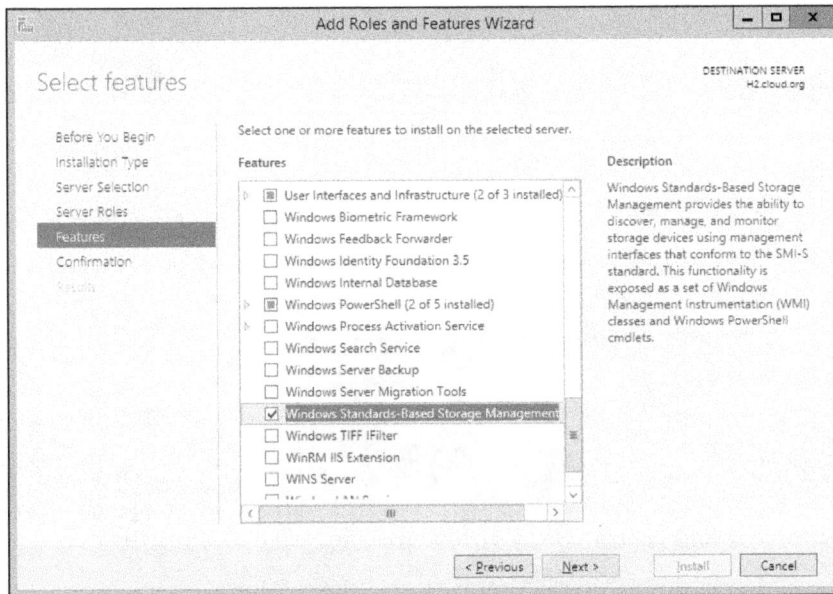

Figure 5-21: The Windows Standards-Based Storage Management Feature

The Windows Standards-Based Storage Management service was first used by VMM 2012 and later added to Windows Server 2012. It allows users to interface with the SMI-S provider from vendors. The storage service gets activated with the installation of VMM 2012 and R2, but with Windows Server 2012 and R2, this is an optional Windows feature and can be installed via Server Manager or PowerShell. It can be used alongside the file and storage services role in Server Manager.

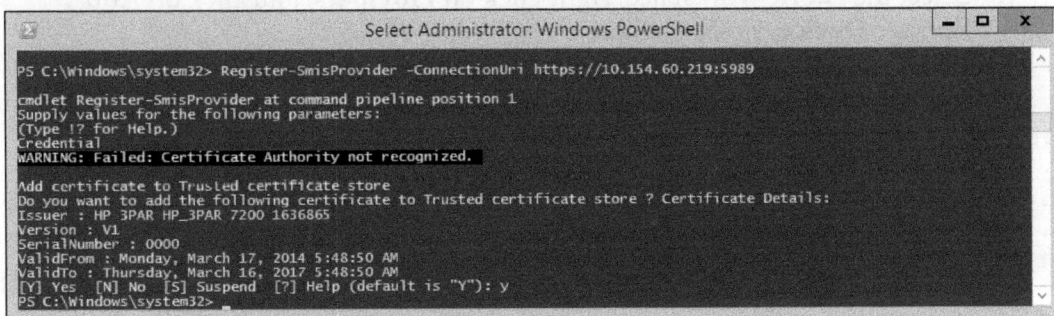

Figure 5-22: Register SMI-S provider

Once the storage service is installed, you will need to register the SMI-S providers from the vendors allowing the service to discover, provision, and monitor storage resources. The iSCSI target SMI-S provider comes integrated with Windows Server 2012 R2.

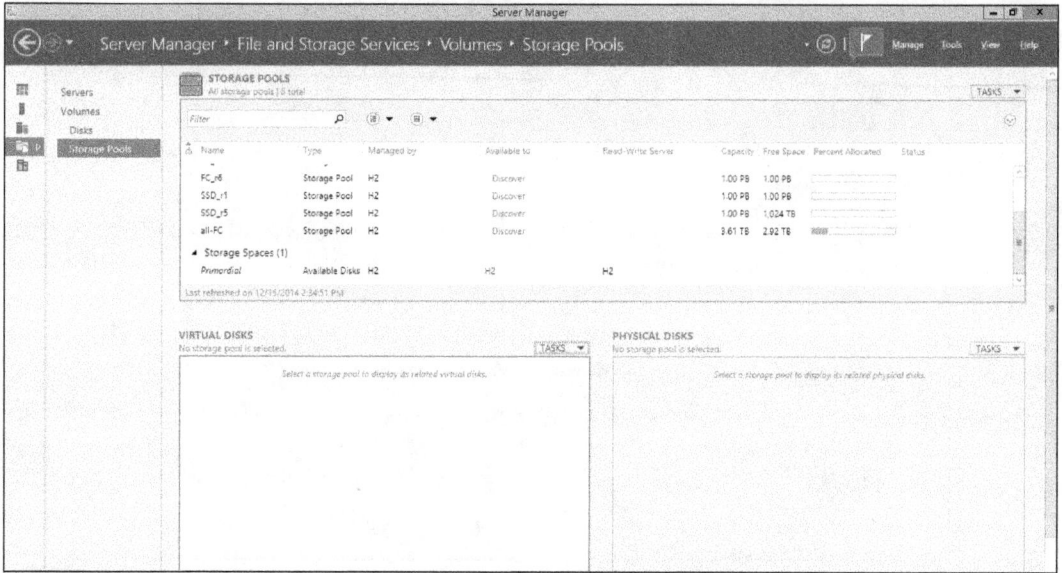

Figure 5-23: Server Manager – File and Storage Services-Storage Pools after Registering SMI-S provider

Server Manager gives a basic array configuration, but System Center Virtual Machine 2012 and R2 give you more granular control over the storage. VMM is beyond the scope of this book, but consider this as a little bonus. The following is a series of steps that will take you through the basic task of adding an iSCSI provider, and thereafter, LUN creation.

1. Select the **Fabric** workspace, right-click on **Providers**, and click on **Add Storage Device**, as shown here:

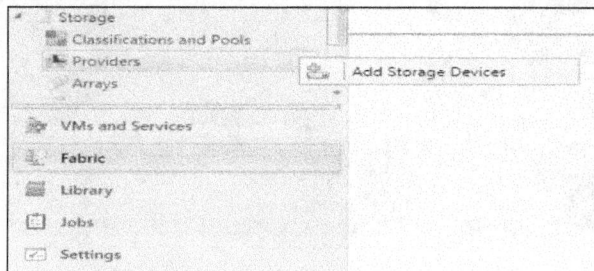

Figure 5-24: SC VMM – Add Provider

2. In **Add Storage Devices Wizard**, select the provider type screen, select **SAN and NAS devices discovered and managed by a SMI-S provider**, and click on **Next**, as shown in the following screenshot:

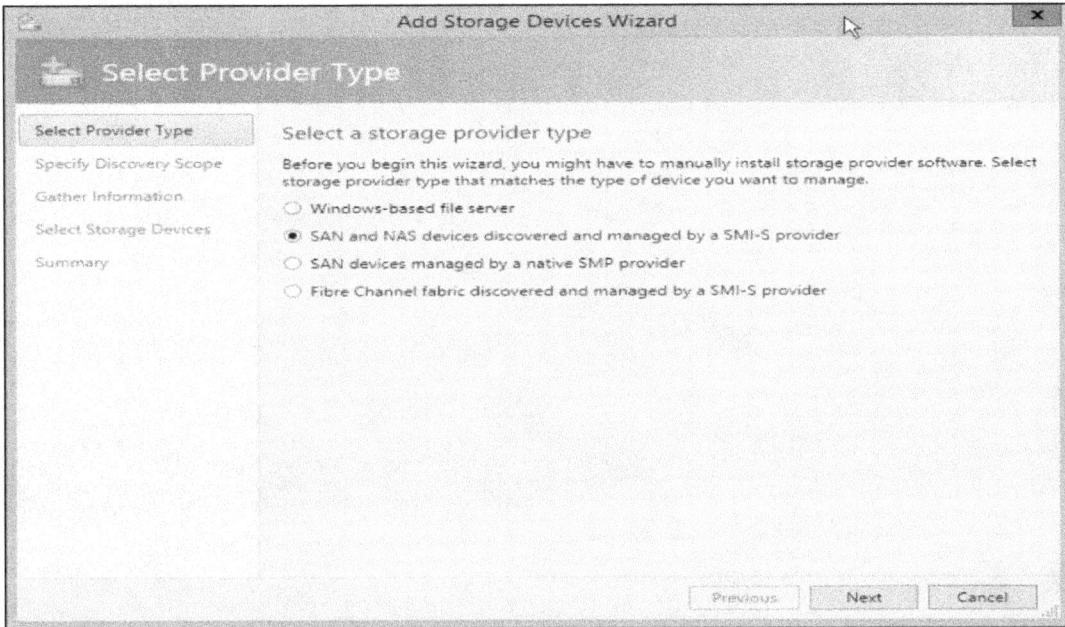

Figure 5-25: Add Storage Devices Wizard – Provider Type

3. In the next screen, **Specify Discovery Scope**, update the relevant details, such as **Protocol**, the FQDN name of the target, and **Run As account**. Then click on **Next** and move forward to the next screen, called **Gather Information**.

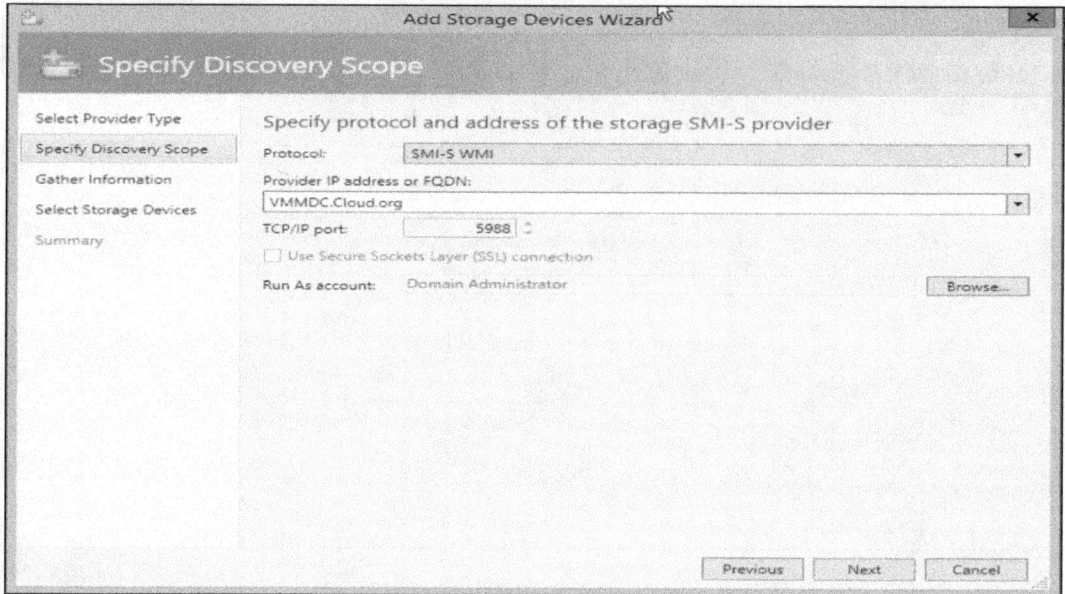

Figure 5-26: Add Storage Devices Wizard – Specify Discovery Scope

4. On the **Select Storage Devices** screen, select the specific device. Then click on **Create classification...** and make the update for that device.

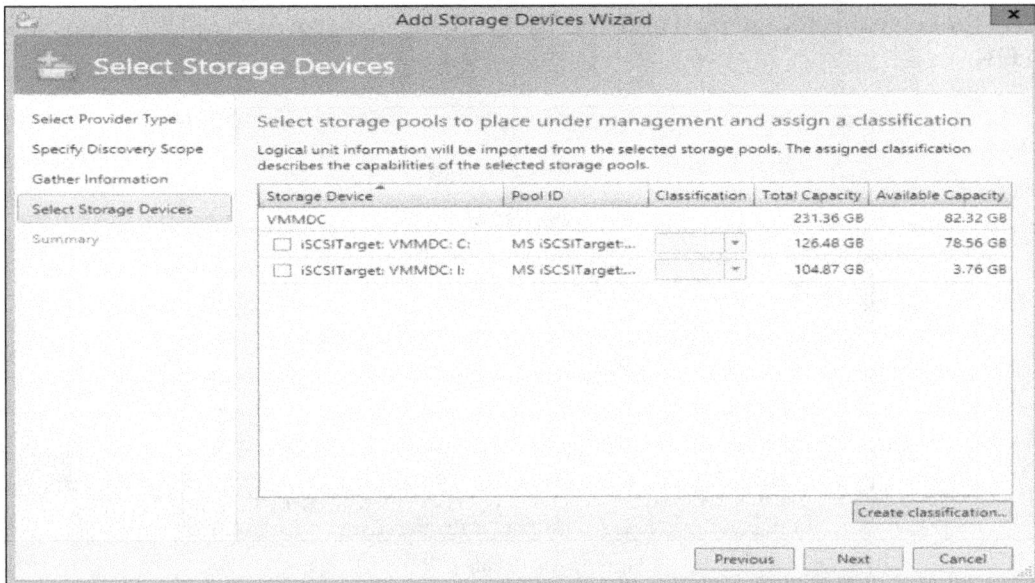

Figure 5-27: Add Storage Devices Wizard – Select Storage Devices

5. In the **New Classification** applet, as shown in *figure 5-28*, fill in the **Name** and **Description** fields. Then click on **Add**. This takes you back to the **Select Storage Devices** screen. Select the device and update the classification as per the new classification created in the screen shown in *figure 5-28*:

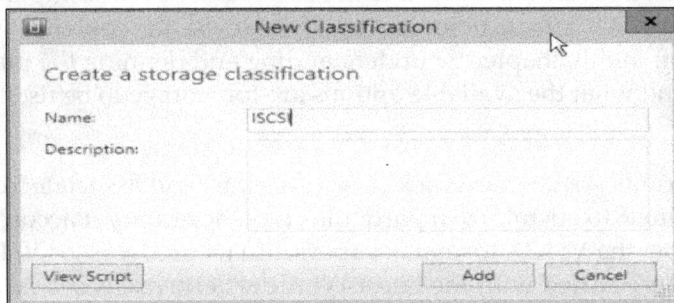

Figure 5-28: Add Storage Devices Wizard – Create Classification

6. On the **Summary** screen, click on **Finish**.

Voilà! You can now create a LUN in VMM. All you need to do is select the **Fabric** workspace and go to **Storage Node**. Thereafter, click on **Create Logical Unit** on the actions ribbon, which in turn invokes the **Create Logical Unit** wizard. In this wizard, select the relevant storage pool and specify the name and size of the LUN. Then click on **OK**.

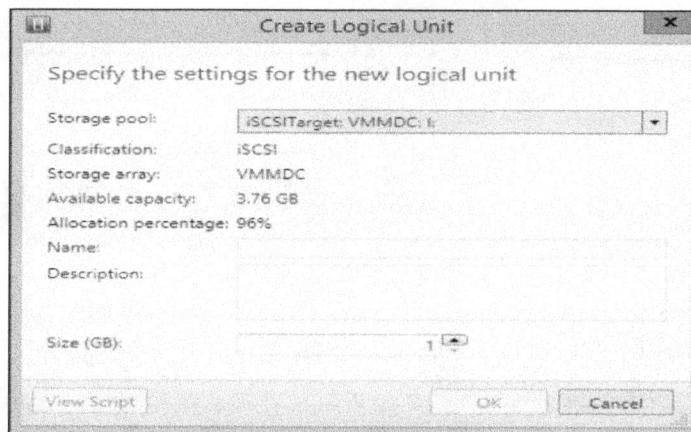

Figure 5-29: Create LUN

This brings us to the end of the discussion on SMI-S, and the chapter.

Summary

As we conclude the fifth Chapter, it is going to be quite a realization that we have covered almost all the basic attributes and aspects required for a simple Windows Server 2012 R2 Hyper-V infrastructure setup. If we revise the contents, we will notice this: we started off in this chapter by understanding and defining the purpose of virtual storage, and what the available options are for storage to be used with a virtual machine.

We reviewed various virtual hard disk types, formats, and associated operations that may be required to customize a particular type or modify it accordingly. We recounted how the VHDX format is superior to its predecessor VHD and which features were added with the latest Window Server releases, namely 2012 and 2012 R2. We discussed shared VHDX and how it can be used as an alternative to the old-school iSCSI or FC LUN as a shared storage for Windows guest clustering.

Pass-through disks are on their way out, and we all know the reason why. The advent of the virtual fibre channel with Windows Server 2012 has opened the doors for virtualization of high-performance workloads relying heavily on FC connectivity, which until now was a single reason and enough of a reason to decline consolidation of these workloads. We also saw how to set up a Virtual SAN and what its underlying attributes are.

Towards the end, we briefly looked at the SMI-S feature and how it can be utilized to simplify storage provisioning and management.

From the next chapter onwards, the onus will shift to advanced topics related to Hyper-V and VM management.

6
Planning a Virtual Machine's High Availability and Mobility

High availability (HA) means planning a system design that delivers operational continuity and stands through any unplanned contingencies or planned downtime over a period of time. Microsoft offers HA solutions with failover clustering and **Network Load Balancing (NLB)** for several of its applications and services (roles). Both of these HA strategies serve different purposes.

Failover clustering involves configuring a group of servers, called **nodes**, to act as one server and serve one or more roles. One of these nodes acts as the active node, and rest nodes supplement as secondary or passive nodes for a particular role. When the primary, or active, node fails, any one of the passive nodes takes over the role, limiting the downtime and thereby increasing availability. The process in which the role is passed from the active node to a passive node is referred to as **failover**.

The NLB cluster is a collection of servers, referred to as **hosts**, running as a single system and providing load balancing for a server application. Each host runs an isolated copy of the application, and client requests for access to the application are distributed among all the hosts, based on an algorithm. NLB is generally used to serve web applications.

Hyper-V does not provide any inherent clustering. However, Hyper-V hosts can be configured as failover cluster nodes to provide HA for VMs as roles. If we go further down the virtualization stack, HA can be planned for the workloads running inside virtual machines using NLB or failover clustering. Throughout this chapter, we will focus on the Hyper-V host failover clustering and VM HA.

One aspect of availability is VM mobility, which has been improvised a lot in Windows Server 2012 and R2 releases, presenting admins with multiple options: live migration, storage live migration, and shared nothing live migration.

The dependence on expensive traditional shared storage for HA and mobility has also been nullified, as you can now achieve the same results with SMB 3.0 shared storage, or even better results with **Scale-Out File Server** (**SOFS**) with SMB 3.0.

In this chapter, we will broadly cover the following topics:

* Hyper-V failover cluster setup and deployment
* Cluster operations, covering Cluster Aware Updating, and installing BitLocker on Cluster Shared Volumes
* An insight into the Scale-Out File Server
* Virtual machine mobility

Hyper-V failover cluster deployment

Failover clustering provides fail-safe availability for a dedicated application or service (role). Clustering allows you to build a collection of servers with similar configurations under a virtual computer name, called a **CNO** (short for **cluster name object**). A CNO retains all the enterprise and network attributes of any normal computer/server in the environment. It has a presence in the active directory and can be accessed in the network.

As mentioned in the chapter's introduction, one of the servers in the cluster setup maintains the active state for a particular role and addresses all the transactions for the hosted role. The rest of the servers stay in the passive state, and one of the passive nodes takes over the active state only in the event of a failure of the original active node. The failure could be either hardware-, software-, or network-oriented. This setup is called **active-passive clustering**.

This design paradigm leaves a little dent in both the **capital expenditure** (**CAPEX**) and **operational expenditure** (**OPEX**) figures, wherein the former is the business cost of procuring assets and the latter is the expenditure on continuity and functioning of the business. If the active-passive concept is followed in its entirety, hardware resources on the passive nodes will stay unutilized. A better approach is to keep one or more roles on all the nodes, each node being active for a particular role and the other nodes supplementing as passive once. This means that all the nodes will be active for one or more roles, and on standby as passive nodes for roles hosted on other nodes. This setup is called **active-active clustering**.

In a Hyper-V cluster, all nodes host multiple virtual machines, just as they would if they were independent servers. VMs are hosted as roles, and one node is active for more than one such VM. The rest of the nodes pose as passive for the same VM or set of VMs. At the same time, the passive nodes act as an active node for some other VMs. The VMs can be live-migrated or failed over from one node to another in the cluster, depending on the availability of compute, memory, and network resources.

Failover clustering has been the HA solution for Hyper-V since its very onset, as it has been for other MS applications and roles. However, it lacked supporting features for early releases of Hyper-V. Windows Server 2012 and Windows Server 2012 R2 have built on clustering to deliver Hyper-V as a solid product for all businesses — small- and medium-sized enterprises (SMEs) and larger enterprises alike.

Prerequisites for the Hyper-V cluster setup

The failover clustering feature can easily be installed from the Server Manager. However, prior to deployment of the feature, it has to be planned out well so that you get a robust solution that stands against all contingencies. Windows Server 2012 and R2 allow you to scale up to 64 nodes in a cluster, unlike their predecessor, Windows Server 2008 R2, which limited the setup to 16 nodes. The nodes or members of the cluster have to be set up as per guidelines and prerequisites spanning across the same set of resources, namely compute, memory, storage, and network. The feature requires you to run the "validate a configuration" test to determine whether all the requirements have been met or whether there is any possible misconfiguration. The following are the parameters which you should consider from the prerequisite perspective.

Server hardware

The participant nodes should ideally be the same or similar with respect to hardware specifications. This takes us back to *Chapter 2, Planning and Deploying Microsoft Hyper-V*. It is essential that the underlying hardware should be Windows Server 2012 R2 certified before you can deploy the Hyper-V role and join the server to a cluster. To support virtual machine mobility, the server hardware should preferably be alike or the same. From the CPU perspective, there's a trade-off, which allows us to use different CPUs. However, they should be from the same vendor. We will review the processor compatibility requirement for live migration in a later section.

Another important aspect is the storage controller (or controllers) on the servers. If the storage assigned to the nodes is DAS or FC, it is imperative that all the components for the storage stack installed on the servers should be alike. The host bus adapter (HBA) and its corresponding drivers and firmware should be the same, along with installed MPIO and DSM versions. If you plan to use different HBAs, ensure that your storage vendor supports the configuration.

If the cluster storage is going to be iSCSI, ensure that your network adapters are uniquely profiled. There should be dedicated adapters to support network communications and iSCSI storage separately, and traffic should not converge.

Storage prerequisites

Shared storage is one of the building blocks of a failover cluster. The shared disk is utilized both for the Quorum Model (as a witness disk) and the file storage provided for clustered applications and services (roles). For Hyper-V, Windows Server 2012 and R2 are no longer reliant on the traditional shared storage and can utilize SMB 3.0 file shares. SMB 3.0 shares can be used as shared storage for Hyper-V clusters. If you are using iSCSI or FC LUNs, there are some gotchas you should remember:

- Ensure that storage compatibility is checked as per the Windows Server Catalog
- Use MPIO or LBFO
- Mask the LUNs per cluster and ensure isolation of LUNS via zoning
- If you wish to utilize native disk support, then use only basic disks. For Cluster Shared Volumes (CSV), NTFS-formatted volumes are preferable (ReFS volumes are also supported)

Software prerequisites

This aspect is mostly expected but still worth a mention. All the members should run the same version of the operating system, be at the same service pack level, and have a set of patches or software updates installed. This is imperative for proper functioning of the cluster.

Environment prerequisites – Active Directory and network configuration

With all the underlying requirements considered, let's focus on how the cluster fits into the environment. A Hyper-V cluster, as would be the case for any other role that is clustered, will get a cluster name, with which it will be identified in an infrastructure like any other server. When you create a cluster, its name gets registered in the Active Directory as a CNO (cluster name object) which is a virtual computer object. You may also opt to prestage (or precreate) the CNO prior to creating the cluster. This is available when the user group responsible for creating the failover cluster does not have permission in the Active Directory to create an object. It is recommended to keep all the computer accounts and CNO of a cluster in their respective OUs. This not only improves manageability, but if your enterprise practices security hardening, or in situations where GPO restrictions are implemented, the same can easily be filtered to avoid any mishaps in the functioning of the cluster.

From the networking perspective, Windows Server 2012 and R2 promote converged networking (which is assumed to be a boon). Unlike their predecessors (which required separate physical network paths for cluster-specific traffic), Windows Server 2012 and R2 Hyper-V allow convergence of all the traffic over one network path by employing Windows network teaming (multiplexor) and a Hyper-V External Virtual Switch.

When planning a Hyper-V cluster, there are multiple traffic channels required to address various needs. Each of the traffic channels can be assigned a virtual NIC, and QoS can be enabled for the same, so that any one of the virtual NICs does not hog the entire available bandwidth and isolation is ensured. The primary network traffic for a Hyper-V cluster can be segregated as follows:

- **Management**: This is the network for Hyper-V host connectivity and management. It ensures that the host has an enterprise network presence.
- **Cluster**: This network is primarily for cluster-specific traffic involving cluster heartbeats and Hyper-V-specific cluster shared volume redirection.
- **Virtual machine access**: This ensures that the virtual machines on the host have a network presence.
- **Live migration**: VM mobility occurs over this channel.
- **Hyper-V Replica**: To be covered in detail in *Chapter 7, Building a Secure Virtualization Environment*, this network channel is focused on VM replication using the Hyper-V Replica.

- **Storage**: Primarily used for iSCSI, and nowadays for SMB as well.

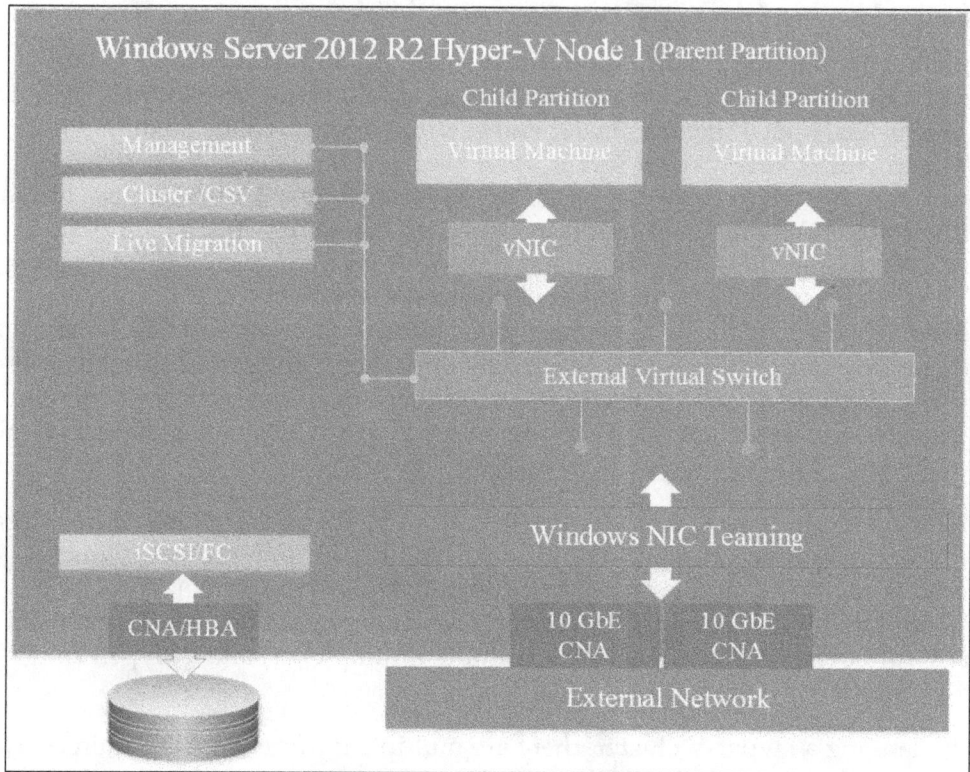

Figure 6-1: Cluster Node Configuration

Installing and configuring the failover clustering feature

Once you have ensured that all the prerequisites are in place, it's time to deploy the feature and add the virtual machines. The installation of this feature can be achieved via the Server Manager or PowerShell, as we have seen in previous chapters.

With PowerShell, it's a straight slam dunk for this feature:

```
Install-WindowsFeature -Name Failover-Clustering -
IncludeManagementTools
```

With the Server Manager, it's a sequential set of steps again, where you add the failover clustering feature from the list. Also, install the multipath I/O feature if you intend to use a robust storage solution for a shared storage resource. Once you have the failover clustering feature installed, the console looks like this:

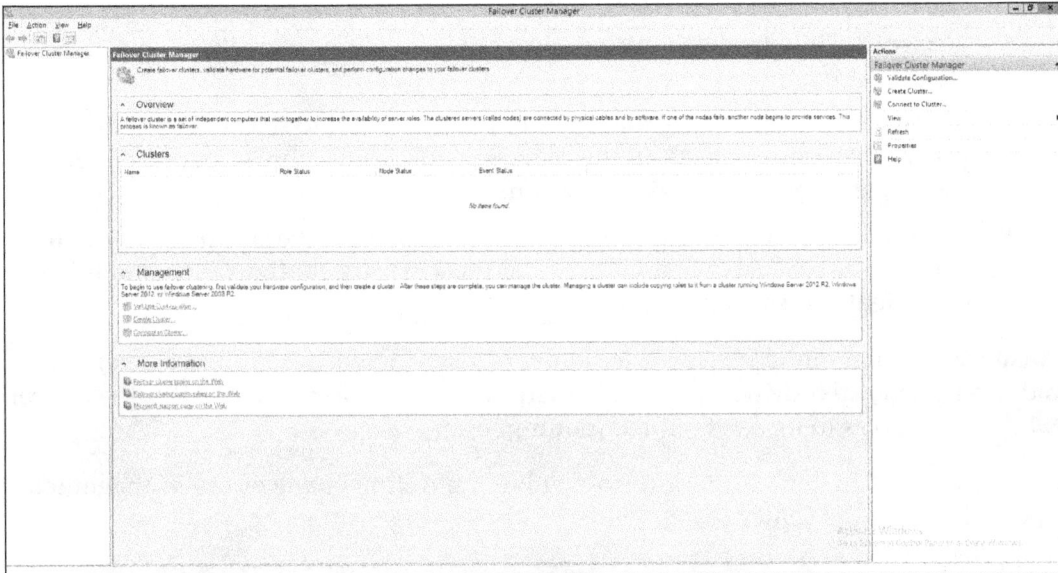

Figure 6-2: Failover Clustering Console

The next action to be performed is **Create a Cluster** and then you can set things in motion. However, before you proceed, Windows ensures that you have followed the prerequisites and validates the configuration you are planning to deploy. Thereafter, you can create a cluster of similar server nodes and add the virtual machine role (or roles) to be hosted on the cluster.

Cluster validation

In the **Failover Cluster Manager** console, in the center pane or the **Actions** pane, you can see the **Validate Configuration** link. It allows you to perform tests against prospective nodes even before you add them to the cluster. The feature prompts you to run the wizard even when you initiate cluster creation. The wizard runs a battery of tests against the nodes, confirming the compatibility and health state of the contributing components in the cluster. The tests invoked fall under five headings, as follows:

- **Hyper-V Configuration**: The set of tests is listed only when you have the Hyper-V role installed. It checks against the basic Hyper-V settings, prerequisites, and hardware compatibility.

- **Cluster Configuration**: The older set of tests, run only on existing clusters. Validate if the nodes are properly configured.

- **Inventory**: As the name indicates, the purpose of these tests is to build an inventory of hardware, software, and the corresponding settings, and then build informative lists accordingly.

- **Network**: This checks the Windows networking functionality from a clustering perspective.

- **Storage**: The tests ensure that the storage presented to the cluster nodes or prospective nodes meets all the requirements from a cluster perspective, including reservation and arbitration.

- **System Configuration**: The final set of tests ensures the compatibility of the software as well as the hardware, and the software configuration should be consistent across all the nodes.

Cluster validation found its way into failover clustering with Windows Server 2008, and has become an indispensable tool when staging a cluster. Let's review the cluster validation process to understand the requirement:

1. Invoke **Cluster Validation** from either the **Actions** pane or the **Management** frame in the center pane.

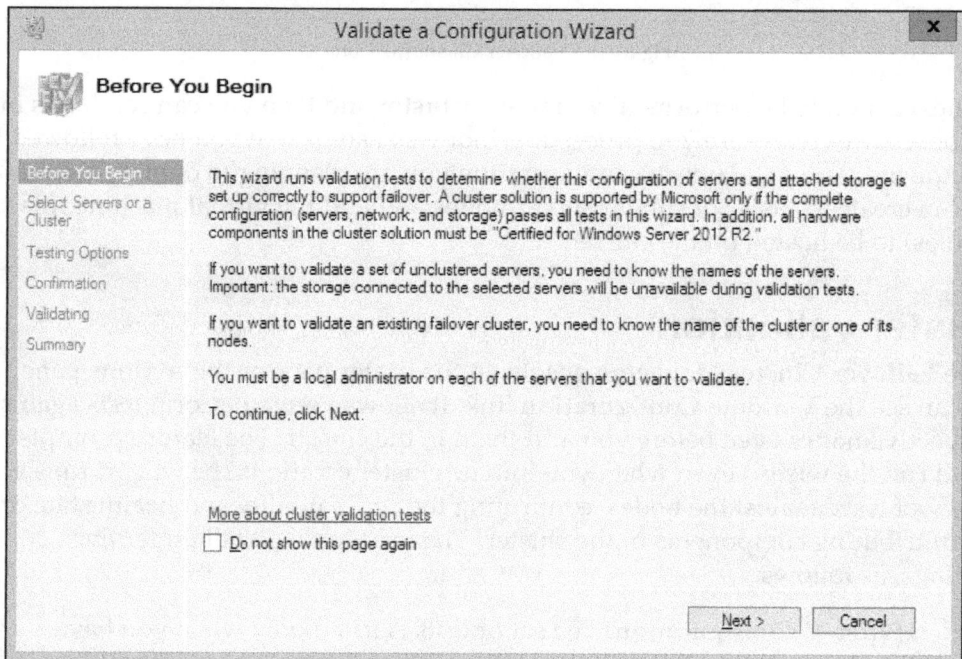

Figure 6-3: Cluster Validation Wizard

2. Add the servers or nodes you wish to validate for a cluster setup. Alternatively, if you wish to validate an existing cluster, you can enter the name (or names) here. Then click on **Next**, as shown here:

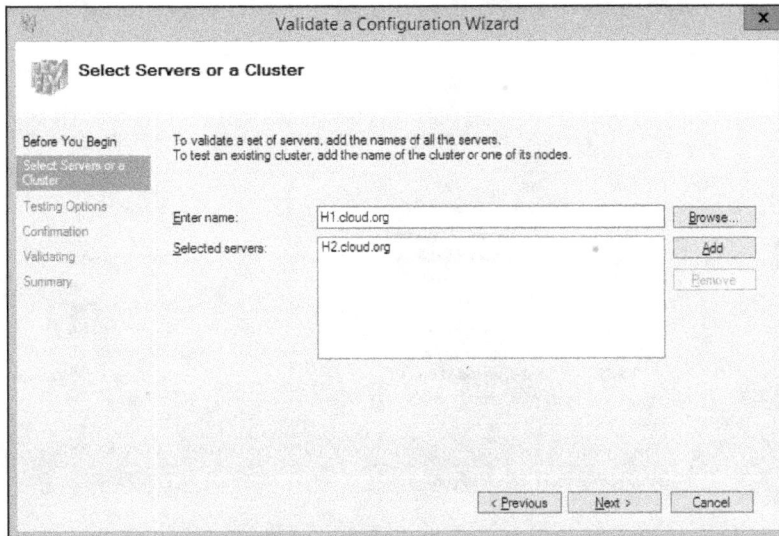

Figure 6-4: Select Servers or Cluster

3. In **Testing Options**, you may choose to run all the tests or select the relevant test from the **Test Selection** screen. After that, click on **Next**.

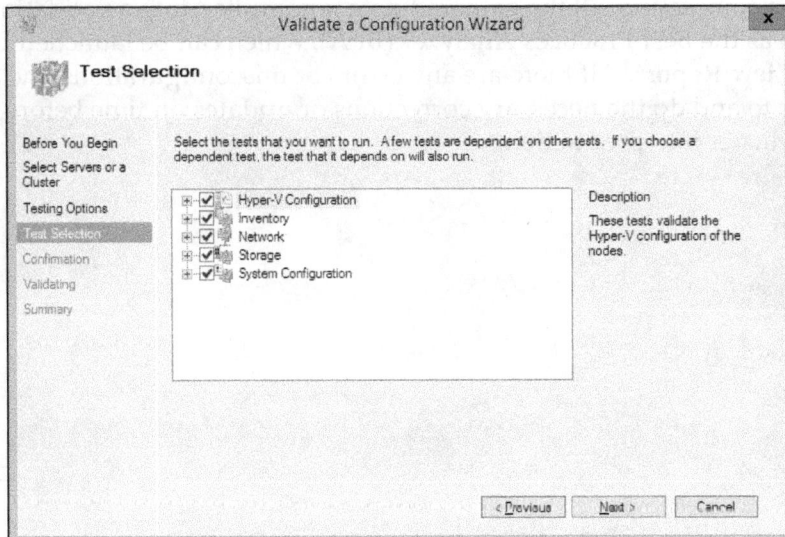

Figure 6-5: Select Tests to run against the nodes or the cluster

4. Once you have confirmed the tests, the validation process initiates and performs routine checks against the selected nodes, like this:

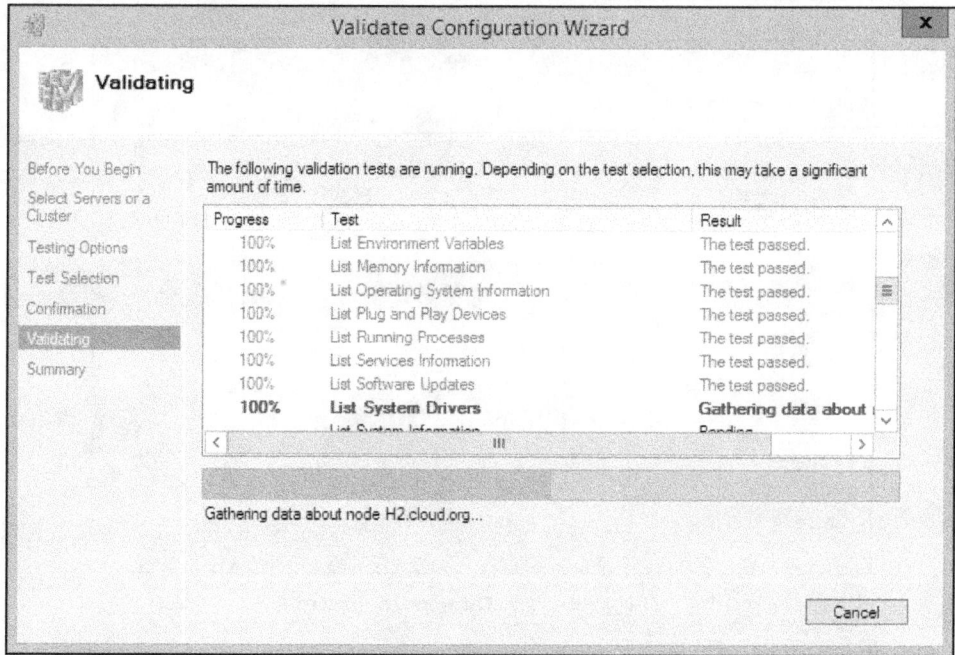

Figure 6-6: Validation in progress

5. Upon completion, all the gathered data is compiled into a validation report, such as the Best Practices Analyzer (BPA), which can be launched by clicking on **View Report....** If there are any errors or misconfigurations, the admin can refer to and do the necessary corrections or updates on time before pushing the cluster into production.

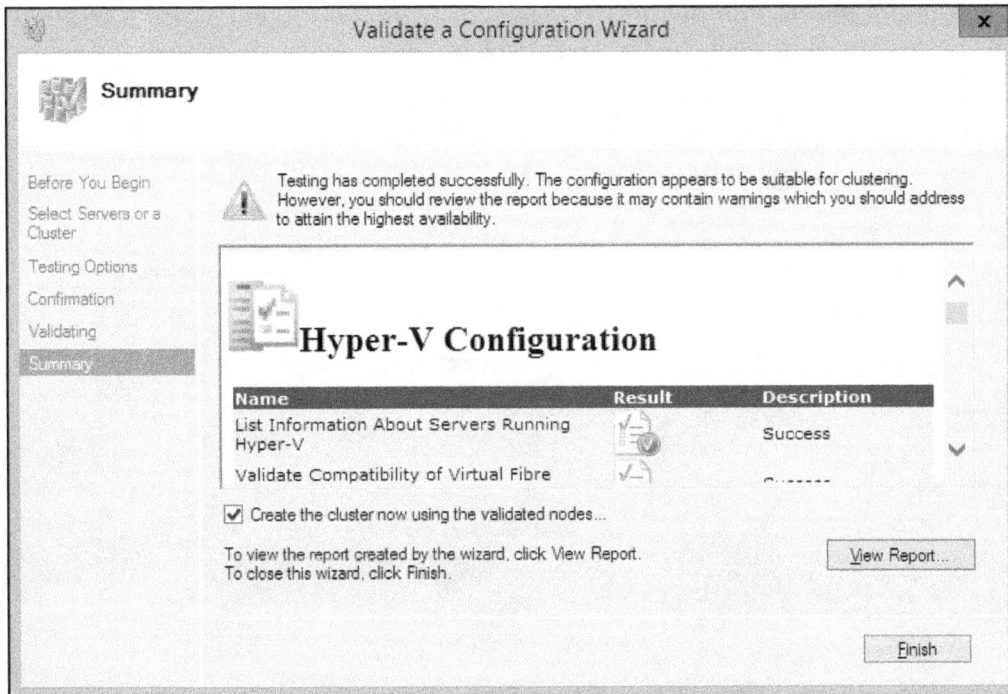

Figure 6-7: Final Report

6. Once you have clicked on **Finish**, you can choose to continue putting the tested nodes into the cluster if the tests are positive, or postpone doing so.

The PowerShell cmdlet used to achieve the same goal is as follows:

```
Test-Cluster -Node H1,H2
```

Setting up a failover cluster

You have met the prerequisites and installed the failover clustering feature on your Hyper-V nodes. Thereafter, you have validated the server configuration. The next logical step is to create the cluster involving the tested nodes. The action takes place from within the **Failover Cluster Manager** console or via PowerShell:

1. Invoke **Create Cluster Wizard** from the **Actions** pane or the **Management** frame in the center pane.

2. Ignore **Before You Begin**, and select the respective Hyper-V nodes to be added to your new cluster. Then click on **Next**, as shown here:

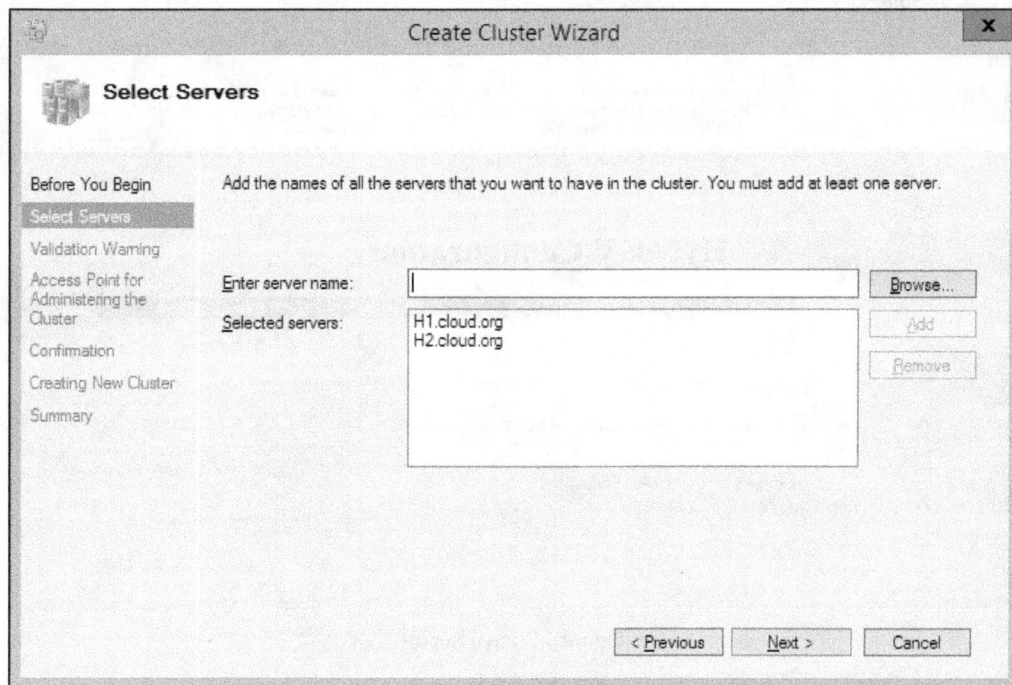

Figure 6-8: Select the Servers

3. You may encounter a **Validation Warning** window if you ran the validation tests and some warnings or errors were reported. Some warnings can be ignored, while others should be addressed accordingly. Thereafter, Windows prompts you to run the tests again or proceed further as is. Select **Yes**—ideally—and click on **Next**, as shown in this screenshot:

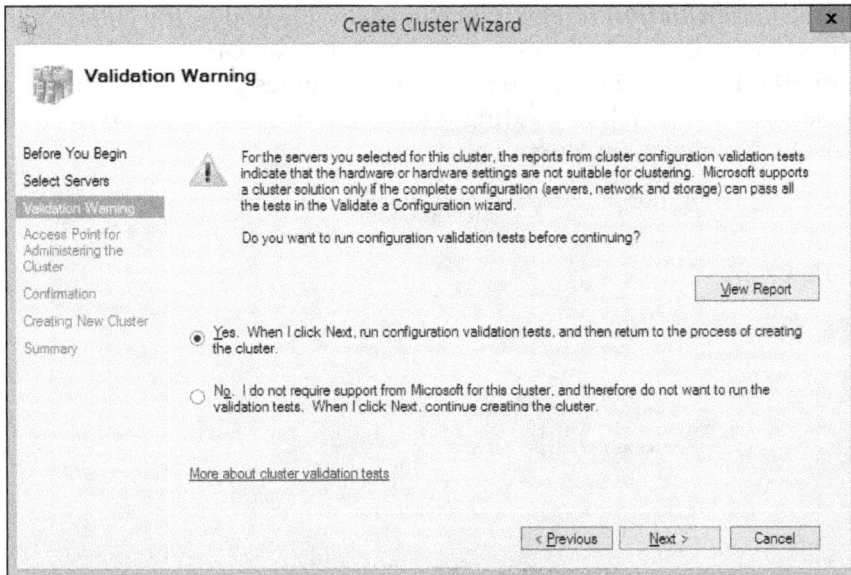

Figure 6-9: Validation Warning

4. As you can see in *figure 6-10*, here you have to update a unique IP address and a cluster name (virtual computer name object) for the cluster you are creating. If there are multiple networks, deselect the inappropriate or internal networks, and click on **Next**.

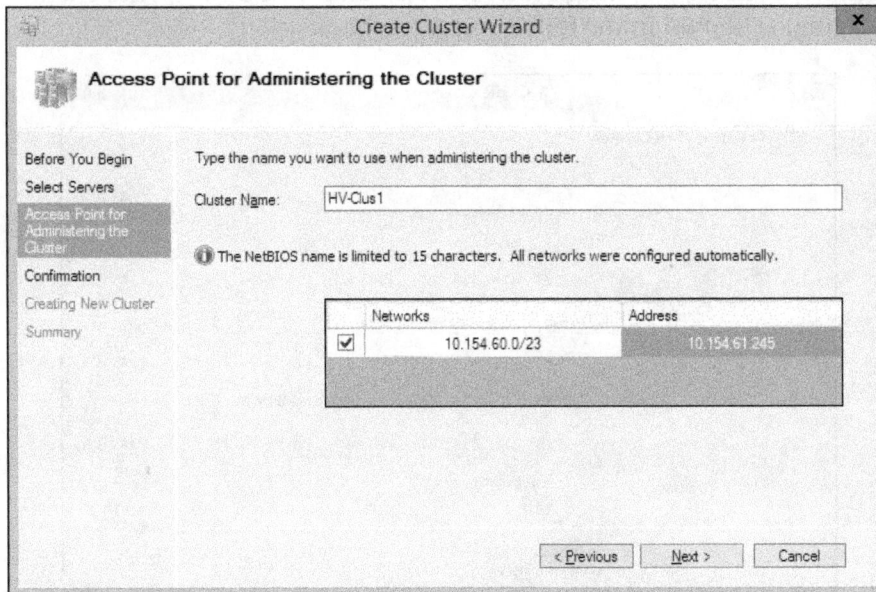

Figure 6-10: Access Point for Administering Cluster

5. On the **Confirmation** screen, you can verify the nodes, the cluster name, and the associated IP address. At the bottom, you can see a checkbox saying **Add all eligible storage to the cluster**. This gives you the flexibility to add presented storage while creating the cluster, or add it later on from the console. Now click on **Next**.

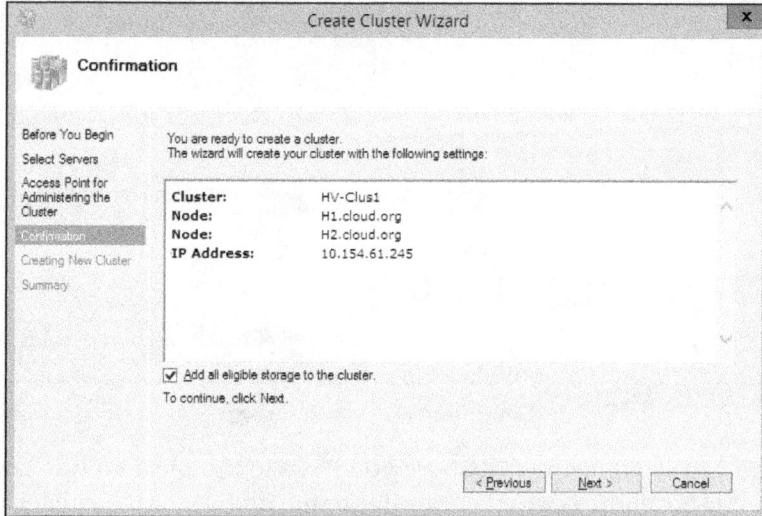

Figure 6-11: Confirmation screen

6. The next screen, **Creating New Cluster**, takes you through the cluster staging, as shown in the following screenshot:

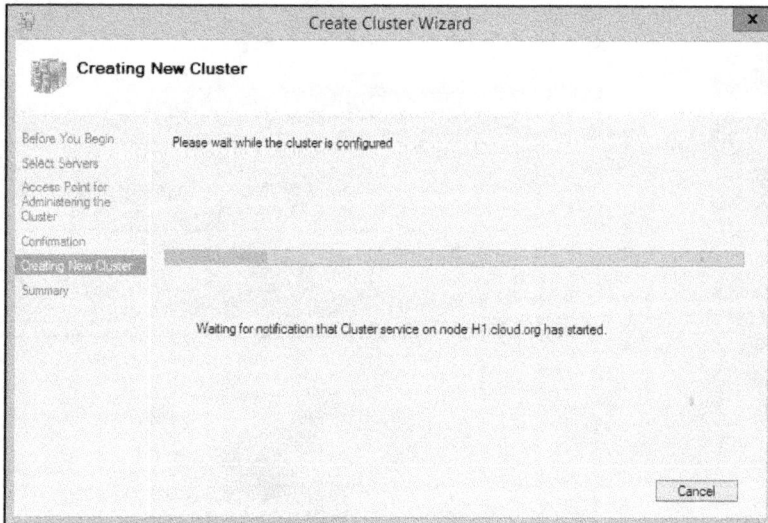

Figure 6-12: Cluster Creation in progress

7. The final screen gives you a positive update about the process of cluster creation in **Summary**. Click on **Finish**, as shown in this screenshot:

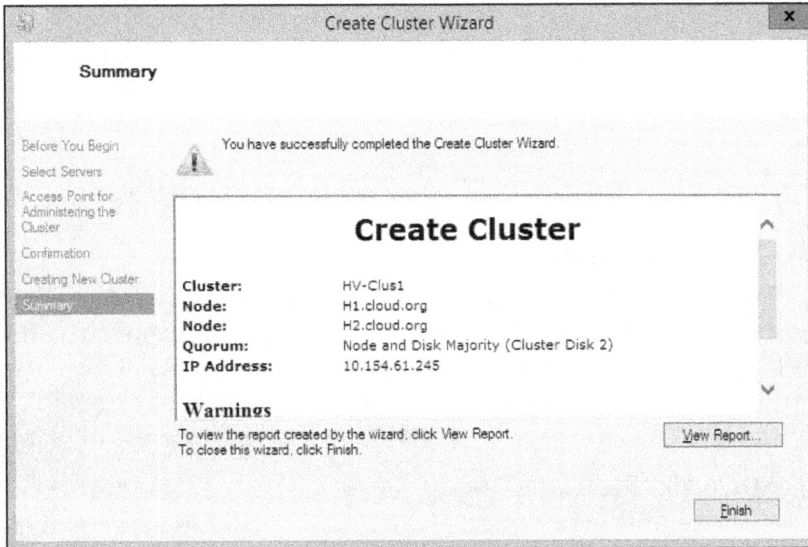

Figure 6-13: Summary

8. In *figure 6-14*, you can see what the new cluster looks like in the console:

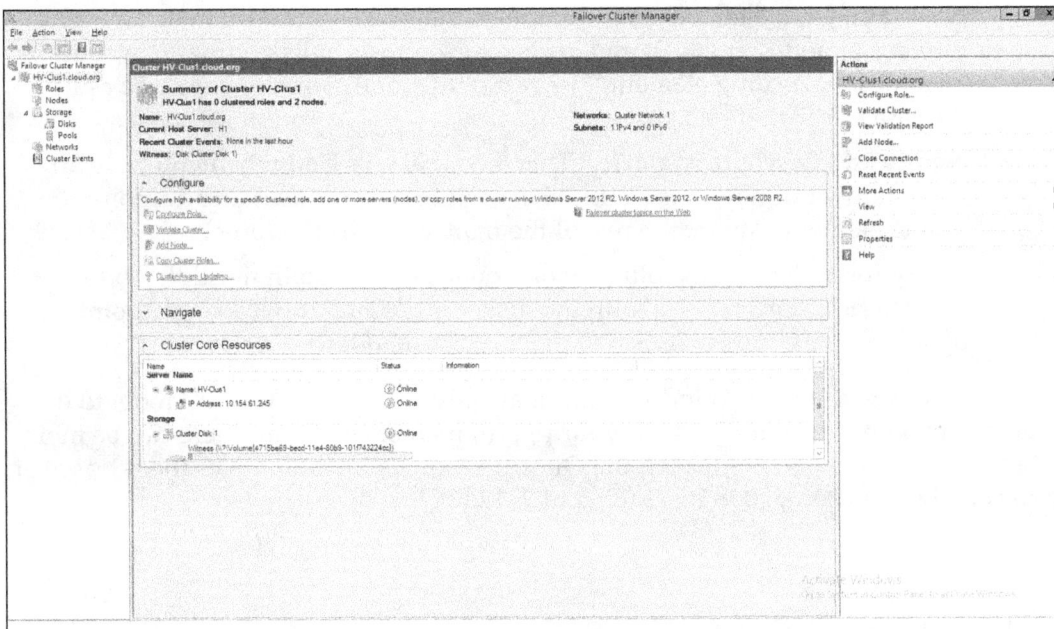

Figure 6-14: New Cluster

The preceding action can be simplified with the help of a cmdlet, as specified here:

```
New-Cluster -Name HV-Clus1 -Node H1,H2 -StaticAddress
10.154.61.245
```

If you don't wish to add the available storage to the cluster, append the switch:

```
-NoStorage
```

The bit can easily be performed later on via the console or PowerShell.

The Quorum Model

An important aspect of a cluster is **Quorum**. A cluster is a bunch of physical hosts presented as a virtual server, and in the event of a failure of one or two nodes, the cluster stays consistent. This is maintained by the Quorum state of the cluster. Each node has a vote for Quorum, and if you have a witness (disk or file share), you get one more voting element, which helps sustain the cluster in the event of a failure.

The Quorum Model has evolved quite a lot since the days of Windows Server 2003, and in the current era of Windows Server 2012 and 2012 R2, it is pretty dynamic. There are four standard Quorum Models, as follows:

- **Node Majority**: This model is suitable when you have an odd number of nodes and can sustain failure of half the nodes minus 1.

- **Node and Disk Majority**: This model is followed when you have an even number of nodes and a shared disk (referred to as a disk witness) introduces an additional voting element. The rest of the math remains the same as in the case of the node majority.

- **Node and File Share Majority**: This model is followed when you have an even number of nodes and a file share witness introduces an additional voting element. Again, the rest of the math remains the same.

- **No Majority**: This is the old-school model. It can sustain multiple node failures, as Quorum stays with the disk witness making it a single point of failure. This, however, is no longer recommended.

When you create a cluster, Windows automatically assigns a Quorum Model to it. You may choose to modify it as per your requirements. However, there can be more customization than just modifying the Quorum Models included over the releases of Windows Servers 2008, 2008 R2, 2012, and 2012 R2:

- **Node vote assignment**: This feature, included in Windows Server 2008 and 2008 R2 by a hotfix update, allowed you to add or remove the voting power of a node, giving you more control over the Quorum state. However, it could only be applied via PowerShell. Windows Server 2012 brought it into the GUI and also introduced Dynamic Quorum Configuration, wherein the vote for a node would be removed when it was removed from cluster membership and assigned again when it rejoined the cluster. The actions are performed automatically by the failover cluster after determining the states of the nodes.

- **Dynamic witness**: Introduced with Windows Server 2012 R2, this is an improvement over Dynamic Quorum Configuration. It updates the vote of the witness as per the requirement and availability of nodes.

- **Tiebreaker for split brain scenarios**: Another improvement to Dynamic Quorum Configuration allows the enabling and disabling of voting elements of the nodes and witness alike, ensuring an odd number of votes to uphold Quorum. This sounds practical in a geoclustering setup.

Adding storage and Cluster Shared Volumes

When you create a cluster and select the option of adding storage, Windows intelligently adds the cluster-suitable (read shared) storage, keeping it ready for use with the role that is meant to be clustered. If you wish to exercise more control over the deployment, you may choose otherwise and add the disks later on. However, with Hyper-V, there's a "step two" after adding the available storage; you need to add the cluster storage to Cluster Shared Volumes. Most of the action in GUI is easily applied from the failover clustering console. Let's first look at how to add the disks to available storage, and then we will discuss CSV a bit more:

1. To add available disks to a cluster, if your cluster is not listed, you have to first add the cluster to the console by selecting **Connect to Cluster** from the **Management** frame in the center pane or the **Actions** Pane.

2. Then expand **Cluster name** in the left pane, expand **Storage**, and select **Disks**.

3. In the **Actions** pane, select **Add Disk**.

4. Check the boxes of the required disks and click on **OK**.

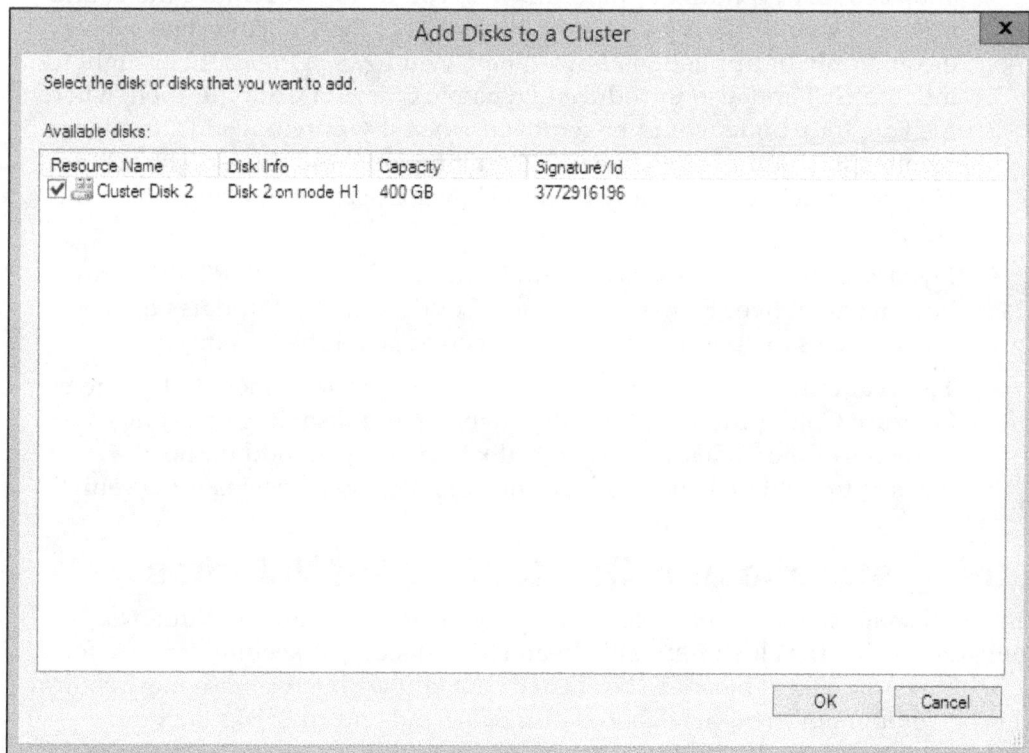

Figure 6-15: Add Disks to a Cluster

Now, the next stage is to add the disk from **Available Storage** to **Cluster Shared Volumes**. Invoke the **Add to Cluster Shared Volumes** option from the **Actions** pane after selecting the newly added disk in the pane, and you are sorted. The new disk is no longer listed under the available storage but is now mounted as a cluster shared volume.

Cluster Shared Volume

The **Cluster Shared Volume (CSV)** feature was released with Windows Server 2008 R2. Prior to CSV, there was a dependence on shared storage ownership, which was limited to retaining only one VM per LUN. You could only maintain one VM per LUN for a successful live migration or failover to another node, as ownership of a LUN could stay with one node in the cluster. This is an old limitation for NTFS because it was never a cluster filesystem. Even with its predecessor, the MSCS, every resource group was required to have its own dedicated LUN to get independent failover ability.

CSV works around this limitation and allows multiple nodes to access a shared storage without any hassle. This enables storing multiple VMs on a single LUN, and thus enables mobility of VMs across nodes in an unaffected and seamless way.

The design requires one of the nodes to play the lead role in CSV synchronization. The role is referred to as a **coordinator node**. A coordinator node is assigned per LUN in a cluster, assuming that it is assigned to all the nodes. If there are multiple LUNs, the coordinator node role can be distributed evenly among all nodes for each presented LUN. The nodes that sync with the coordinator node are called **data servers**. In other words, one node can be a coordinator for one LUN and a data server for another. The coordinator node is responsible for updating changes in metadata and blocking redirected I/O from other nodes to the NTFS stack. The CSVFS architecture ensures the all nodes get direct I/O to the underlying disk, and in the event of failure of connection to the shared disk, redirected IO would happen over the coordinator node.

To add all the storage to the CSV section, the following are the PowerShell cmdlets:

- To add a specific disk from the available storage:

```
Add-ClusterSharedVolume -Name "Cluster Disk 1"
```

- To add all the disks in the available disk storage:

```
Get-ClusterResource *disk* | Add-ClusterSharedVolume
```

CSV attributes

CSV 2.0 has more to offer than its predecessor, and still more with R2 of Windows Server 2012. The attributes have some underlying prerequisites that ought to be met before implementation, and offer a few additional improvements in Windows Server 2012 R2. They are as follows:

- CSV requires the client for Microsoft networks and the file and printer sharing services to be enabled on the NIC configured for cluster communication.

- CSV requires that the system drive letter across all nodes should be the same, as it hosts the admin share for Clusterstorage$.

- CSV maintains the same namespace for the mapping folder and mount points across the nodes. The default location for the ClusterStorage mapping folder (it also has an AdminShare linked to it) is C:, and as the volumes are added to the folder, they get named Volume1, Volume2, and so on. The path to one volume will be like C:\ClusterStorage\Volume1, and it will be consistent across all nodes. If you rename Volume1 to something else, HRD for example, the change will be replicated across all the nodes to reflect the change in path as C:\ClusterStorage\HRD.

- CSV requires NTLM to be enabled on all nodes.

- CSV can be enabled on both NTFS and ReFS volumes in Windows Server 2012 R2.

- CSV on Windows Server 2008 R2 were based on reparse points, but from Windows Server 2012 they are mount points to volumes.

- Support for data deduplication, storage spaces using parity, and tiering.

- Support for SQL 2014.

- Support for BitLocker encryption.

BitLocker

The BitLocker drive encryption feature was brought forth with the release of Windows Vista and 2008. It adds the ability of effective data protection to Windows by encrypting and protecting disk drives. In the event of a theft or loss, it ensures that the data on the drives stays inaccessible, and removes the vulnerability clause from decommissioned machines and servers as well. In the subsequent releases of Windows platforms, Microsoft enhanced this security feature even further. Windows Server 2012 was equipped to use this feature on cluster storage and CSV, ensuring protection of shared storage as well.

Let's discuss a few aspects of BitLocker from the failover clustering perspective. BitLocker can be enabled on volumes either prior to adding to cluster or later. You may keep other unshared volumes on a cluster encrypted as well. To enable BitLocker on a Windows Server 2012 or 2012 R2 Hyper-V cluster, you will need to complete these prerequisites:

- A Windows Server 2012 or R2 Domain Controller accessible by all the nodes in the cluster.

- The Group Policy enabled—choose how BitLocker-protected fixed drivers can be recovered.

- Ensure that the drives are formatted with NTFS or ReFS (Windows Server 2012 R2 only). If the drive is already added to the cluster, it has to be placed into maintenance mode before enabling encryption on it.

- Finally, the BitLocker drive encryption feature should be installed on all the nodes.

The feature can be installed like any other Windows roles or features via the Server Manager, or with the help of PowerShell:

```
Install-WindowsFeature BitLocker -IncludeAllSubFeature -
IncludeManagementTools -Restart
```

When you enable BitLocker on a volume, you may decide on a password protector for it, and also a recovery password protector. The latter can be used to recover the drive from encryption in the event of malicious activity or if the CNO of the linked cluster is accidentally deleted.

To enable the BitLocker against a volume or a CSV with a password protector, run the following cmdlet. Then you will be prompted to provide the password:

```
Enable-BitLocker <drive letter or CSV mount point> -PasswordProtector
```

Likewise, you may use the cmdlet for the recovery password protector. However, the recovery string is randomly generated and it is best practice to back up the key in the Active Directory:

```
Enable-BitLocker <drive letter or CSV mount point> -
RecoveryPasswordProtector


$protectorId = (Get-BitLockerVolume <drive or CSV mount
point>).Keyprotector | Where-Object {$_.KeyProtectorType -eq
"RecoveryPassword"}

Backup-BitLockerKeyProtector <drive or CSV mount point> -
KeyProtectorId $protectorId.KeyProtectorId
```

It is advisable to add an AD security identifier of the cluster name object to a CSV disk. This allows manageability of BitLocker-enabled volumes by the cluster service:

```
Add-BitLockerKeyProtector <drive letter or CSV mount point> -
ADAccountOrGroupProtector -ADAccountOrGroup CNO$
```

To disable BitLocker, use this cmdlet construct:

```
Disable-BitLocker <drive letter or CSV mount point>
```

Cluster Aware Updating

Automation is the key to peace of mind. Windows Server 2012 did just that with the **Cluster Aware Updating (CAU)** feature, by automating patch management and automatic resource failover. Prior to Windows Server 2012, patch management on cluster nodes was a manual and a laborious task, and required quite a lot of planning, and even maintaining a night watch over the entire process. The process of patching the nodes became tedious when ensuring failover and failback of the resources while keeping resource utilization under tab. Also, there was always a window for human error and, thereafter, service outages.

CAU was released with Windows Server 2012. It is an add-on feature with failover clustering. It ensures automated and controlled deployment of patches and updates on the nodes. The objective of releasing CAU was to reduce outages subject to human error in manual management, and it is tailor-made to achieve that goal. The clause here is that CAU works with Windows Server 2012 and onwards, and is compatible with clustered roles hosted on Windows Server 2012 failover clusters.

The server or machine hosting the CAU role is called the update coordinator. Role hosting also adds a level of differentiation for the coordinator role, as follows:

- **Self-Updating Mode**: The coordinator role is maintained on one of the cluster nodes. There are quite a few merits to this one. One is that the CAU role itself becomes fault-tolerant and highly available. Also, you can schedule an update task in this mode.

- **Remote-Updating Mode**: Remote mode can be enabled on a Windows Server 2012 or R2 server sitting outside the cluster, or can even be set up by installing RSAT failover clustering on a Windows 8 client machine.

There are certain prerequisites to this role that you will need to consider before you set out to deploy it:

- The cluster nodes should be accessible to the coordinator node.

- Ensure that **WMI Remote Management (WinRM)** is enabled on all the nodes. The same can be enabled from the Server Manager or via PowerShell:

```
Set-WsManQuickConfig
```

- Ensure that PowerShell and PowerShell remoting are also enabled. The same can be enabled via PowerShell:

```
Enable-PSRemoting
```

- Ensure that .NET Framework 4.5 is installed. If not, install it from the Server Manager or via PowerShell.

- Another important configuration is to allow remote auto-restarts. This can be enabled via Windows Firewall inbound rules or via a PowerShell cmdlet:

```
Set-NetFirewallRule -Group "@firewallapi.dll,-36751" -Profile
Domain -Enabled true
```

- It is advised not to enable automatic updates on cluster nodes, but if there is a WSUS infrastructure, CAU can be configured accordingly. Otherwise, you can use CAU to apply updates using its default `Microsoft.WindowsUpdatePlugin` plugin on the cluster nodes.

- Prestage a computer account for CAU before you set it up if you wish to control the naming convention. Otherwise, CAU will create an account for itself with a random name.

Installing Cluster Aware Updating

Once you know the nitty-gritty of a feature, it becomes easier to install and configure. In this section, we will focus on the Self-Updating Mode only. Let's look at the steps required to enable this intelligent feature:

1. Invoke the Cluster Aware Updating (CAU) feature applet from the failover clustering console, from either the node or the remote client machine. It is listed in the **Configure** frame.

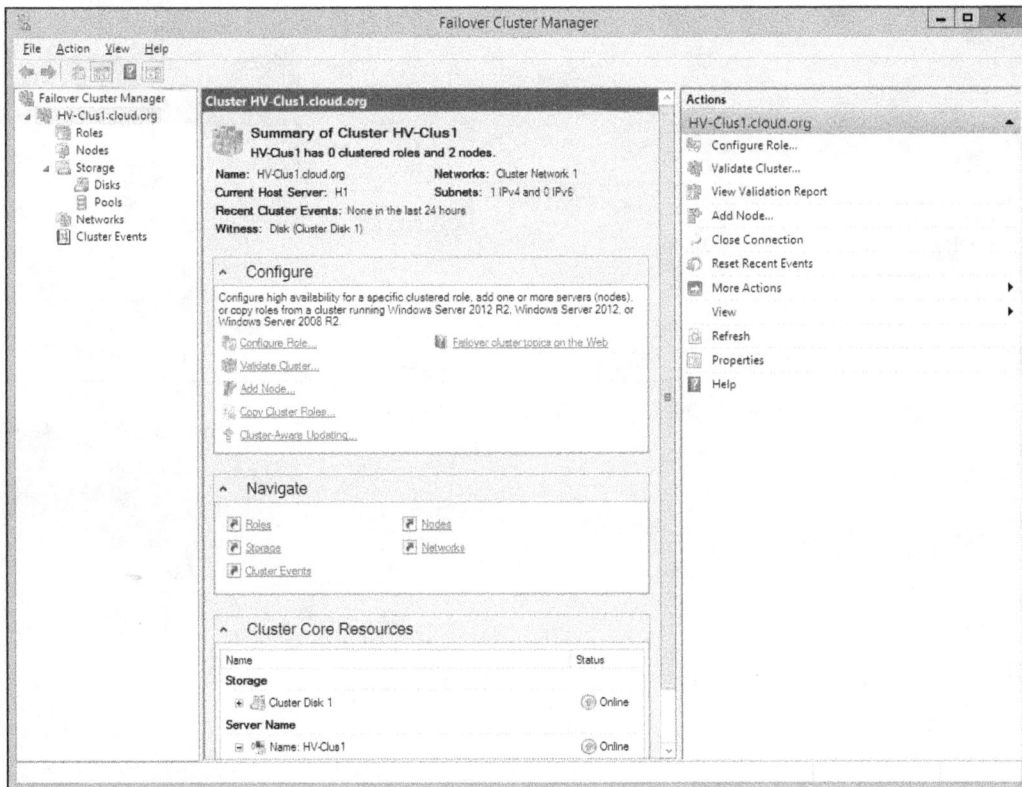

Figure 6-16: Configure – Cluster Aware Updating

2. The applet selects the cluster by default if launched from the supposed self-updating wizard. Otherwise, you can connect to the desired cluster by clicking on **Connect**.

    Here's the separation point; for the Self-Updating Mode, you have to select **Configure cluster self-updating options**, and for the Remote-Updating Mode, you simply have to select **Apply updates to this cluster** and let it follow its default course.

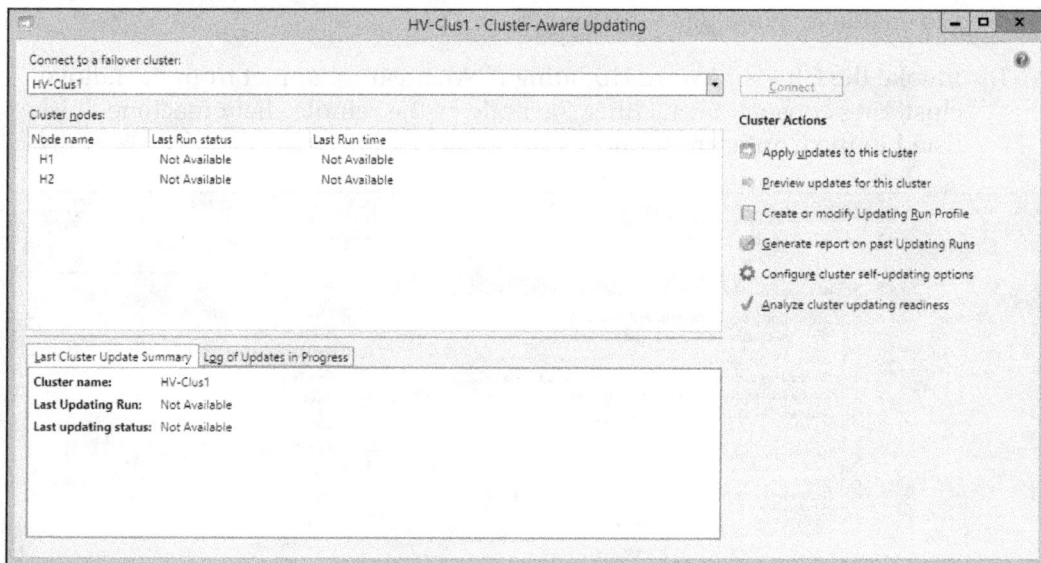

Figure 6-17: Cluster-Aware Updating Selecting Updating modes

3. Invoke the self-updating wizard and click on **Next**.

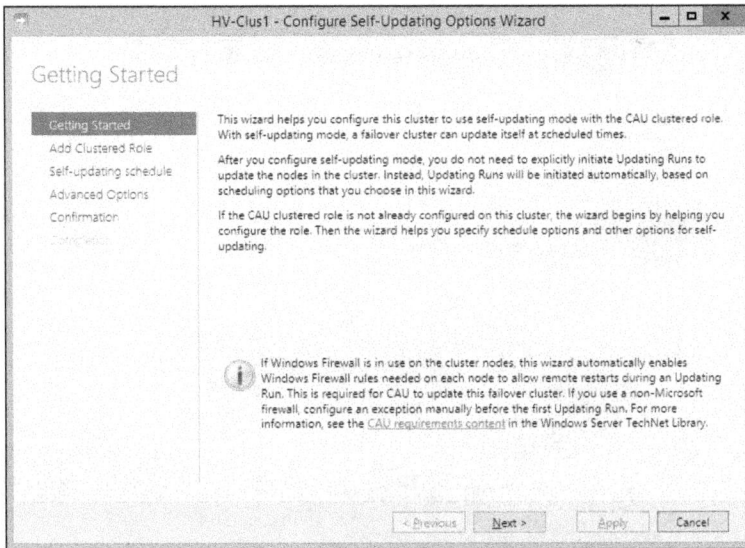

Figure 6-18: Configure Self-Updating Options Wizard

4. In the screen for **Add Clustered Role**, check the box for **Add the CAU clustered role, with self-updating mode enabled, to this cluster**. If you have the CAU Computer object prestaged in the Active Directory, you may check the second box. Otherwise, leave it unchecked, and the wizard will do the object creation bit. After that, click on **Next**.

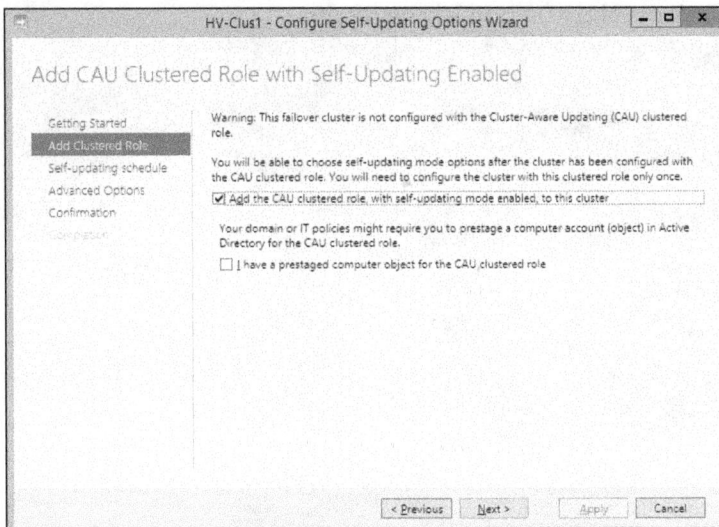

Figure 6-19: Add Clustered Role

5. In the following screen, you may fix an update schedule for the cluster nodes. Then click on **Next**.

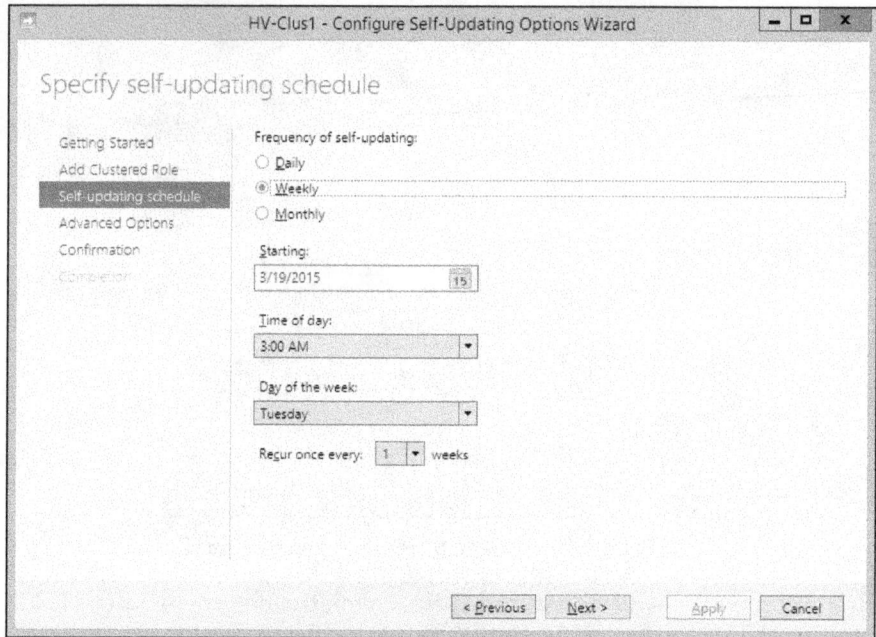

Figure 6-20: Self-updating schedule

6. The screens for **Advanced Options** and **Additional Options** can be left as they are with the default options, unless you wish to further customize the plan. Click on **Next** on both the screens.

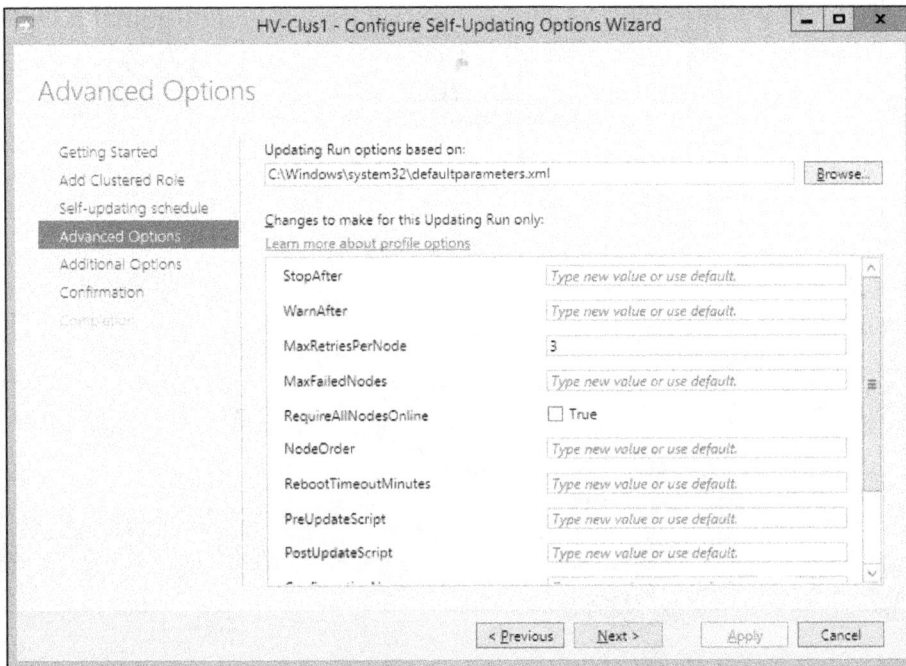

Figure 6-21: Advanced Options

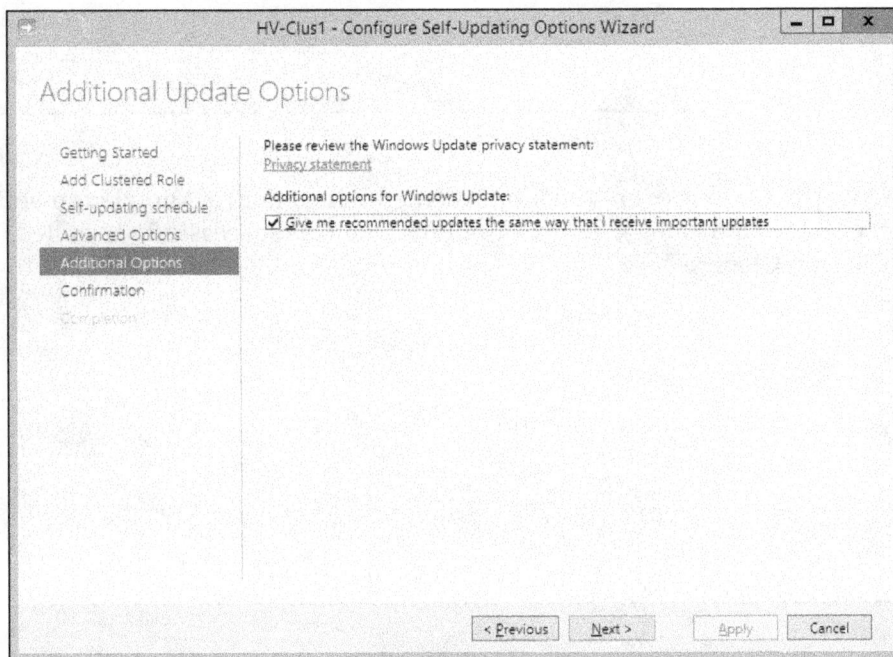

Figure 6-22: Additional Options

7. The last leg is the **Confirmation** screen, which lets you do a final review of your preferences. Then click on **Next**, as shown here:

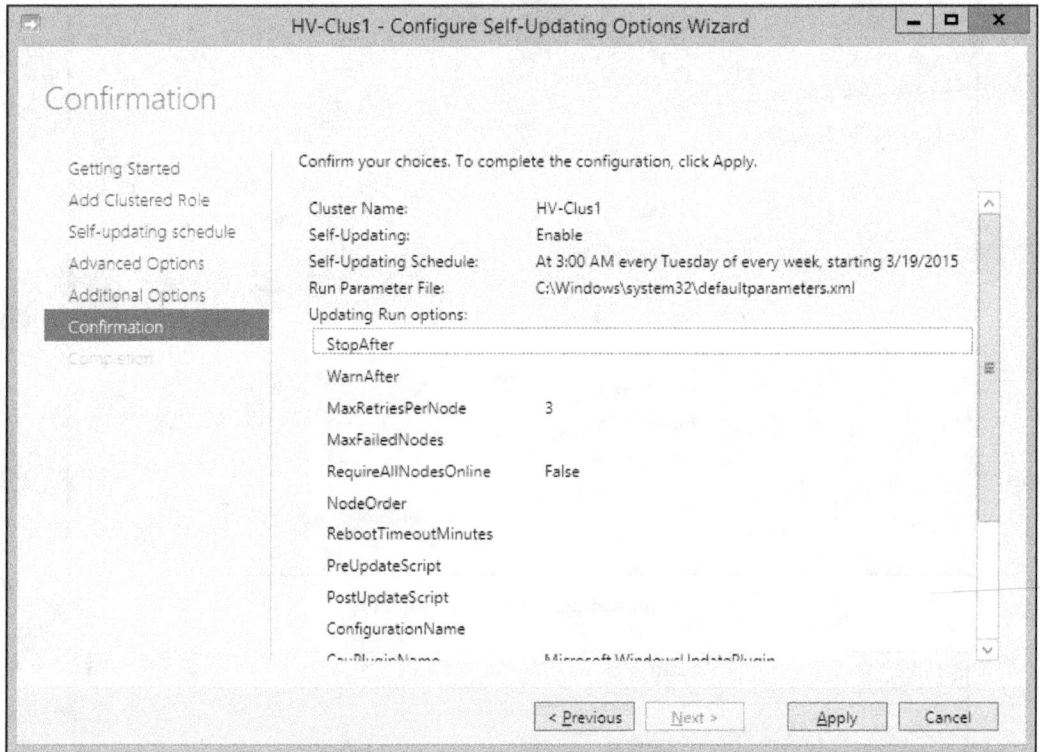

Figure 6-23: Confirmation

8. Once the setup is over, you are presented with a final acknowledgment screen that indicates whether or not the role was successfully installed. Click on **Close**.

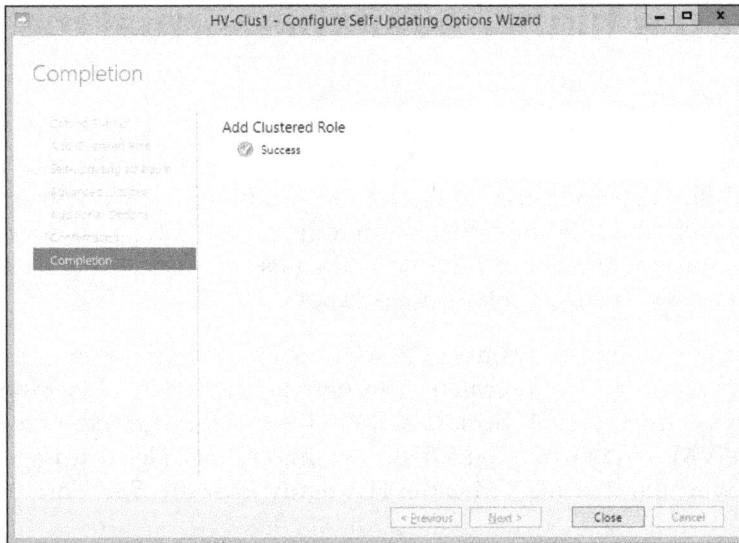

Figure 6-24: Completion

This completes the configuration of CAU for you. A final tip would be PowerShell:

```
Add-CauClusterRole -CauPluginArguments @{ 'IncludeRecommendedUpdates'
 = 'True' } -CauPluginName Microsoft-WindosUpdatePlugin -ClusterName
HV-Clus1 -DaysOfWeek 4 -EnableFirewallRules -Force -MaxRetriesPerNode
3 -StartDate 3-22-2015 -WeeksOfMonth 3
```

A virtual machine's high availability and mobility

The purpose of Microsoft failover clustering is to provide high availability and fault tolerance to the R2 Hyper-V cluster. Alternatively, we can create a VM on the cluster itself, and thereby create a highly available VM. This takes care of the availability of the VM, but failing over would require restarting of the VM on the passive node, which may just—only just— sound feasible in the event of the primary node going down with an acceptable turnaround time. However, in situations involving maintenance of the cluster infrastructure, you cannot afford to take down VMs to load them onto a different node. You migrate them live and running to another running node (well, until Windows Server 2012) with a negligible—almost unnoticeable—downtime. This is called **VM mobility**. Windows Server 2012 R2 adds more spice to better an almost perfect recipe, with shared nothing live migration, which does not require the VM to be clustered for mobility. We will look at the options gradually as we build an understanding of this concept.

Setting up a highly available virtual machine (HAVM)

Windows Server 2012 and R2 Hyper-V are focused on increasing the VM density on the Hyper-V hosts and clusters and, at the same time, retaining the robustness of the Hypervisor solution. At any time, an HAVM would be running on one of the cluster nodes, pretty much like running a VM on an independent Hyper-V host. However, it has the capability to fail over or migrate to the passive node or the backup node when the need arises, ensuring a fail-safe solution.

Setting up a VM on a cluster is almost the same as bringing it up on a single Hyper-V host if you are building it from scratch. Alternatively, you may also import a VM running locally on the Hyper-V host directly to the cluster. But there's a gotcha when you import the VM—the virtual hard disk will linger on the local storage and hence you will get a warning that the VM is not HA ready later on. There are two ways to fix this:

- The first action is pre-emptive. You can have the VM set up on CSV prior to Cluster import.

- Alternatively, you can use **Storage Migration** later, and move the VM and its files to CSV after the cluster import.

Let's preview the steps for importing an already hosted guest machine and running locally on a Hyper-V node (the same as for an independent Hyper-V host):

1. Invoke **Failover Cluster Manager**. In the navigation pane, expand the cluster and select roles.

2. In the **Actions** pane, select **Configure role**. This leads to the **High Availability Wizard**. On the **Before you Begin** screen, click on **Next**.

3. Select **s** and click on Next.

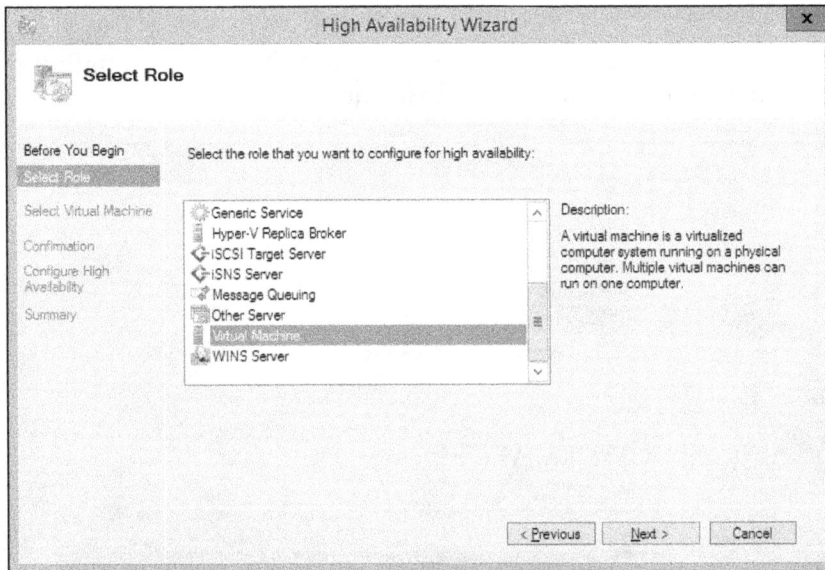

Figure 6-25: High Availability Wizard – Select Role

4. On the next screen, you will get a list of locally hosted VMs on either of the cluster nodes. Select the one you need to make the HA and click on **Next**, as shown here:

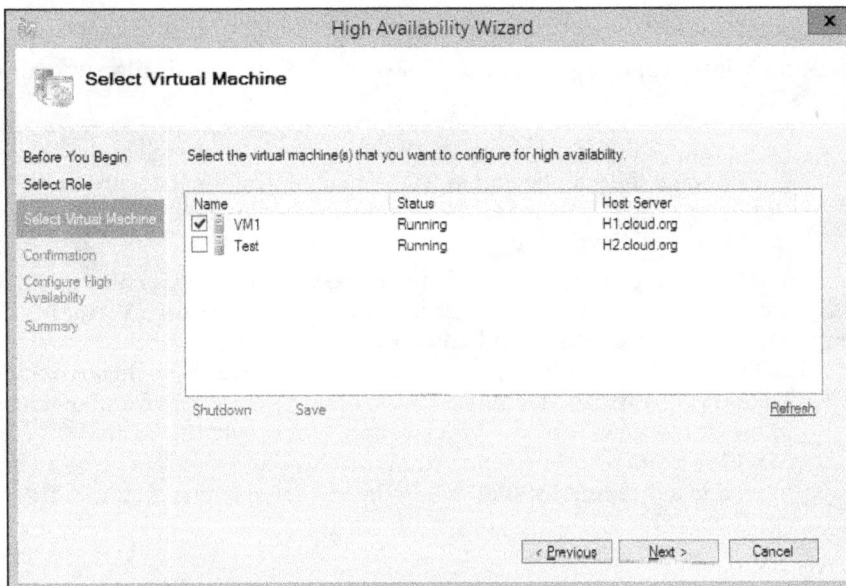

Figure 6-26: High Availability Wizard – Select Virtual Machine

5. Click on **Next** on the **Confirmation** screen as well.

6. On the **Summary** screen, you will see that the VM is now a highly available virtual machine (HAVM), but with a warning.

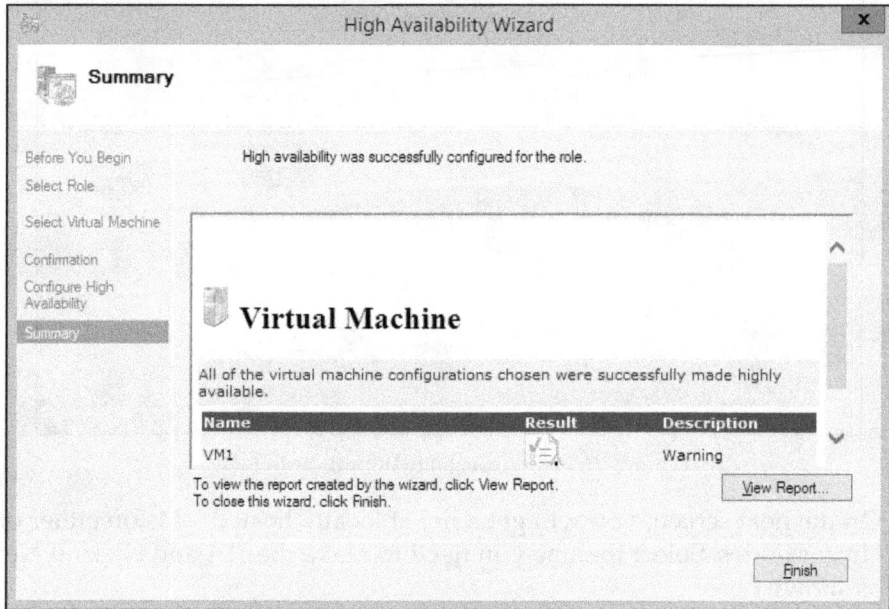

Figure 6-27: High Availability Wizard – Summary

7. Click on **View Report**, and you will see the following, similar warning:

Disk path `C:\Folder Name\VM1` is not a path to storage in the cluster or to storage that can be added to the cluster. You must ensure this storage is available to every node in the cluster to make this virtual machine highly available.

You can change the location of the virtual machine and its files to a valid cluster-managed storage location, or use the **Move Virtual Machine Storage** dialog in **Failover Cluster Manager** (or the `Move-VMStorage` Windows PowerShell cmdlet) to move the virtual machine. To open the **Virtual Machine Storage** dialog, select the virtual machine in the **Roles** view, then the **Move** action, and finally the **Virtual Machine Storage** option. The virtual machine and its files can be moved to a different location while the virtual machine is running.

8. The next action is to move the VM to Cluster Shared Volume (CSV). In the navigation pane, select **Roles**. Then select the new HAVM. From the **Actions** pane, select **Move** and then **Virtual Machine Storage**, as shown in this screenshot:

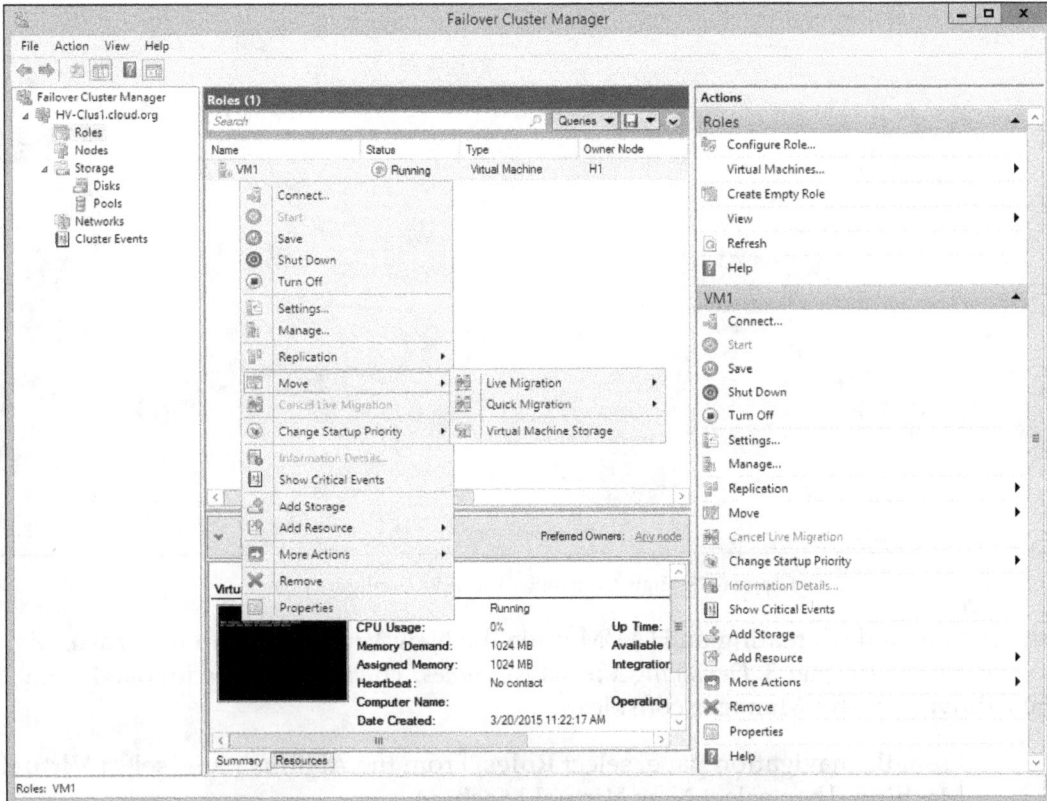

Figure 6-28: Move VM to CSV

9. In **Storage Migration**, select **s** and drag and drop it into the desired location or folder on CSV.

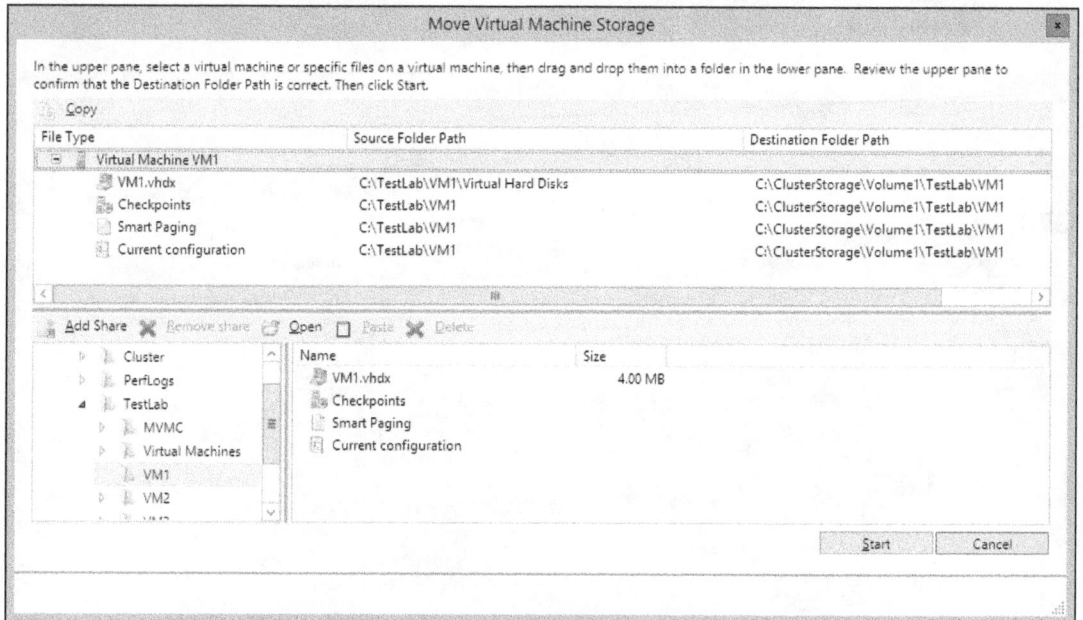

Figure 6-29: High Availability Wizard – Configure Role

Another method of creating an HAVM is via the **New Virtual Machine Wizard**, as you learned in *Chapter 3*, *Deploying Virtual Machines*. The same can be invoked from the **Failover Cluster Manager** console:

1. From the navigation pane, select **Roles**. From the **Actions** pane, select **Virtual Machine**. Then select **New Virtual Machine**.

2. It invokes an applet, prompting you to select the target cluster node (*figure 6-30*).

3. Select the node and click on **OK**. Voilà! You see the same old **New Virtual Machine Wizard**. Follow it religiously!

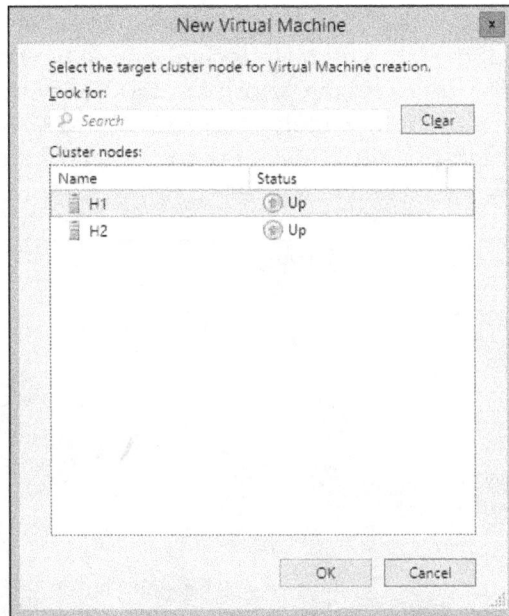

Figure 6-30: Select the target Cluster Node for a new VM

Virtual machine failover and management options

We now have an HAVM ready. However, it is imperative to understand its new nitty-gritty within a failover cluster. There are new property settings, which help you plan the failover and priority of the running VM in comparison to other VMs hosted in the cluster. To better understand this, let's review the property sheets. In the navigation pane, select **Roles** and then select the HAVM. From the **Actions** pane, select **Properties**. You get to see two property sheets in this applet: **General** and **Failover**.

On the **General** page, you can see a list of preferred owners, which sets a criteria or preferred sequence for a VM to be started in the event of a node failure hosting the VM. In a situation where the preferred owners are not set, the VM would be started on the possible owner, where the VM could be placed anywhere. If the preferred owners list is configured, the VM will be launched on the next host in the sequence given in the list. Also, you get to set the priority of the VM with respect to other VMs in the event of a failover situation, namely **High**, **Medium**, **Low**, and **No Auto Start**. As per this setting, the high-priority VMs get placed or started by the cluster before the medium- or low-priority virtual machines.

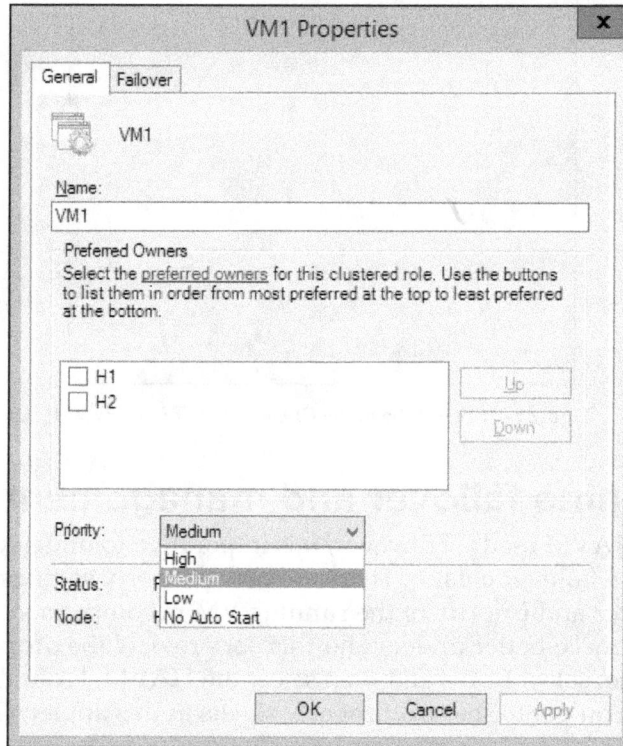

Figure 6-31: Failover Policies

On the **Failover** page, you have to specify the failover policies for the VM, describing the number of attempts to restart the VM over a stipulated time. You also have to keep a tab on the failback if the most preferred node or the original node hosting the VM returns to a healthy state.

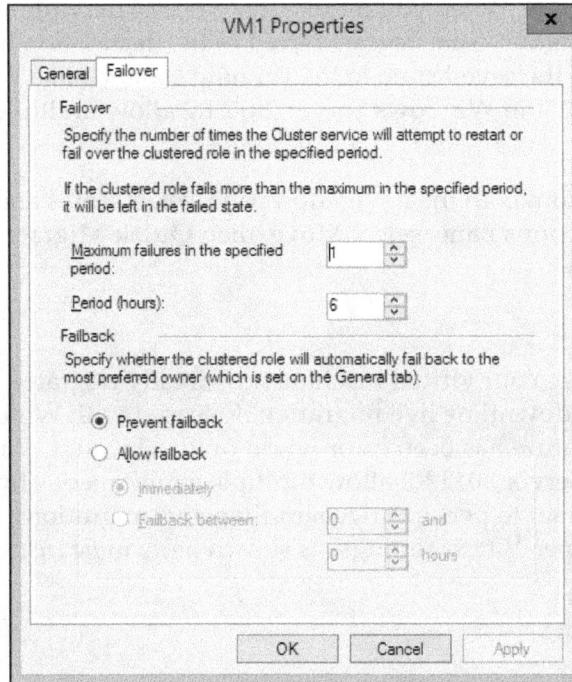

Figure 6-32: Failover Policies

VM mobility scenarios

Hyper-V has come a long way, starting from quick migration, then live migration, followed by storage migration, and now shared nothing live migration. The terms used are not intended to baffle you. However, it is in your best interest to realize the progress of the product. All of these VM mobility options are here to ensure high availability and better manageability of virtual machines. Let's check out the migration options.

Quick migration

The quick migration option was released with the first offering of Hyper-V, and it is still present with the latest offering, which is Windows Server 2012 R2. Enabled on a Hyper-V cluster, this feature allows you to move the running VMs to another host, with minimal downtime. When you invoke the process, the running VM goes into a saved state and its memory state is transferred to the destination host. Thereafter, the VM is returned from the saved state to the running state. Unlike their predecessors, Windows Server 2012 and Windows Server 2012 R2 allow multiple simultaneous quick migrations.

Quick migration is simple. In the navigation pane, select **Roles** and then select the HAVM. From the **Actions** pane, select **Move**, then **Quick Migrate**, and finally the **Node** to migrate to.

Live migration

You don't lose a blink. Your virtual machine has already migrated to the other node, and you didn't see a downtime live migration. Released with Windows Server 2008 R2, this migration feature has been improvised quite a bit, and Windows Server 2012 and Windows Server 2012 R2 allow multiple simultaneous live migrations. By default, the hosts are set to perform two simultaneous migrations, but the setting can be updated from Hyper-V host settings, as shown here, in *figure 6-33*:

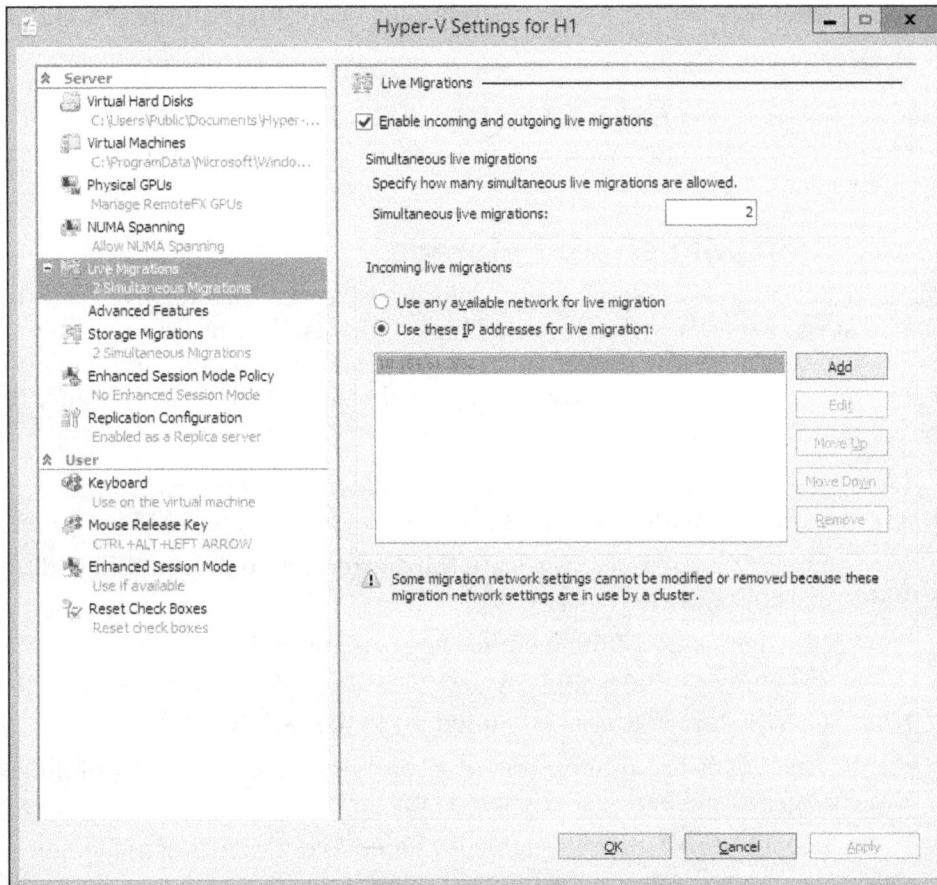

Figure 6-33: Hyper-V Host Settings: Live Migration

Live migration has three variants in Windows Server 2012 and 2012 R2 Hyper-V, namely **live migration with shared storage**, **live migration without shared storage (shared nothing live migration)**, and **live migration with SMB shared storage** (released with Windows Server 2012). In all of these three options, a running VM is migrated from one host to the other without any downtime. They are mostly alike on the surface, with just a few underlying differences. But before we dig deeper into these concepts, let's cover the basic requirements for live migration (which is standard for all forms):

- Two or more servers installed with Windows Server 2012 or Windows Server 2012 R2 and Hyper-V role enabled, supporting hardware virtualization and using processors from the same vendor (either all Intel or all AMD)
- The servers should be listed in the same Active Directory

- Guest machines should have virtual hard disks or virtual fibre channel disks
- A private network for performing live migration of virtual workloads

These requirements stay consistent. Now let's move our focus to the various forms of live migration offered with Windows Server 2012 Hyper-V and Windows Server 2012 R2 Hyper-V.

Live migration with shared storage

The standard live migration offering since Windows Server 2008 R2, live migration with shared storage works with clustered Hyper-V hosts. This feature requires Hyper-V hosts enabled with failover clustering and shared storage running CSV. Under the hood, the live migration of a VM goes through multiple stages until it gets loaded on the destination host:

1. Live migration is initiated, where a session is set up between two hosts, the VM structure is created on the destination, and adequate RAM is allotted.
2. In the next stage, memory pages are transferred to the destination and a VM state replica is gradually set up.
3. Next is the delta sync of the memory pages and building of the final state of the VM on the destination host.
4. Now, the VM storage access is handed off to the recipient host.
5. Finally, the VM is brought up on the second host, and the owner of the VM changes in the **Failover Cluster Manager**.
6. At the network level, the ARP table is altered and a request for change of MAC address is sent to the network switch.

Live migration without shared storage (shared nothing live migration)

Shared nothing live migration was released with Windows Server 2012, and has caught everyone's attention. It does not have a dependency on failover clustering or shared storage, but in turn gives flexibility in the placement of virtual machines. The drawback is that the setup is not highly available, unlike in the previous one. The VM state and its files are migrated completely to a different host, but within the same domain.

It is easier and more convenient in more than one way. You may migrate a VM between two failover clusters or one from an independent host to a failover cluster. You can also segregate VM components during migration, wherein you may move the VM and VM storage to separate locations.

The process of handoff to another host or cluster includes the following steps:

1. The contents of the source VHD are replicated to the destination VHD, while the VM disk writes still continue at the source disk.

2. Next, disk operations are mirrored on both sections, and if there are any pending changes between two disks, they are completed in the background.

3. Once the disks are in sync, the VM live migration process begins as discussed earlier.

4. Once the migration is over, the files and content of the VM are purged on the source server.

Live migration with SMB shared storage

Alright! So you don't wish to invest in expensive storage equipment for clustering and yet still want to own live migration abilities. Windows Server 2012 provides you with this and keeps it plain and simple. You can now put your VM and its components onto an SMB 3.0 share, instead of a regular server or shared storage, and live migrate its state from one Hyper-V host to another seamlessly. It can't get simpler than this. However, there's a gotcha; you have to ensure that the SMB share has all the Hyper-V hosts added in the ACL.

Storage migration

Storage migration is a bit different from what we have discussed so far. In the previous two cases, we were concerned about migrating the VM state or VM state with VM storage from one host to the other. Storage Migration, introduced with Windows Server 2012 Hyper-V, allows you to move or migrate the storage of a running VM without affecting its state or causing downtime. We saw a demonstration of this at the beginning of this chapter, when you were learning how to set up an HAVM. The feature can have multiple use cases. To name a few, add more storage to a cluster or an independent host and then move the VM back and forth, or move along the storage hierarchy from the expensive shared storage to the inexpensive SMB 3.0 share storage.

Scale-Out File Server (SOFS)

IT is driven by costs, and every now and then, we look at options to keep the CAPEX and OPEX under check. Storage is one of the primary investment areas that have to be planned as per changing requirements. The currently available options in DAS and SAN (iSCSI or FC) come with their own set of merits and demerits. However, if you look towards increasing the merit list, you end up increasing your costs. With Windows Server 2012, Microsoft introduced an excellent storage option with the Scale-Out File Server (SOFS) and SMB 3.0 protocol.

SOFS, in essence, is a file server cluster, but in comparison with the traditional clustered file server cluster, it is quite different. SOFS is an active-active cluster, and file shares hosted by SOFS are active and accessible on all nodes, unlike the standard file server cluster, which follows the active-passive concept. Also, file server clusters have a wider usage. However, SOFS is so far confined to but recommended for Hyper-V over SMB or SQL over SMB. Still, SOFS has other merits, which include better bandwidth utilization, as bandwidth utilization is the sum total of bandwidths of all nodes and all nodes are holding an active instance of the share. It uses the CSV platform, and so forwards all the benefits of CSV. It is also easier to manage and features self-tracking and automatic balancing of SMB connections to the SOFS file share to all cluster nodes.

Let's look at a demo for setting up an SOFS role, after which we will create an SMB share-applications:

1. Launch **Failover Cluster Manager** and select **Roles** in the navigation pane.

2. From the **Actions** pane, select **Configure Role...**.

3. On the **Before You Begin** screen, click on **Next**.

4. Under **Select Role**, select **File Server**. Then click on **Next**.

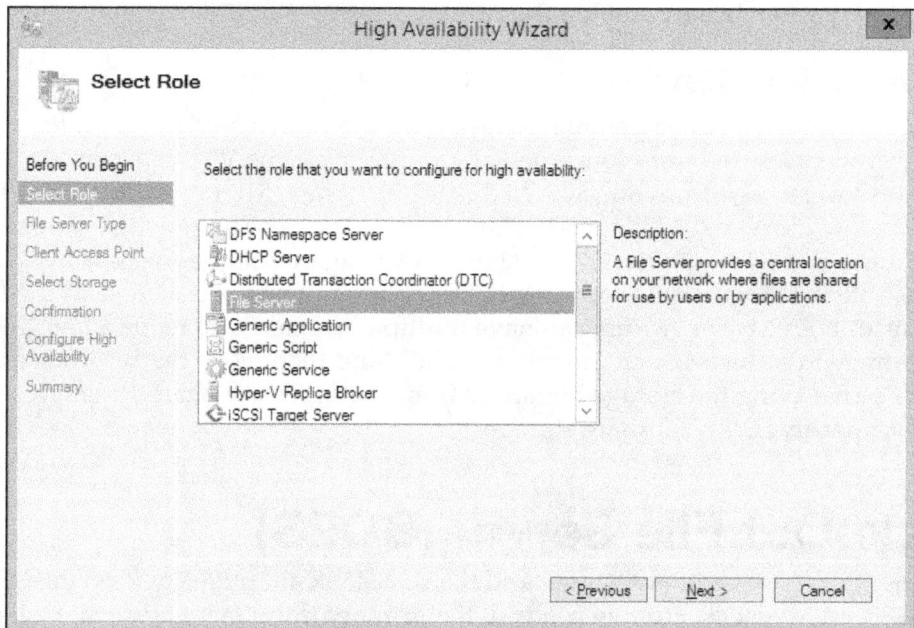

Figure 6-34: Select Role – File Server

5. In the **File Server Type** screen, select **Scale-Out File Server for application data**. The other option, **File Server for general use**, is the traditional file server cluster. Click on **Next**, as shown here:

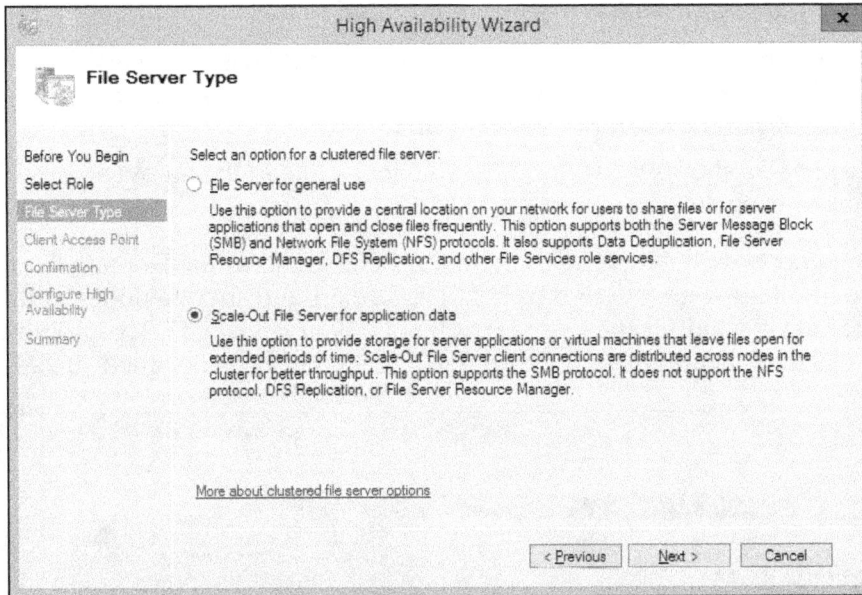

Figure 6-35: Select Roles – File Server Type

6. For **Client Access Point**, or CAP, specify a suitable name. It will be the virtual computer object (VCO) in AD and serves for authentication and authorization. Again, click on **Next**, as shown in this screenshot:

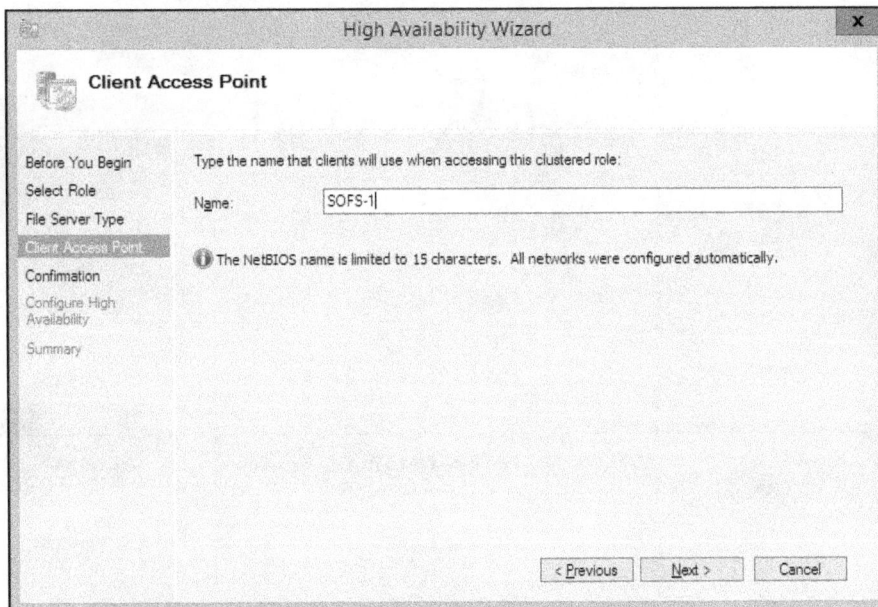

Figure 6-36: Select Roles – Client Access Point

7. On the **Confirmation** screen, click on **Next**.

8. It will proceed by creating the SOFS role, and then give the result on the **Summary** Screen. You can use **View Report** to view the report of the configuration setup. Click on **Finish**.

   Figure 6-36 shows what the SOFS role looks like in the failover cluster console.

9. If you review the DNS snap-in on the DNS server or the Domain Controller, you will see there are two **Host (A)** records (there are two nodes in this cluster) created for the VCO for SOFS. Look at *figure 6-37*. The previous three steps help us understand that the SOFS role has been installed successfully.

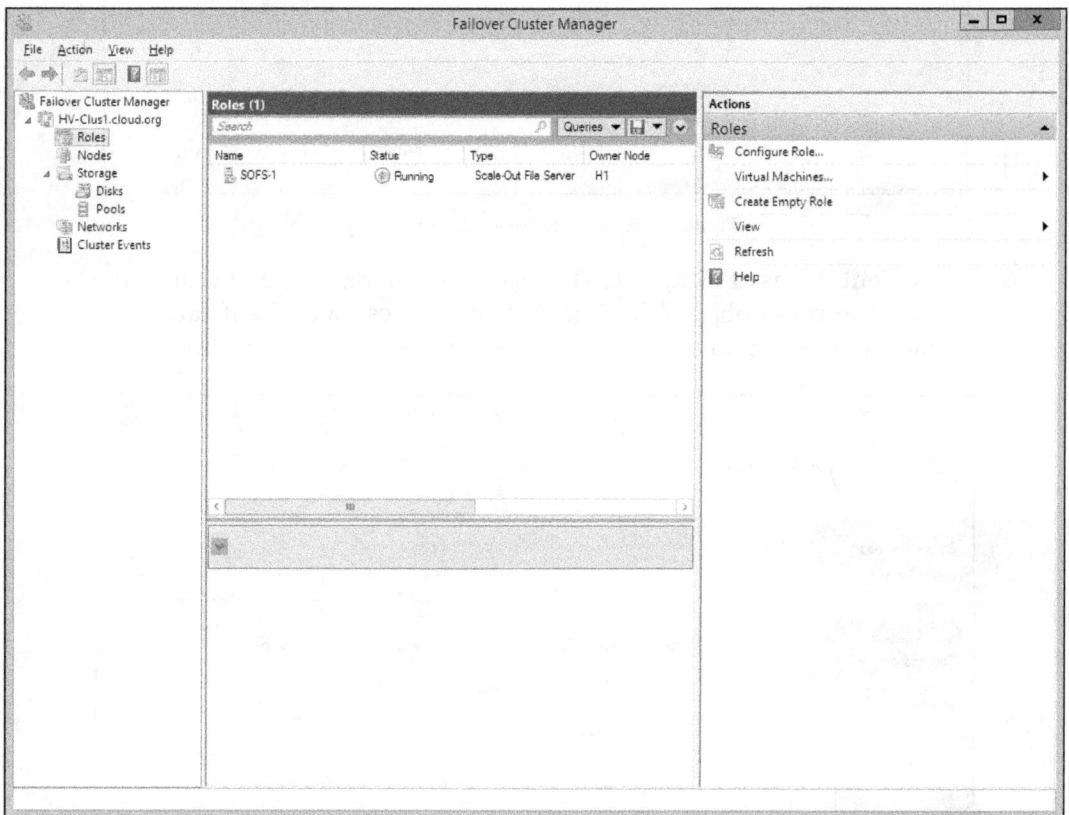

Figure 6-37: The Scale-Out File Server role

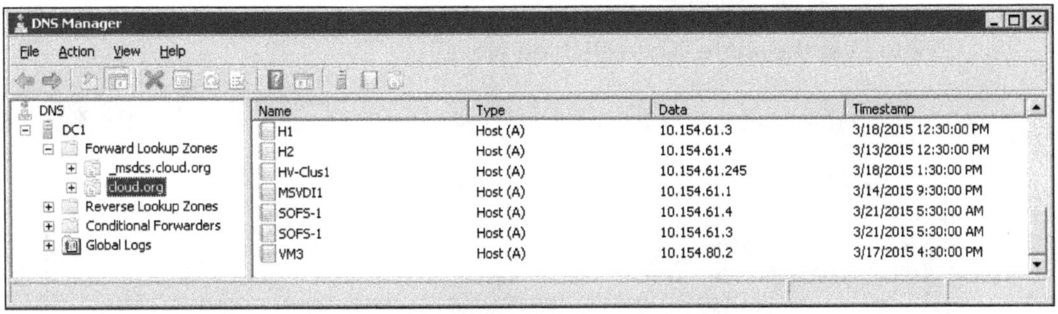

Figure 6-38: DNS Host (A) records for the Scale-Out File Server role

So far, you have witnessed how to set up the Scale-Out File Server role. Let's proceed with creating the SMB share under the role:

1. Select the SOFS CAP in the **Failover Cluster** console, and from the **Actions** pane, select **Add File Share**.

2. In **Select Profile**, select **SMB Share – Applications**, which is suitable for Hyper-V and SQL workloads and not for generic file share access. Click on **Next**.

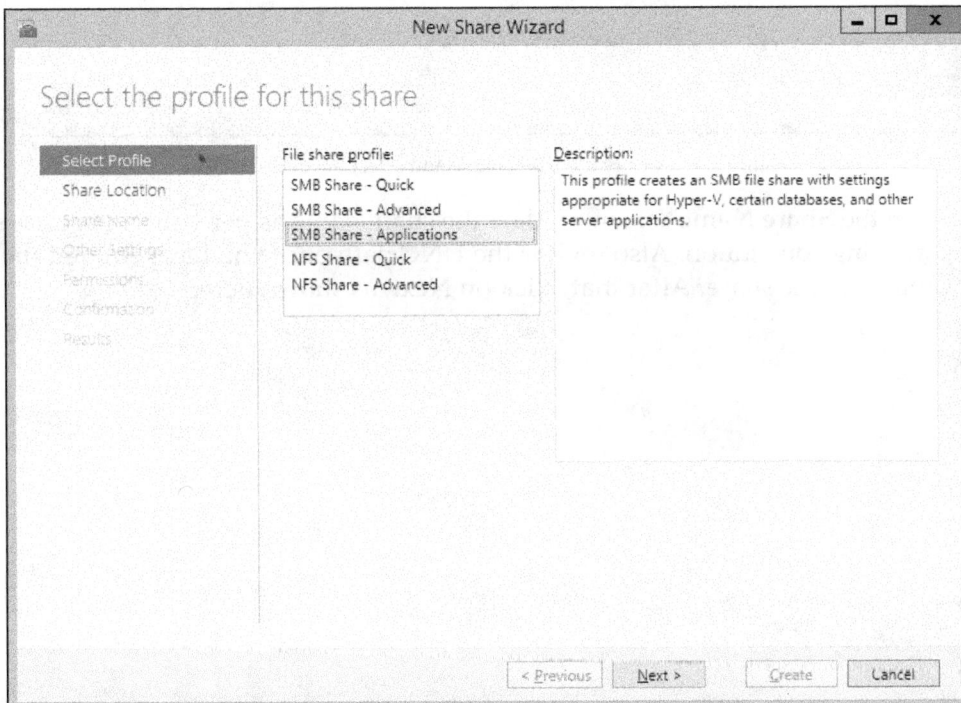

Figure 6-39: SMB Share – Applications

3. On the **Share Location** screen, select **VCO for SOFS** and select the desired CSV to host the share. Then click on **Next**.

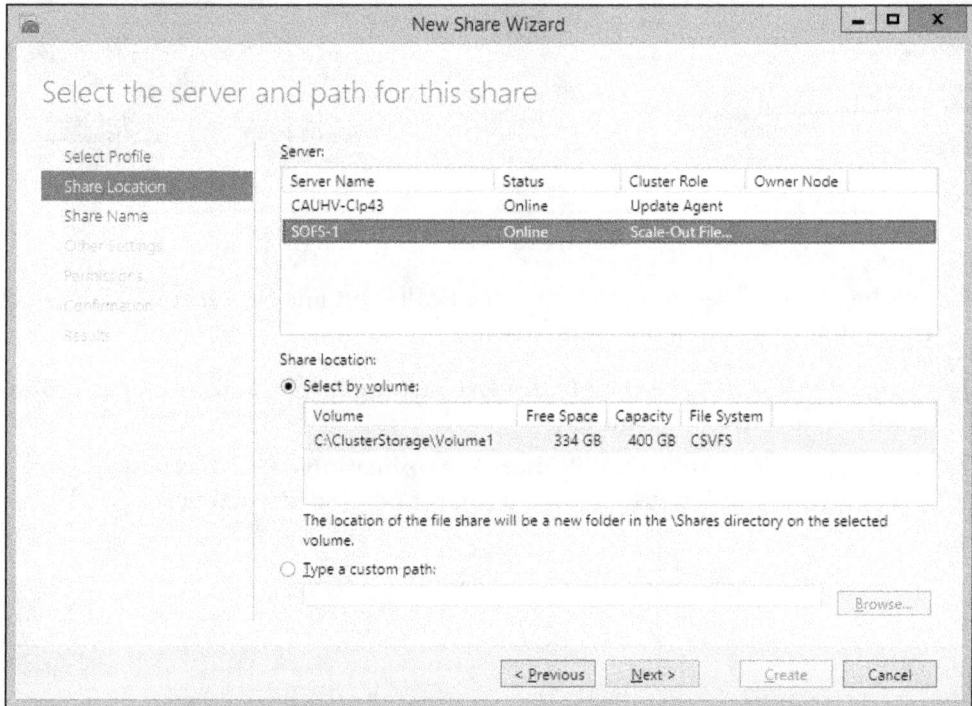

Figure 6-40: Specify the SOFS name and select the desired CSV

4. On the **Share Name** screen, update the share name as per your enterprise's naming convention. Also review the UNC path once you have entered the name of the share. After that, click on **Next**, as shown here:

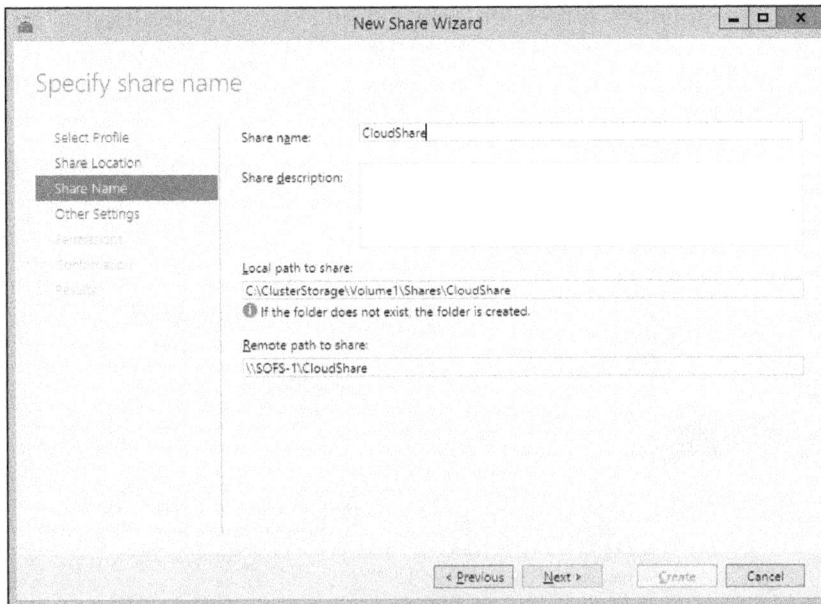

Figure 6-41: Specifying a suitable name for the share

5. Under **Other settings**, you have various other options to consider. You can either choose to enable access-based enumeration and encrypt data access, or just leave it at the default setting. Click on **Next**.

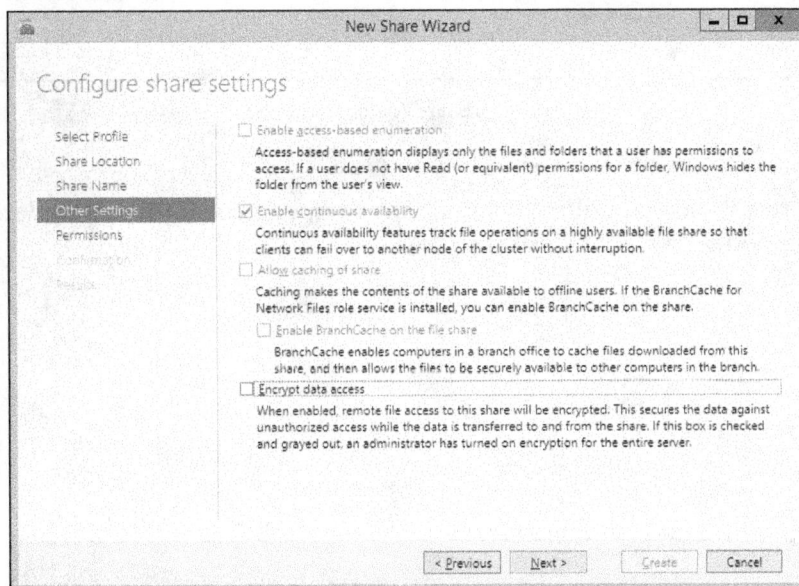

Figure 6-42: SOFS Share settings

6. On the **Permissions** screen, ensure that you have the security principals in place. If you will be using the share for Hyper-V, ensure that the Hyper-V hosts' machine accounts are also added to the ACL. Then click on **Next**, as shown here:

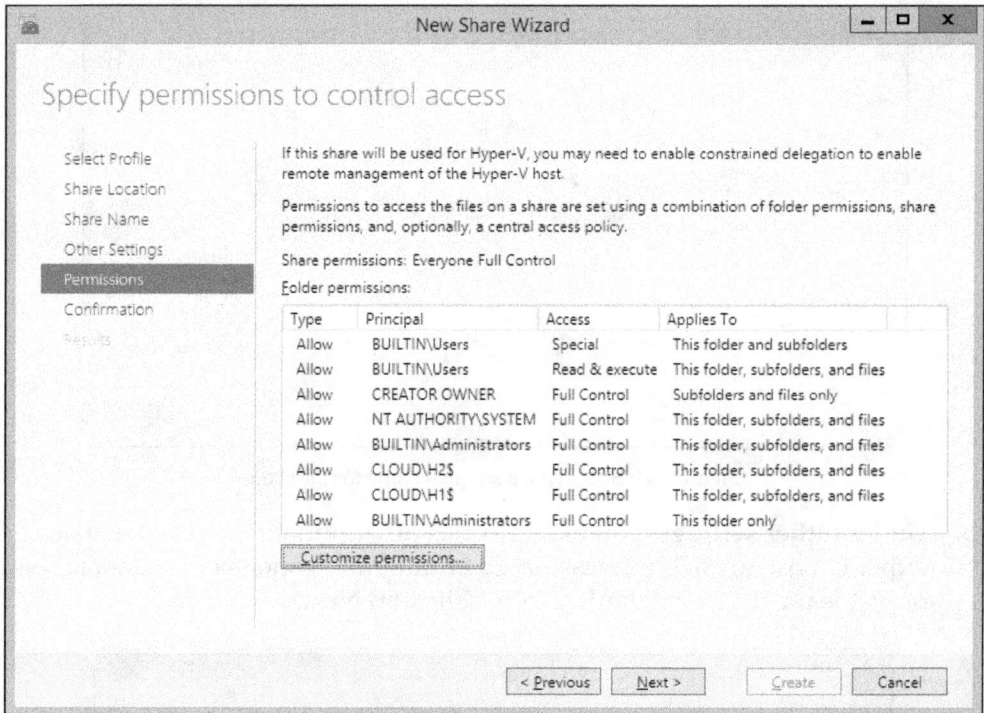

	New Share Wizard	— □ X

Specify permissions to control access

Select Profile
Share Location
Share Name
Other Settings
Permissions
Confirmation
Results

If this share will be used for Hyper-V, you may need to enable constrained delegation to enable remote management of the Hyper-V host.

Permissions to access the files on a share are set using a combination of folder permissions, share permissions, and, optionally, a central access policy.

Share permissions: Everyone Full Control
Folder permissions:

Type	Principal	Access	Applies To
Allow	BUILTIN\Users	Special	This folder and subfolders
Allow	BUILTIN\Users	Read & execute	This folder, subfolders, and files
Allow	CREATOR OWNER	Full Control	Subfolders and files only
Allow	NT AUTHORITY\SYSTEM	Full Control	This folder, subfolders, and files
Allow	BUILTIN\Administrators	Full Control	This folder, subfolders, and files
Allow	CLOUD\H2$	Full Control	This folder, subfolders, and files
Allow	CLOUD\H1$	Full Control	This folder, subfolders, and files
Allow	BUILTIN\Administrators	Full Control	This folder only

Customize permissions...

< Previous   Next >   Create   Cancel

Figure 6-43: Share Folder Permissions

7. On the confirmation screen, click on **Next**.

8. The results screen will take some time to update, as it fetches updates from other nodes as well. Click on **Close**.

9. If you select the SOFS role in the cluster console, it will show you the shares created under the role.

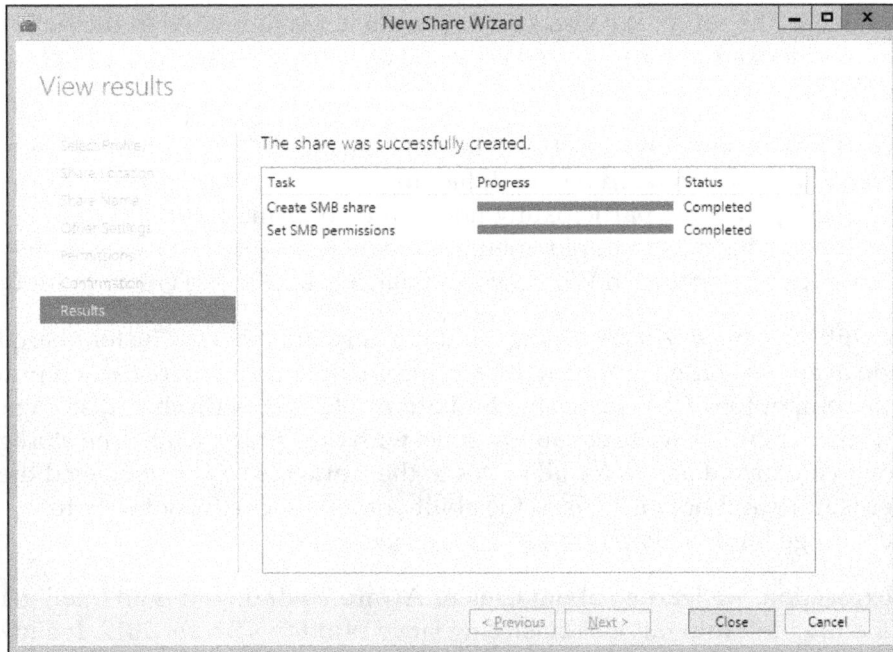

Figure 6-44: The Scale-Out File Server Role

SOFS is beneficial for Hyper-V and SQL workloads, so use it wisely.

Summary

This brings us to the final section of the chapter on high availability. This was the first of the advanced topics for Hyper-V, and we have more in store for you. The objective of this chapter was to tell you the principles of high availability and what Microsoft offers in this space. Microsoft promotes Hyper-V along with its solid failover clustering as a stable and dependable solution. The HA function is not limited to the host level, and the guest machines running on a Hyper-V cluster can have HA functions enabled for their specific workloads (by utilizing failover clustering or NLB), some of which we saw in the previous chapter.

In this chapter, you learned about the deployment principles of the Windows failover clustering feature, and reviewed the related prerequisites from server, storage, network, and Windows software perspectives. These prerequisites are indispensable to the setup. We also saw how a cluster is identified in the Active Directory, and looked at other related concepts of failover clustering applicable to a Hyper-V deployment.

Following this, you saw how to set up a failover cluster. MS recommends running the **Cluster Validation Wizard** before deploying a cluster. The wizard performs a battery of tests against the participating nodes and confirms that the configuration is suitable for a stable cluster deployment. Thereafter, we gave a brief overview of the new concept of Quorum in Windows and various applicable Quorum Models.

Then we shifted focus to cluster storage and the very interesting Cluster Shared Volume feature. The latter proved to be a game changer for Hyper-V when pitted against its competitors. CSV solves the limitations of NTFS with shared storage, where the ownership or write capability stays with one node owning the storage. CSV allows concurrent access for all nodes to the storage. We also reviewed the BitLocker feature and how it adds to the ability of data security, not only to standard storage but to CSV as well.

In the next section, we learned about Cluster Aware Updating. It is an intelligent add-on feature built into failover clustering since Windows Server 2012. It allows automated Windows update patching on cluster nodes without the need for human intervention.

Finally, we moved on to setting up high availability and mobility for a virtual machine, the essence of this chapter. This section covered how to add a VM as a clustered role on a Hyper-V cluster. Thereafter, we reviewed various concepts of VM mobility, both old and new: quick migration, live migration, storage migration, and the new kid on the block — shared nothing live migration.

In the penultimate section, we reviewed the Scale-Out File Server (SOFS) feature. We got to know its various attributes and benefits, and you learned how to configure the role and create an SMB share for application data.

The next chapter will get more exciting. We will discuss the security aspects of the Hyper-V infrastructure, and identify the suitable methods and means to maintain the security sanity.

7
Building a Secure Virtualization Environment

Threats and vulnerability are common terms in IT vocabulary and an IT administrator would have a fearful association with these two words. Securing an IT environment has different facets and every facet will have a vulnerability clause. An IT infrastructure or environment is a generic term indicative of a site or collection of sites with a certain user base and set of computers. The site could be a hub or a headquarter hosting a data center for an enterprise or an SME office or just a branch site with a skeleton staff and low end machines to fulfill a business requirement. The present assets at the site serve a purpose, and to ensure they continue to do so, it is imperative that their continuity is consistent. Security is one of the planning aspects to guarantee this continuity.

With an increase in the number of assets, servers and the installed roles and apps in an environment, there is greater vulnerability exposed. Planning security measures and the follow-up implementation to check on the vulnerabilities is an important task on the checklist. In broader terms, the security framework may begin with enforcing physical security of the premises, setting up a DMZ, maintaining a firewall and proxy for your network traffic, encrypting onsite data and inbound and outbound traffic on the wire, ensuring security hardening of your servers and on it goes until you create awareness in users about data security. One loophole can open a Pandora's box of troubles for the organization, regardless of it being small, large, or somewhere in the middle.

Virtualization adds a new facet to your IT infrastructure and thereby another aspect of complexity to your security design. The concept puts a virtual datacenter within the real datacenter; imagine the equation now. There are multiple components to the underlying equation too, namely the Hypervisor, the Management OS (ring 3), the virtual network, guest instances, applications, and so on. Each of these has to be assessed and managed to avoid any future complications arising out of operational threats or efforts to take advantage of any other exposed vulnerability. For example, an inadequately managed environment could result in virtual machine sprawl. VM deployment allows you to quickly roll out VMs, which at times stay untracked and unpatched. An unpatched VM could end up as a backdoor entry to your domain or enterprise, let alone your virtual infrastructure. Likewise, in another situation, if we consider the example of the virtual network traffic, it should be considered as equally critical to the network traffic. Sensitive data passed on between the VMs, and then on to wire, often goes unchecked and unmonitored. Monitoring and tracking performance data for better traffic management adds up as a to-do item in the workspace and then there are several other to-do items.

Before we delve into other possible threat areas that make you worry about any zero-days attacks, let's bring the attention back to the virtualization platform of our interest—Microsoft's Hyper-V. All the mentioned possible situations, including both infrastructure and hypervisor, are both applicable to our platform as well. There is more to security than what meets the eye, and in this chapter we will focus on only a subset of the security-related attributes pertaining to Windows Server 2012 R2 Hyper-V. With a Hyper-V host, the implication are greater than with a physical server hosting one role, as apparently we are hosting multiple servers on one heavy-duty virtualization host. A compromised host does not mean a single failure or even a domino effect for the guest machines. It would be a small black hole.

In the course of this chapter, the focus will be on the following areas:

- Security aspects of the hypervisor and the Management OS
- Security aspects of the virtual switch and the virtual network in Hyper-V
- Security aspects of guest machines
- Other security best practices

Hypervisor and Management OS security

Let's reminisce about what we discussed in the initial chapters of this title. At the onset, we looked at installing and configuring a Windows Server 2012 R2 host in various installation modes. Thereafter, we looked at how the Hyper-V role was installed, allowing for effective abstraction of physical hardware and enabling the pooling of resources comprising of compute, memory, network, and storage. The latter action moves the original Windows installation into a parent partition hosted on the type 1 hypervisor (Hyper-V) and it is referred to as Management OS and sits at ring 3. The Management OS is responsible for setting up communication via VM hypercalls in between VMs and the Hyper-V, as well as performing management tasks. These two entities, Hyper-V and Management OS, must be protected under various subsections. We may switch between three Windows installation modes, ensure the Hyper-V host is patched per both security and cumulative updates, and enable anti-malware protection across the nodes, hosts, and so on. In the following sections, we will review these methodologies more closely.

Reducing the attack surface

Microsoft Windows has always been noteworthy for one major aspect—an intuitive user friendly interface. Of course, we are not going down the memory lane of GUI as we all are aware of the history and merits of GUI. However, a graphical interface is more prone to remote execution and zero-day attacks than a command-driven interface. Windows Server 2012 and R2 provide you with three installation modes, which can be switched on the fly, namely **full**, **minimal server interface**, and **server core**. The quick switch makes it easier for the administrator to check and customize the deployment perspective. It is recommended that you use the latter two options and even the more, the lattermost option, server core, when deploying a virtual infrastructure. Server core removes the Windows shell and MMC snap-ins and offers only PowerShell for server management purposes. The lack of Windows Shell and MMC reduces the attack surface on your Hyper-V host and makes it less vulnerable, and the preferred choice from a security perspective. The free Hyper-V Server 2012 and R2 are available only in server core mode.

The **Minimal server interface** (or **MiniShell**) does away with the Windows Shell but retains Server Manager and other GUI aspects like Internet Explorer and some control panel applets. This provides an easier mode to manage the host for folks who are not comfortable with PowerShell and command line. Moreover, this is certainly a better choice when it comes to picking a less vulnerable option when compared to a full installation mode. The minimal server interface is not a default Windows installation option and can be invoked via Server Manager or PowerShell later on.

Another aspect we should consider when looking at the attack surface is to retain one role per server and then focus on servicing and securing Windows from that perspective only. Each role generally requires separate servicing, patching, and security design considerations. A delayed or missed patching schedule of one role may affect the overall security of the server. For an ideal deployment, it is recommended that you don't install any add-on roles on a Hyper-V host.

Windows updates

People tend to ignore patching their server due to some reserved notions. OS and software vendors release patches as per a defined cycle to enhance or improve their products and features, and patch vulnerability in their code, with demarcation as a feature update or a security update and then a cumulative update. The latter is a bulk package, a collection of pre-released updates over a cycle. Security updates are inclined towards patching vulnerabilities in developer code to prevent any possible remote execution or **zero-day attack** or a **denial of service (DoS)**.

Microsoft releases Windows updates in the third week of every month, entailing both security and other updates, for its current running operating systems and software releases. The patches are intended to correct bugs or correct vulnerability clauses in the code.

> One of the dreaded vulnerability threats discussed quite a bit that seemed too good to be true was VM escape, or guest-to-host attack. It was discussed as a remote possibility in the last decade, but has been reported by CERT KB 649219. Not Hyper-V but Windows guest machines were affected and resolved by the Security Bulletin MS12-042.
>
> Another situation is a DoS attack situation on Windows VMs where they could be rendered unmanageable by VMM. The vulnerability is corrected by a the recently released Security Bulletin MS15-042.

The Windows updates can be delivered to a Hyper-V host in more ways than one:

- **Windows updates – automatic or manual**: Patching a Hyper-V server is no different than updating a Windows server, and the simple way to apply the patches is by enabling automatic updates, which takes care of streaming and applying the patches or downloading the hotfixes and installing them manually. Automatic updating is generally avoided both at SME and bigger organizations as it becomes imperative to first test the patch prior to deployment. Testing patches before full-scale deployment is an essential Windows updating strategy nowadays.

- **Cluster Aware Updating (CAU)**: An intuitive feature rolled out with Windows Server 2012, which we learnt about in the previous chapter. As the name indicates, this add-on feature is applicable only for clustered hosts and not independent hosts. It eases Windows update patching on cluster nodes by seamlessly synchronizing updates across the nodes in a sequential way. The task sequence is scheduled and controlled by a machine hosting the CAU role which is referred to as an update coordinator.

  The update coordinator role can be installed on one of the cluster nodes or it can deployed on remote client or server machines and thereafter can be used to schedule patching. It is recommended not to enable automatic updates on the cluster nodes once CAU is enabled, as CAU can benefit from an intra-environment WSUS setup or it can also employ its default plugin for Windows updates.

- **SCVMM and WSUS**: The level of control and automation is taken to the next level with this setup, however you need to shell out for the System Center License if you wish to benefit from using this. You can integrate SCVMM with WSUS to orchestrate patching of Hyper-V hosts and clusters.

  The best practices and complete configuration are beyond the scope of this book, but we will delve a bit into the subject. The integration has to be enabled from within the SCVMM console, and you may choose to add your WSUS or WSUS with SCCM. Thereafter, create a new baseline for patching and select the updates to be added to the list. Next you would define the scope for the baseline, in other words, the Hyper-V host(s) you wish to be updated as per the new baseline. The follow-up process requires you to scan the host as per the scope to verify if the updates have been applied successfully.

Anti-malware protection

Anti-malware protection is a necessity and sometimes mistaken as the sole defense against all vulnerabilities. Administrators often assume that an antivirus is the one-stop solution to all kinds of threats, undermining the complete definition of threat. Antivirus or anti-malware software forms a part of the arsenal that you should employ to build an all-round security boundary for your infrastructure.

Microsoft recommends not to install an anti-malware software, however, if you do (you should) install it there are a few considerations and exclusions that need to be implemented for an uninterrupted operation. The first point to consider that is evident, and which should be practiced without fail, is keep your antivirus software updated along with the virus and malware signatures and definitions. Anti-malware utilities work on certain algorithms and are triggered by rigorous file access activities, and they identify Hyper-V and clusters actions as anomalous, hence the exclusions.

The exclusions encompass the directories where you would store the VM files (e.g. VHD(X), AVHD(X), XML, BIN, and VSV) as well as executable for vmms.exe and vmwp.exe. The directories could be the default stores, specified new locations, or the ClusterStorage mount points for **Cluster Shared Volumes**. Do not forget, we need to ensure the failover cluster related exclusions as well. The following are primary directories to be excluded:

- The cluster database on witness disk
- The %Systemroot%\Cluster folder

Isolating the management network

The management network, or the network for the virtualization hosts over which you perform the administrative functions on the hosts or nodes, is ideal for every virtualization infrastructure. The management network allows Hyper-V host connectivity and ensures the host has an enterprise network presence. It is recommended to segregate the network traffic on Hyper-V hosts whether independent or clustered. The segregation can be done via physical network paths or via converging network traffic on a Windows Multiplexor Adapter, segregated via virtual NICs, VLAN tagging, and QoS thereafter.

The objective is to keep the network traffic for various functions separate and enforce restricted access on service VLANs. The management VLAN is primarily used for servicing hosts and VM management and deployment, hence it would have a more lenient security policy unlike a service VLN or user VLAN. Isolation also ensures there's no escape from the user VLAN to the management network and thereby compromising the host.

Securing communications between hosts

In Hyper-V there are few situations when two or more Hyper-V hosts or nodes would set up communication with each other: cluster communications, VM migration, and VM replication. VM migration, as we have discussed in the previous chapter, encompasses live migration, storage migration, and shared-nothing live migration; all are VM mobility scenarios that we covered in the previous chapter. VM replication is a disaster recovery technique that is available as a free add-on feature on Windows Server 2012, R2 Hyper-V, and free Hyper-V platforms of the same releases. The feature is referred to as the Hyper-V Replica, which is the subject of the next chapter.

Cluster communications

Cluster communications involve heartbeats, node status, updating files on network shares, and CSV access. All of the state updates and changes are signed traffic, and this is by default in Windows failover clustering. However, you may choose to raise the bar further and encrypt the cluster communication traffic using PowerShell.

The cmdlet allows you to modify the security level of the communications among the three states, which may be set as per your requirements. The requirements depend on how your cluster is configured within a LAN or a WAN (geo or multisite clustering). The first two are preferred options for within a LAN, and the latter may be employed when traffic goes over the WAN:

- Clear text or 0
- Signed (default state) or 1
- Encrypt or 2

The following cmdlet helps you adjust the security level as per your requirement:

```
(Get-Cluster -Name HV-Clus1).SecurityLevel = 2
```

VM migrations

VM migrations can be broadly classified as cluster-based live migration, storage migration, and shared-nothing live migration. Live migration on a cluster is enabled by default and only transfers the VM state from one node to the other node with no apparent downtime and it is by far the fastest of the three. Storage migration helps in moving selected VM files and stores to the desired location, which may be a local storage or shared storage on a host or an SMB share, though the VM state continues to run on one Hyper-V host only. Shared nothing was quite the breakthrough, as it allows you to migrate both the VM state and the stores to another host and the selected storage, and it should be understood it will be slowest of the three (though it's still very fast) as the handoff is longer and again there is no visible downtime.

Live migration

Live migration is an attribute of the Hyper-V cluster and is enabled by default on the nodes participating in the cluster. The live migration traffic is not encrypted. To secure the traffic you may either choose to isolate the channel, or encrypt, or employ both.

In the **Failover Cluster** console, you may invoke the **Live Migration** settings and dedicate a physical network for live migration, thereby ensuring isolation. If you are using converged networking, you may do the same by assigning a virtual NIC for live migration, assigning a VLAN tag, defining a bandwidth, and enabling QoS for the channel.

Should you choose to encrypt the traffic, you may employ IPsec to encrypt the channel. The current day processors and advanced NICs perform IPsec offloading efficiently, hence the performance impact would not be a reason to worry.

Storage migration

This traffic again lacks inherent encryption in its default state. However, in different situations, we can employ two encryption techniques. If the source and end destinations use SMB 3.0 share, SMB signing and encryption is an easier and available methodology. IPsec could be set up between the host and the share as well to ensure protection. Another recommendation is to isolate the SMB channel access.

Shared nothing live migration (SNLM)

Windows Server 2012 introduced this amazing feature, which removed the dependency of keeping shared storage and failover clustering for VM state migrations. Also, it allows for cross-version upward migration from a Windows Server 2012 to Windows Server 2012 R2 Hyper-V; however, downward migration is not possible. Nonetheless it's only a mobility solution and should not be considered as an alternative to failover clustering which ensures the high availability of virtual machines. Failover clustering also takes care of live migration and basic authentication settings since both the nodes are domain joined and clustering is AD dependent. With SNLM you would have to consider the prerequisites and plan accordingly.

Pre-requisites encompass:

- The hosts should be part of the same domain or trusted domains
- The hosts should have at least a 1 Gbps network connection to support the migration
- The hosts should have the same names for the virtual switch in use by the VM
- The user account should be a local administrator and part of the Hyper-V admins group on both the servers
- VMs should not be using pass-through storage (well, are you still using it?)

Live migration is not enabled by default on independent Hyper-V hosts, so you would have to enable live migration and decide on the authentication methodology to kick-start the setup. The settings can be accessed once you invoke Hyper-V settings of the hosts and select **Live Migrations**. Check the box for **Enable incoming and outgoing live migrations**, and then under **Incoming Live Migrations** you can set up isolation by selecting **Add to update the IP address information** or else select **Use any available network for live migration**.

The second option is in the left pane **Advanced Features**. Here you are prompted to select the authentication protocols for verification when the live migration is initiated. There are two options, look at *figure 7-1*:

- **Credential Security Support Provider (CredSSP)** requires local logon on the Hyper-v host to initiate the migration process. With CredSSP, the user logon can only go one hop hence the local logon.

- **Kerberos** allows administrators to perform the migration remotely as it allows more than one hop for authentication and the prerequisite is to enable constrained delegation for the hosts in the AD. Look at *figure 7-2*:

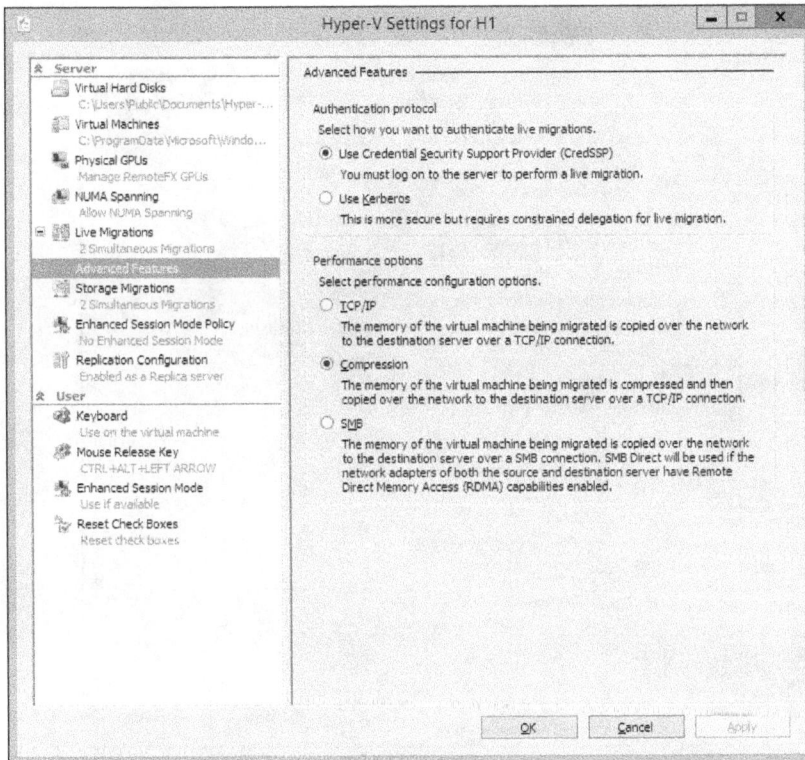

Figure 7-1: Hyper-V Settings Live Migration Advanced Features

Enabling constrained delegation for live migration specifically is a straightforward process:

1. Invoke **Active Directory Users And Computers**.

2. Identify the Hyper-V server(s) in the designated OU or, if their location has not been altered, in the **Computers** container. Right-Click on **Properties**.

3. Select the **Delegation** tab. Then select **Trust this computer for delegation to specified services only** and under the settings select **Use Kerberos only**.

4. Click on the **Add** button. Click on **Users and Computers** on the **Add Services** applet.

5. In the next applet, type the name of the recipient server and click **Check names** to verify and then click **OK**.

6. Add services **cifs** and **Microsoft Virtual System Migration Service** and click **OK**.

7. Verify that the services are listed under the **Delegation** Tab.

8. Now repeat the process for the other Hyper-V host.

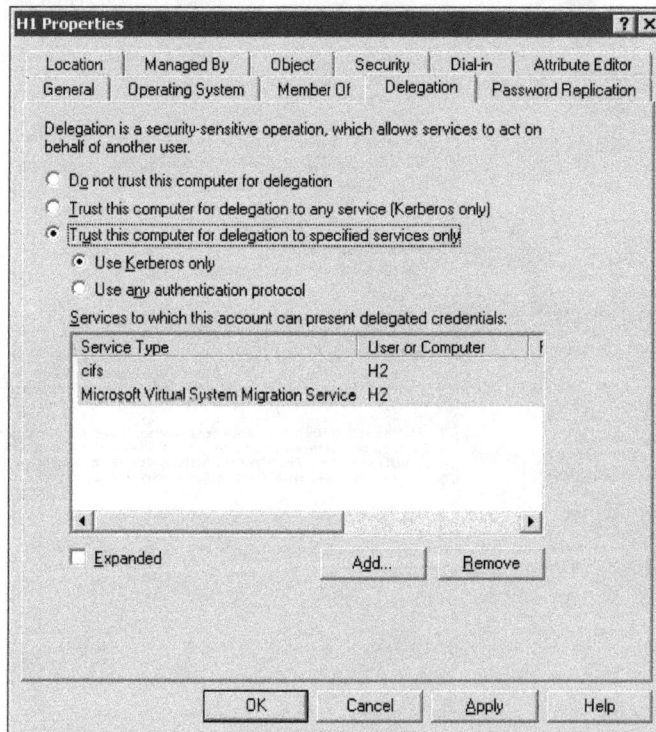

Figure 7-2: Enabling Constrained Delegation for the Hyper-V host

The preceding steps help you with the authentication piece. Next you may consider the performance options by working out your options between TCP/IP, compression, or SMB.

For further security encryption using IPsec is applicable here as well.

VM replication (Hyper-V Replica)

Hyper-V Replica is a disaster recovery mechanism built-in to Windows Server 2012 Hyper-V and enhanced further. We have a dedicated chapter coming up next on the subject, so hold on to your seats. However, we will discuss it here a bit so that security and threat management for this aspect falls in sync with the entire structure.

The objective of Hyper-V Replica is to build a dormant secondary copy of a VM on a replica server that can be invoked in case the primary VM goes down due to unseen or unplanned contingency. The process involves sending out an initial replication from the primary to the replica server; thereafter only tracked changes on the VM are transmitted to the replica server. You may be keeping the primary and replica server on the same site that means the traffic is intra-site and less prone to security threats. However in a general case, if the **disaster recovery (DR)** site is a remote location far from the primary site and receives the traffic over a dedicated VPN or a WAN the latter makes it prone to eavesdropping or packet sniffing.

To address vulnerabilities for possible VM access and exposed traffic, Hyper-V Replica presents three security parameters. To avail and customize them, we need to invoke Hyper-V settings of the Hyper-V host, and expand the **Live Migrations** option and then select **Replication Configuration** tab. On the right side of the applet, you may see the checkbox **Enable this computer as a Replica server**. No points for guessing what enabling that checkbox will do.

Once you enable the server for receiving incoming VM replication, you need to configure the various security settings, as depicted in *figure 7-3*, encompassing authentication, authorization, and consolidation settings to ensure effective and uninterrupted replication of changes.

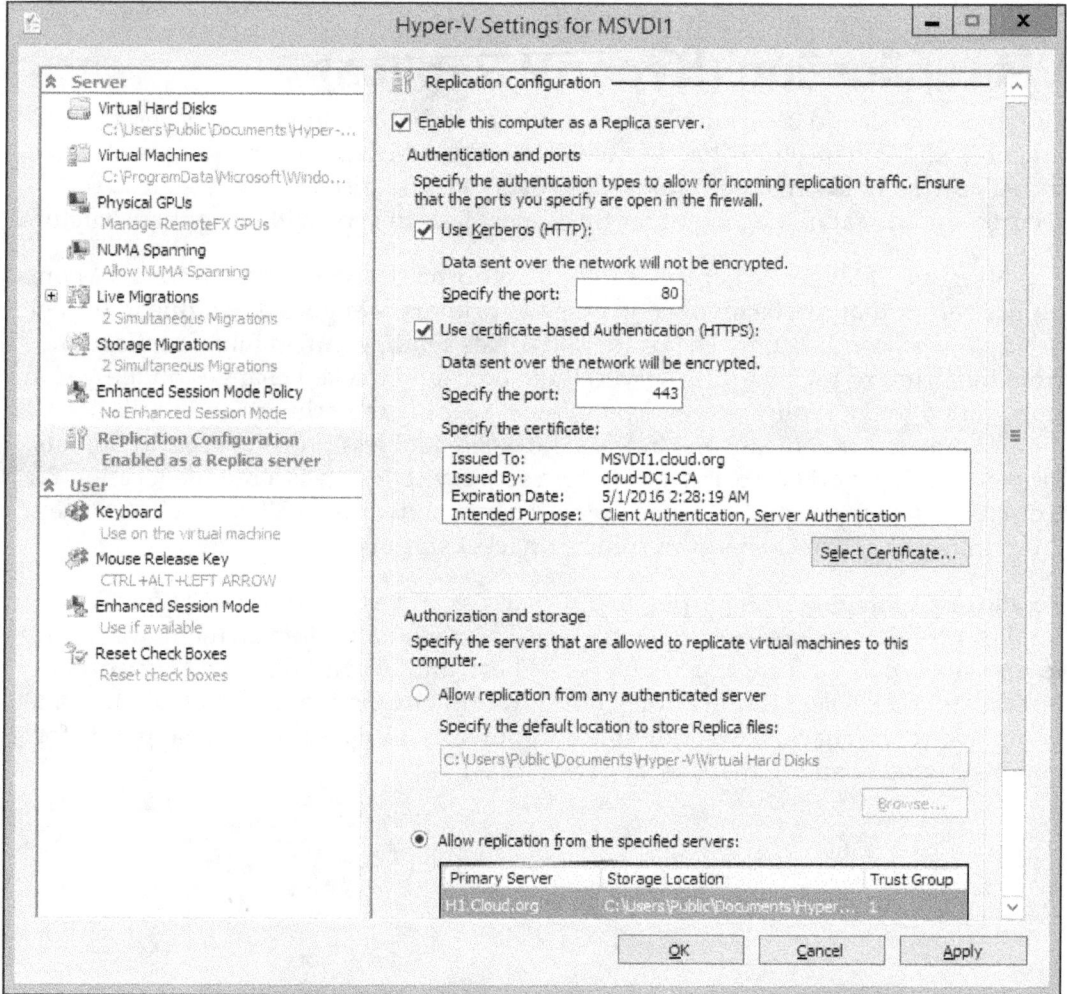

Figure 7-3: Enabling Constrained Delegation for the Hyper-V host

The first section under the applet is **Authentication and Ports**, which helps you select the authentication protocol and port for transmission of changes. There are two options, namely **Use Kerberos (HTTP)** and **Use certificate-based Authentication (HTTPS)**. The former is faster and uses Kerberos for authenticating primary and replica servers with each other and uses HTTP port 80 for transmitting changes. The traffic sent via this channel is unencrypted and insecure. The choice of selecting this mode depends on the setup, as if the transmission is within a LAN and intra-site, this channel can be adopted. If it is going to a DR site in a VPN tunnel then it is going either way via an encrypted route. If it's not, you may opt for the second method of **Certificate-based Authentication**, employing SSL over HTTP on port 443. The setup requires a certificate with **Enhanced Key Usage** (EKU) both for client authentication and server authentication. The certificate needs to be imported to the local machine store of the replica server(s), and selected in the replication configuration. An important point is that the issuing CA should be trusted at both primary and replica servers. If you are using a popular third party CA, it is easily addressed. If, however; you are using ADCS based CA, the CA cert needs to be deployed in the domain or at the very least imported in to the Trust Root CA store of the participating Hyper-V hosts.

The next section is **Authorization and Storage**, which prompts you to either let any authenticated server use this secondary server as a replica as per the agreed mechanism or specify the FQDN of the primary Hyper-V server from where the replication would be seeded and updated. There are two options: **Allow replication from any authenticated server** and **Allow replication from the specified server**. If you select the latter, click on the **Add** button and specify the relevant FQDN. This also prompts for the third important setting — the trust group. The trust group assists in grouping primary hosts, and ensures the replica server does not lose track or override changes to a VM if the changes are coming from more than one host for the same VM. The replica server would only consider the concurrent changes for a particular VM from two different VM if they are part of the same trust group.

BitLocker protection

Securing the data on the storage devices whether local or on CSV, is as imperative as any other threat-evading measure. We have discussed this topic at length in the previous chapter, however the feature deserves a mention in this chapter as well in order to understand how to benefit most with all the abilities put together. BitLocker features on Windows platforms, since Windows Server 2008 and Windows Vista and is an encryption ability that is used to protect disk drives effectively. The objective is to protect data against any theft involving physical drives being stolen or via data access over the network. BitLocker also ensures that the deleted data is harder to recover.

The prerequisite for BitLocker, the **Trusted Platform Chip** (**TPM**), is normally present on all current computers and servers, however, with later versions of TPM, 1.2 or 2.0, it is able to use its enhanced abilities to scan for any altered changes to boot components and identify if the disk is on the original computer.

The encryption can be implemented both on local disks and cluster volumes as well as on both Windows filesystems, namely NTFS and ReFS (an ability added from Windows Server 2012 R2). The feature can be installed and enabled using server manager or PowerShell cmdlets. It allows you to generate a password protector and a recovery password protector, with the option of storing the latter in the Active Directory presenting you with a quick recovery option in the event of an unforeseen situation.

Securing the virtual network

Let's move the focus a bit away from the hypervisor to discuss the security aspects of the new extensible virtual switch and virtual network of VMs. Windows Server 2012 and Windows Server 2012 R2 saw major changes to the Hyper-V design. One notable difference was the virtual switch that Microsoft offered in the current releases. It is completely different from the standard virtual switch offered with earlier platforms and referred to as the Extensible Virtual Switch (EVS).

The EVS, apart from performing its layer 2 responsibilities, can be programmatically enhanced (using published Windows APIs) by adding extensions for monitoring, modifying, and forwarding traffic to the extensible ports. Unlike VMware where the vSwitch is replaced, Hyper-V allows third party developers to build extensions, which are MS certified filter drivers based on the **Network Driver Interface Specification** (**NDIS**) and **Windows Filtering Platform** (**WFP**). There are three extensions that can be installed on the EVS: capturing, filtering, and forwarding. Each possesses the capabilities of the previous extension, with forwarding extension placed in the first layer and possess attributes for both filtering and capturing, whereas the filtering extension is the middle layer extension and possesses capabilities of capturing extensions as well. There are some popular third party extensions which assist in beefing up the security of your Hyper-V infrastructure. To name a few:

- *Cisco Nexus 1000V Switch for Microsoft Hyper-V* (forwarding extension)
  `http://www.cisco.com/c/en/us/products/switches/nexus-1000v-switch-microsoft-hyper-v/index.html`

- NEC ProgrammableFlow PF100 (forwarding extension)
  `http://www.nec.com/en/global/prod/pflow/pf1000.html`

- 5nine Cloud Security 4.1 NEW for Hyper-V (filtering extension)
  `http://www.5nine.com/5nine-security-for-hyper-v-product.aspx`

Beyond extensions, Windows Server 2012 and Windows Server 2012 R2 have a few more enhanced security features built-in with the virtual switch. They are setup through virtual machine settings or via PowerShell.

Protection via virtual NIC ports

There are attributes available on virtual NICs of VMs that assist in the overall protection of the virtual network from the VM perspective. All these attributes are referred to as **advanced features**, each assigned with a dedicated role against a particular network service. To access and customize the settings, you need to invoke the **Virtual Machine** setting from the **Hyper-V Manager** or **Failover Cluster Manager**, and expand the **Network Adapter** tab and select **Advanced Features** to get a view of the security aspects. Some attributes can be invoked through PowerShell only.

The Port Access Control List

The **Port Access Control List (ACL)** is a very helpful feature rolled out with Windows Server 2012 and was referred to as the basic port ACL and then later enhanced with Windows Server 2012 R2 as the extended port ACL. The Port ACL allows for the isolation of traffic by blocking all traffic and allowing transmission to and from a dedicated set of VMs or ports. An important consideration is that you enable ACL on the virtual NIC rather than the virtual switch when you are creating an exception.

With the basic port ACL, you can create exceptions using IP or MAC addresses between virtual adapters:

1. First you create the ACL to block all the traffic (incoming and outgoing):

   ```
   Add-VMNetworkAdapterAcl -Action Deny -Direction Both -
   VMName VM6 -LocalIPAddress 0.0.0.0/0
   Add-VMNetworkAdapterAcl -Action Deny -Direction Both -
   VMName VM6 -RemoteIPAddress 0.0.0.0/0
   ```

2. Second you create an exception to allow transmission with the desired IP:

   ```
   Add-VMNetworkAdapterAcl -Action Allow -Direction Both -
   VMName VM6 -LocalIPAddress 10.154.61.3
   Add-VMNetworkAdapterAcl -Action Allow -Direction Both -
   VMName VM6 - -RemoteIPAddress 10.154.80.14
   ```

3. Once you have configured the ACLs, you may query to get a complete list.

   ```
   Get-VMNetworkAdapterAcl -VMName VM6
   ```

Extended the ACL takes it one step ahead where rather than accepting all traffic from the VM, you can restrict the traffic from one port and enable stateful communication. Also, you can assign a weight to the connection. Unlike the basic port ACL, you cannot set both as a direction parameter in the extended ACL and you will need to create two separate rules for inbound and outbound traffic. In the following example we are depicting the inbound rule only:

```
Add-VMNetworkAdapterExtendedAcl -Action Deny -Direction Inbound -
VMName VM6 -Weight 1 -RemoteIPAddress *
Add-VMNetworkAdapterExtendedAcl -Action Allow -Direction Inbound -
VMName VM6 -Weight 50 -Protocol TCP -RemoteIPAddress 10.154.80.14
-LocalPort 389 -Stateful $true
```

The MAC address

Every machine, physical or virtual, ought to have a unique **Media Access Control (MAC)** address. In the physical machine the MAC address is hardcoded, whereas as we discussed earlier for VMs, there's a pool of range defined under the **Virtual Switch Manager** settings of the Hyper-V host. The pool range can be altered and so can the VM's MAC as well. You may set it to static as per your requirements for certain apps binding to a definite MAC, especially in the event of live migration when the moved VM gets a new MAC in case of a dynamic assignment, or if you have a defined range for the setup.

The next option is a checkbox **Enable MAC Address spoofing**. Enabling MAC spoofing (less secure) has some merits though, which includes enabling VMs to receive broadcasted unicast packets when used alongside promiscuous mode which assists in analyzing network traffic. Now since this also enables the port to send and receive packets from any MAC address, it helps the layer 2 virtual switch in building the forwarding table. You may also need the setting enabled for the **Network Load Balancing (NLB)** service.

The DHCP guard

This is a preemptive setting to ensure DHCP operations run as per the authorized standards and don't fail due to a rogue or silly DHCP deployment. The DHCP follows a DORA process and the DHCP client, as per the process, sends out a broadcast packet in the segment, which is answered by the authorized DHCP server. This setting ensures that the guest machine does not answer to any DHCP client request if there's an accidental or incidental DHCP deployment running on it.

The router guard

The router guard is one of the new attributes released with Windows server 2012. It is again a preventive measure like the previous one. It is quite possible that a VM might be running a rogue routing and remote access service deployment or any third party routing software, which would end results as routing advertisements and redirection messages into the network. When you enable the router guard, you plug the hole for letting out these packets and ensuring a stable and safe network.

The protected network

This is a failsafe feature introduced with Windows Server 2012 R2 to ensure user access to the VM continues unaffected. It is used alongside failover clustering and employs live migration. Now the inherent behavior of failover clustering is to provide high availability by consistently monitoring the health state of the HAVM and cluster resources, including storage and network. With this setup, we got a bit more granular by way of monitoring the VM's network.

In the event of the network being used by the VM goes down, the VM is live migrated to the next available node with adequate resources to address the VM state and requirements. If the destination node also reports the network required by the VM is unavailable then the VM would not be migrated. If there are multiple VM migrations queued and the failed network comes back, the pending migrations would be cancelled and the VM would be retained on the original node.

Port mirroring

Port mirroring is more of a diagnostic setting rather than threat prevention and is utilized to perform network traffic analysis of a particular machine by mirroring its network port on the diagnostic virtual machine. This is done under a situation wherein you can't install diagnostic tools on the desired VM, however, since you mirror the port, you get the mirrored traffic for analysis on the diagnostic machine.

To configure, you need to set the **Mirroring mode** to **Source** on the problem VM, and the **Destination mode** on the diagnostic machine. Please note that Hyper-V only provides traffic duplication, however for diagnosis, administrators need to install their tools on the diagnostic VM.

The private VLAN (PVLAN)

The **private VLAN (PVLAN)** is a security networking concept fixated around the isolation of traffic and scalability rather than filtering or encryption. It is brought into effect to address the size limitation of available VLANs ranging to a max of 4096 as the VLAN ID is a 12 bit number. The PVLAN is a switch port property and before you go ahead with this consult your network administrator to see if you are really going to benefit from this setup. It is imperative to understand the following concepts around PVLAN:

- **Primary VLAN**: This is the standard VLAN to which the secondary VLAN would attach. The PVLAN maintains the VLAN ID of the primary VLAN as part of its identifier.

- **Secondary VLAN**: The secondary VLAN links to the primary VLAN, and through which its members find a network presence.

- **Isolated port**: This is a PVLAN mode. An isolated port can connect with only promiscuous ports in the secondary VLAN and none other. It can connect with the primary VLAN as well. To configure a vNIC in isolated mode, use the following cmdlet:

  ```
  Set-VMNetworkAdapterVlan –VMName VM5 –Isolated –
  PrimaryVlanId 4 –SecondaryVlanId 10
  ```

- **Community port**: This is the second PVLAN mode. The community port can connect with the other community ports and promiscuous ports in the secondary VLAN, and with the primary VLAN as well. To configure a vNIC in isolated mode, use the following cmdlet:

  ```
  Set-VMNetworkAdapterVlan –VMName VM5 –Community –
  PrimaryVlanId 4 –SecondaryVlanId 10
  ```

- **Promiscuous port**: This is third PVLAN mode. The promiscuous port can connect with all entities in the secondary VLAN and primary VLAN as well. Using this mode, membership can be extended to multiple secondary VLANs. This mode is more suited to the router role. When configuring, you may like to add a list of secondary VLAN IDs (cmdlet parameter `SecondaryVlanIdList`), if need be.

  ```
  Set-VMNetworkAdapterVlan –VMName VMRouter –Promiscuous –
  PrimaryVlanId 4 –SecondaryVlanIdList "10, 20, 30"
  ```

Protecting the guest machines

We will now move to the center of the Hyper-V universe—the guest machines. The objective of virtualization is to abstract the underlying hardware, setup a pool of resources and then disseminate them between the hosted machines, but then the objective is not just efficient utilization by the VM but also to ensure the VM runs securely and without failure. Securing VMs has two facets. First, set up protection for it as an entity within Hyper-V, and second, protect it as you would do to a normal computer or server. One cannot be undermined for the other, and both aspects need to be considered with equal weight. Some of the security parameters we discussed earlier do assist with the first scenario. In the following sections, we will broadly discuss the security recommendations, and certain best practices should be leveraged religiously.

Secure boot

In *Chapter 2*, *Planning and Deploying Microsoft Hyper-V*, you were introduced to Generation 2 (Gen-2) virtual machines, which are supposedly going to succeed the Gen-1 VMs in future Hyper-V deployments. We discussed the reasons why the Gen-2 is the worthy successor when we reviewed the benefits. The prime differentiator is that they boot off the **Unified Extensible Firmware Interface (UEFI)** instead of the standard BIOS. UEFI defines a feature called **secure boot** as part of its specification, and Hyper-V in its Gen-2 VM has a partial implementation for the technology piece.

The secure boot mechanism employs **public key infrastructure (PKI)** for verification of the OS image. The public key stays with the firmware and the private key is with the OEM (for example. Microsoft). If the verification is confirmed, the boot image is loaded unless the boot process fails.

This ability is limited to the latest Windows platform offerings from Microsoft, namely Windows 2012 and R2 from the server operating systems, and Windows 8 and 8.1 from the client side. The secure boot has no specific prerequisites and should be employed when you are deploying Gen-2 VMs. The feature is enabled by default when a Gen-2 virtual machine is created and if you have a reason to toggle it off you can easily do so as well. Invoke the VM settings of the desired guest machine from the Hyper-V Manager and select the **Firmware** tab and then, on the right hand side, uncheck the **Secure Boot** checkbox.

Planning authorization and NTFS security as it is bye-bye AzMan

Windows Authorization Manager (**AzMan.msc**) is no longer a handy utility as it has been deprecated since Windows Server 2012 and cannot be used to set up authorization policies for Hyper-V. Windows Server 2012 and R2 have a new built-in group called Hyper-V administrators, which is entitled to control over the Hyper-V Management operating system and virtual machine operations. So if you wish to assign users access to Hyper-V operations, you no longer need to add them to the local administrators group. This is referred to as **simplified authorization**. For more granular control, you may employ the System Center VMM. Also, further security hardening around Hyper-V administrators group can be performed using **Group Policy**, and one such tool that comes in handy to create a Group Policy baseline is the Security Compliance Manager, which we will discuss in a later section of this chapter.

Apart from authorization and hardening, the other aspect that requires consideration is ensuring the correct NTFS permissions on VM default stores or VM storage locations. One standard security principal you shall see populating the ACL is virtual machines. It is not a domain based or a generic local SAM based principal. The security principal is associated with the VM ID for the relevant virtual machine whose folder's ACL we are looking up. In an ideal situation, do not customize the ACL of the virtual machine folder or its underlying contents. If, for some reason, this principal is removed, the VM would fail to start and you will be playing around with icacls to restore everything back to normal. The permissions are well handled by Hyper-V wherever they need to be adjusted, whether for local storage or a CSV. Rather, toying with hardening the ACLs ensure your groups have the right membership and ensure you have auditing enabled for VM folders even to just keep an eye on the trustworthy Hyper-V administrators, as to err is human.

Setting up auditing for VM access

It is always in your best interest to keep track of access to your virtual infrastructure. Security hardening may protect against unauthorized access, however, auditing helps with detecting potentially erroneous or harmful actions by users and administrators. To enable file level auditing on the virtual machine folder, you would first need to enable the Group Policy for object access: Audit filesystem, thereafter pick up the relevant folder and, via Windows Explorer, enable auditing accordingly. The Group Policy used could be domain-based or local GPO, whichever suits your requirements. A word of caution though, auditing gets really chatty and you may like to exercise discretion when enabling on certain folders, unless the need is otherwise, you may very well ignore it at times, unless imperative. Let's do a quick rundown of the steps.

Enabling Local Group Policy for object access – audit filesystem

Here we will look at the basic steps to enable Group Policy for auditing filesystem access via the Local Security Policy:

1. From the **Administrative Tools**, invoke the **Local Security Policy** snap-in.

2. Select **Computer Configuration**, and expand in sequence: **Windows Settings | Security Settings | Advanced Audit Policy Configuration | System Audit Policies – Local Group Policy Object | Object Access**.

3. On the right-hand pane, select and double-click on **Audit File System**.

4. In the **Audit File System Properties** applet, check the box **Configure the following audit events checkbox**.

5. Check the checkboxes for **Success** and **Failure**.

6. Click **OK**. Close the **Local Security Policy** snap-in.

Enabling file-level auditing on the VM stores

Now we will see how to enable file level auditing in the relevant folders and subdirectories:

1. Open **Windows Explorer** via the **Taskbar**.

2. Browse to your **Default Stores** or folder where your VM is stored.

3. Select the **File** menu and click **Properties**.

4. Invoke the **Security** tab and then click on the **Advanced** button.

5. Select the **Auditing** tab and click on the **Add** button to open the auditing entry for the folder applet.

6. Click on the hyperlink **Select a principal**. This opens the **Select User, Computer**, or **Group** dialog box. Type Everyone in the box and click on **OK**.

7. This returns us to the **Auditing Entry** applet. Select type as **All** from the dropdown menu and apply to **This Folder, subfolder and files**.

8. Under **Basic Permissions**, select **Full Control**.

9. Check the box **Only apply these settings to object and/or containers within this container**.

10. Click **OK** on following screens to close them out.

To verify if the mentioned changes have been successfully implemented, you may run a quick access test and check in the security event log for the audit success or failure event under the task category – filesystem.

Antivirus and backup software inclusions for virtual machines

Basic security requirements for virtual machines are set up in the same way as that of a physical machine. Anti-malware or antivirus is not preferred on the management operating system, even with all the exclusions in place, as it affects performance and the Hyper-V employed memory and I/O operations are sometimes detected as anomalous, as discussed earlier.

Guest machines host roles and applications and have a greater attack surface exposed to threats. Protecting a VM internally in turn ensures the protection of the host and the infrastructure. An attacker would first attempt to access a vulnerability in the guest to gain access to the host or the infrastructure, and antivirus protects against such actions.

The last leg in the scheme of things is backup for the VMs, a preferred means for protecting VMs against a contingency. Your backup strategy may involve a host-level backup which ensures backup of the Management operating system as well as VMs or a VM internal backup, which is like the backup of a physical machine or a hybrid strategy. Using either of the strategies, whichever is deemed fit for your infrastructure, you can feel safe against an unseen VM or host failure. We will be looking at backup strategies in *Chapter 9, Backup and Recovery Strategies for Hyper-V Solutions*.

Other best practices

The strategies we have discussed so far are based on best practices and assist in devising a stable security plan pertaining to both the management operating system, the VMs and the underlying framework. Microsoft offers tools to help you identify exposed vulnerabilities, and suggests best practices to further harden your environment and also streamline the hardening procedures. Let's look at a few of the freely available tools and see how they fit the purpose.

The Microsoft Baseline Security Analyzer

The **Microsoft Baseline Security Analyzer (MBSA)** is a free utility available on the Microsoft downloads site and is primarily used to identify vulnerabilities against a predefined security baseline. You may download it from here:

```
http://www.microsoft.com/mbsa
```

The tool has a simple installation process and may require elevated privileges during install and launch. Once installed, you may easily invoke the executable from the programs list and it will present you with its GUI. The MBSA allows you to scan a local computer, a remote computer, or multiple remote computers at once. In the scan options you can see it is not listing Hyper-V as a separate option but performs Windows generic administrative vulnerabilities, though it works just fine picking the pieces from a Hyper-V host perspective. It also checks for relevant security updates that may need to be applied against the system being scanned. Look at *figure 7-4*:

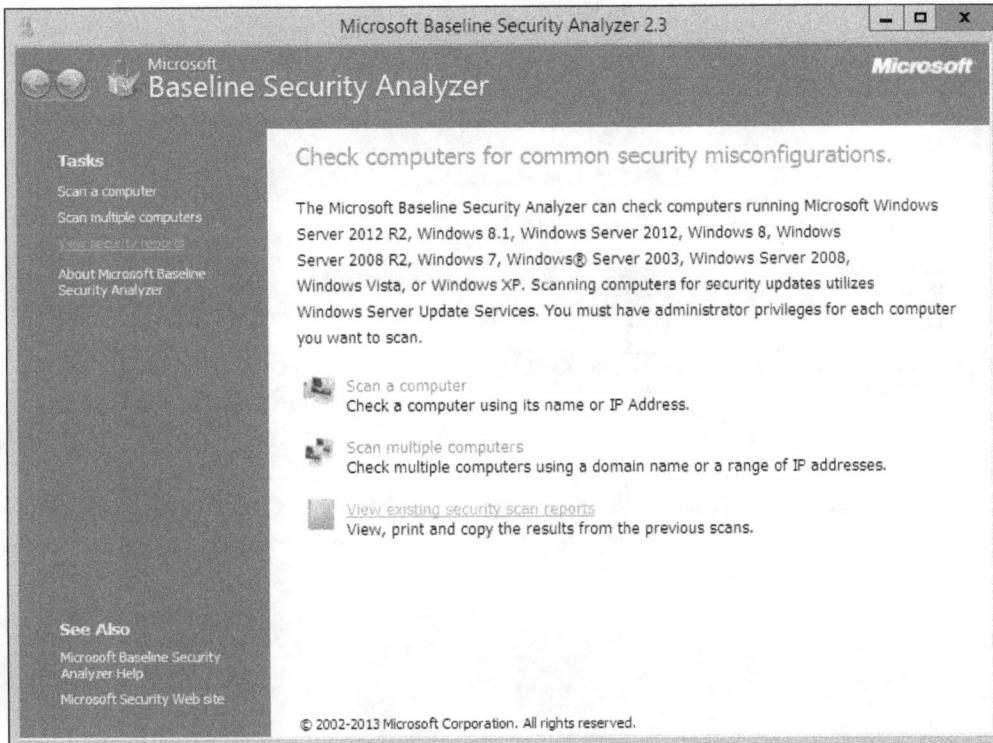

Figure 7-4: MBSA – Scan Options

Ensure the scan is performed with administrative privileges, otherwise some of the tests will fail. Once the scan is complete, the end screen depicts what parameters the server was scanned for and what the score outcome was as indicated in *figure 7-5*. If the situation is critical or warning oriented, a remedy is also suggested. The scan reports are saved locally and can be accessed later on as well using the **View security reports** link (*figure 7-4*). The MBSA scan should be performed at regular cycles to keep track of pending requirements and any new vulnerabilities.

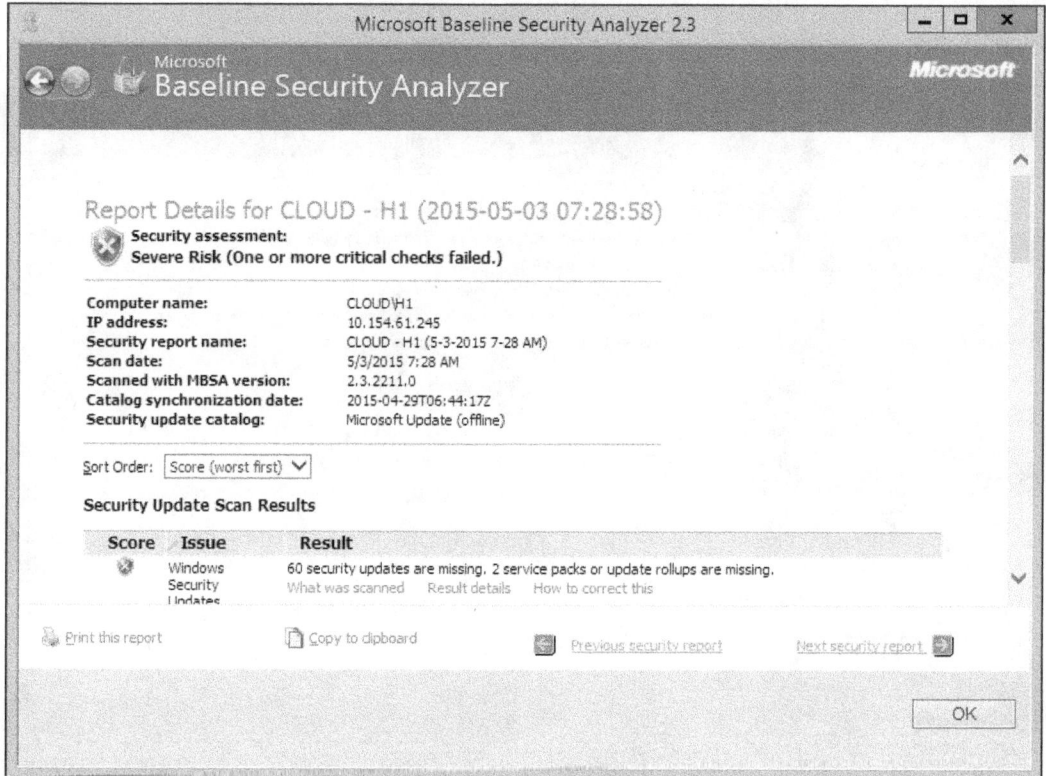

Figure 7-5: MBSA – Scan results

The Best Practices Analyzer

The **Best Practices Analyzer (BPA)** is part of the built-in arsenal in Windows Server 2012 and R2 Hyper-V. The utility performs a battery of tests against a Hyper-V host to check for common configuration issues and other aspects. The BPA scan can be invoked from the Server Manager as well as PowerShell. Both the Server Manager and PowerShell allow the flexibility to perform the scan on multiple hosts at once.

In the Server Manager, you can add multiple servers to the dashboard; they get easily segregated as per their installed roles. Select Hyper-V on the left pane, and scroll down to the **Best Practices Analyzer** frame. On the right, under the **Tasks** menus, click **Start BPA Scan**. It prompts a box to select the server to run the scan against, so select the specific servers and click on **Start Scan**. The results are displayed in the next frame with a problem statement and more information around it.

The same can be achieved using PowerShell. If you wish to see all the available modules, run the following cmdlet:

```
Get-BpaModel | Format-Table -Property Id
```

The BPA scan is initiated using the `Invoke` cmdlet, however the `log` folder must be precreated before launching the scan:

```
Invoke-BPAModel -ComputerName H1, H2 -ModelId Microsoft/Windows/
Hyper-V -RepositoryPath D:\TestLab\BPAScan
```

Security Compliance Manager

The **Security Compliance Manager (SCM)** is a solution accelerator offering from Microsoft and is a one-stop solution for many requirements. It offers Group Policy baselines for Microsoft platforms and applications as well DCM configuration packs. The SA can be downloaded from the following link:

```
http://www.microsoft.com/SCM
```

Though you can do quite a bit with the SCM, our interest is with Hyper-V Security 1.0 baseline group policies. The SCM installation is simple and requires SQL Express as a backend or preexisting SQL installation. Once it is installed, launch the utility and on the left pane expand as per the sequence – **Microsoft Baselines | Windows 2012 | WS2012 Hyper-V Security 1.0**. It has listed settings for Windows Server 2012 but should work fine for the Windows Server 2012 R2 as well. Set up the required parameters as per your hardening guidelines and export the GPO backup using the option in the right pane.

The GPO backup can be easily imported into a new domain GPO using the **Group Policy Management** console and the desired setting can be deployed seamlessly. If you have standalone Hyper-V hosts that are non-domain joined, the same GPO backup folder can be imported using the Local Security Policy ensuring the same hardening as you would have achieved on the domain joined Hyper-V hosts. Look at *figure 7-6*:

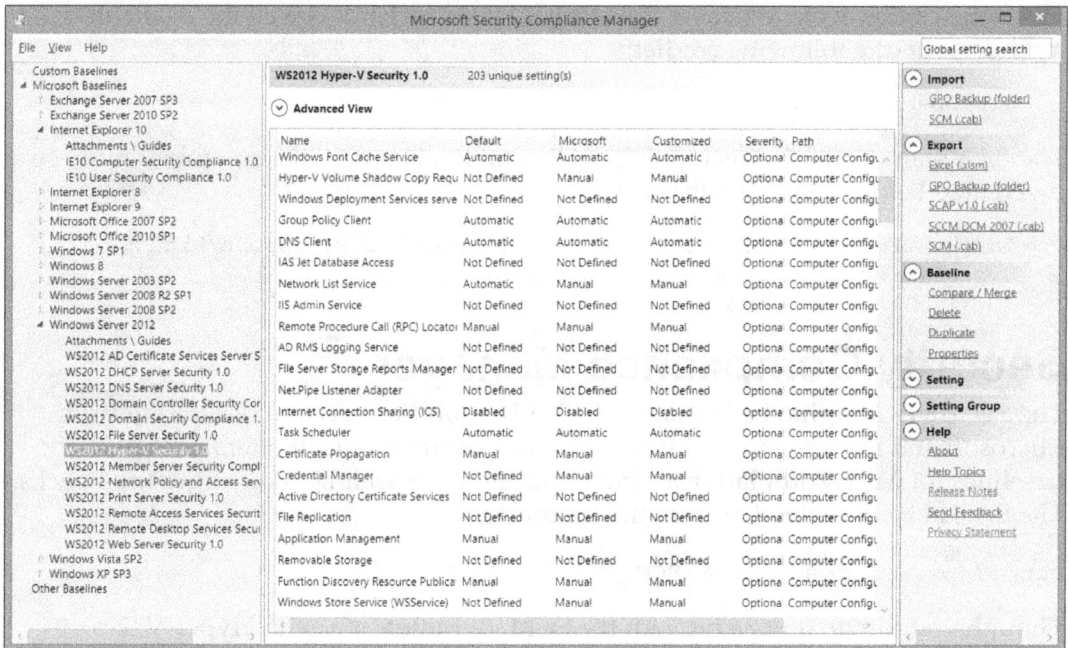

Figure 7-6: Microsoft Security Compliance Manager

The Enhanced Mitigation Experience Toolkit

The **Enhanced Mitigation Experience Toolkit (EMET)** is an interesting tool from Microsoft, which has great utility and is quite elaborate as well. The utility is used to identify and mitigate security threats in your systems thereby building a vigilance against cyber attacks. It puts to use effective mitigation techniques like **Data Execution Prevention (DEP)** and **Address Space Layout Randomization (ASLR)** to prevent attackers from exploiting vulnerability in installed programs. In an ideal situation you would not be installing programs on a Hyper-V server so EMET may not have much of a role but nonetheless it still can be used as an effective tool. EMET is a complex tool and more emphasis on it would be beyond the scope of this chapter. For more information you can refer to the EMET user guide.

Both the utility and guide can be downloaded from here:

`http://www.microsoft.com/EMET`

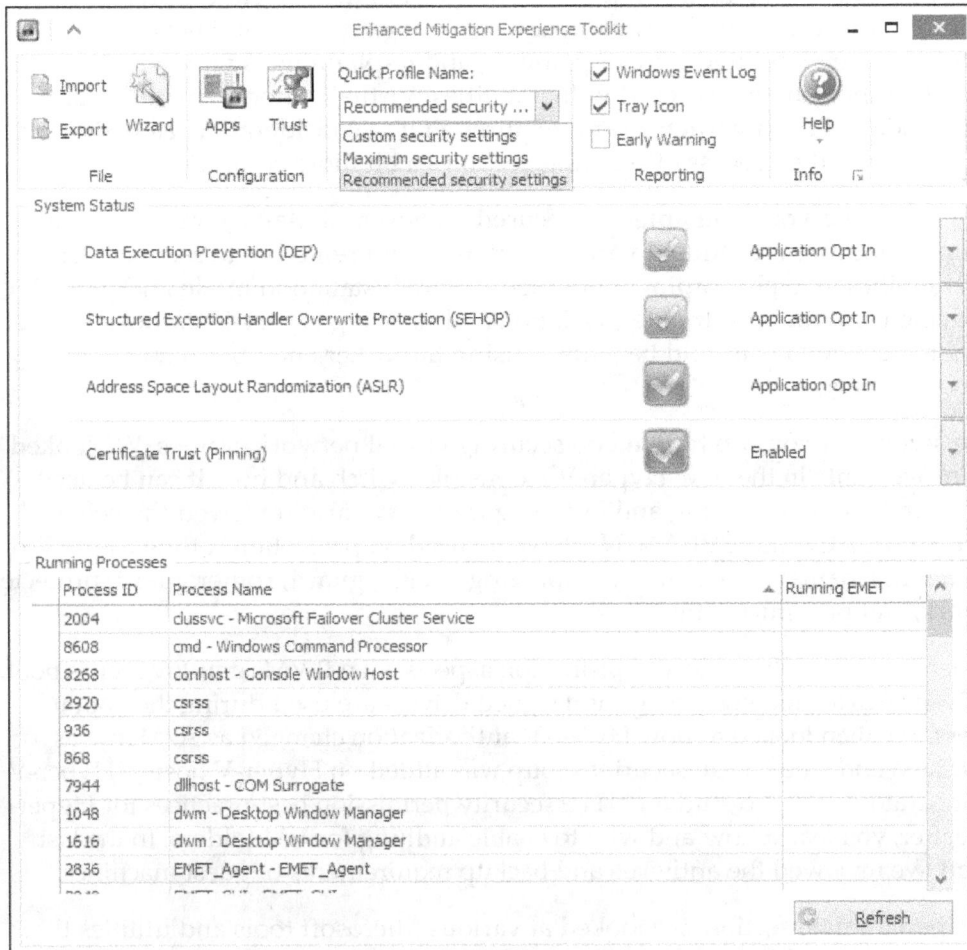

Figure 7-7: Enhanced Mitigation Experience Toolkit

Summary

As we conclude one of the most complex topics and get ready for the next one in line, let's quickly recap as to what you have learnt in the current chapter. Security and threat assessment in IT environment is a tedious process and hence before an infrastructure goes live, a lot of planning and re-planning is worked out to ensure that there are no exposed vulnerabilities. Virtualization is an important facet in today's IT infrastructure and requires a lot of consideration, as with nested infrastructures, the process of securing becomes a bit more complex.

In the first section of the chapter we focused on host and Management operating system protection. We studied various measures and remedies to reduce exposed vulnerabilities, namely employing the server core installation mode for Hyper-V deployments, Windows updates, isolation and securing Hyper-V traffic on clustered and non-clustered hosts, and benefits of using BitLocker encryption for protecting Hyper-V storage.

In the second section, we focused on securing virtual network entities. We looked at improvements in the new Hyper-V Extensible Switch and how it can be used to filter and secure incoming and outgoing traffic. We also reviewed the benefits of using port ACL and PVLAN. Next, we focused on protection settings added to virtual NICs, namely MAC address spoofing, DHCP guard, router guard, protected network, and port mirroring.

We then moved the focus to VM protection aspects. Gen-2 VMs employ secure boot, which ensures a valid boot image and signed drivers are used during the boot up process. We then looked at how Hyper-V authorization changed as AzMan was deprecated and a new local security group was added on Hyper-V hosts — Hyper-V administrators. We also studied NTFS security permission best practices for Hyper-V. Thereafter, you learnt how and why to enable auditing for VM folders. In the last section, we reviewed the antivirus and backup requirements of guest machines.

In the penultimate section, we looked at various Microsoft tools and utilities that assist you with building security hardening policies and detecting vulnerabilities in your Hyper-V setup.

In the next chapter, we will learn how Hyper-V is equipped to deal with disasters and contingencies.

8
Hyper-V Replica

Destiny favors the prepared! An efficient data center with high-end servers and zipping storage delivering throttling performance for your Hyper-V clusters and independent hosts. Sounds as if your script is almost complete. Maintaining virtual workloads on clusters, and ensuring a decent backup strategy does take care of any short-lived or predictable contingency in your environment. However, if you overlook disaster recovery or other major contingencies in your design, then your deliverables are far from complete. **Business Continuity Planning (BCP)** is a norm for enterprises. BCP ensures that the solution designs stand robust, and are able to sustain any major disruptions to the primary data center. Disruptions can arise in the event of a natural disaster, catastrophe, a site wide power outage, or even SAN failure on site, to name a few. Enterprises resort to SAN level replication to a secondary site, but the same adds a big bill to the CAPEX and OPEX, and also adds a bit more complexity to the design.

Microsoft yet again surprised everyone with another classic Hyper-V feature in Windows Server 2012—Hyper-V Replica. It was quite the news when the feature was announced. Hyper-V Replica is a built-in attribute with Windows Server 2012 and Windows Server 2012 R2. Hence, it comes to you at no additional costs. It enables a host-based replication for virtual machines, and can be configured across independent hosts and Hyper-V clusters alike. Also, it is available on all the variants of Hyper-V platforms. In the current release of the Hyper-V platform, Windows Server 2012 R2, and Hyper-V Server 2012 R2, the replica feature adds more flexibility and scalability to the initial offering, as it now allows you to add a tertiary recovery site. If you wish to savor more, MS Azure offers **Azure Site Recovery (ASR)** service as a caveat. ASR runs on the cloud, but assists you in building a disaster recovery plan, allowing for automation, remote health monitoring, recovery, and more. ASR offers many options. It can help you kick-start services on an on-premise secondary site, or keep your secondary site on Azure cloud, should you chose to move up to the cloud. Well, ASR comes with a price tag!

Let's look deeper into the subject. In this chapter, we shall learn about:

- Hyper-V Replica features and attributes
- Design considerations
- How to configure and set up VM replication

Hyper-V Replica overview

Hyper-V Replica is a disaster recovery add-on feature for Hyper-V. The feature was released with Windows Server 2012, and has been enhanced further with the release of Windows Server 2012 R2. The add-on is offered for free, and is present in all Hyper-V variants, regardless of whether it be Standard or Datacenter edition, or even free Hyper-V Server 2012 R2. The Hyper-V Replica is not a VM mobility concept or a backup strategy. Its purpose is to maintain a standby replica copy of virtual machines, running on your Hyper-V host or in your data center. In case your host goes down or even the entire data center goes down, the VMs can be brought online on the secondary site or data center to resume services with a very minimal downtime and data loss, which is defined as per the **Relative Time Objective (RTO)** and **Relative Point Objective (RPO)** in your BCP.

Hyper-V Replica enables asynchronous replication of virtual machines between two or more Hyper-V hosts. The replication engine running under the hood ensures that the traffic can safely travel over a standard IP-based network by enabling encryption. The engine provides asynchronous replication, which means the changes on the VMs are not applied instantly or immediately to the replica copies. Though in the current release, the interval of synchronization has been reduced to 30 seconds, which improves the normalization between the original and replica to a greater extent. Also, asynchronous replication puts lesser load on the primary server as well as the network.

Hyper-V Replica is a storage agnostic and workload, or an application agnostic. It is not dependent on a shared storage, and does not have any specific storage requirement similar to failover clustering. From a VM workload perspective, it will replicate any workload that supports virtualization on Hyper-V. This feature is quite simple to configure, and can be used under a variety of scenarios. The participants can be independent hosts or Hyper-V clusters, or a combination of both and being domain joined is not a prerequisite. Replica can work with or without an AD domain presence.

An important realization will be that the Hyper-V replica is neither a failover clustering alternative, nor a backup strategy. Often confused with either the former or latter, in a business continuity plan, all three have an important place. Failover clustering ensures high availability of a VM and its mobility across hosts, whereas replica maintains an older copy of the VM. Likewise, replica is assumed to be an alternative for a backup solution, but it isn't, and should be used in tandem with your backup strategy. You will need to use your backup drives in the event of a data corruption, bad patching, user errors, and so on.

What's new in Hyper-V Replica?

Windows Server 2012 R2 was packed with a volley of new features and improvements. Hyper-V Replica was loaded with a couple of enhancements as well. Let's quickly review the goodies:

- **Upgrade to Windows Server 2012 R2**: Windows Server 2012 R2 provides an easier upgrade path from its predecessor in Windows Server 2012. Post the upgrade, there will be no need to reset the replication of your VM replicas, as Hyper-V replica, just as other features, picks up from where the things were left off. Windows Server 2012 R2 also provides the flexibility of upgrading the primary and secondary sites at different time intervals, as the replica will continue its replication from the Windows Server 2012 environment to the Windows Server 2012 R2 environment without an interruption during the upgrade process.

- **Linux support**: With an aim for a greater support to non-Windows guest machines, Hyper-V Replica was capable of replicating any supported workload. In its current release, it is more tightly coupled with the internal operations of the Linux and other supported non-Windows VOSE's.

- **Recovery points**: Windows Server 2012 offered a limit of 16 recovery points for the VM replicas, which got bumped up to 24 recovery points, offering a greater retention and resiliency for the VMs.

- **Replication frequency**: Previously Hyper-V replica had a predefined replication time interval of 5 minutes post untill, the changes were pulled to the replicas. In its current release, the feature offers more flexibility, allowing end users to define the replication frequency suited to their requirements. The frequency is offered in the range of three time intervals—30 seconds, 5 minutes, and 15 minutes. You may chose the one that suits the best for your VM workload and its preferred RPO.

- **Tertiary site replication**: This improvement was pretty much in demand after the first offering of Hyper-V replica, as it was designed to retain the replicas till the secondary site. Windows Server 2012 R2 offered extended replication to a third or tertiary site from the secondary site. However, the offered replication frequency are of only two time intervals — 5 minutes and 15 minutes. If you chose 15 as a replication frequency between first and second, it will be understood that you cannot choose 5 minutes as an interval between secondary and tertiary sites.

- **Better performance**: Hyper-V Replica has been tweaked to ensure better performance by checking on IOPS and storage resource requirements by its predecessor. Windows Server 2012 R2 implements the "undo-logs" architecture in Hyper-V Replica, which reduces the IOPS required by the replica server. There's one minor drawback; undo-logs cannot be directly exported or imported, unlike as we able to do in the previous version.

- **Hyper-V Recovery Manager/Azure Site Recovery**: Another one which caught the headlines. Hyper-V Recovery Manager or HRM was launched as an Azure service to automate, manage, and orchestrate the Hyper-V replica failover process between your primary and secondary sites (private cloud on VMM 2012 SP1 and R2). However, there was no provision to replicate the VM to the Azure cloud. Now, it is improved as Azure Site Recovery, which does more than just orchestrating failovers between on-premise sites. You can now host and failover to your replica VMs in Azure via VMM 2012 R2 providers.

The working of Hyper-V Replica

So far, we learned a bit regarding the knowhow of the features. Before we jump on the setup and configuration, let's look under the hood and see how the replication tracking and changes are parsed and passed on to the replication partner on the DR site. In architecture, the following are the prime components:

- **Replication engine**: The running force for the vehicle, the replication engine, is responsible for maintaining the replication configuration details and ensuring initial replication and sync and thereafter, the delta changes and test-failover and failover operations. It ensures that there's no corruption arising due to VM mobility actions, and tracks and interrupts the replication process during the mobility event.

- **Change tracking**: The module is responsible for tracking changes on VHD for the VMs that are tagged for replication. The mechanism tracks the write operations on the VHD, and then generates the **Hyper-V Replication Log (HRL)** files. It updates the changes with the replication engine. The module works agnostic of the underlying storage technology in use for the VM.

- **Network module**: As the name indicates, the module provides a network traffic channel between the primary and secondary sites, and ensures data compression for a better network bandwidth utilization. The network transmissions use either HTTP or HTTPS protocol, and provide support for certificate based authentication and optional encryption.

We will briefly review the replication process for the Hyper-V Replica. It will make sense once you know the components and their roles in the entire scheme of things:

1. First, configure the replica host for inward replication. The configuration will require you to flag the authentication mechanism to be Kerberos-based (Active Directory) or certificate authentication.

2. On the primary server, enable replication on the required virtual machines. You may choose to exclude virtual disks on the guest machines.

3. Now, the replication engine kicks in, and performs the initial replication. Then, it creates a replica VM. Once the standby VM is created, the change tracking module takes over and starts tracking changes.

4. The change tracking module follows its routine and tracks write operations on the VHD and generates an HRL. As per the defined replication frequency interval (30 seconds, 5 minutes, or 15 minutes), the older HRL is flushed to the replication engine, and then a new one gets created.

5. Replication engine will pass on the old HRL in reverse order to the replica host to ensure that they append the latest writes. The transmission is sent in compressed form.

6. The VMs are replicas of the originals and stay in a turned-off state, unless invoked via a failover.

7. A test failover can be performed to ensure that it works as expected by the disaster recovery planning (DRP). Planned failover and failovers are performed in the event of a major contingency and reverse failover, back to the primary site/server, is invoked once the situation is averted.

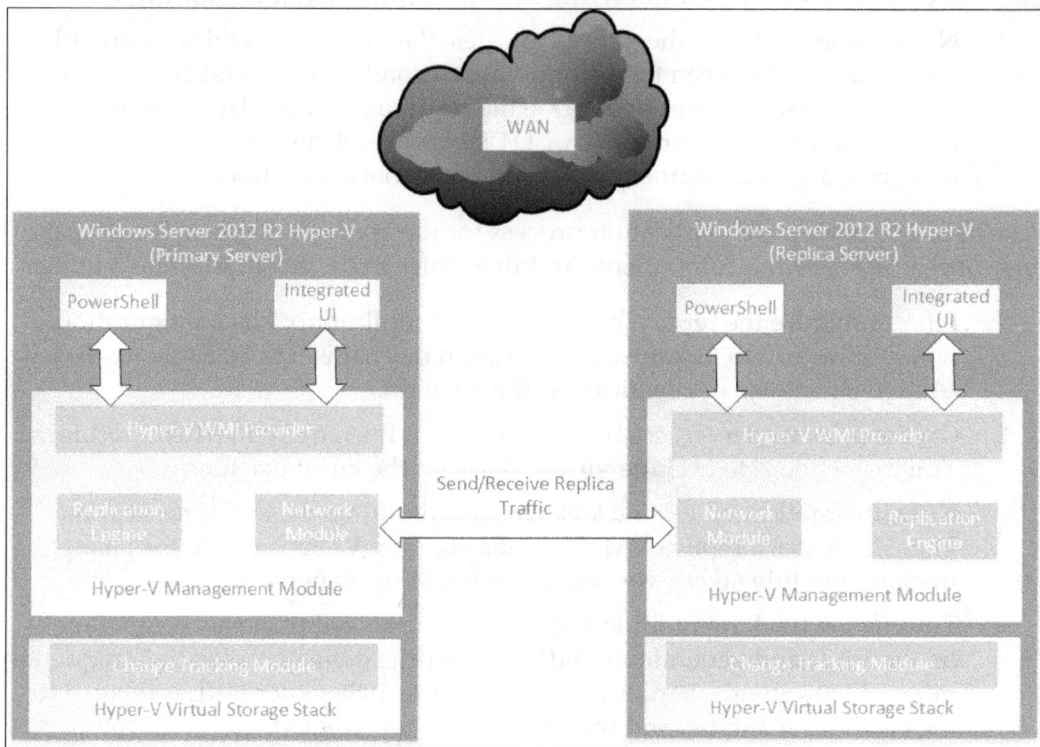

Figure 8-1: Hyper-V Replica Process Flow

Hyper-V Replica setup and configuration

In the following sections, we will review the process and requirements to setup Hyper-V Replica for independent hosts and failover clusters. We will also briefly look at the steps required to extend the replication to a tertiary site. There can be various replication scenarios depending largely on how your Hyper-V hosts are setup and placed, whether they are in failover cluster or independent hosts, and if they are in the same or different domain, or even in a workgroup. All these aspects add up as design elements to your disaster recovery plan. It is now time to begin the process of setting up your first replica. However, just prior to this, you need to understand basic prerequisites of the implementation.

Hyper-V Replica terms and their significance

It is always in your best interests to understand the native language before you tread into a country. Hyper-V Replica has a lingo that is quite legible. You will be able to pick up the terms when you start to configure the feature. To name a few, as indicated by Microsoft:

- **Recovery Time Objective (RTO)**: This is another expression for **Service Level Agreement (SLA)**. The term is used to refer to the duration of time within which a business is restored post a major contingency, or in other words, how much downtime you can bear for a system without it impacting on your business?

- **Recovery Point Objective (RPO)**: This is used to quantify your data recovery and loss, and is used to indicate the amount of data loss acceptable in the event of a downtime.

- **Primary server**: This term is used to refer to the Hyper-V hosts or cluster, hosting the protected virtual machines.

- **Replica server**: This term is used to refer to the Hyper-V hosts or cluster, hosting the replica or copied virtual machines.

- **Standard copy/replica**: This is a crash-consistent copy of a protected virtual machine.

- **Application-consistent copy/replica**: This is a thorough process but provides an application transactional recovery, and requires VSS enabled writers.

- **Test failover**: As the term indicates, this is a test sequence to ensure that the replica VM/VMs are working as expected.

- **Planned failover**: This is a manual intervention event where the administrator will initiate a planned failover under some requirement to bring the replica site or VM online gracefully.

- **Failover**: This is an unplanned event, in the event of a major contingency, when the replica site or VM are brought online.

Hyper-V Replica prerequisites

As a subset of the Hyper-V role, most of the requirements for setting up a replica are already met when you prepare a host for setting up an independent Hyper-V server, or a part of a Hyper-V failover cluster. The requirements are consistent on both primary and replica servers. And some of them are as follows:

- Windows Server 2012 or Windows Server 2012 R2 with Hyper-V role enabled or Hyper-V Server 2012 or Hyper-V Server 2012 R2 on Hyper-V capable hardware

- Ensure you have ample storage available on both sides

- There should be suitable network connectivity and considerable bandwidth for failover operations, and do not forget the firewall rules to pass through the desired network communications

- Servers should be a part of the same Active Directory domain, or should be employing a certificate for SSL authentication and encryption of traffic

Hyper-V Replica capacity planner

One of the aspects of prerequisite verification is to ensure that adequate resources are available to deploy a particular role or feature. Resources in all four areas are — compute, storage/IOPS, memory, and network bandwidth. Microsoft offers a free tool to assist you with the maths, referred to as **capacity planner** for Hyper-V Replica. The results may not be exact but will help you build an estimate, based on the VM that you intend to protect.

> You can download the capacity planner for Hyper-V Replica from https://www.microsoft.com/en-us/download/details.aspx?id=39057.

There are some gotchas before you set sail with this one — one being that you can have multiple independent primary hosts to monitor in one monitoring instance. But you cannot merge independent hosts, and then cluster them under a monitoring cycle. Also, for every cluster, there has to be a separate cycle. Hosts running different releases of Windows Server 2012, namely the initial release and R2, should be monitored separately.

Let's review the steps and learn how to use the utility:

1. Locate the HVRCapacityPlanner.exe utility. Select and right-click on it and opt for **Run as Administrator**.

2. Now, launch the wizard for the capacity planner for Hyper-V Replica. On the **License Terms** screen, select the radio button **I accept the license terms** and click on **Next**.

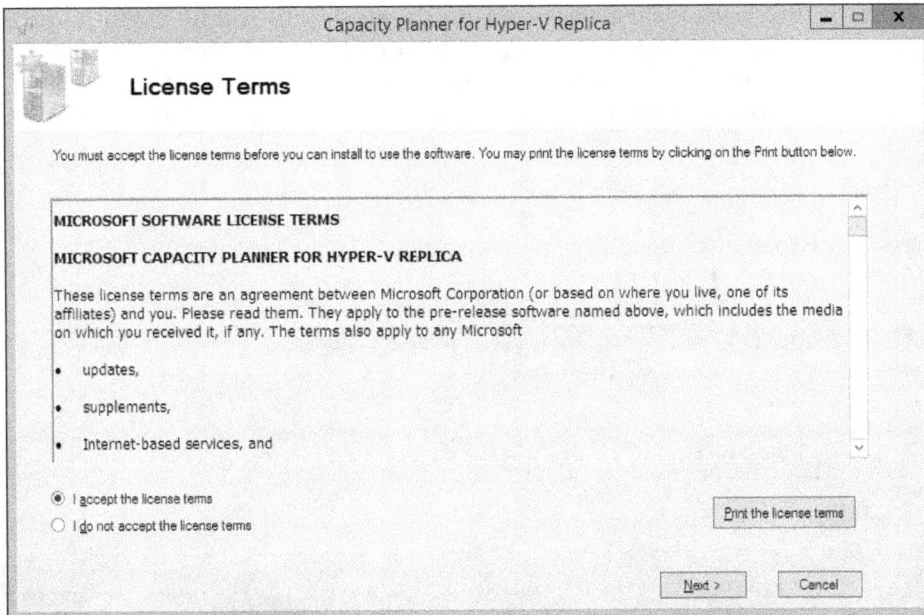

Figure 8-2: The HVR Capacity Planner – License Terms

3. On the first screen of **Before you Begin**, specify the duration that you wish to measure the resource utilization. Click on **Next**.

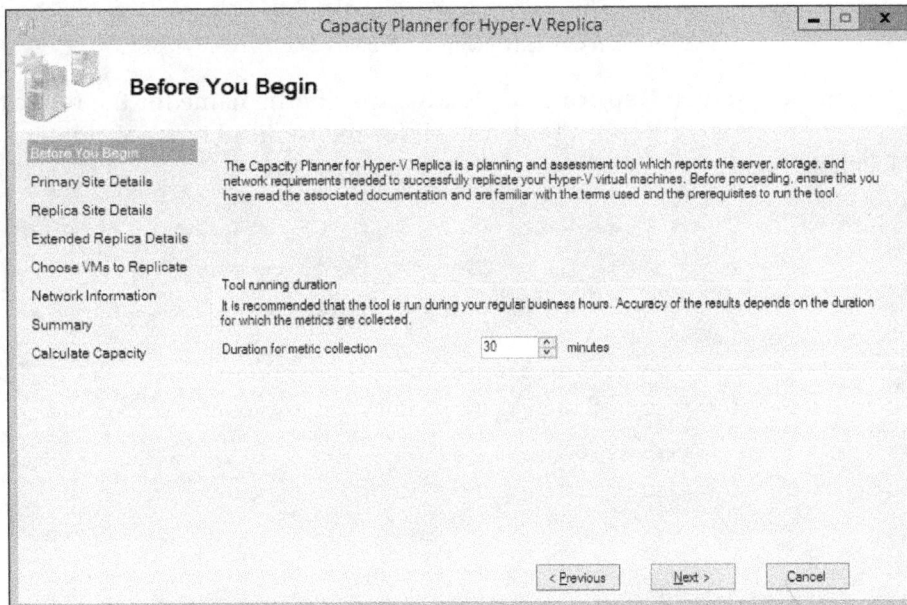

Figure 8-3: HVR Capacity Planner – Metric Collection

4. On the next screen **Primary Site Details**, specify the name for the source server or Hyper-V Replica broker CAP for the source Hyper-V cluster (we will discuss the HVR in a later section of this chapter). Click on **Add**. Once the host name or the HVR broker name gets populated, click on **Next**.

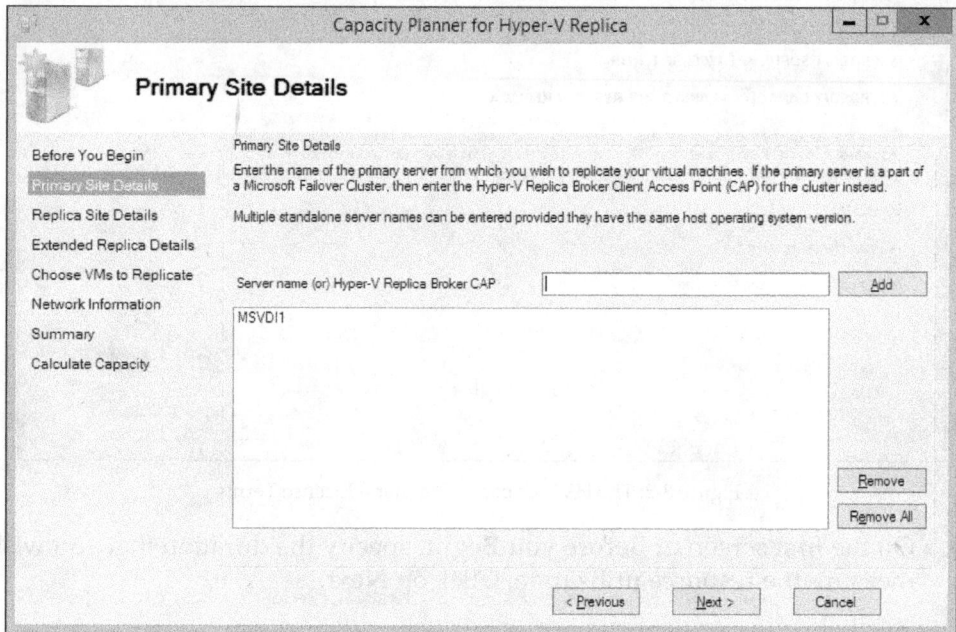

Figure 8-4: The HVR Capacity Planner – Primary Site/Server Details

5. On the next screen **Replica Site Details**, specify the name for the replica server or Hyper-V Replica broker CAP for the replica Hyper-V cluster. Click on **Next**.

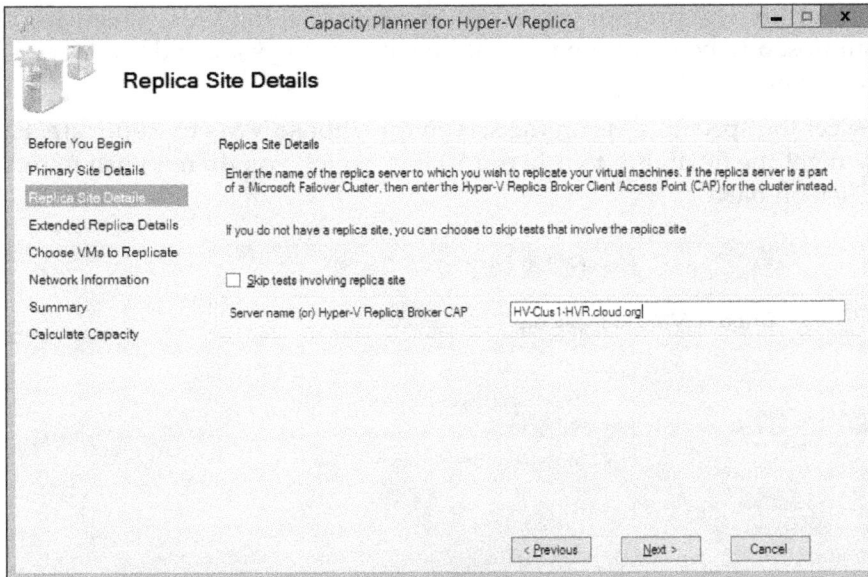

Figure 8-5: HVR Capacity Planner – Replica Site/Server Details

6. On the next screen **Extended Replica Details**, specify the name for the replica server or Hyper-V Replica broker CAP for the Replica Hyper-V cluster hosted on the tertiary site. Click on **Next**.

You may also choose to skip this test if you do not have a third site.

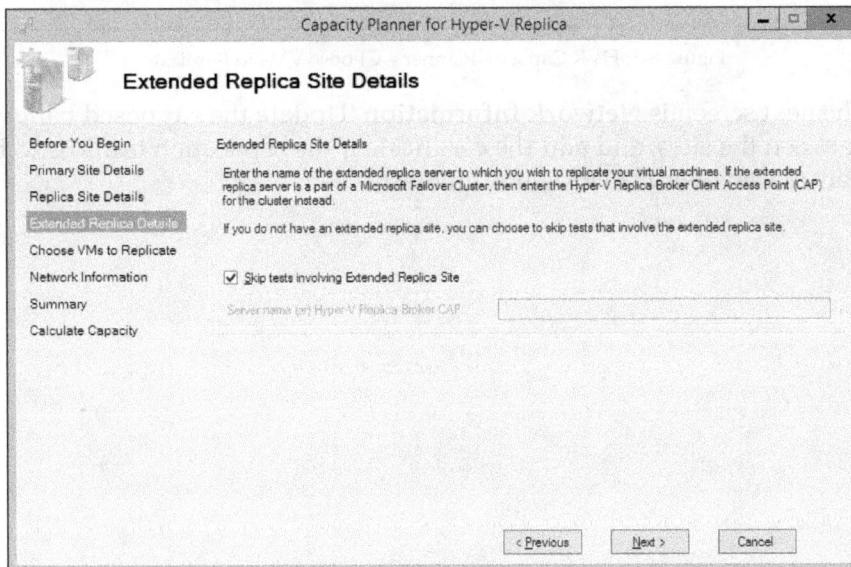

Figure 8-6: HVR Capacity Planner – Extended Replica Site/Server Details

7. The utility will prompt you with a message that the VMs, which are supposed to be monitored, should be in running state and not tagged for replication as of yet.

8. Select the specific VMs on the screen for **Choose VMs to Replicate**. Here, you get the flexibility to rule out VHDs, which you do not wish to replicate. Click on **Next**.

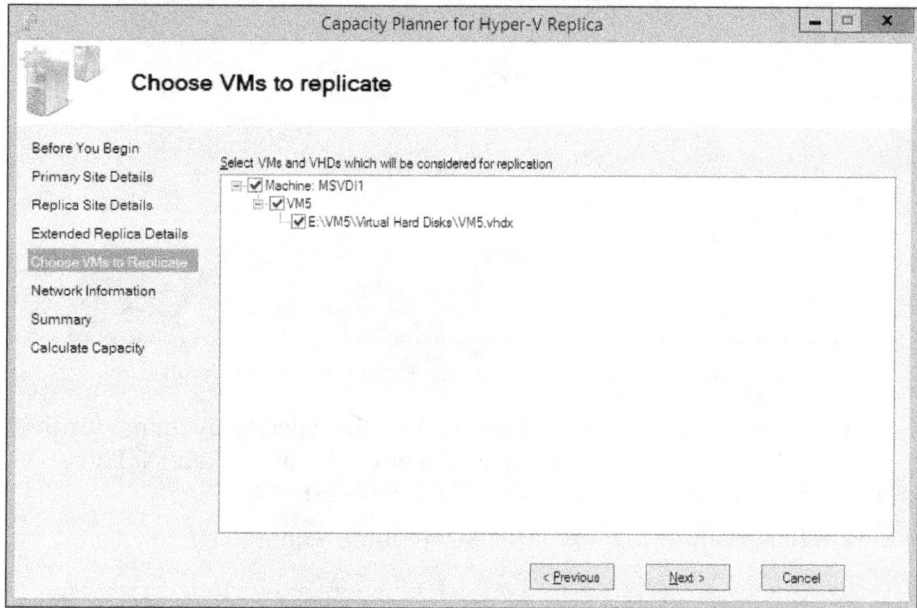

Figure 8-7: HVR Capacity Planner – Choose VMs to Replicate

9. The next screen is **Network Information**. Update the supposed bandwidth between the sites, and add the certificate if the replication traffic is to be transmitted over HTTPS. Click on **Next**.

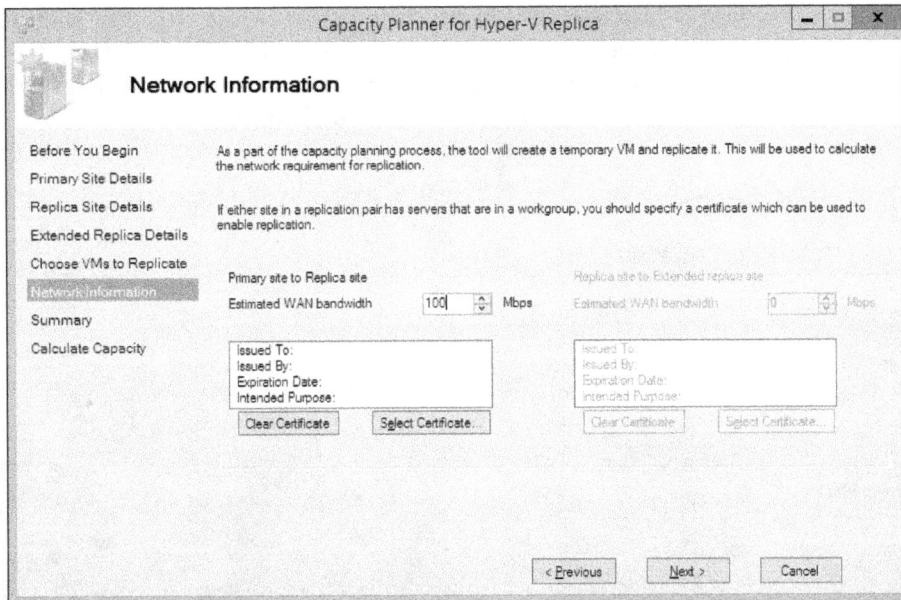

Figure 8-8: HVR Capacity Planner – Network Information

10. The penultimate screen is **Summary** of the selected parameters for you to review. If you intend to make any changes, you may go to the previous screens and update, else click on **Next**.

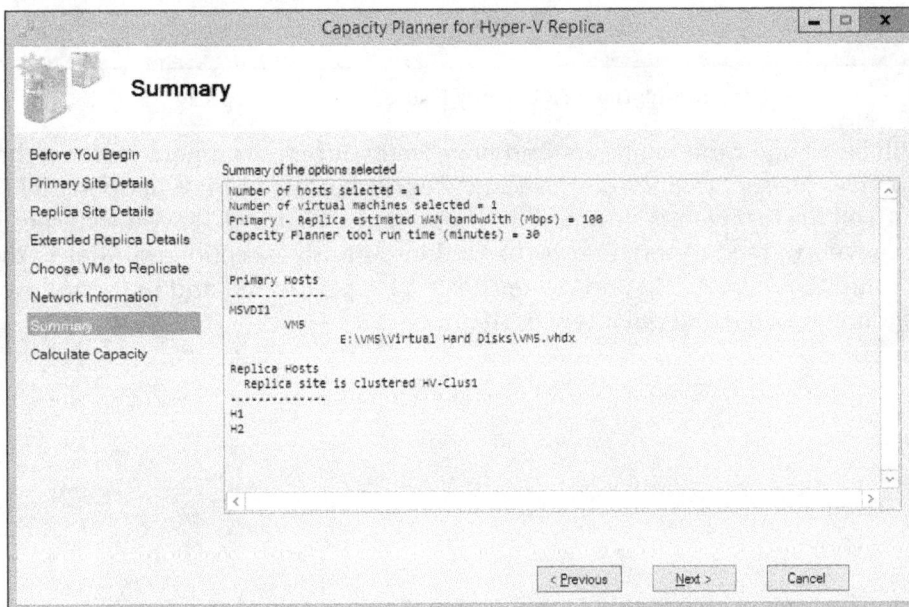

Figure 8-9: The HVR Capacity Planner – Summary

11. The next screen is **Calculate Capacity**. The utility, as per the parameters provided, runs a battery of tests against all the entities involved, and generates a success or failure report. You may choose to view the report for more information. Click on **Exit** to close the utility.

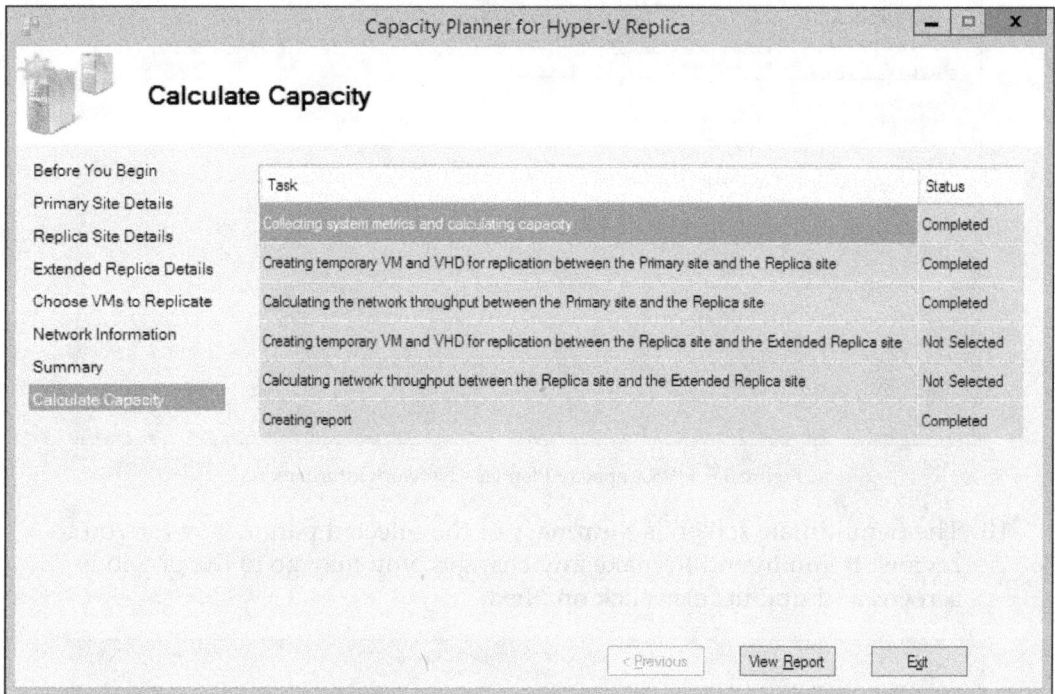

Figure 8-10: The HVR Capacity Planner – Calculate Capacity

Now will be a good time to understand how well your environment fared in the tests. To view the report, click on the **View Report** button and it will open an HTML page with all the test results dumped in. If you look at *figure 8-11*, you will see that it is a well-framed report, and is divided into multiple sections similar to the cluster validation report. There were multiple tests performed and in the following screenshot, you will make out a few of them:

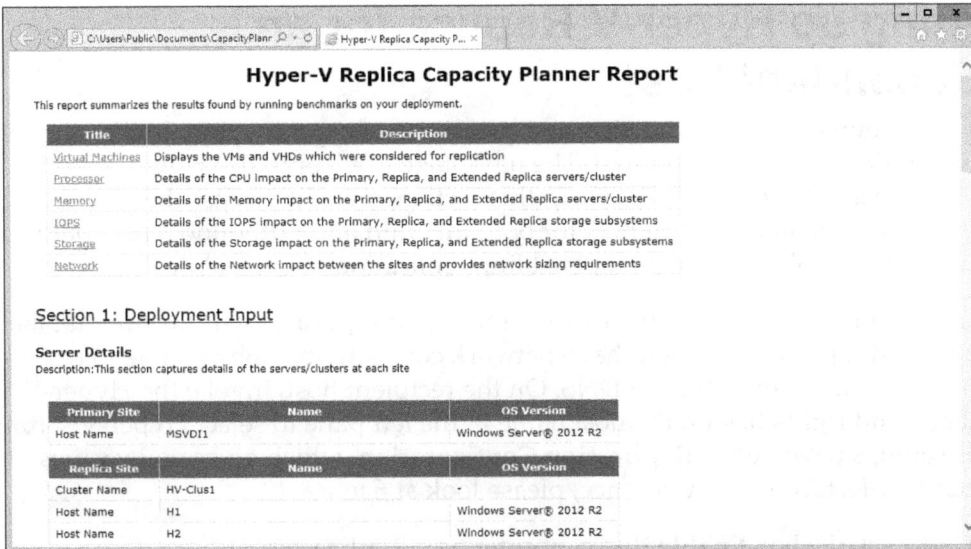

Figure 8-11: The HVR Capacity Planner Report

If you dig into the results, you will see two facets. One will be the resource utilization prior to enabling VM replication, and the second will be after testing VM replication against the set of available resources. The fields will show, as per the number of VMs that you intend to replicate, the expected spike in the resource utilization. For example, in the following screenshot, we see an over 3 percent of additional overhead for both processor and memory on both the primary source server and replica cluster. Likewise, you need to consider the test results for storage, network, and IOPS to ensure if the resources need to be bumped up accordingly, or whether you should leave them just as it is.

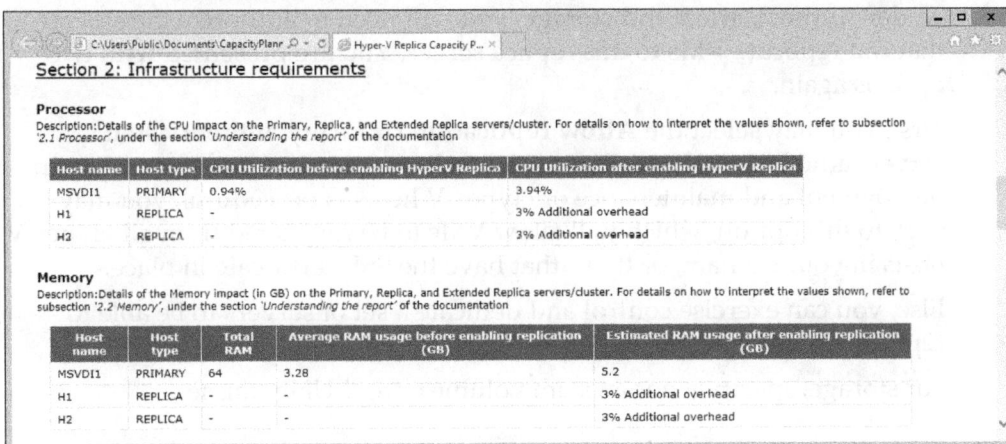

Figure 8-12: The HVR Capacity Planner Report – Processor and Memory Views

Setting up Hyper-V Replica for an independent host

We now understand the perquisites and principles of capacity planning for the setup of a Hyper-V Replica environment. The next stage is to configure Hyper-V Replica (HVR), Hyper-V hosts, and clusters. In this section, we will discuss the nitty-gritty of configuring an independent host for both inbound and outbound VM replication; and thereafter, look at the steps for enabling replication on virtual machines.

First, you will need to enable the recipient host as a replica server. Ensure that the primary and replica server both have network connectivity, and are able to resolve each other's names, or FQDN in DNS. On the recipient host, invoke the Hyper-V Manager, and right-click on the host name in the left pane to select Hyper-V settings. In the settings page, select **Replication Configuration**, which gives you various options to select from. For reference, please look at *figure 8-13*.

1. Check the box **Enable this computer as a Replica server**.

2. Under **Authentication and ports**, you will need to specify the protocol and the supposed port. For example, if you plan to replicate the VM between servers in the same forest or domain, and the link is secure, you may opt for Kerberos over HTTP at port 80. You may change the port. However, the traffic on the wire will not be encrypted.

   You may opt for certificate-based authentication if the servers are not in the same forest, or in case, the communication line is not secure. The second option uses SSL over HTTP (HTTPS) at port 443, and can be opted for even when the servers are in the same forest. You will need a X.509 v3 certificate to be imported for the purpose of authentication.

3. Under **Authorization and storage**, you will need to authorize the servers that can replicate VMs to this replica server. You are presented with two options again.

   First, you may select the **Allow replication from any authenticated server** radio button. If you have a controlled server environment wherein deployment and maintenance of Hyper-V hosts is procedural, you may stick to this option, which will allow VMs to be replicated from all Hyper-V hosts in your domain, or those that have the SSL certificate in place.

   Else, you can exercise control and dedicate a set of servers to be able to replicate to this specific Hyper-V Replica server.

   For storage, specify a non-system volume or an LUN volume.

4. Click on **OK** to save the settings.

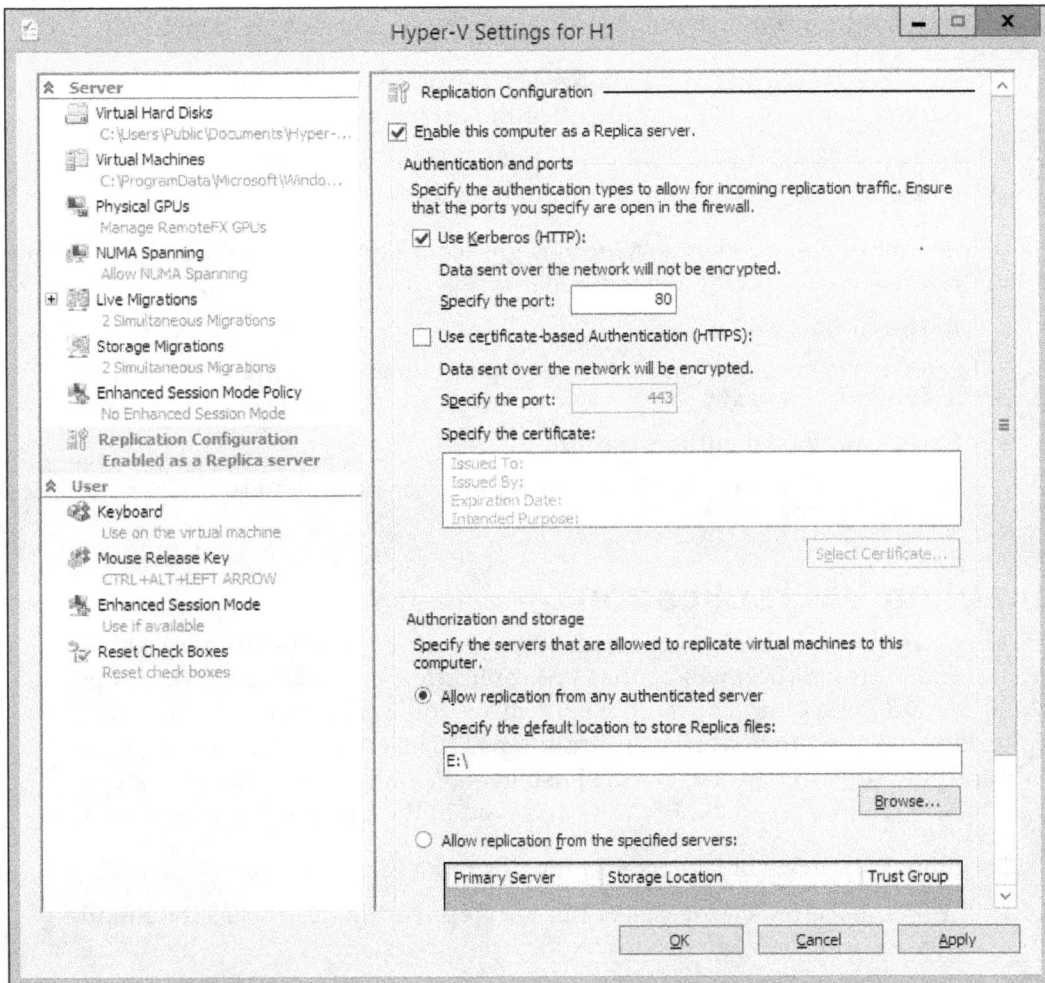

Figure 8-13: Hyper-V Settings – Replication Configuration for HVR

The next action will be to ensure that the communications are allowed over the firewall. There are two inbound rules to consider, and you will need to enable one of them, based on the authentication type that you have selected previously:

- **Hyper-V Replica HTTP Listener (TCP-In)**: Enable this rule if you intend to use the Kerberos/HTTP authentication on the replica server

- **Hyper-V Replica HTTPS Listener (TCP-In)**: Enable this rule if you plan to use the SSL/HTTPS authentication on the replica server.

The same can be enabled via the Windows Firewall with **Advanced Security** console, or you may use the following PowerShell tips.

- **Kerberos authentication**:

```
Enable-NetFirewallRule -DisplayName "Hyper-V Replica HTTP
Listener (TCP-In)"
```

- **Certificate-based authentication**:

```
Enable-NetFirewallRule -DisplayName "Hyper-V Replica HTTPS
Listener (TCP-In)"
```

Enabling VM replication

The next stage is to enable replication on the desired VM on the primary server. An important observation will be that VM replication has to be enabled on a per VM basis, and you get more granular control, as you get to select which VHD to replicate as well. In other words, replication has to be enabled separately on all VMs and cannot be generalized at the host level. We will now look at the steps to do this, and explain some intricacies involved in the process:

1. From Hyper-V Manager, select the desired VM.

2. From the **Actions** pane, select **Enable Replication**. It invokes the **Enable Replication for VM6** wizard.

3. On the **Before you Begin** screen, click on **Next**.

4. On the screen **Specify Replica Server**, update the replica host name or FQDN, as shown in the *figure 8-14*, and click on **Next**.

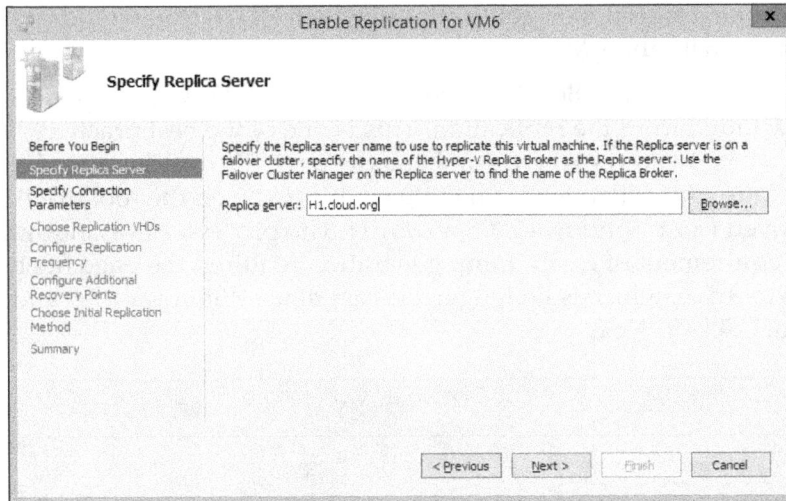

Figure 8-14: Enable Replication – Specify Replica Server

5. On the next screen, **Specify Connection Parameters,** select the authentication protocol and port as per your environment preference and click on **Next**. Please check the checkbox for **Compress the data that is transmitted over the network**. The field is self-explanatory, indicating the lesser load on your network when you enable data compression. Then, there is a trade-off between data compression, and decompression that puts the CPU load on the Hyper-V hosts. The decision will be based on your infrastructural requirements.

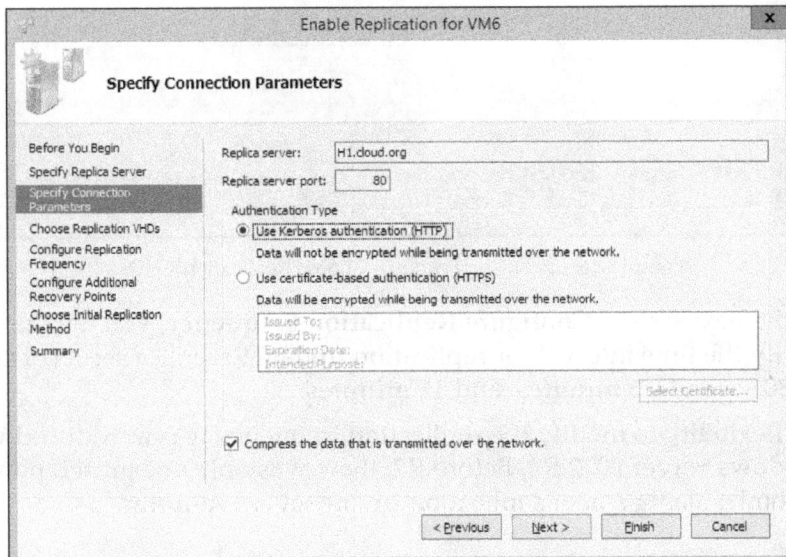

Figure 8-15: Enable Replication – Specify Connection Parameters

6. On the next screen, you get to choose which VHDs you would prefer to replicate with the VM.

As per the Hyper-V Best Practices Analyzer, VHDs with page files should be excluded from the replication. This is one of the best practices being followed nowadays where you keep the page file on a separate VHD. This is because the dependence on the page file, to be on the root drive, has been removed from Windows 2008 onwards. The processor in Windows 2003 for the requirement of crash dump generation required the page file to be on the system drive, which is no longer the case since Windows 2008 and Windows Vista. Click on **Next**.

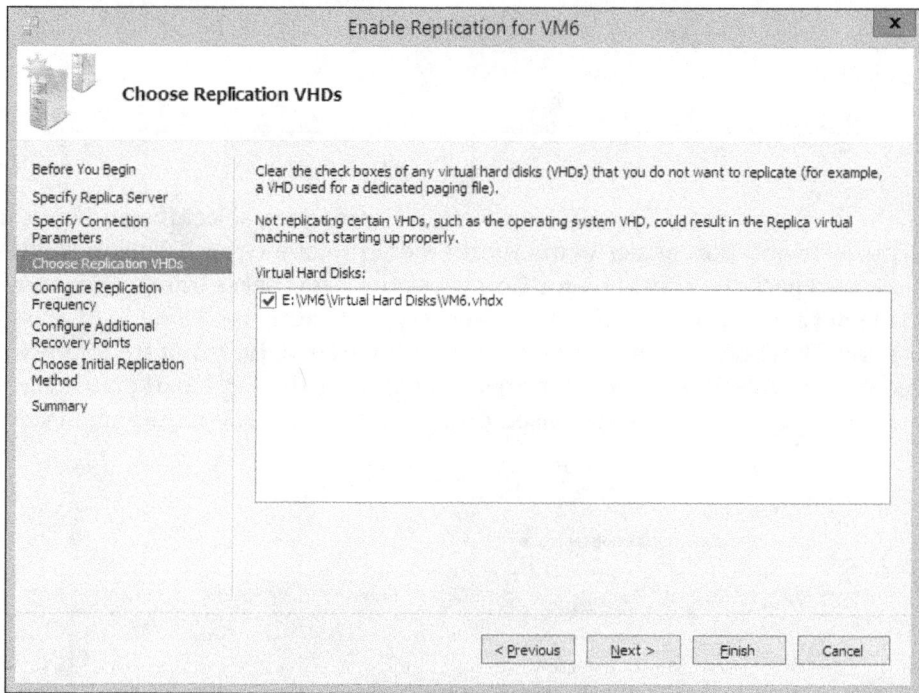

Figure 8-16: Enable Replication – Choose Replication VHDs

7. On the next screen, **Configure Replication Frequency**, you will have to specify the time interval for replication update to replica server. The options are **30 seconds**, **5 minutes**, and **15 minutes**.

The flexibility to modify the replication frequency was introduced with Windows Server 2012 R2. Before R2, there was only one preset, non-customizable figure for replication frequency — **5 minutes**.

Select **30 seconds** and click on **Next**.

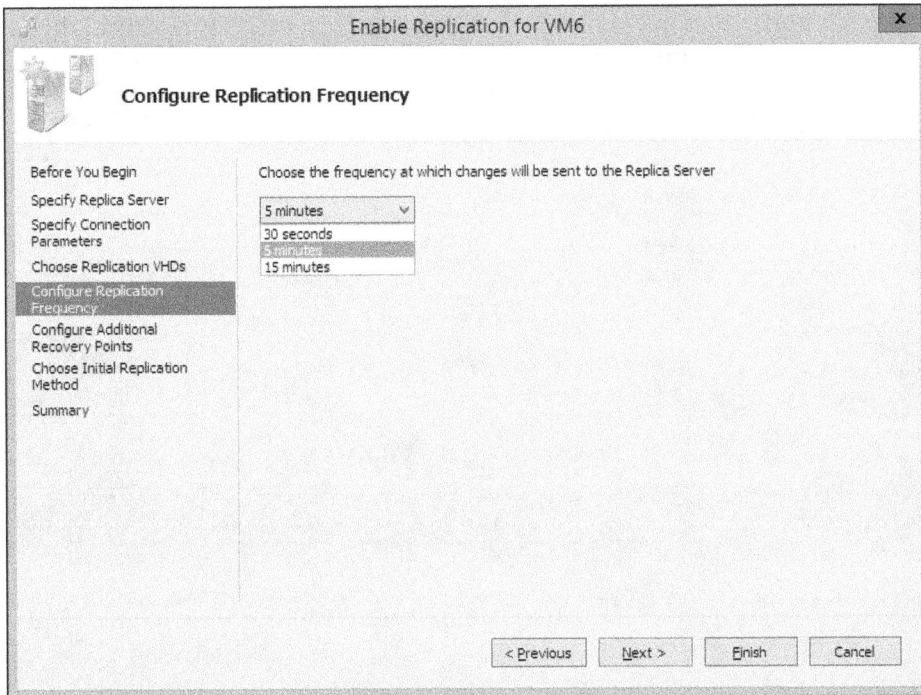

Figure 8-17: Enable Replication – Configure Replication Frequency

8. The next screen **Configure Additional Recovery Points** is an important configuration setting. The first option is to set the latest recovery point (read one), which does not maintain any historical recovery points. If you wish to go in more depth and enable options to roll back in time, you can select the second option, and create additional hourly recovery points. This enables checkpoints to be created for the VM, and provides you with the flexibility to pick a specific restore point out of the available list.

Also, you can enable VSS to capture application-consistent data, and perform incremental data quiescing, as per the specified frequency. In the *figure 8-18*, we have specified to capture incremental data every 2 hours. Select the desired options and click on **Next**.

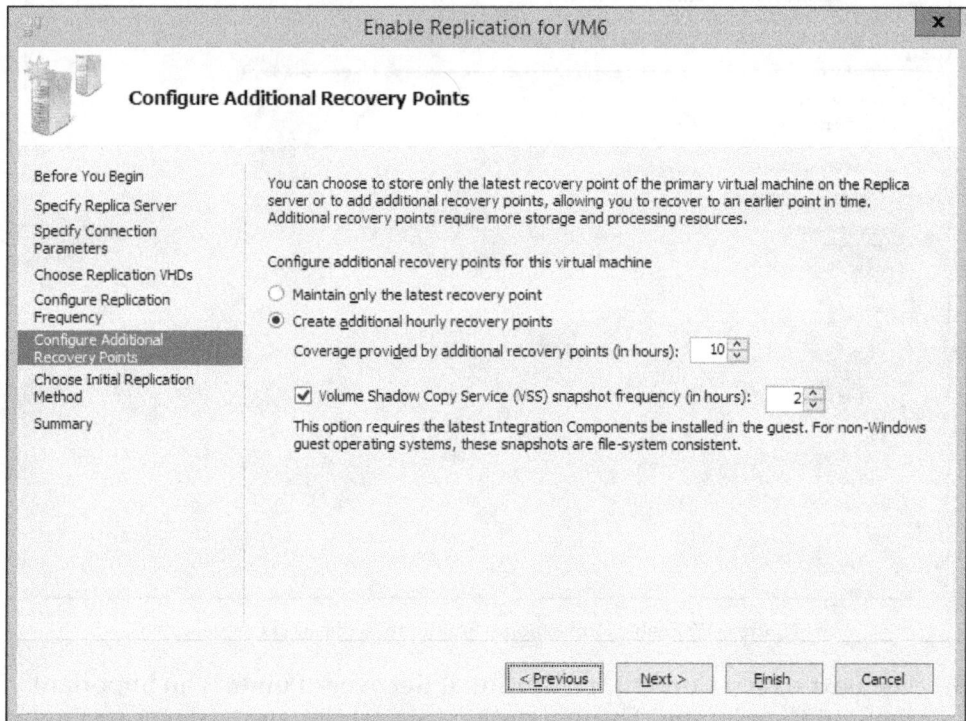

Figure 8-18: Enable Replication – Configure Additional Recovery Points

9. Another important configuration screen is **Choose Initial Replication Method**. When enabling replication for a VM, you are presented with three options:

    ° **Send initial copy over the network**: This amounts to sending the VM data that is to be sent over the network wire, and has a bill for bandwidth utilization

    ° **Send initial copy using external media**: This can be used to prestage replication data over a media, and sent to the replica server for extraction and import

    ° **Use an existing virtual machine on the Replica server as the initial copy**: This can be an older VM that is extracted from a backup or a previously replicated VM, and may be in a disabled state

On the same screen, you get the option as to whether to invoke the replication immediately or at a later schedule, preferably during the off-business hours.

Select the first option from both settings, and click on **Next**.

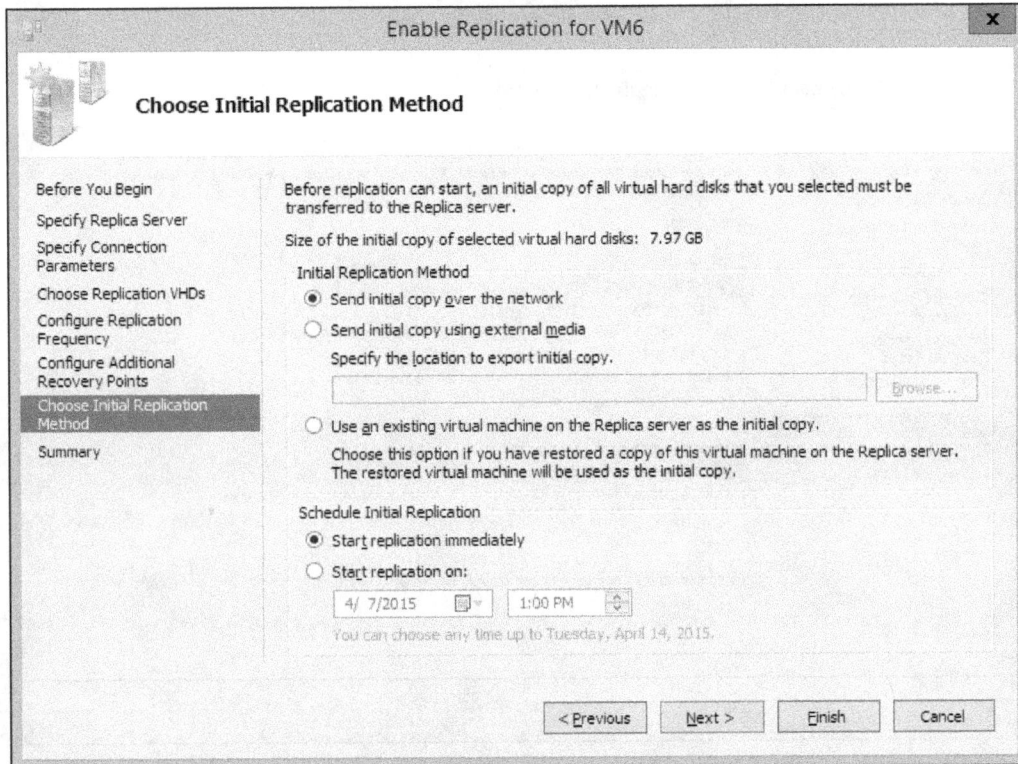

Figure 8-19: Enable Replication – Choose Initial Replication Method

10. The last screen is **Summary** for you to review and consent with your settings. Click on **Finish** and the replication will be enabled for the VM on the replica server.

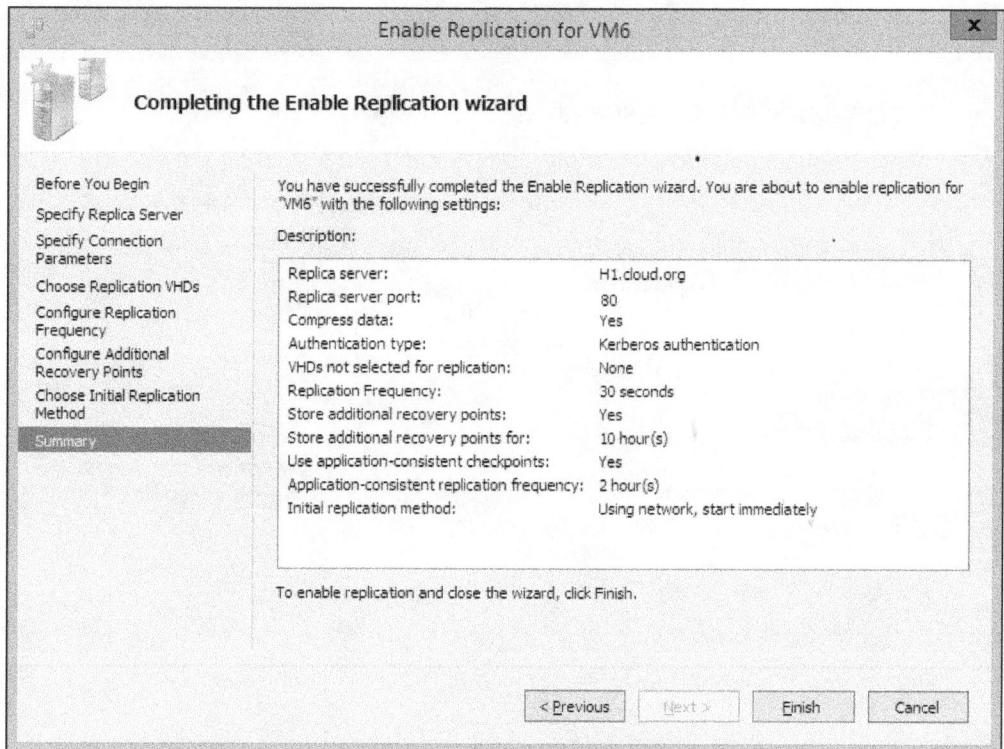

Figure 8-20: Enable Replication – Summary

The previous exercise can be done via PowerShell in the following way:

```
Enable-VMReplication -VMName VM6 -ReplicaServerName "HV-Clus1-
HVR.cloud.org" -ReplicaServerPort 80 -AuthenticationType Kerberos
-RecoveryHistory 10 -VSSSnapshotFrequency 2 -ExcludedVhdPath
"E:\VM6\Virtual Hard Disks\VM6-Pagefile.vhdx"

Start-VMInitialReplication -VMName VM6
```

One important aspect to consider when enabling VM replication is to check on the IP address handoff on the replica site. There will be a difference of IP ranges and VLANs at two sites, and when planning a DR design, this ought to be worked out. This is done so that post the failover, the VM does not lose network connectivity, and users still have access to it. The IP settings have to be supplied at the primary server, as depicted in *figure 8-21*.

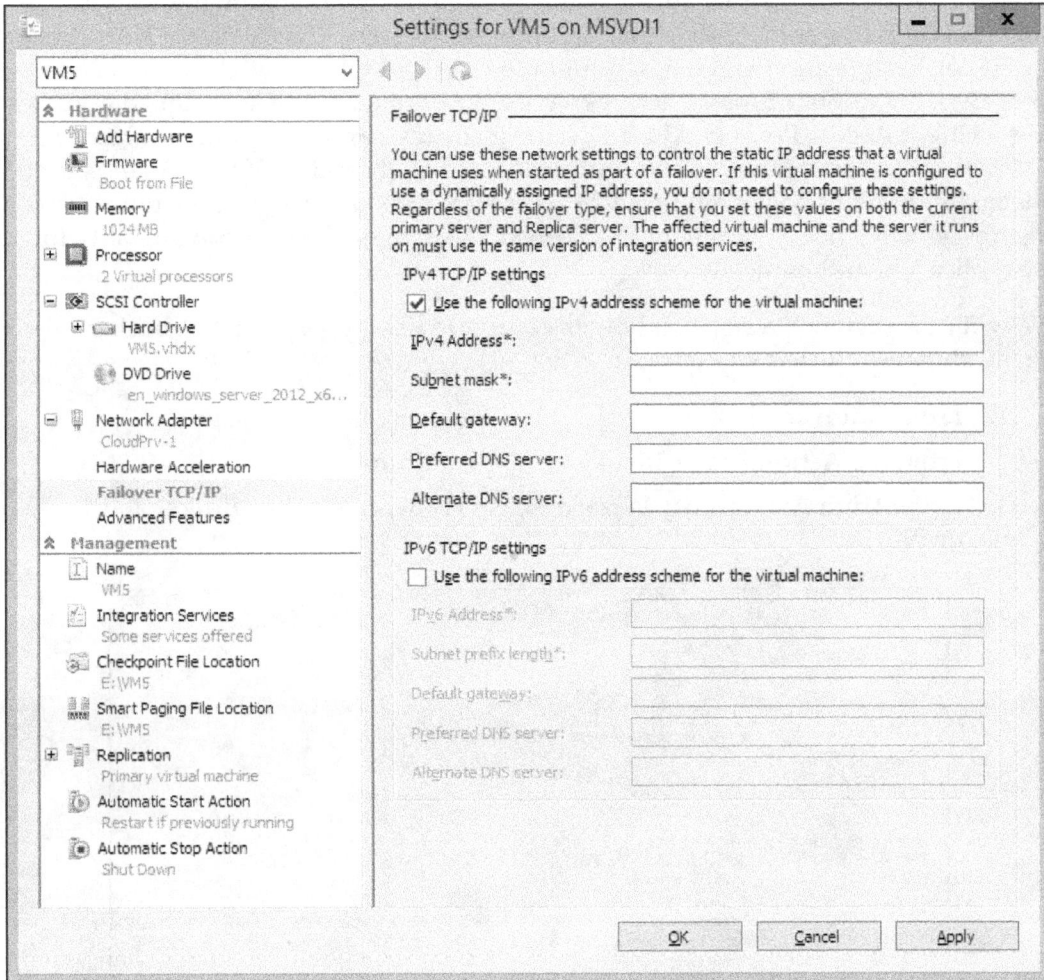

Figure 8-21: Enable Replication – Summary

Setting up Hyper-V Replica for a Hyper-V failover cluster

Let's add a layer of high availability to your Hyper-V setup, and see what else can be required to achieve VM replication. In contrast to when hosting a VM on an independent host, the VM(s) ownership is distributed across multiple nodes in the cluster. Due to some maintenance schedule or manual intervention, the VMs can be migrated from one node to the other. In order to track the VM location on the cluster for Hyper-V replication tagging, we ought to create a highly available role referred to as Hyper-V Replica Broker. A Hyper-V Replica Broker role gets assigned a VCO in AD, a **Client Access Point (CAP)**, a DNS host address, and an IP address. Hence for VM replication, both inwards and outwards, the FQDN and IP of the broker is used. The broker role not only simplifies VM access for outbound replication, but it also ensures effective node placement of a replica VM, and enables high availability for the replica VM automatically.

We will now review the steps on how to configure the Hyper-V replica broker role on the Hyper-V cluster.

1. From **Failover Cluster** console, select the name of your cluster.

2. From the **Actions** pane, invoke **Configure Roles**.

3. In the **High Availability Wizard**, select **Hyper-V Replica Broker**. Click on **Next**.

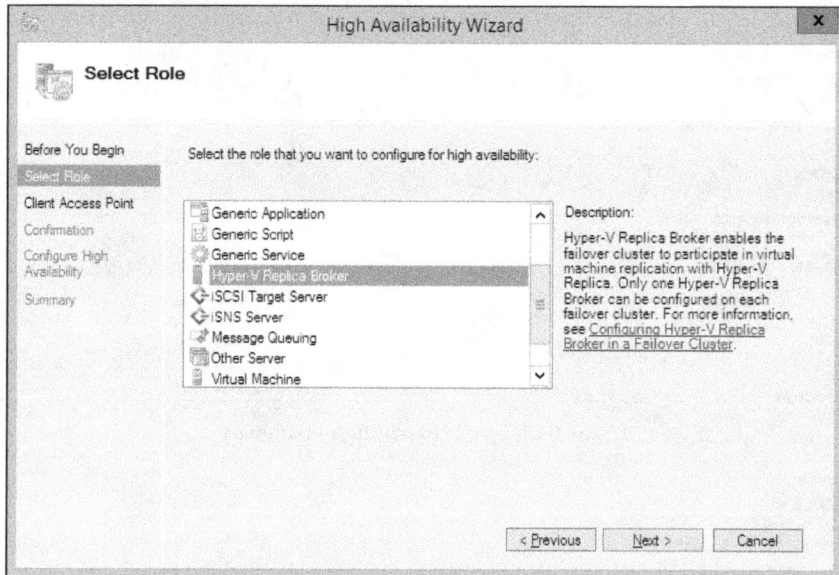

Figure 8-22: Hyper-V Replica Broker – Configure Role

4. On the **Client Access Point** screen, update the client access point and specify the IP address. Click on **Next**.

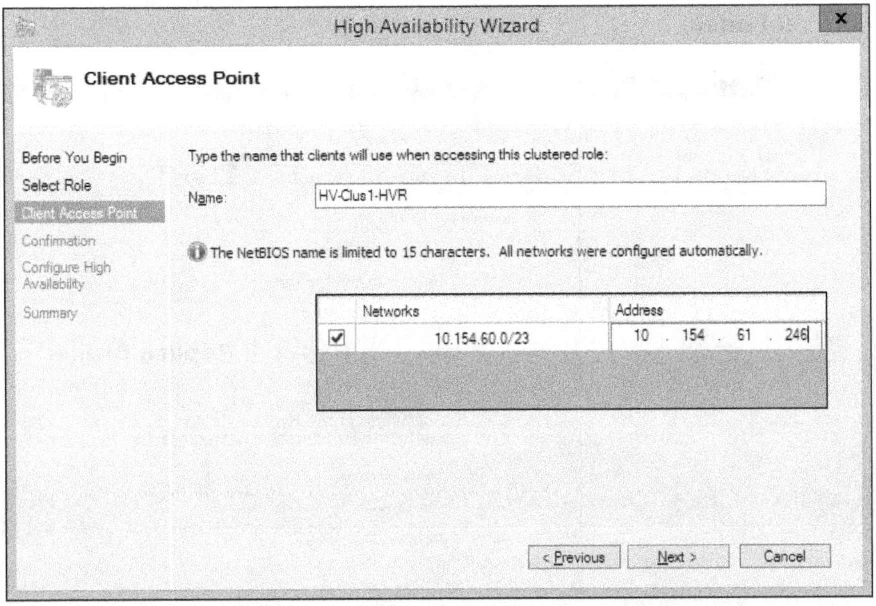

Figure 8-23: Hyper-V Replica Broker – Specify CAP

5. On the **Confirmation** screen, review the parameters and click on **Next**.

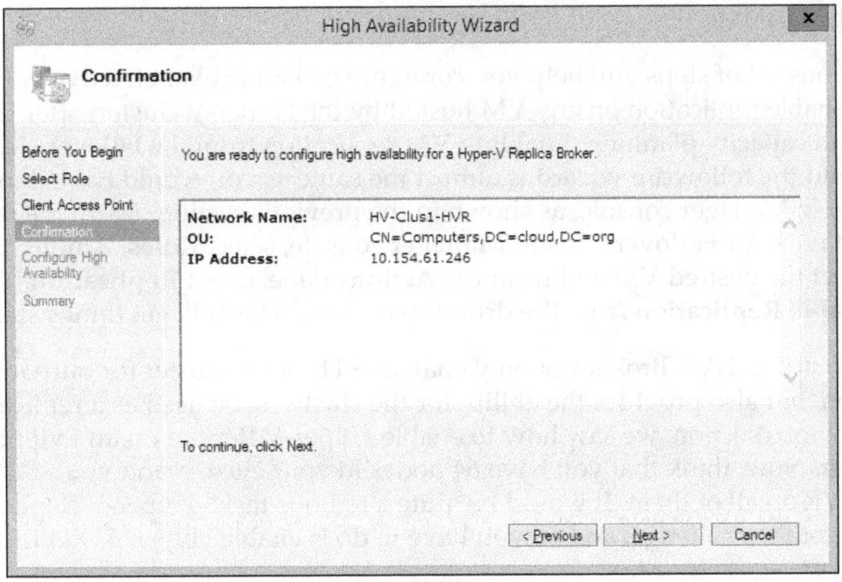

Figure 8-24: Hyper-V Replica Broker – Confirm Role

6. The next screen configures the role for high availability, and then prompts you with the **Summary** screen with success, warning, or a failure message. For more details, you can click on **View Report....** On the **Summary** screen, click on **Finish**.

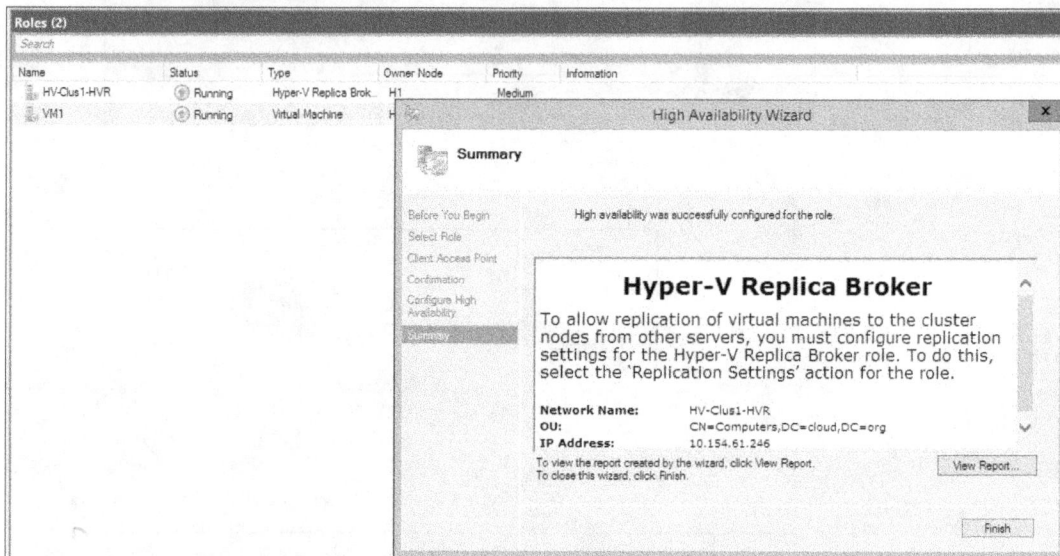

Figure 8-25: Hyper-V Replica Broker – Role Summary

7. The **Hyper-V Replica Broker** role will now be listed as a HA role alongside the HAVMs.

The previous set of steps will help you configure a HVR Broker effectively. Post this, you can enable replication on any VM hosted by the Hyper-V cluster, after thorough testing and capacity planning. Enabling VM replication from the failover cluster console and the follow-up wizard is almost the same as you would have done via the Hyper-V Manager console, as shown in the previous section. To do the needful, in the left pane for **Failover Cluster Manager** console, select **Roles**. Among the listed VMs, select the desired VM and from the **Actions** pane, select **Replication**. Then, select **Enable Replication** from the dropdown menu. This will get things started.

As stated earlier, HVR Broker not only enables a Hyper-V cluster for outbound VM replication, but also provides the ability for the cluster to be used as a replica server. In the previous section, we saw how to enable Hyper-V Replica on an independent single host. Now, think that you have 64 nodes in your cluster, and you will need to enable HVR on all of them. It would be quite a tedious task!. Hyper-V Replica Broker takes care of the challenge, and all you have to do is enable Hyper- V Replica on the HVR Broker.

To accomplish this, the steps are as follows:

1. In the left pane of **Failover Cluster Manager** console, select **Roles**.

2. Select the **Hyper-V Replica Broker** role, and from the **Actions** pane, select **Replication Settings**.

3. The replication settings will be similar to the replication configuration in Hyper-V settings.

4. Enable the settings as desired, as we did for the Hyper-V host, in the previous section.

5. Under the **Authorization and storage**, you may choose to allow replication from any authenticated server in the domain, or a specific set of servers or HVR Brokers.

6. For the default location to store the replica files, update the suitable CSV on the cluster.

7. Ensure that firewall inbound rules are enabled on all nodes. The same can be done via **Windows Firewall Advanced** settings, or through the small PowerShell script shared here.

   For Kerberos authorized replication, perform the following:

   ```
   Get-ClusterNode | ForEach-Object {Invoke-Command -
   ComputerName $_.Name -ScriptBlock {Enable-NetFirewallRule -
   DisplayName "Hyper-V Replica HTTP Listener (TCP-In)"}}
   ```

   For Certificate-based authentication replication, perform the following:

   ```
   Get-ClusterNode | ForEach-Object {Invoke-Command -
   ComputerName $_.Name -ScriptBlock {Enable-NetFirewallRule -
   DisplayName "Hyper-V Replica HTTPS Listener (TCP-In)"}}
   ```

8. You can now use the HVR Broker CAP FQDN to use a replica path from primary servers.

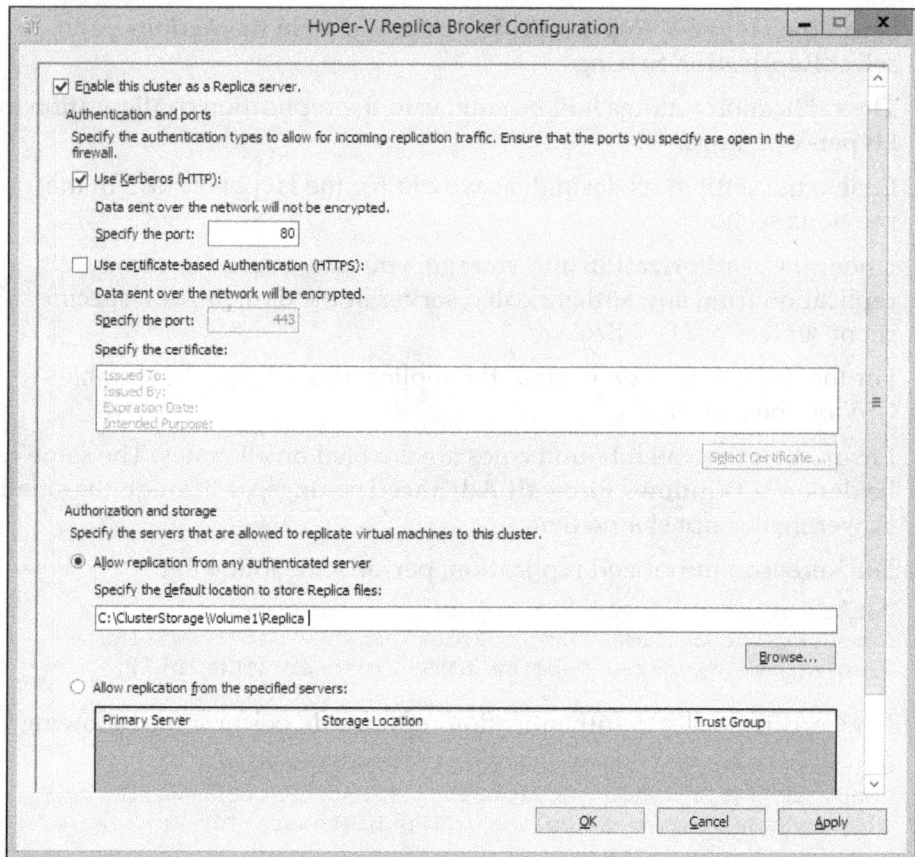

Figure 8-26: Hyper-V Replica Broker – Enabling cluster as a Replica server

Extending replication

This ability is a new addition to HVR, and pertains to Windows Server 2012 R2 Hyper-V and Hyper-V Server 2012 R2. The feature add-on enables enterprises to maintain yet another replica site in the scheme of things, which draws its replication feed from the secondary site. This site can be on-premise or off-premise in the cloud as per the BCP. This was an in-demand feature, post the introduction of Hyper-V Replica in Windows Server 2012. This allows for an additional layer of protection to your setup, and you can easily think of reasons to employ this. For example, you may keep the primary and secondary servers in the same site or data center, and keep the third in a remote site. It gives you more control on expediting the recovery actions, and yet have a standby copy safely being collected at its end.

Extending the replication for a guest machine is fairly simple. From the console of the replica server or broker, right-click on the VM and select **Replication**. In the follow-up dropdown menu, select **Extend Replication**, and then you will get prompted for **Extend Replication** wizard, as seen in the next screenshot. The wizard has the same screens for same parameters, as we discussed earlier. All you need to provide is a name for the replica server or HVR Broker.

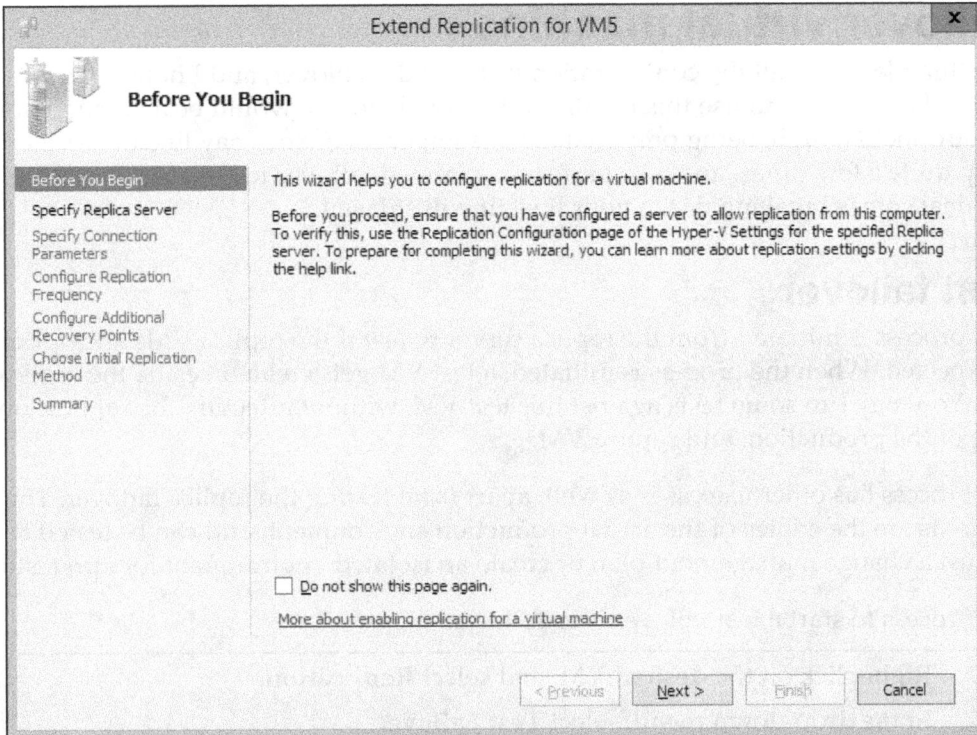

Figure 8-27: Extending Replication to third site

There are some points that you should bear in mind when you are deploying a tertiary site:

- The replication frequency for the tertiary site will be greater than what you would specify for the secondary replica site. For example, if you have opted for 30 seconds for primary-secondary, then you will have two options to select for secondary-tertiary — 5 or 15 minutes.

- If you have enabled application-consistent replicas, then the replication frequency doesn't change.

- You can change the initial replication method to keep a check on the bandwidth utilization.

The PowerShell tip (same as earlier, but this time from the secondary replica server) for this is as follows:

```
Enable-VMReplication -VMName VM6 -
ReplicaServerName"downsouth.cloud.org" -ReplicaServerPort 80 -
AuthenticationType Kerberos-ReplicationFrequencySec 300
```

Failover virtual machine

One thing left after all the configuration is to test the failover, and I hope that you will never have to use this feature. Why? Well, no one would be a game for a catastrophe! Though, being prepared for it is imperative. You may like to test the setup quite a few times, and also perform a planned failover to ensure when the real deal comes breaking down your boat, it will still sail.

Test failover

This process is initiated from the replica server to test if the replica VMs are working as expected. When the process is initiated, a test VM gets created beside the replica VM. You may run some tests against this test VM, without affecting the replication, state of the production, and replica VM.

The process has other use cases as well, apart from testing the replica failover. The test VMs are the copies of the actual production environment, and can be tested against a change management plan or create an isolated environment for app testing.

The process to start a test failover is as follows:

1. Right-click on the desired VM, and select **Replication**.
2. In the drop-down menu, select **Test Failover**.
3. If you see the multiple recovery points, select the one that you wish to load for the VM.

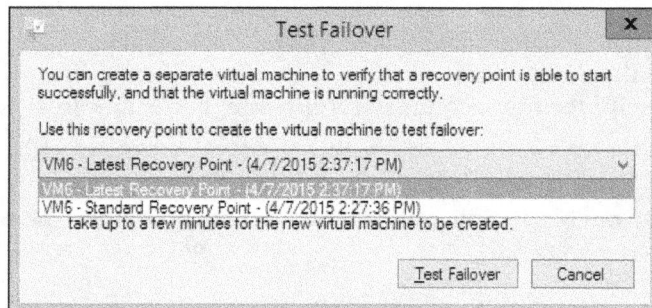

Figure 8-28: Test Failover – Select Recovery Point

4. In the console, you will now see a copy of the replica VM, created and appended with a suffix -Test.

5. Start the VM manually and perform your testing.

6. Once the testing is done, to perform the clean-up, right-click on the replica VM again, select **Replication**, and then from the drop-down, opt for **Stop Test Failover**.

7. Stop failover deletes the test replica VM without affecting any other entity in the replica setup.

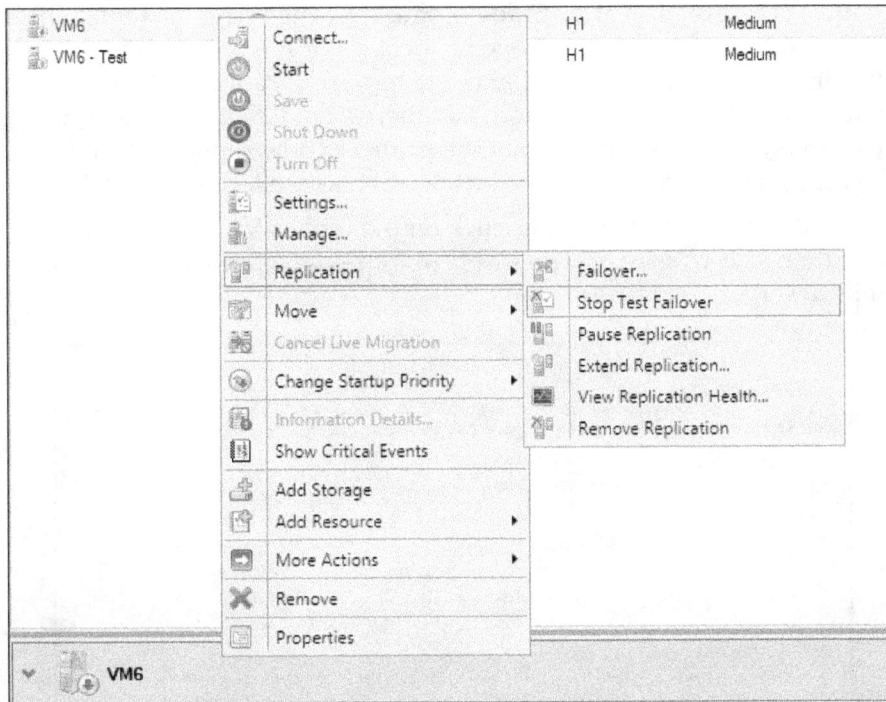

Figure 8-29: Test Failover – Stop the Test Failover event

Planned failover

Planned failover is a proactive action in the wake of a possible natural disaster warning or a power outage. Under the circumstances, you can decide to failover to the replica site to ensure the continuity of the business processes without any visible downtime. You may also perform the action in the event of any maintenance task, or even as a test failover to check the feasibility and sustenance of the setup. The planned failover procedure requires actions on both primary and replica servers.

The process for invoking this action is as follows:

1. On the primary server, right-click on the VM (Hyper-V Manager/Failover Cluster Manager) and select **Shut Down** or **Turn Off**. One of the prime prerequisites for planned failover is that the VM to be failed over should be turned off.

2. Right-click on it and select **Replication**.

3. Then, from the dropdown, menu click on **Planned Failover**.

4. In the **Planned Failover** applet, there are two checkboxes: **Reverse the replication direction after failover** and **Start the virtual machine after failover**. By default, the first one is unchecked. It is recommended to check the first checkbox to ensure that the reverse replication to the production VM, which will receive data, ensures that there's no data loss after the process. However, this also requires that the primary (now replica) should be configured to receive inward replication as well. Click on **Failover**.

5. Go to the replica server. Right-click on the replica VM, select **Replication**, and then select **Failover**. The VM now gets started and functions on the replica server.

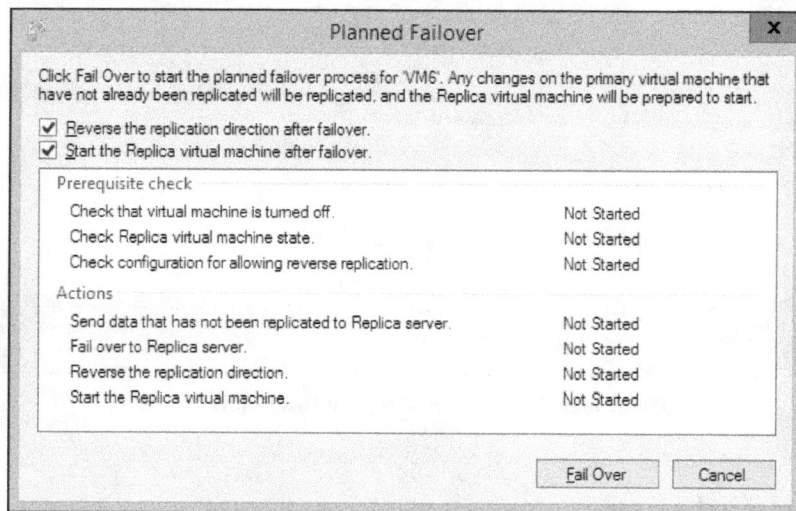

Figure 8-30: Planned Failover – Configuration

6. To bring the VM to the primary server, we need to repeat the previous actions from the replica server in the same order.

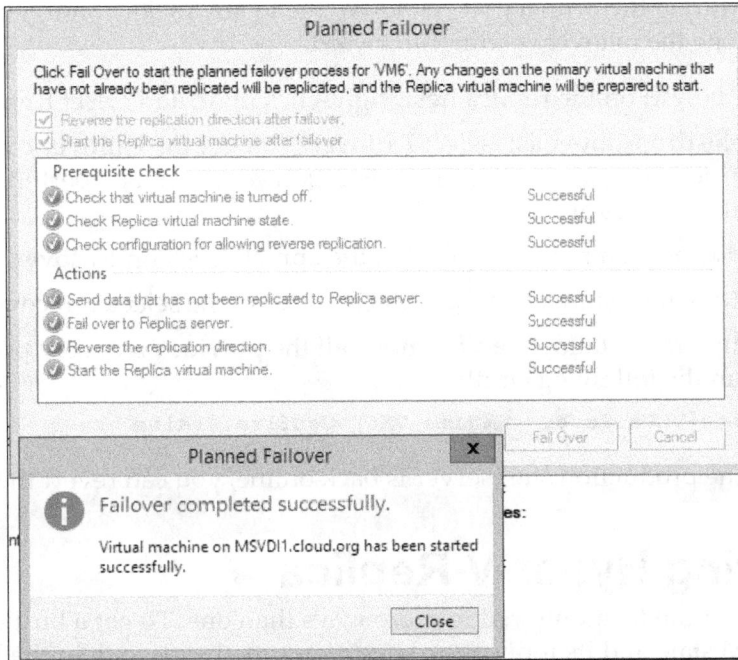

Figure 8-31: Planned Failover – Reverting Failover

The previous can be achieved via PowerShell using the following script:

```
$SourceVM = "VM6"
Stop-VM $SourceVM
Start-VMFailover -VMName $SourceVM -prepare
```

Next, proceed to the replica server:

```
$ReplicaVM = "VM6"
Start-VMFailover -VMName $ReplicaVM
Start-VM $ReplicaVM
```

Now, the replication revert:

```
Set-VMReplication -reverse -VMName $ReplicaVM
```

Failover

The failover is the last and least hoped-for action in the setup. You will invoke the failover procedure if the primary site is down due to any major contingency. The process to invoke the failover is straightforward:

1. Select the VM on the replica host, right-click on it, and select **Replication**.

2. From the drop-down list, select **Failover**. You get the **Failover configuration** applet indicating a warning that this action should not be performed until the primary VMs are down.

3. Select the desired recovery point in the applet. Click on **Failover**.

4. The VM will be started off the replica server to the selected recovery point.

5. To complete the failover and remove all the previous recovery points for the VM, run the following cmdlet:

```
Complete-VMFailover -VMName VM6 -Confirm:$false
```

6. Once the production site/server is back online, you can revert the replication.

Monitoring Hyper-V Replica

Hyper-V Replica can be monitored in more ways than one. To get a bird's eye view of the VM state and its replication state, you can always look in the Hyper-V Manager or failover cluster manager. When you select a VM, the bottom pane will show VM status summary. If you select the **Replication** tab in the bottom pane, if depicts the replication state along with the primary and replica servers. Look at the figures here:

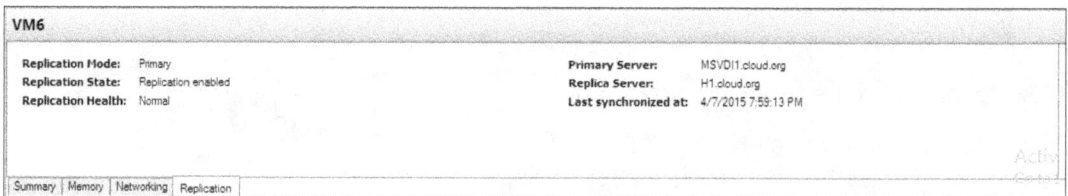

VM6			
Replication Mode:	Primary	**Primary Server:**	MSVDI1.cloud.org
Replication State:	Replication enabled	**Replica Server:**	H1.cloud.org
Replication Health:	Normal	**Last synchronized at:**	4/7/2015 7:59:13 PM

Summary | Memory | Networking | Replication

Figure 8-32: Hyper-V Manager VM Summary and Replication

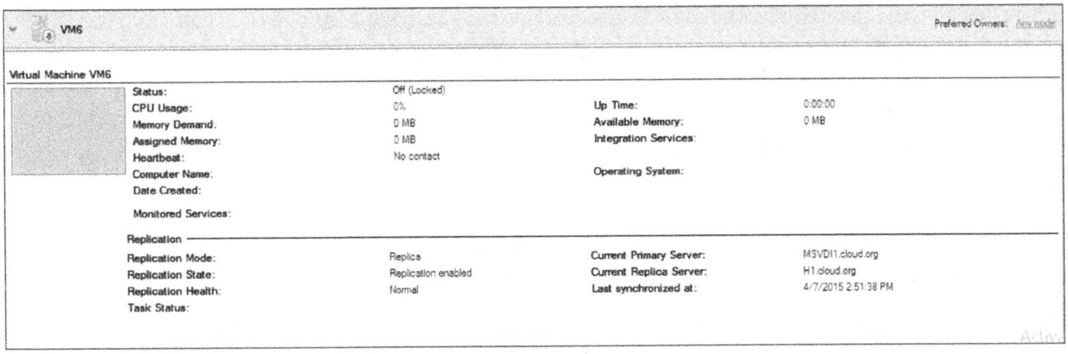

Figure 8-33: Failover Cluster Manager VM Summary and Replication

If you want a more granular approach, you can pull up the replication health of a VM. Steps to draw the replication health is same for the Hyper-V and failover cluster manager. Right-click on the VM name, select **Replication** and from the drop-down list select **View Replication Health**. The **Replication Health** view gives you the state and other statistics of the VM replication as depicted in the following *figure 8-34*:

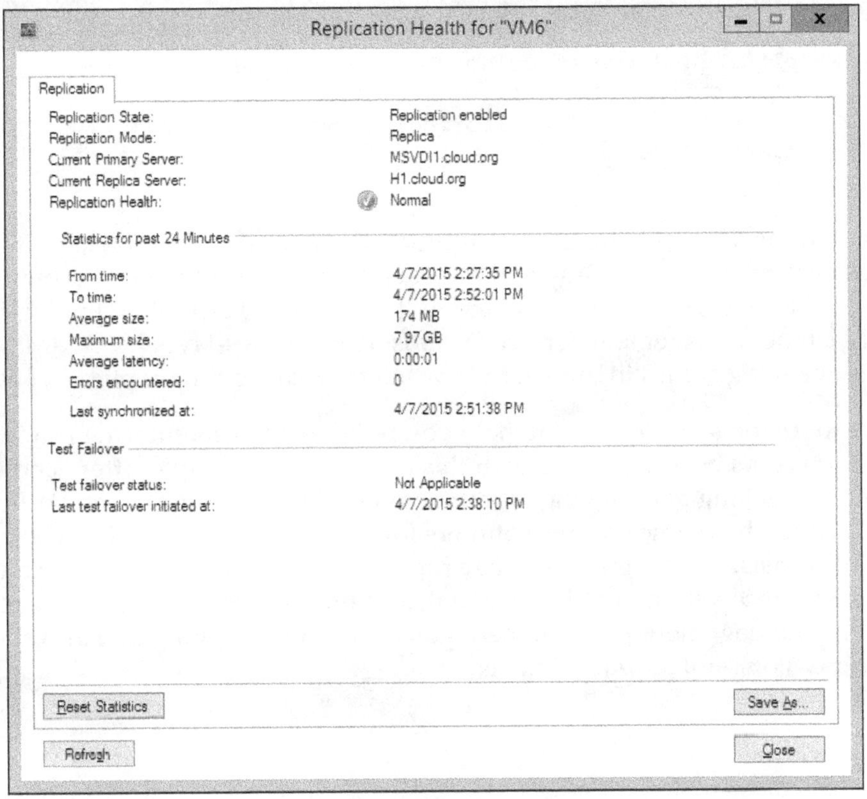

Figure 8-34: Replication Health

The replication health report has a few indicative fields. The replication health parameter can have four possible values—not enabled, normal, warning, and critical indicating, only if the VM replication has been successful over a time interval or if there's any delay or latency. The average latency should be lower as per the HVR replication frequency. Then, there are other important variables such as average size, maximum size, and errors encountered.

PowerShell has its own set of cmdlets that can do more for you with regards to monitoring Hyper-V Replica, VM, and replication.

The following cmdlet fetches the VM replication configuration for all the VMs:

```
Get-VMReplication
```

If you need to view replication stats about VMs in the table form, then, the next cmdlet is for you:

```
Measure-VMReplication
```

To view and change the default monitoring interval of a Hyper-V host, use the following cmdlets. By default, the interval is set to 12 hours:

```
Get-VMReplicationServer | Select MonitoringInterval,
MonitoringStartTime
Set-VMReplicationServer –MonitoringInterval "05:00:00" –
MonitoringStartTime `
"00:00:00"
```

Another Windows built-in monitoring utility is the **Eventlog** that tracks and generates events triggered by any and almost all Windows and on-Windows objects. For Hyper-V Replica, events are updated in the standard Hyper-V event log for Virtual Machine Management Service (Microsoft-Windows-Hyper-V-VMMS\admin log). This event log comes in quite handy when troubleshooting replica issues.

There are more tools and utilities to help you build a better monitoring framework. However, this falls beyond the scope of this chapter. For example, after keeping performance tracking and logging in mind, you can always fall back on Perfmon and SCOM. Perfmon has some specific counters for Hyper-V Replica that can be invoked on a per-VM basis. For example, average replication latency, average replication size, network bytes received, network bytes sent, and more. From SCOM's perspective, the Hyper-V management pack can help you quite a bit in setting up rules and alarms as per your suited requirements.

Azure Site Recovery

Microsoft has been keen on promoting Azure and Azure services all this while. There have been sessions, IT camps, and even conferences set up specifically to discuss and present the Azure strategy, and how to utilize its services in improving your IT experience. There are many services offered around public cloud. One of the interesting options, Azure Site Recovery, is poised around assisting disaster recovery management. In its initial offering, the support was for protecting a failover between the primary and secondary SCVMM sites only. However, the services have been evolved to do a lot more, as follows:

- Protect an on-premises VMM site to Azure
- Protect an on-premises VMware site to Azure
- Protect an on-premises physical server to Azure
- Protect an on-premises VMM site to another VMM site
- Protect an on-premises VMM site to another VMM site with SAN
- Protect an on-premises VMware site to another VMware site

Azure Site Recovery or **ASR** ensures that you get your peace of mind and ease of management when it comes down to planning and activating your DR strategy. It takes care of automation and orchestrated recovery for your site. Also, it assists you with tracking the site health and customizes the site recovery plans accordingly.

Azure Site Recovery is a paid service, and may require additional inclusions on premise, such as SCVMM and its deployed private clouds. For more information, refer to the proprietary portal at `http://azure.microsoft.com/en-us/services/site-recovery/`.

Summary

As we conclude this chapter, let me congratulate you on your progress as an advanced learner. This chapter threw light upon one of the most important subjects for virtualization with Hyper-V-: Hyper-V Replica. A feature free to use, it was released with Windows Server 2012, and later, it was enhanced with Windows Server 2012 R2. The HVR feature is available on both editions of Windows, and is also available with the free edition of Hyper-V Server 2012 and R2.

In the initial sections of this chapter, we reviewed the new attributes offered with Hyper-V Replica released with Windows Server 2012 R2, and also discussed the underlying architecture and process flow for HVR.

In the following section, we discussed some more HVR aspects from a setup and configuration standpoint. You learned about the terminologies that are in use for the technology, which comes in handy to understand when you are enabling the role. Then, we considered the requirements for the role, and learned how to ensure that the same are met for a successful deployment.

One aspect of planning a successful deployment is to closely review the capacity and sizing requirements for the role. Microsoft offers a free tool called capacity planner for Hyper-V Replica to address this requirement. We learned the functioning of this handy utility.

Next, we proceeded towards configuring VM replication. This has two stages. The first stage is to enable inward replication on the replica server or cluster. The second stage is to enable replication on VMs on the source Hyper-V host. Replication on VMs has to be enabled per-VM basis and not at host level. We also learned about the Hyper-V Replica Broker role, and its significance when configuring replica feature on a Hyper-V cluster. Windows Server 2012 Hyper-V offered HVR, which limited VM replication to a secondary site. Windows Server 2012 R2 adds the ability to extend VM replication to a tertiary site.

We then looked at the failover options available with the HVR- test failover, planned failover, and (unplanned) failover. We discussed how and when to use these procedures, and their benefits and limitations. Thereafter, you learned how to monitor the VM replication state, and how to monitor and measure Hyper-V Replica health.

In the penultimate section, we covered Azure Site Recovery, which is one of the recent Microsoft offerings. ASR is a paid service that helps you to build further upon Hyper-V Replica. ASR assures automation, remote health monitoring, and orchestration of the site recovery procedures, and much more. There's a free trial available for the service from Microsoft.

In the following chapter, we will study yet another feature that will find its way into BCP as an indispensable contingency remedial option — backup and recovery.

9
Backup and Recovery Strategies for Hyper-V Solutions

Any solution design is incomplete without a clear backup and recovery strategy in place. As we approach the final contents of this book, this chapter will help you understand and build backup readiness for your Hyper-V infrastructure. Business continuity has multiple facets, and in the earlier chapters, we have already traversed through two important subjects from the Hyper-V perspective—high availability and disaster recovery planning. Maintaining backup in BCP comes second to neither of the two aforementioned options. Often used alongside disaster recovery (DR), it is in fact the DR option for a small shop or an SME, but then again, it isn't. DR options are a costly affair, requiring SAN replication (quite expensive) or host replication (Hyper-V replica) to a designated offsite (well, primarily a skeleton site). This also adds a major overhead to the acquisition and maintenance costs. Backups can be maintained off-site or on-premises, depending on your planning and willingness to increase the CAPEX.

Before the advent of virtualization, backups had a simple but long-drawn-out process. We could come up with a few terminologies about the concerned action when performing a backup of a physical server, such as full, system state, incremental, and differential. With Hyper-V, things have become even simpler but, at times, a bit more complex. Your physical server is now your Hyper-V host, and the critical data to be backed up are from your guest machines. From a different viewpoint, guest machines are emulated physical machines hosting role-specific or app-specific data that needs to be retained as a critical backup. It may sound like a single backup, or maybe a backup within a backup, as we have nested roles under the layers of virtualization. In other words, your backup plan's inception depends on your perception of the fundamentals.

In this chapter, we will focus on:

- Hyper-V backup strategies and options
- The built-in backup utility for Windows—Windows Server Backup (WSB)
- An insight into the System Center Data Protection Manager 2012 R2

Hyper-V backup strategies and options

A Hyper-V host, whether independent or clustered, is like any other physical server, and the virtual machines hosted on the host are a collection of files; well, almost! The clause here is that VMs run OSEs (short for Operating System Environments), and when performing a backup, we need to ensure that the present state of the virtual machines is retained as well. Hence, in the event of a storage loss or an equipment failure, the last known good state of the VM can be recovered and restored. A turned-off VM will not pose such a challenge, but what good is a turned-off VM?

With VMs and virtualization, it is not just the standard backup methodology. There are alternative methods. They may be avoided in other Windows roles, but work fine in the Hyper-V space. These alternative methods include copying VHDs/VHDXs, exporting VMs, importing them later on, and capturing checkpoints (VM snapshots). The alternative methods are not recommended as prominent backup methodologies, but still find a place in the scheme of things. The standard methodologies involve keeping backups via VSS on the Hyper-V host, which ensures that the VM state is captured, or performing a backup of roles and apps from a VM using the traditional approach. All of these procedures have a set of gotchas, use cases, and—of course— some demerits. In the following sections, we will cover each one of them so that you get to decide which ones you could choose to use or avoid.

Copying VHD/VHDX

Copying VHD/VHDX is as simple as it sounds. All you need to do is copy and save the VHD/VHDX of the desired VM (or VMs) from your designated Hyper-V-assigned storage to an effective external medium, LUN, or even a file share. The copy operation allows you to capture the desired state of the VM in question and keep it saved for later access. This process does help you with maintaining in-time captures of the VHD. Then you leave out the VM configuration files. The drawback here is that you will end up creating a new VM using the wizard or PowerShell, and attach the copied/saved virtual disk to the new VM.

Another drawback is the lack of automation, storage utilization, and network utilization each time you perform the operation. Moreover, due to the lack of automation, you won't have an incremental list. Instead, you will be overwriting the new with the previously copied virtual disk. This option is simple, but not very feasible from the production standpoint, and finds suitability only within a lab environment or small shops.

A practical situation you may run into is when you use a previously active VHD in a new VM, but the VM does not start. Instead, it prompts you with an access denied error. This happens because the new VM has a different SID from the VM to which the VHD was originally linked, and the new VM also does not have access permissions to the AVHD or VHD. The remedy to this is to grant full access to the VM SID for VHD access, which is achieved using icacls in the command line:

```
icacls <VHD/avhd/vhdx PATH> /grant "NT VIRTUAL MACHINE\<New VM SID
>":(F)
```

Exporting virtual machines

Now we're going to go ahead and raise the bar from the previous action. We export the entire virtual machine, including the configuration, state, checkpoints, and virtual disk (or disks). It is more of an administrative task allowing the Hyper-V admin to move machines from one host running with low resources to another. However, this is also utilized as a backup operation. This is more feasible and manageable than the previous one, but it comes with almost the same set of demerits from the backup capture standpoint.

The process involves just a few clicks, and the location where you would like to export the guest machine configuration and state:

1. In the Hyper-V Manager console, select the VM to be exported in the virtual machines frame in the center pane.
2. Either right-click on the VM or select **Export** from the **Actions** pane.
3. In the **Export VM** applet, specify the path of the exported VM. Click on **Export**.
4. The export process and state are visible under the **Status** column in the **Virtual Machines** frame.

The exported VM can be imported to any Windows Server 2012 R2 Hyper-V host—independent or clustered—when required. The import process is similar to the export process. You need to select **Import Virtual Machine** from the **Actions** pane in the Hyper-V Manager.

Checkpoints (snapshots)

A snapshot or checkpoint (this is a new name borrowed from the VMM scheme) is not a new concept, but has been around since the older Hyper-V platforms. The procedure assists in maintaining system restore points stacked together, each with the capability of taking your VM back in time to when the checkpoint was created. The creation of checkpoints is a sequential process and can be applied, merged, or removed as required, as discussed here:

1. Let's say you create a VM and install a vanilla OS. Also, you have a control image. You save a checkpoint, **No. 1**, for this state.

2. Thereafter, you go ahead customizing the OSE and save another checkpoint, **No. 2**, for the customized OSE.

3. Next, you install certain apps to give a role definition to your VM. Incidentally, one of the apps acts up and your VM misbehaves.

4. To undo the changes, you won't have to redo the entire VM, but just revert to checkpoint No. 2, and you will have the state where you had customized the OSE post the OS installation but prior to deployment of the app on the VM.

5. If all goes well and you figure out that the VM deployment was successful, you can continue to run it as is, with no need to revert to any checkpoints. Also, you may very well merge the snapshots.

Windows Server 2012 allows you to live-merge the checkpoint with no requirement to shut down the VMs, unlike its predecessor, which required the VMs to be shut down or turned off for the merge function.

The current release of Hyper-V allows a maximum of 50 snapshots. For each checkpoint, there's a differencing disk created, which may be an AVHD or AVHD(X), depending on the native virtual disk format (for example, VHD or VHDX). The differencing disks are linked to their immediate parent, which may be the VM's virtual disk or, in the event of multiple checkpoints, a previously generated AVHD(X). This is often the not-so-recommended way for backup or recovery measures, as it creates notable performance degradation at the host level when there are multiple checkpoints for a VM. A single access involves the entire dataset of AVHDs for the VM to be accessed, and thereby increases CPU cycles and IOPS.

There are a few more noteworthy facts about Hyper-V checkpoints. They can be exported along with the virtual machine, and the entire set of virtual disks is rolled out without a merger. You might remember from *Chapter 8, Hyper-V Replica*, that additional recovery points are nothing but checkpoints created for the replica VM.

There are a few gotchas when you use checkpoints/snapshots for Hyper-V guest machines:

- The hosted app or role in the VM should be snapshot aware. If not, it is pretty much a mishap in the making. There used to be a classic case of USN rollback with domain controllers running on earlier Windows platforms. However, from Windows Server 2012 onwards, the concern has been alleviated, with the addition of a new AD attribute called the **VM-GenerationID**.

- Perform the merger of checkpoints in time, as a bigger count creates a performance drift towards the lower side. For every read or write operation, a pre-read operation is performed on all the parent disks involved in the chain.

- Perform a standard merge operation from the console or PowerShell, and avoid deleting AVHDs from the virtual machine stores if the VM goes into a paused state due to low hard drive space. An accidental deletion of AVHD breaks the chain of hierarchy, and all the following checkpoints become orphaned and useless.

The traditional backup methodology

So far, we have observed options that could be used as a backup alternative. These options lack automation and require manual intervention for granular control. Mostly, they will not seem feasible on the long run or if you are working out a plan for a medium-sized business or a larger enterprise. The backup solution, whether it is a built-in Windows server backup or a vendor-specific solution, provides you with greater control over the backup philosophy. The backup tools mostly use the **Volume Shadow Service (VSS)** to achieve successful backups of VMs. Moreover, the backup can be performed at the host level, providing you with the flexibility of selecting the VMs that to be backed up in full. Alternatively, you may choose to install the backup agent on the VM and perform the backup as you would on a physical machine.

Windows Server 2012 R2 has one more twist with respect to all of this. The advancements in its current release digress a bit from host-side VSS with respect to VM backup, and use a VM checkpoint instead of a VSS snapshot, which finally gets appended to the host VSS snapshot. In the following sections, we will look at the formerly discussed aspects, but with a more detailed approach.

The Volume Shadow Service

The **Volume Shadow Service (VSS)** is a Windows service designed to capture volume snapshots or shadow copies of storage volumes that have been enabled for the VSS. This ability allows the backup of open files and performs consistent backup of running systems without the need to take them offline. VSS snapshots should not be confused with Hyper-V checkpoints (snapshots), as both are different in origin and function. VSS operates at the block level of the filesystem, and thereby provides an effective backup infrastructure for Windows platforms. The fundamental principle behind the point-in-time capture with VSS to effectively freeze the filesystem is write I/O, and thereafter thaw. In this process, flush out the buffers to deliver a data-consistent shadow copy. VSS architecture has primarily four components working on top of storage volumes, namely **VSS** the service, **writers**, **providers**, and the **requestor**. *Figure 9-1* is an illustration of this concept. Let's look at how these components fit into the system:

- **VSS**: The heart of the framework, the volume shadow service, or volume shadow copy service, caters to function calls made by other components, and thereby delivers a VSS snapshot to the requestor as the end result.

- **Requestor**: The requestor is typically a VSS-enabled backup application that calls the VSS to enlist the VSS writers and invoke the shadow copy capture. The requestor also syncs with writers to identify the dataset to be backed up and the ideal process of doing so. Examples can be the standard Windows server backup or an enterprise backup application, such as Data Protection Manager or Symantec Backup Exec.

- **Writers**: These modules are associated with VSS-aware applications and are responsible for ensuring crash-consistent shadow copies. They have a twofold role. First, when invoked by the VSS, they freeze the specific application writes and flush their data stores to the shadow copy. Second, they update the attributes to assist in the retrieval of the application identity (name, icons, and so on) and data during the restore process. The maximum timeline for a scheduled pause is 60 seconds.

  Not all applications have writers added for them, so there lies a window of inconsistent data within a shadow copy. The inconsistent data may be due to open files during a write operation or buffered data yet to be written. This moves the focus of the snapshot to crash consistent from application consistent, from the app perspective.

- **Providers**: Providers are responsible for creating shadow copies for VSS-enabled volumes. VSS keeps track of the snapshot process by first invoking the writers. Then it invokes the providers to create and retain a shadow copy until the process is successfully closed. Once the snapshot process is complete, the provider returns the location of the snapshot to the requestor or the backup application.

There are three types of providers, and they are called in the following sequence: hardware, software, and system:

- ° **Hardware**: This provider is an interface between the VSS and the hardware level, being worked on by a storage controller or HBA. The process of creating a VSS snapshot is addressed by an HBA or a storage controller. This is mostly seen with SAN snapshots and CSV snapshots of the LUN. You can enable the providers on your hosts only if the vendor supports it.

- ° **Software**: This provider is pretty much a user mode DLL and a kernel mode filter driver working in conjunction. It is confined between the filesystem and the volume manager and is used to track the process I/O.

- ° **System**: This provider is inherent to the Windows OS and creates a shadow copy of a volume by utilizing its free space.

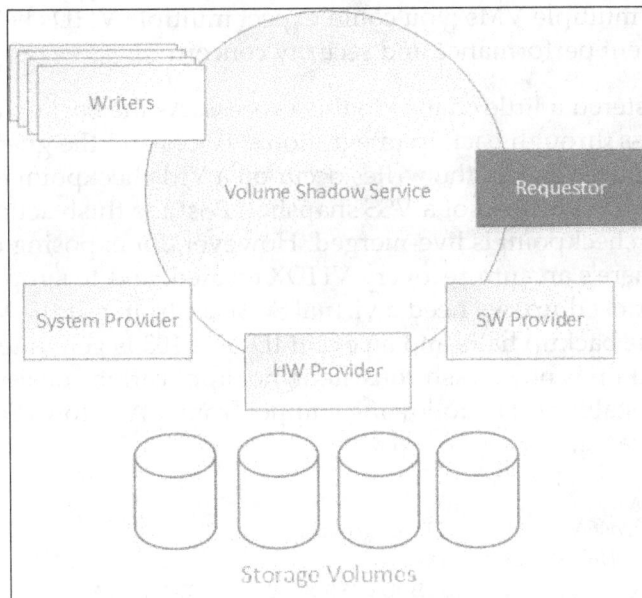

Figure 9-1: VSS Architecture

The Hyper-V backup process in Windows Server 2012 R2

In this title so far, we have reiterated quite a few times the new features that Windows Server 2012 R2 brings onto the scene. There was a significant change in the backup process for Hyper-V until Windows Server 2012. In the current release, the focus at the host level is moved from the VSS snapshot to the Hyper-V snapshot or checkpoint for backup task execution. The live merge ability of checkpoints, as introduced with Windows Server 2012, is put to good use in the backup procedure of Windows Server 2012 R2. Under both the circumstances, to ensure that VMs are captured live and not put to the saved state, make sure that Integration Services for backup (volume checkpoint) is enabled for the VM under VM settings. We discussed VM settings in detail in *Chapter 3, Deploying Virtual Machines*. One more indispensable addition to the VM setting would be a virtual SCSI controller. It's just a controller; no virtual disk is required. You will come to know the reason for this in some time.

In the old procedure, the action was around the standard VSS shadow copy process. It usually started off with a backup application requesting backup of a VM, and Hyper-V would invoke the backup integration service on the VM. In a chain reaction, the next entity called upon was the VSS inside the guest machine. The VSS puts all the VSS-aware services into a quiescent state in the VM and prepares the snapshot. Then the snapshot is mounted on the host, merged with the host snapshot, and thereafter dismounted. The process left room for inconsistency, as discussed earlier, and in the case of multiple VMs, you could expect multiple VHDs being mounted, which is an apparent performance and security concern.

Microsoft administered a little change to this process. As the backup application invokes the process through backup integration services and the guest machine VSS instance completes its job, the writes occur on a VM checkpoint differential disk (AVHD/AVHDX) instead of a VSS snapshot. Post the flush action to the host snapshot, and the checkpoint is live-merged. However, for exposing the snapshot back to the VM, there's an auto-recovery VHDX created, and to support its hot-add to the VM being backed up, we need a virtual SCSI controller. If the VM lacks the SCSI controller, the backup halts and an event ID of 10103 is generated. The clause is that the VM backup is now crash consistent, not application consistent. However, this ensures more stability. The following snippet from a Windows Server Backup log illustrates the same:

```
Backed up E:\
Backed up E:\VM6\
Backed up E:\VM6\Snapshots\
Backed up E:\VM6\Snapshots\B9D3C599-DF0E-45DC-B04A-
1CCF12258930.xml
Backed up E:\VM6\Virtual Hard Disks\
```

```
Backed up E:\VM6\Virtual Hard Disks\VM6-AutoRecovery.avhdx
Backed up E:\VM6\Virtual Hard Disks\VM6.vhdx
Backed up E:\VM6\Virtual Machines\
Backed up E:\VM6\Virtual Machines\346A879A-6864-4DE5-9A6D-
5737CA6E3893.xml
Application backup
Writer Id: {66841CD4-6DED-4F4B-8F17-FD23F8DDC3DE}
    Component: 346A879A-6864-4DE5-9A6D-5737CA6E3893
    Caption    : Online\VM6
    Logical Path:
```

Apart from the preceding code, there's one more welcome change, which is better support for Linux guest machines. With Windows Server 2012 R2, you can perform live backups of Linux VMs without pausing them. Linux does not have an inherent VSS, so that removes the possibility of an application-consistent backup. However, it is possible to capture a crash-consistent backup of a Linux VM with the help of a new snapshot function built into Hyper-V 2012 R2.

CSV improvements in Windows 2012

Another major improvement was around CSV 2.0 with Windows Server 2012. In Windows Server 2008 R2 Hyper-V, due to redirected I/O, the VM backup was never parallel and the coordinator role was transferred from one node to whichever node got invoked for backup. The backups stayed serialized. In addition to this, another limitation was no incremental backup. These were addressed with the new version of CSV that rolled out with Windows Server 2012.

In the new framework for CSV, the backup of VMs across all nodes was synchronized with one backup node in the cluster, which invoked the CSV writer to track VM locations across the nodes via their Hyper-V VSS writers. Then initiate a CSV LUN snapshot was initiated, placing all the VMs in a quiescent state, and releasing them once the snapshot was captured. The change in the CSV framework was a breakthrough, with major merits such as faster and parallel backups, and ensuring that the CSV coordinator role does not move during a backup.

Backup policies

Beyond the framework, next in line is the backup strategy, which helps you identify what to back up and how to back up. A well-defined approach makes it easier to justify and execute the backup plan. Backup plans and methods differ for different organizations and still get altered as per their changing requirements. Let's discuss the fundamental methods and see how they fit into a particular backup plan.

Host-level backup

Just as we discussed in the previous sections, in the host-level backup approach, the backup agent of a VSS-aware backup solution gets activated at the host level. The VSS framework is intelligent and ensures that snapshots are captured in a consistent way, at both the host and the guest levels. The flow starts with the requestor or the backup agent, invoking the VSS. The Hyper-V VSS writer identifies the volumes where the VMs are hosted. Thereafter, the VSS provider creates shadow copies of those volumes. The VSS at the guest machine gets invoked through the backup Integration Service and sets a quiescent state to all application writes. The end result is a merged snapshot from the guest and host levels, ensuring a crash-consistent or application-consistent backup, depending on the Windows platform and VOSE of the VM.

The host-level backup approach is pretty easy to manage and execute. In the event of a recovery, recovering a VM is simpler than an application restore. The demerit of this method is the additional storage requirement, as it requires space to store the entire VM rather than just the application data.

Virtual machine-level backup

The virtual machine-level backup is the old-school method of capturing a backup, as the process is the same as enabling backup on a physical server. In this method, the backup agent is installed locally on the VM. It allows the backup administrator to protect only the required options rather than the entire VM. The depth allows you to select the required files, app data, or system state and avoid capturing the entire VHD.

This approach may seem more efficient. However, if all the VMs are hosting the backup agents, it affects the overall performance of your Hyper-V setup. A backup instance running on a physical machine requires a good section of server resources. Imagine multiple VMs, if not all (the backup admin will schedule it), launching the backup instance. It might just result in a performance crunch.

Hybrid backup

The ideal approach would be to use the preceding strategies in conjunction with each other and gain the merit of both the forms. You may opt for more frequent virtual machine internal backups and host-level backups that support business-critical data, complemented with host-level backups captured at long, defined intervals. This applies to both Windows and non-Windows VOSE, as Windows Server 2012 R2 Hyper-V supports live capture of Linux machines as well.

Azure backup

Another approach to the backup plan, but with additional costs, is to employ the Azure backup service. The Azure backup agent can integrate with an x64 client and servers, and to benefit our cause, it can integrate with DPM and ensure an offsite backup of our virtual workloads.

Windows Server Backup

After discussing all the aspects of capturing a successful backup, it's time to look at a backup solution in action. There are many vendors who offer enterprise backup solutions with different abilities, and Microsoft does this too, as part of its System Center 2012 R2 suite of applications called **Data Protection Manager**. Although these solutions are beyond the scope of this chapter, and this book as well, we will briefly look at DPM 2012 R2 towards the end of this chapter. In this section, we will focus on the Windows Server Backup utility.

Windows platforms come bundled with an inherent backup utility called **Windows Server Backup (WSB)**. WSB was rolled out with the release of Windows Server 2008, and its predecessor was the NTBackup utility. WSB is not a role on Windows Server 2012 R2, but a feature that you can install via Server Manager or PowerShell. It is capable enough to capture Hyper-V backups both for VMs running on independent hosts and on a CSV on clustered hosts. However, it should be understood that WSB is a local server feature, and so it will assist in performing backups locally only. This ability cannot be extended to a remote server or nodes. If you wish to extend the backup ability to all nodes, then the feature needs to be enabled across all nodes. Now, let's have an overview of the installation and management of the WSB feature.

Adding the Windows Server Backup feature

Windows Server Backup is a not a role, but a feature that you can install like any other Windows role or feature, either via Server Manager or through PowerShell:

1. In Server Manager, click on the **Manage** menu and select **Add Roles and Features**.
2. On the **Before you Begin** screen, click on **Next**.

3. On the **Installation Type** screen, select **Role-based or feature-based installation**. Click on **Next**, as shown in this screenshot:

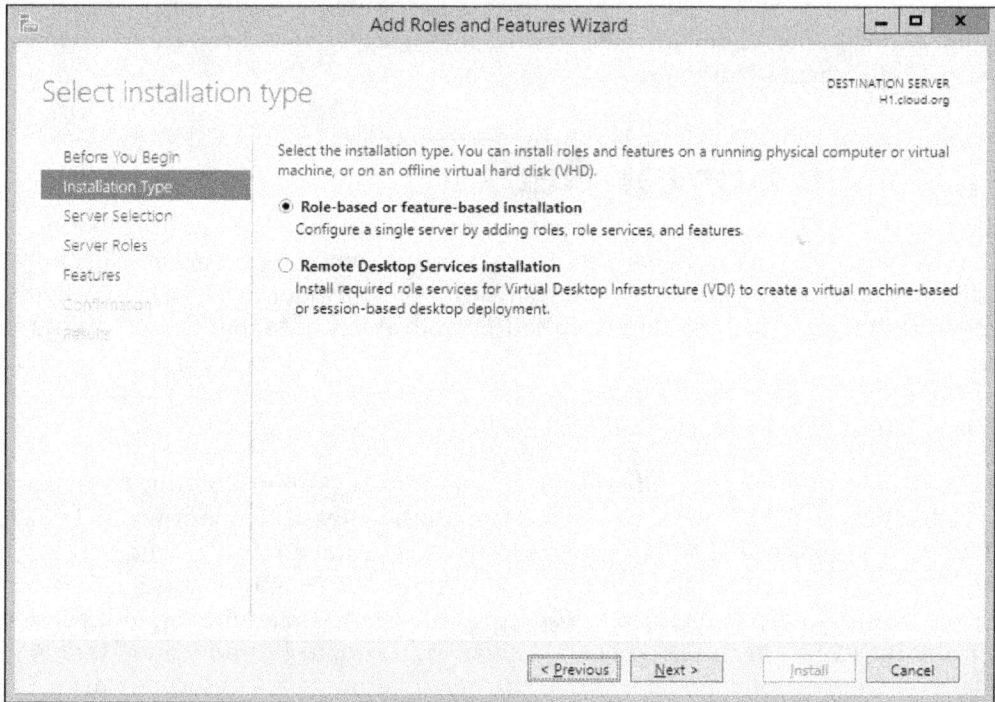

Figure 9-2: Feature-based Installation

4. On the **Server Selection** screen, you can choose the local server or select the remote server you wish to deploy the service on. Then click on **Next**, as shown in the following screenshot:

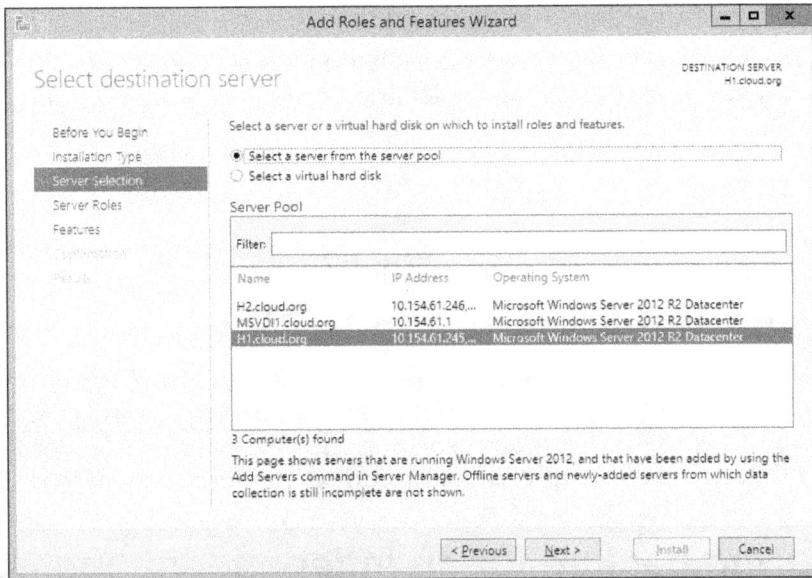

Figure 9-3: Server Selection

5. On the **Server Roles** screen, click on **Next**.

6. On the **Features** screen, enable the checkbox for Windows Server Backup. Then click on **Next**, as shown here:

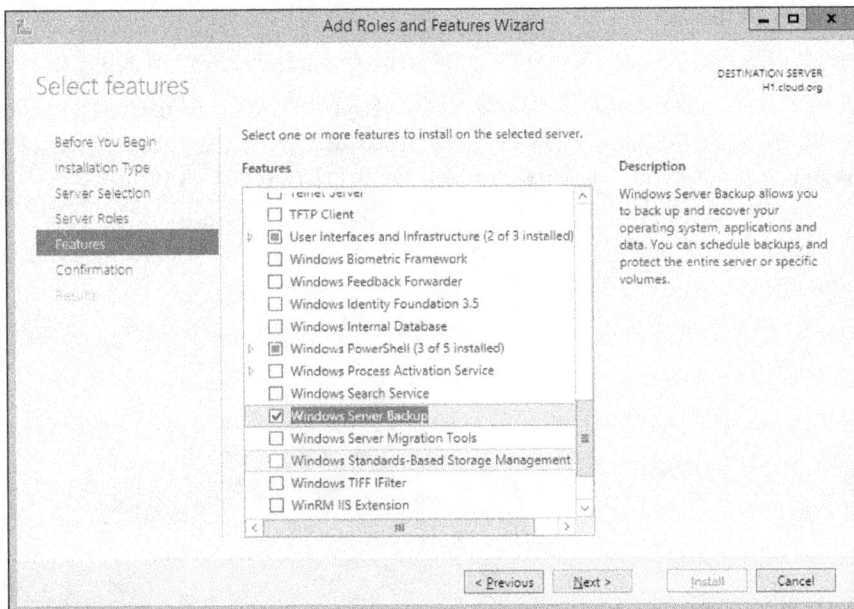

Figure 9-4: Enabling the Windows Server Backup feature

7. On the **Confirmation** screen, click on **Install**.

8. On the **Results** screen, once the installation has succeeded, click on **Close**. You may choose to close the applet after initiating the installation process as well.

The preceding result can be achieved via a PowerShell cmdlet, like this:

```
Install-WindowsFeature Windows-Server-Backup
```

Managing backups using WSB

Once the feature is installed, you have access to its console and PowerShell module. As stated earlier, WSB is not an enterprise application and backup control is limited up to localhost only. Each host that needs to be protected has to be enabled for the WSB feature locally. Let's review the process of capturing a backup on an independent host.

Configuring backup for an independent host

WSB provides you with two wizards to configure backups: backup schedule and backup once. As their names indicate, the former is used to define a schedule and the latter is used to capture a just-in-time backup. The settings are more or less the same. Hence, we will review the backup schedule wizard and look at its details:

1. In the **Windows Server Backup** console, under the **Actions** pane, select **Backup Schedule**.

2. On the first screen of the wizard, **Getting Started**, click on **Next**.

3. On the next screen, **Select Backup Configuration**, opt for **Custom**. The purpose of this demo is to depict the granularity of the process and focus on the VM backup. The host backup is simplified. Click on **Next**.

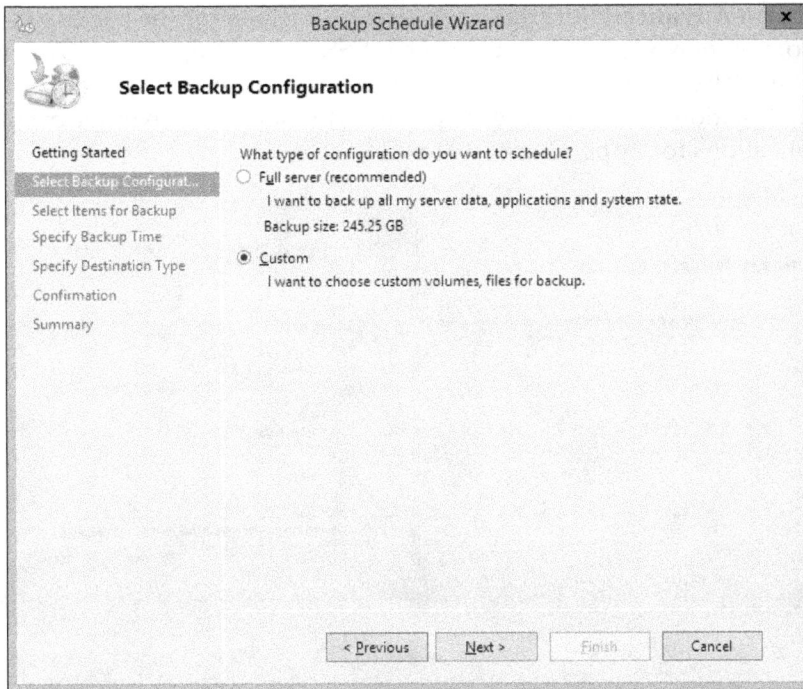

Figure 9-5: Backup Schedule Wizard – Select Backup Configuration

4. On the next screen, **Select Items for Backup,** click on **Add Items**. This takes
    you to an applet window with expandable and collapsible options. These
    can be backed up using WSB. You may notice in *figure 9-6* that WSB allows
    granular recovery for the host, and the options range from bare metal
    recovery and system state to the Hyper-V host or its VMs. Then there are
    other options too. You may opt for selective VMs and choose host as an
    option as well. Click on **OK**.

Click on **Advanced Settings** to set any exclusions for the backup capture. Also, you may set this backup to be a VSS full backup or a VSS copy backup. The former is used when WSB is the preferred tool for the backup of applications, and the latter is preferred when you use other backup applications for apps. Click on **Next**.

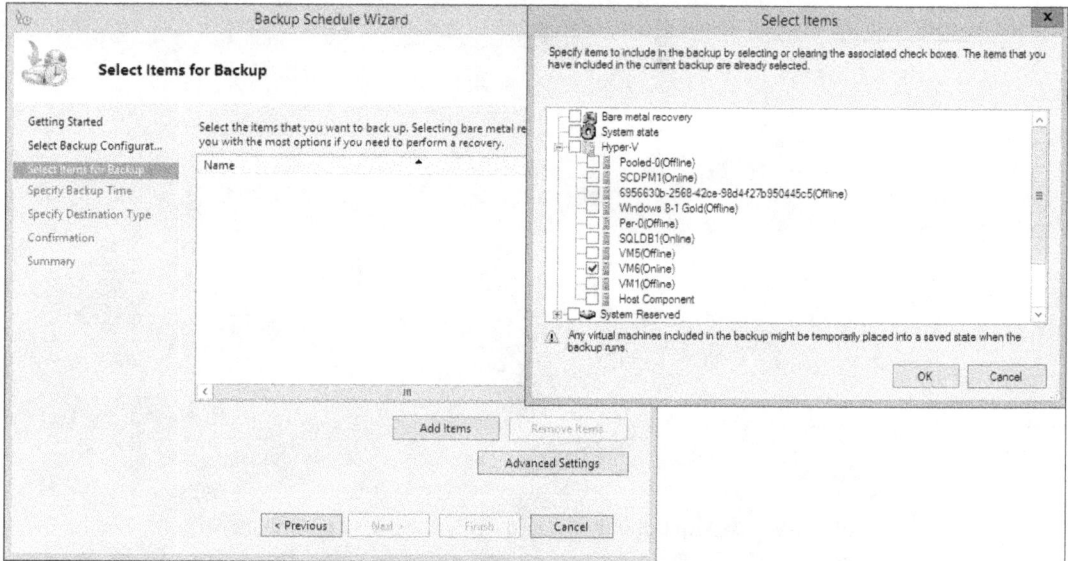

Figure 9-6: Backup Schedule Wizard – Select Items for Backup

5. **Specify Backup Time** is shown in *figure 9-7*. This screen requires you to affix a schedule to protect your VMs. The default is once a day, though you can opt to alter the schedule to ensure that the backup occurs more than once a day at different time intervals. Click on **Next**.

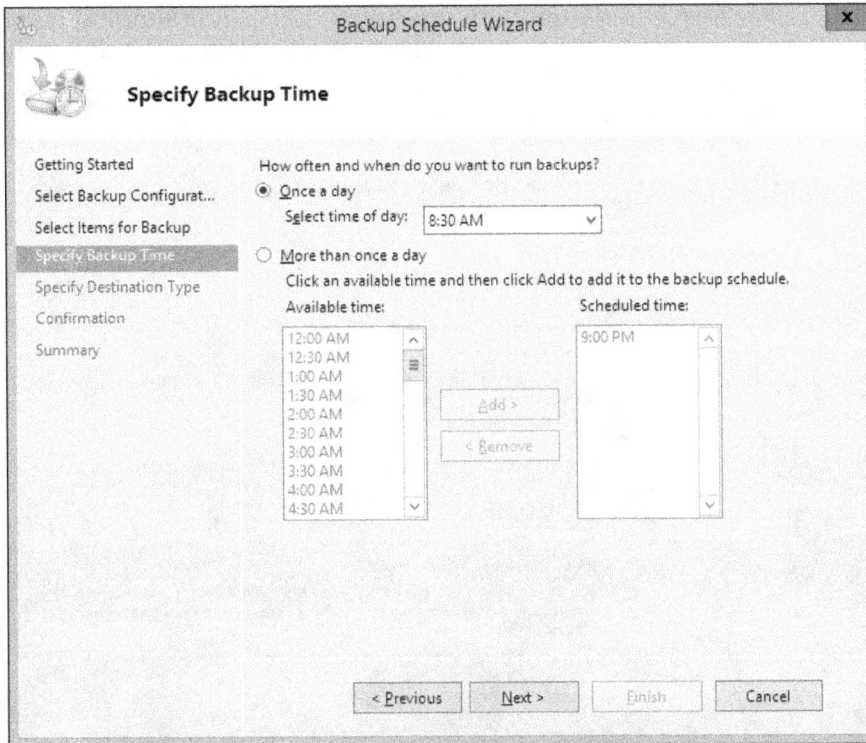

Figure 9-7: Backup Schedule Wizard – Specify Backup Time

6. Now comes an important parameter field — **Specify Destination Type** (*figure 9-8*). Here, you are presented with three options for the preferred location where you can store your backups. Select any one of the following options and click on **Next**:

    °   **Back up to a hard disk that is dedicated for backups (recommended)**: This is the recommended option, wherein you should preferably dedicate a LUN or a USB drive to store backups. In the event of a failure, connect to the storage and recover the virtual workloads.

    °   **Back up to a volume**: This seems a feasible and easy option, but presents a single-point-of-failure situation. You have to store the backups of your virtual workloads in a local volume on the host. In a possible situation where there is a small contingency and you end up losing the server completely, you end up losing the backups as well.

○ **Back up to a shared network folder**: This is the simplest of all the listed options. You select a file share on a remote file server with ample storage and security, and the backups are easily accessible for recovery whenever required.

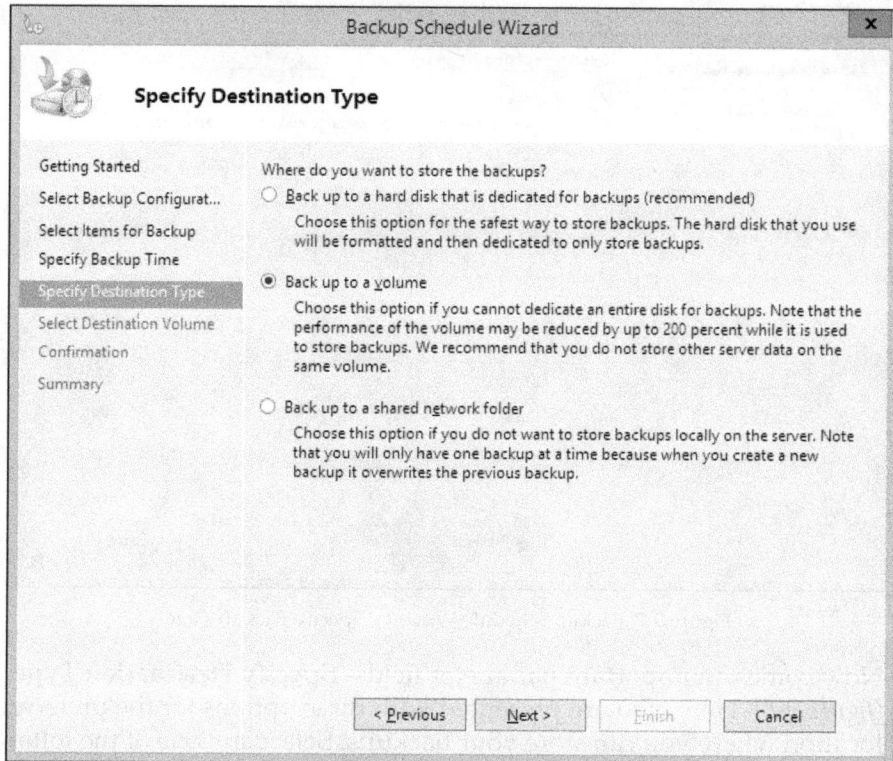

Figure 9-8: Backup Schedule Wizard – Specify Destination Type

7. The next screen will be a follow-up screen for any of the three options that you selected in the previous screen. Update the fields and click on **Next**.

8. On the **Confirmation** screen, review the selected parameters and click on **Next**.

9. On the **Summary** screen, you will receive an acknowledgement that a backup schedule has been successfully created.

10. To review the backup schedule task, you may look up **Task Scheduler** and verify, as shown in this screenshot:

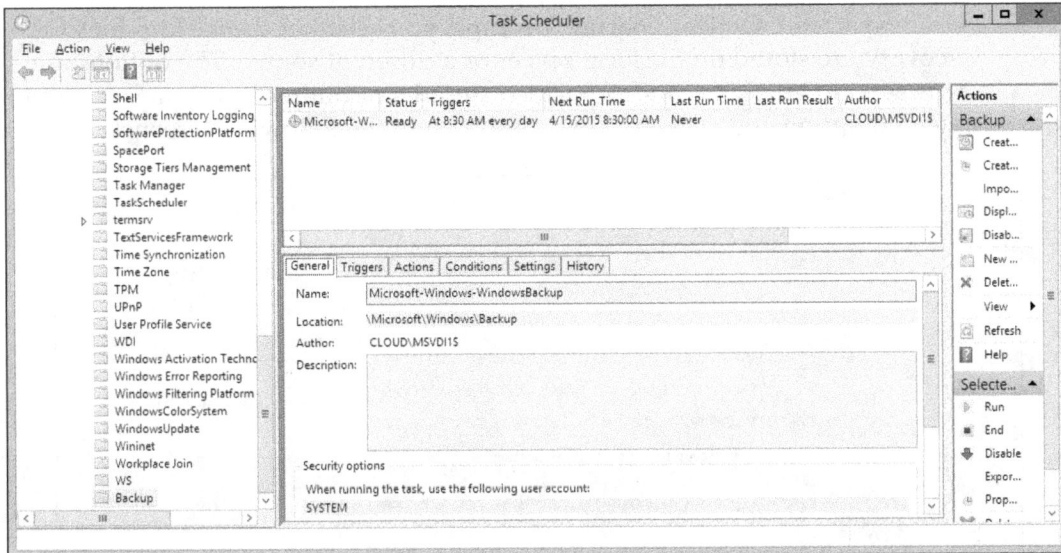

Figure 9-9: Task Scheduler – New Backup Task

Performing a recovery

In this section, you will learn how to recover a setup using the backup we captured just now. As best practice, the restoration of your virtual workloads should be tested time and again to ensure that when there's a real failure, you are not at a loss. The recovery process outlined via WSB is straightforward and simple.

Let's walk through this process:

1. From the **Actions** pane, select **Recover**. This invokes **Recovery Wizard**.

2. The next screen, **Getting Started**, prompts you whether the backup files for recovery are stored on the local server or a different source. The options are **This server (MSVDI1)** and **A backup stored on another location**. Select the relevant option and click on **Next**, as shown in the following screenshot:

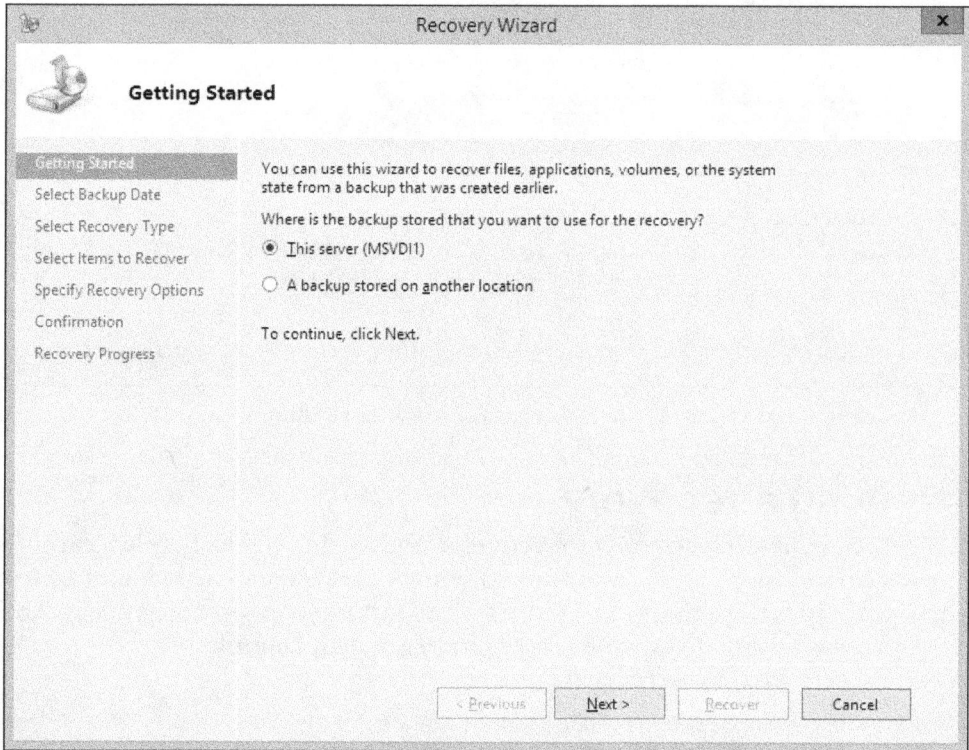

Figure 9-10: Recovery Wizard

3. Once the location is identified, the backup policy and details get loaded. The next screen, **Select Backup Date**, requires you to select the date and time of the backup file captured earlier for the VM. Select the options to get the desired state of the VM and click on **Next**, as shown here:

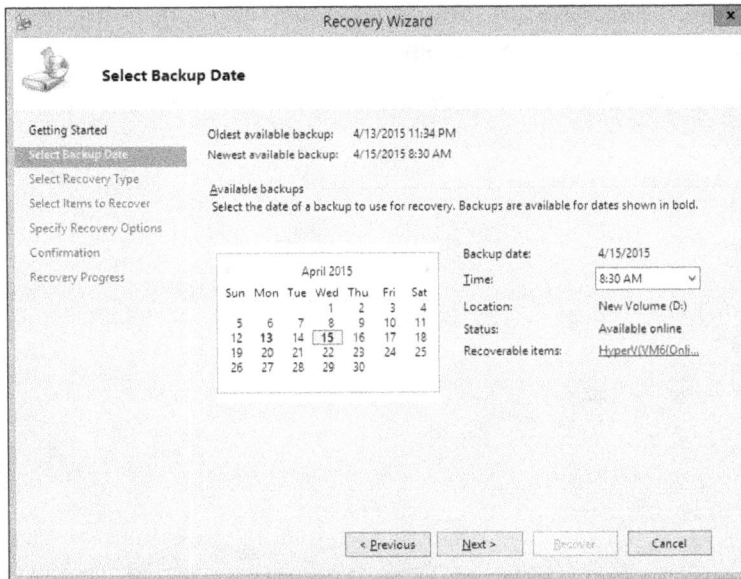

Figure 9-11: Recovery Wizard – Select Backup Date

4. Once the date and time to be loaded have been specified, in the next screen **Select Recovery Type**, the wizard prompts you to select the type of data you wish to recover from the backup file. Select **Hyper-V**, as shown in the following screenshot, and click on **Next**:

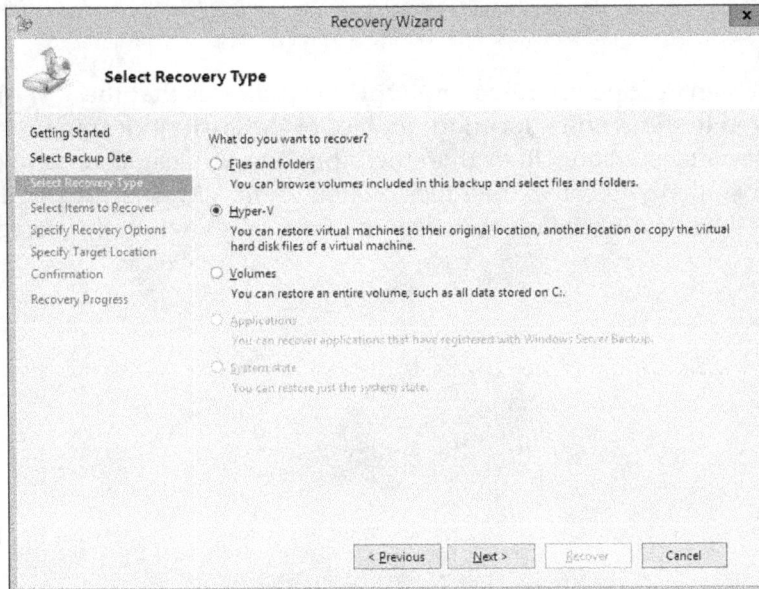

Figure 9-12: Recovery Wizard – Select Recovery Type

5. On the next screen, **Select Items to Recover**, check the VMs you intend to restore. Then click on **Next**, as shown here:

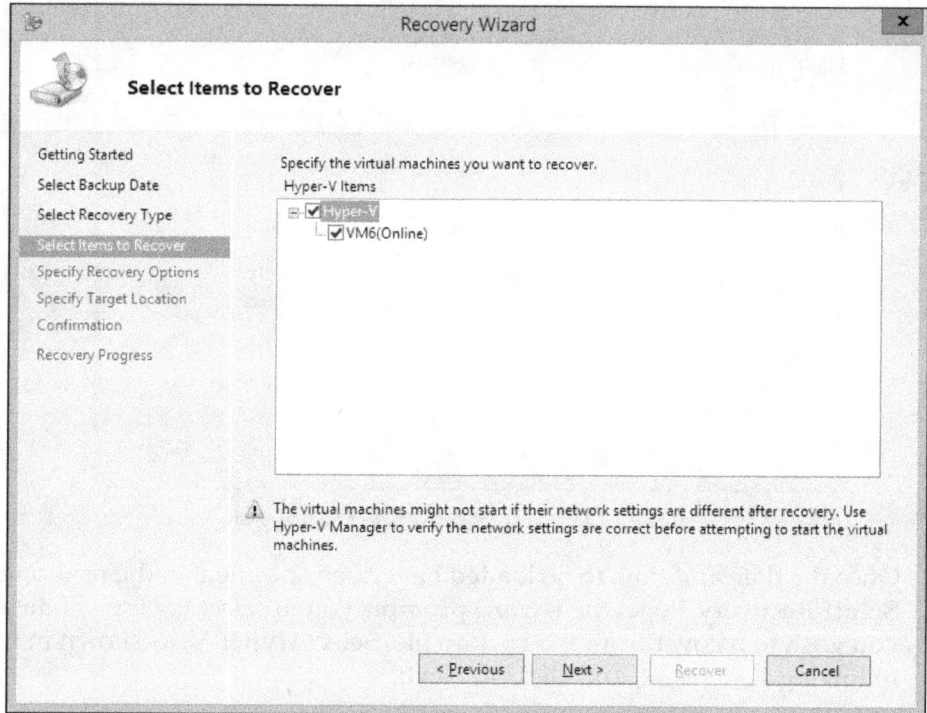

Figure 9-13: Recovery Wizard – Select Items to Recover

6. The screen for **Specify Recovery Options** indicates that the VM can be restored to the original location in place of the current running instance, or an alternate location. Other than these options, you can choose to copy to a folder so that you can extract files related to the VM, specifically the VHD. Select the relevant option and click on **Next**, as shown in this screenshot:

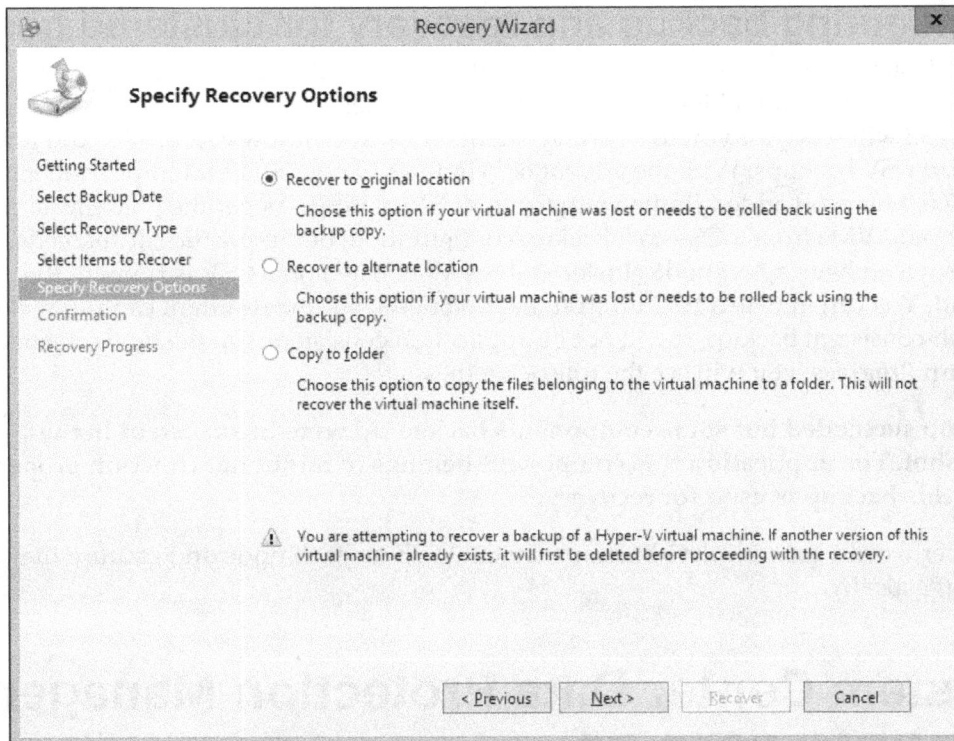

Figure 9-14: Recovery Wizard – Specify Recovery Options

7. On the **Confirmation** screen, review the VMs you are recovering and click on **Recover**.

8. The next screen, **Recovery Progress**, shows you the status of the VM restoration process. Click on **Close** once you are done, or you can close it prior to completion as well.

9. Once the process is complete, you should check the state of the restored VM. It will be in the *off* state. Start the VM. It will begin the merge process. Then check whether it is running in the desired state or not.

Configuring backup and recovery for clustered hosts

For a cluster setup, you should opt for an enterprise solution. However, assuming you do not wish to opt for a bigger solution for cost or other reasons, Microsoft has ensured that WSB will work for you to a certain extent. Prior to Windows 2012, WSB did not support CSV backups. With the advent of Windows Server 2012 and improvements in CSV 2.0, Microsoft added limited support for CSV in WSB. As per the guidelines, you cannot add VMs from a CSV to a backup configuration, but in practice, it succeeds. Let's say you have a two-node cluster and the VM hosted on a CSV is running the second. You can initiate a backup from the first node, but the resultant capture will be a crash-consistent backup. It will not be application consistent. On the final screen for **Backup Progress**, you will see the following message:

Backup succeeded but some components backed up were inconsistent in the snapshot. The application this component belongs to might not function properly after this backup is used for recovery.

In other words, for complete backups, install WSB on each node and capture the backups locally.

System Center Data Protection Manager (SCDPM) 2012 R2

DPM is Microsoft's very own enterprise backup solution. It forms an integral part of the System Center suite and private cloud initiative. Initially focused around the protection and backup of Microsoft platforms and applications only, the DPM is poised to become more versatile, with more support for Linux platforms. DPM has been around for some time, though it was never the popular kid from the system center family. The current release, however, packs a wallop. Let's briefly review the new features of the System Center Data Protection Manager (SCDPM) 2012 R2:

- **Support for virtualization**: DPM has official support for deployment as a virtual workload. You can deploy DPM on a physical server, an on-premise virtual machine, as well as an Azure virtual machine. As a virtualized instance, DPM can benefit from VHDS to add to its storage pools. There's a gotcha, however; DPM generally utilizes a tape drive for backup but Hyper-V does not support tape drive emulation as yet. As a remedy, Microsoft recommends using the iSCSI tape drive connected over a dedicated physical NIC at the host level.

- **Azure backup integration**: DPM can be integrated with Azure backup services in order to port on-premise DPM data to Azure backup. The data at Azure can be stored for 3,360 days.

- **Support for the Linux guest machine**: DPM has been tuned to support online backups of Linux virtual machines as part of Microsoft's strategy to promote Linux support within Hyper-V. The gotcha here is that the backup is crash consistent and not application consistent, as Linux does not have an inherent VSS. Also, as of now, Linux VMs are not supported for Azure backup.

- **Support for an SQL cluster as the backend**: In earlier releases, there was a limitation with DPM: using only a standalone SQL server instance, which leaves a window of inconsistency and leads to a lack of resiliency. DPM now allows a clustered SQL instance to be the backend for its indexing and other functions. Using a SQL cluster provides resiliency and scalability, as the application workload grows gradually.

- **Improved consistency**: DPM 2012 R2 has been built over the limitations of its previous releases, and it delivers better performance as an enterprise backup solution. DPM protection groups are integrated with automatic consistency checking, which can be scheduled accordingly after a backup cycle, thereby mitigating any consistency challenges.

Summary

This brings us to the end of the penultimate chapter of this book. This was also the last chapter from the Hyper-V advanced topics series. It focused on the backup and recovery aspects of Hyper-V and the importance of maintaining backups from a business continuity perspective.

At the inception of this chapter, we reviewed alternate options for protecting data, such as maintaining copies of VHDs and exporting virtual machines to safe locations. We again reviewed the benefits of checkpoints (Hyper-V snapshots) and saw how they fare as an alternative to traditional backups.

As we progressed further, we reviewed the traditional backup methodology based on the VSS framework, and you learned the dynamics of VSS under the hood. We also focused on the backup improvements and changes rolled out with Windows Server 2012 R2, and saw how they are going to benefit the consistency of backed-up data. Later on, we reviewed the possible backup strategies for identifying situations such as the following: when to invoke a host-level backup or a virtual machine internal backup, and when to maintain a hybrid backup plan using both the methodologies in moderation and as per the need of the hour.

Windows Server Backup (WSB) is the built-in backup solution offered on Windows platforms. This utility has been tweaked and tuned for better delivery and performance from a Hyper-V perspective, and now it also has limited support for CSV.

We concluded the chapter by reviewing the System Center 2012 R2 Data Protection Manager (DPM) and its new features in the current release. DPM is Microsoft's enterprise data protection or backup solution offering, and is bundled with the System Center suite of applications.

In the last chapter, we will move the focus away from server-side virtualization and touch upon client-side virtualization. There, you will learn about the Microsoft Virtual Desktop Infrastructure.

10
Building a Virtual Desktop Infrastructure

Virtualization did not just stop at the server side; there were meritorious client-side developments too. It started with session virtualization where multiple users would log into a terminal server remotely to get a Windows Server desktop session and experience. This allowed the users to share the server resources effectively. Microsoft along with Citrix has been one of the pioneers for session virtualization when the former offered terminal services, and now **Remote Desktop Services (RDS)**; and the latter offered **MetaFrame Server**.

We are now in the era of mobility where the end users clamor for the flexibility to work from anywhere and look for convenience of using their personal devices to access the work environment, which led to the advent of **Bring Your Own Device (BYOD)**-yet another catchy acronym. The answer to this is called **virtual desktop**, wherein a user can get a virtual machine assigned when he or she logs in.

RDS evolved to address both the requirements under separate server roles. As it now supports remote desktop sessions and virtual desktops, it is presently termed as **Virtual Desktop Infrastructure (VDI)**.

In the final chapter of this book, we will broadly discuss:

- Insight into RDS and VDI
- Benefits of using Hyper-V for VDI
- VDI architecture and improvements
- Implementing a VDI environment

Desktop virtualization

We briefly defined the desktop virtualization concept in *Chapter 1, Introducing Release 2.0*. The fundamentals are similar to what we have discussed in entirety throughout the book. Desktop virtualization is abstracting the user desktop environment and associated applications from the underlying physical hardware. Microsoft offers this feature in three flavors – pooled (shared) virtual machines, personal (private) virtual machines, and desktop sessions along with RemoteApp as an option, which allows an application to be run remotely on a RDS host. All of them can be maintained from one single pane of Server Manager as separate collections via the **Remote Desktop Management Service (RDMS)**.

Microsoft Terminal Services and Remote Desktop Services were quite a success. However, the changes in end-user preferences, where workplace was no longer confined within the boundaries of an office cubicle, led to the advent of Virtual Desktop Infrastructure (VDI). Under the RDS umbrella, MS presents both session desktops and virtual desktops. Session desktops are the standard offering, and are recommended for most remote desktop scenarios that allow for shared sessions on the server. This is the more cost-effective option and provides for a greater user presence per server.

VDI (or virtual desktops) have evolved alongside the Hyper-V roadmap. The purpose is to provide end users with either shared or dedicated desktops that are hosted as virtual machines on a Hyper-V infrastructure. Virtual desktops are employed when certain requirements are not met by session desktops. For example, a user need to be the administrator of his/her desktop or session, or need to use an application that may require a dedicated OSE for committing permanent changes. Virtual desktops provide a more isolated environment than sessions. One more factor that is gradually changing the way of IT is the BYOD, where the users prefer or it is generally preferred that they use their own devices for work environment access. The devices can range from laptops to smartphones or tablets. The mode of access is Remote Desktop Access app that is made available in app stores from various vendors.

There are two deployment choices under virtual desktops: pooled and personal. The names are self-explanatory indicating the mode of deployment. Pooled desktops are a virtual machine pool from where VMs get deployed to the users when they log in. A pooled collection in concept is an aggregated resource pool, shared among the end users. A shared gold image is used as a parent and virtual machines are spawned as children when the users log in. The changes committed during the login are stored on a virtual hard disk, which gets purged when the user logs off, and the virtual machine is returned back to the pool. The setup comes second to session desktops in being cost effective and easily managed, as there's just one gold image to be maintained and serviced.

Personal or private desktops are desktop collections that are permanently assigned to the users. A copy of the gold image virtual machine is exported during the rollout process, and gets assigned to the specific users, such as with a desktop PC. The deployment option allows for personalization and flexibility. However, it generates the same overhead of managing VM as you would do for physical machines, and adds to the OPEX weight a bit more than the former two.

Another deployment option under RDS is the hosted application virtualization called RemoteApp. It's configured the same way as the session desktops, but in this case, the application is streamed down to the user's personal desktop rather than the desktop session.

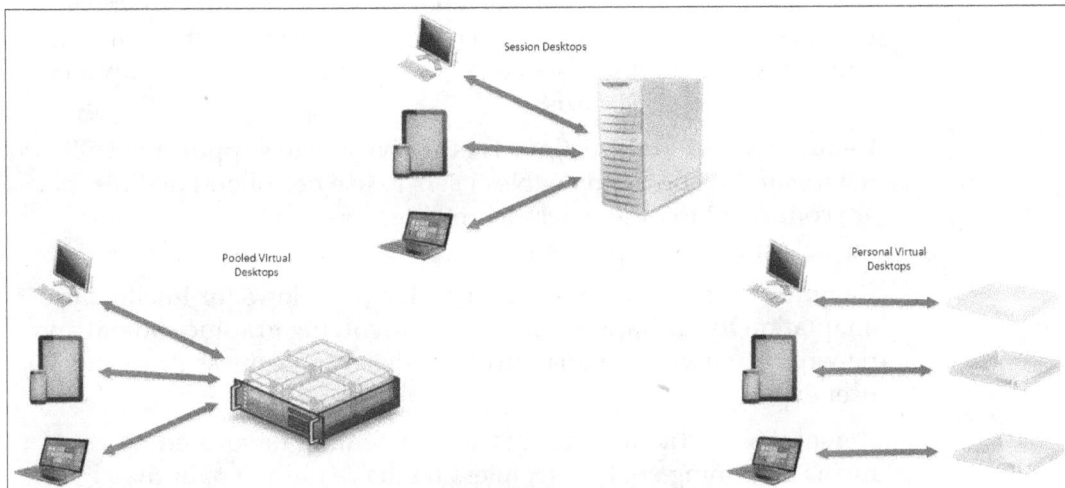

Figure 10-1: VDI Deployment choices

Hyper-V for VDI – the engine under the hood

Hyper-V has had a remarkable evolution, and MS VDI had tagged alongside it for almost the very onset. VDI runs on the Hyper-V platform, Windows Server 2012 R2, or free Hyper-V Server 2012 R2, unlike session desktops on RDS, which is a server role installed on a Windows Server platform. VDI saw the light of the day with Windows Server 2008 R2, and caught the attention with Windows Server 2008 R2 Service Pack 1 when two interesting features were rolled out, namely **RemoteFX** and **dynamic memory**.

Windows Server 2012 and Windows Server 2012 R2 added more attributes to the former two features and introduced furthermore to the arsenal feature. We will discuss them briefly and see their value add-ons:

- **RemoteFX**: An acquired intellectual property, RemoteFX was put to good use and developed further with VDI. The core idea was to give a superior visual experience via the remote desktop protocol, and render the Aero to virtual desktops similar to physical desktops. There are furthermore use cases for this feature, and the new RemoteFX components introduced with each Windows Server release have bettered the previous version.

  - **RemoteFX vGPU**: This allows you to present a virtual instance of a physical GPU to the virtual machines, and enables them to utilize hardware acceleration and render superior graphics for 3D or video gaming within a remote session. The current version now supports DirectX 11.1 on GPU cards.

  - **RemoteFX USB Redirection**: This allows you to support the USB devices redirection and enables users to use peripheral devices that are connected to local machines, or a terminal to be used within virtual machines or sessions.

  - **RemoteFX Adaptive Graphics**: This feature allows for intelligent adaptation to runtime environments, involving graphic content and network bandwidth availability, and delivers seamless Aero and 3D user experience.

  - **RemoteFX Media Streaming**: Complementing the preceding, media streaming enables seamless media rendering over the unreliable networks.

  - **RemoteFX for WAN**: This component ensures that the user experience is not affected over unreliable networks, including WAN and wireless networks.

  - **RemoteFX Multi-Touch**: This feature interestingly supports touch and gesture control over the remote desktops.

- **Dynamic memory and smart paging**: The dynamic memory feature saw improvements with Windows Server 2012 and Windows Server 2012 R2. It allows for pooling of physical RAM and intelligent and dynamic allocation, and ballooning (reclaim) and reallocation of memory to the virtual machines based on their active workloads. The objective of this feature is to increase the VM density on the Hyper-V and virtualization hosts. Thereby, we can have more virtual desktops running on a lesser number of hosts with effective utilization of the capacity.

Smart paging came out with Windows Server 2012 and is used to address VM restart failures on Hyper-V host with a high VM density. If we ponder over the dynamic memory variables, startup, and minimum memory, it is understood that the normal memory utilization figure will be lower than the amount of RAM required during the boot-up of a VM. If the host is under memory pressure, it may not be able to free up RAM to be reassigned to a restarting VM and thereby result in the VM boot-up failure. One way to address this is to install more memory modules. However, this is an expensive choice.

Smart paging is used as a tradeoff between startup and minimum memory figures, and ensures successful startup of VMs. It stores a backup memory page file on the hard disk to address memory requirements. It is evident that hard disks fit in the affecting performance benchmarking and hence, it should be understood that the tradeoff is used to lower the costs with the drawbacks of reduced performance. The options is quite popular, and is used extensively in pooled desktop collections with low workloads.

- **User Profile Disk (UPD)**: This is a means for the user state virtualization wherein the user data is not tied to the user or his/her device, and can be made available on login from an authorized device. Earlier versions of Windows saw the user state being abstracted either via **Roaming User Profiles (RUP)** or **Folder Redirection**. Both these are old mechanisms to achieve the same goal. However, the latter, Folder Redirection, is often used to prevent bloating of the roaming profiles. Of course, the means have their own set of tried and tested demerits. For example, loading and unloading of the RUP results in a slower login. If not maintained properly, it results in a bloated profile and needless to say, even a slower login. RUP may also result in profile corruption and data loss.

  UPD allows for personalization of the user state and storing user and application data on a VHDX file mounted under the user profile. This is an ideal choice with pooled virtual desktop collections. However, it can be put to use with sessions desktop collection as well. It simplifies the profile management
  in VDI.

- **CSV block cache**: Another feature with CSV was rolled out with Windows Server 2012. It is used to reduce the read IO where you have read-intensive workloads. It supports unbuffered IO and enables block level read cache. Unbuffered IO are not cached by Windows Cache Manager, hence when enabled, the CSV cache boosts the performance in a Hyper-V environment.

CSV cache reserves its cache from the physical RAM. An ideal recommended value is 512 MB. However, you may allocate till 20 percent with Windows Server 2012 and a whopping 80 percent with Windows Server 2012 R2 for the CSV write-through cache, from the non-paged pool memory.

To enable and configure, you will need to employ PowerShell.

CsvEnableBlockCache: This property enables caching on the CSV volumes:

```
Get-ClusterResource <cluster disk name> | Set-
ClusterParameter
CsvEnableBlockCache 1
```

SharedVolumeBlockCacheSizeInMB: This is a common property value for clusters that are used to commit the size of the cache.

```
(Get-Cluster).SharedVolumeBlockCacheSizeInMB = 1024
```

- **Cost effective storage options**: Hyper-V packs a volley of low cost storage solutions for VDI deployments, namely storage spaces, SMB 3.0 for Hyper-V clusters, Cluster Shared Volumes (CSV), and Scale-Out File Servers (SOFS).

Storage spaces remove the reliance on traditional storage RAID dependency by utilizing JBOD concept. SMB 3.0 is a new file share protocol and has extensive use for Hyper-V and file server solutions. CSV and SOFS (SMB 3.0), and we have seen the benefits of them in the earlier chapters.

- **Storage tiering and online data deduplication**: Two of the primary promotional features for VDI are that they augment and optimize workloads on your storage. Storage tiering allows for two or more tiers for storing virtual disks. For example, a high performing SSD tier for frequently accessed data (preferably parent), a fast class/SAS drive tier for less accessed data (VMs), and maybe another tier for UPD.

Data deduplication in Windows Server 2012 R2 provides you with yet another cost-saving advantage. The feature has been improvised from the previous offering in Windows Server 2012. Deduplication's purpose is to identify and remove duplication of data without affecting the integrity of the contents. It supports CSV in hosting SOFS and VDI workloads, and optimizes live VDI workloads by performing deduplication of the open files on the fly.

Understanding VDI deployment

VDI, as with any other role deployment, requires homework and planning before you lay down a design and implement your environment. The deployment process requires the same meticulous efforts as we discussed in *Chapter 2, Planning and Deploying Microsoft Hyper-V*. You will need to understand the user-base and the use-case for the suitable deployment that follows the design principles, and then conclude on the deployment choice. Flipping the coin for choosing the deployment model is not an option!

Further on into the VDI deployment, multiple server roles will need to be installed. Hence, you may work out the design plan depending on whether to keep all the roles under one roof (simple not safe) or spread across multiple servers. Also, you may like to ensure that the roles are highly available, which can be achieved by employing measures such as failover clustering, NLB, and so on. The last piece of the puzzle is to understand the RDS and VDI Licensing needs from the server and client side.

You may chose a standard recipe, or garnish it with various caveat options as discussed earlier in this chapter, depending on your requirements and CAPEX budget.

RDS roles

There has been a few additions since the terminal server days, but RDS still has the standard roles, though it further added the VDI supporting roles to the fore. The prime segregation is for two roles: the RD Session Host for desktop sessions or session desktop rendering, and RD Virtualization Host for hosting virtual desktop collections. The rest are supporting roles to these two primary roles. To have a design plan rolled out, you will need to understand the function of these roles and identify how to aggregate these components effectively:

- RD Session Host (RDSH)
- RD Virtualization Host (RDVH)
- RD Connection Broker (RDCB)
- RD Management Server (RDMS)
- RD Web Access (RDWA)
- RD Gateway (RDGW)
- RD Licensing

RD Session Host

The improved terminal server, **RD Session Host (RDSH)**, is required for hosting session desktop and RemoteApp instances. This is more similar to the hosted virtualization where the users' login to their sessions on Windows Server, use installed programs on the server and share resources effectively. The RDSH also allows the users to save files on the server, if permitted.

RD Virtualization Host

RD Virtualization Host (RDVH) is the bridging piece, which gets integrated with Hyper-V and hosts desktop pool collections: personal and pooled virtual desktops. This role facilitates each user to get his or her own virtual machine, uniquely, or dynamically assigned, depending upon the collection that he is assigned to.

RD Connection Broker and RD Management Server

As the name indicates, **RD Connection Broker (RDCB)** is used to break the session or the virtual desktop connections to the users. It allows the users to reconnect to their disconnected connections to sessions desktops, RemoteApp, or virtual desktops, and provides load-balancing abilities in a Session Desktop Farm or Virtual Desktop Collection by distributing the load accordingly among RDSH or pooled desktop collections.

RDCB also provides the centralized management to a remote desktop deployment. Prior to Windows Server 2012, there were multiple snap-ins and consoles for different roles under RDS, namely Remote Desktop Services Manager (tsadmin), Remote Desktop Services Configuration (tsconfig), Remote Desktop Connection Manager (sbmgr), and RemoteApp Manager (remoteprograms). With the introduction of **RD Management Server (RDMS)**, all the previous snap-ins have been deprecated. RDCB is a critical role to a VDI or RDS deployment, and the RDMS service is installed on the same server as RDCB. RDMS is installed as a plugin in the Server Manager and gives full view and control of a Remote Desktop Infrastructure.

RD Web Access

RD Web Access (RDWA) facilitates users to access desktop collections and RemoteApp through the start screen/menu of a Windows client or a web browser. It is not installed as a service but gets installed over IIS as a facilitator for RDS connectivity. IIS is installed as a required component when installing RDWA and thereafter, RD Web Access website is hosted on the IIS server, which aids in the connectivity to all VDI options allowed by RD Connection Manager.

RD Gateway

The **Remote Desktop Gateway** (**RDGW**) server is responsible for allowing authorized connections to the RDS deployment in an internal network from any VDI supported device over the Internet. This is a preferred DMZ role that interfaces between the public and the internal network through a firewall.

RD Licensing

This is a tracker role to ensure that you only use what you pay for. Of course, you may get a free lunch for the initial trial period of 120 days of installing the RDS Host. The RD Licensing server is used to host and manage the RDS **Client Access License** (**CALs**) for a device or user access to a particular or set of hosts. The number of coctions allowed to a RDS deployment is directly proportional to the number of RDS CALs activated.

High availability recommendations

VDI runs on many roles. This means that we may have multiple points of failure. To ensure availability of each role, we need to determine the high availability options suitable for each one of them:

- **RD Session Host (RDSH)**: For high availability of RDSH, we need to follow the old-school way of TS farm by deploying multiple RDSH and configuring DNS Round Robin.

- **RD Virtualization Host (RDVH)**: This is a Hyper-V server, and to ensure that a Hyper-V workload stays highly available, we deploy the workload on a Hyper-V cluster.

- **RD Web Access (RDWA)**: This is a webapp that can be scaled out to a multiple web servers. They can be setup under a Network Load Balancing (NLB) cluster to ensure multiple active connections.

- **RD Gateway (RDGW)**: This role can also be setup under a NLB cluster for a high availability.

- **RD Licensing**: The Licensing role can too be clustered or installed on a virtual machine, which is hosted on a Hyper-V cluster.

- **RD Connection Broker (RDCB)**: RDCB high availability has been improvised since the Windows Server 2008 R2, where it was clustered as an active/passive instance. The Fall Windows Server 2012 and connection broker can be customized from the Remote Desktop Services snap-into function, as an active-active instance against multiple RDCB nodes. The snap-in allows you to migrate RDCB's Windows internal database to a SQL database, to which, multiple RDCB can connect and provision VM logins. RDCB can benefit from dual high availability, as the backend SQL database can be clustered as well.

Server and client prerequisites

An important aspect to every successful role deployment is to understand the prerequisites that need to be addressed beforehand. Identifying prerequisites requires some groundwork to be done, and once the same is achieved, the rest of the process goes smooth.

Server hardware and software prerequisites

A check against the *Windows Server Catalog* website (http://www.windowsservercatalog.com/) is compulsory to ensure that we are running on a supported hardware. Of course, there are processor requirements, namely **Hardware Assisted Virtualization, Second Level Address Translation (SLAT)**, and **Hyper-Threading**. If deploying RemoteFX is on the agenda apart from the former requirements, ensure that the RemoteFX server is capable of GPU.

From the software's perspective, there are just a few caveats that should be understood without mention. However, the same deserves a discussion:

- The server must be running on Windows Server 2012 or R2
- The server must be joined to an Active Directory domain
- The user installing the RDS roles should be a domain admin

Client requirements

Clients could range from a physical desktop or a thin client to a web browser or a smartphone as well. Windows 7 SP1 clients should be updated to Remote Desktop Protocol 8.0 or 8.1; and smartphones and tablets should have the Remote Desktop app installed so that they benefit from the Remote Desktop enhancements.

From a client's perspective, Microsoft has eased its licensing for virtual desktops recently. It also allows for a per-user licensing for **Virtual Desktop Access (VDA)**. So to connect to a VDI environment, you will need both RDS CALs and VDA licensing.

Deploying a simple VDI environment

Now that you know the players and the rules of the game, let's play! In the following section, we will only be demonstrating RD Virtualization Host deployment along with RD Connection Broker and RD Web Access roles.

As with all the roles and features, RDS roles have to be installed via the Server Manager. However, we may choose to install the role on the desired server locally or remotely. Server Manager provides you with a flexible management interface, which allows you to add servers to its pane and from where you can manage and monitor them remotely. To give you a brief idea, you will be able to configure or remove roles, setup performance counters, and even configure NIC teaming.

Installing Remote Desktop Services

The process of initiating the role installation is the same. Thereafter, the wizard takes you through a different route. Let's walk through the process:

1. First you invoke the **Manage** menu, and select the **Add Roles and Features** option. Bypass the default **Before you Begin** option, and select **Remote Desktop Services installation** on the **Installation Type** page. Click on **Next**.

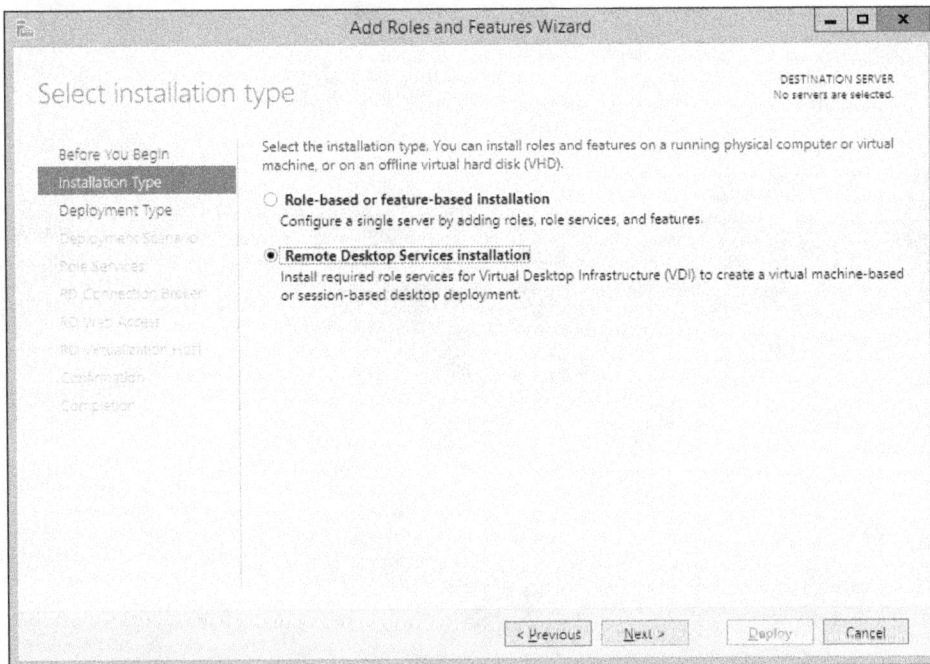

Figure 10-2: Installation Type – Select Remote Desktop Services Installation

2. Under the **Deployment Type** screen, you will be presented with two options: **Standard deployment** and **Quick Start**. The latter, as the name indicates, is opted for a quicker deployment of virtual desktops wherein we do not plan to deploy a complex infrastructure. All the RDS roles, including RD Connection Broker and RD Web Access, will be installed on one server and the VDI will be ready for immediate provisioning of virtual desktops. Select **Standard deployment** and click on **Next**.

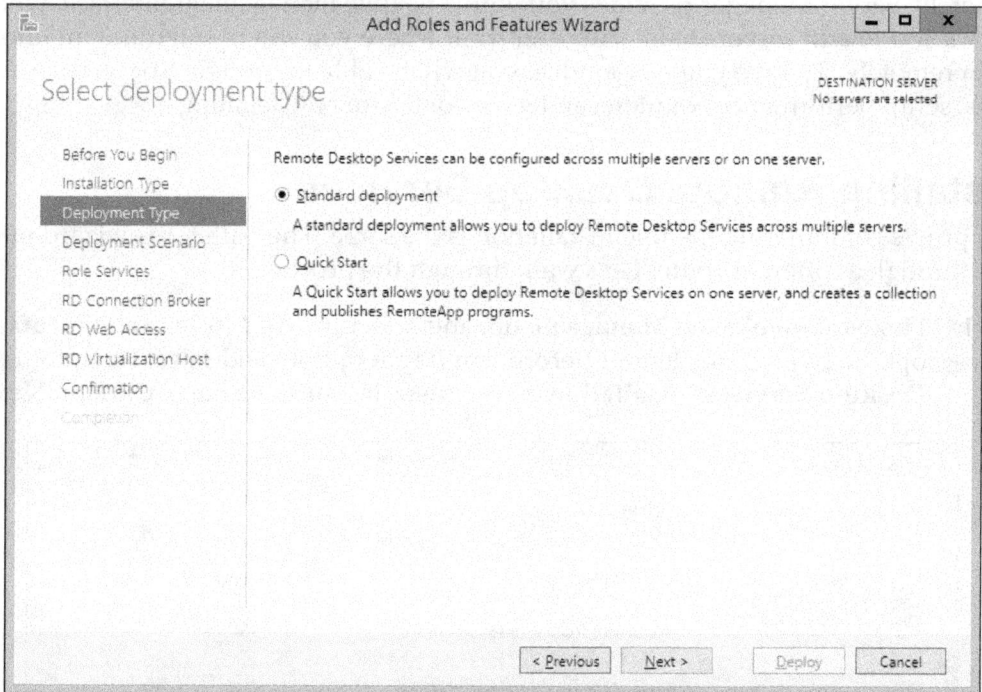

Figure 10-3: Deployment Type – Standard deployment or Quick Start

3. The next screen is **Deployment Scenario**. Here again you will be presented with two options: **Virtual machine-based desktop deployment** and **Session-based desktop deployment**. We select the former and click on **Next**.

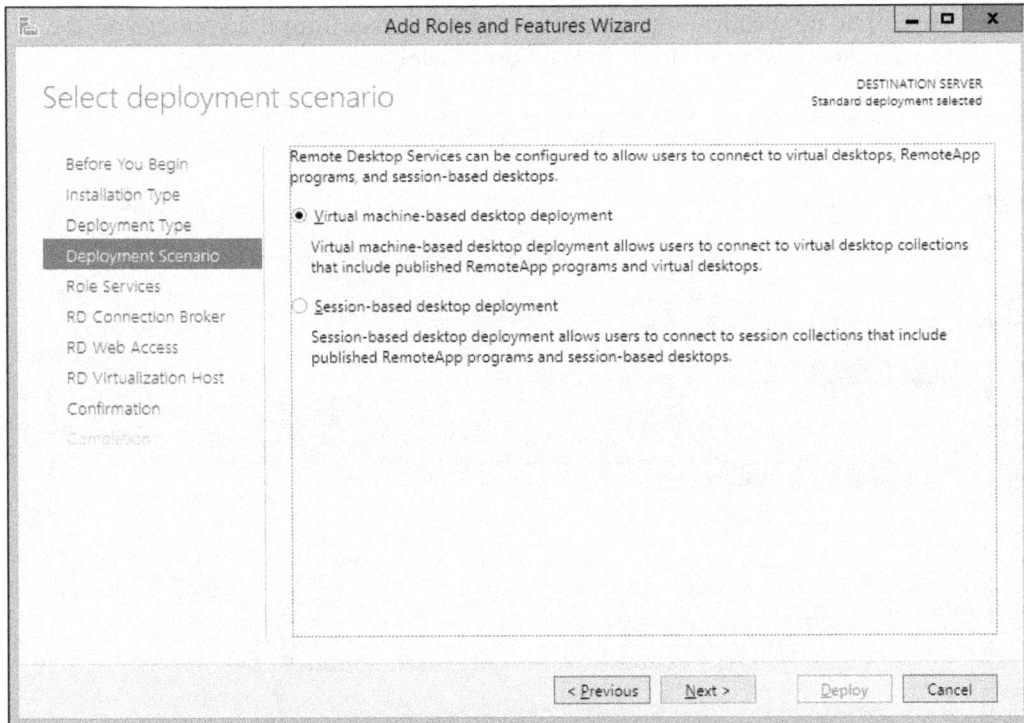

Figure 10-4: Deployment Scenario: Virtual machine-based desktop deployment or Session-based desktop deployment

4. The next screen is **Role Services**, which are available and would differ for either of the deployment scenario. The available services for a virtual machine-based desktop deployment are **Remote Desktop Connection Broker**, **Remote Desktop Web Access**, and **Remote Desktop Virtualization Host**. The next follow-up screens will be for installing the services on the specific servers, pre-added in the Server Manager.

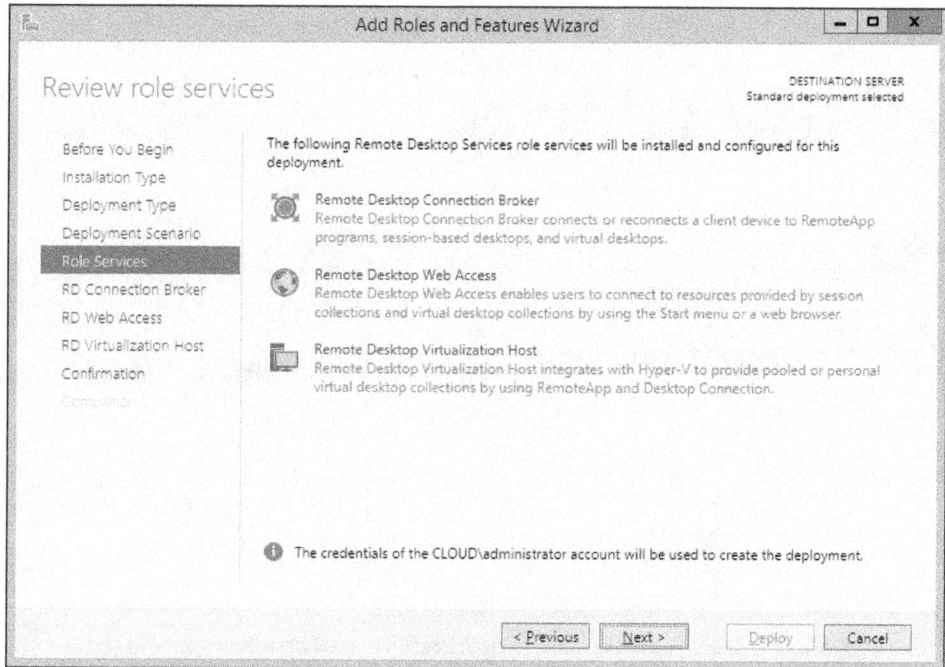

Figure 10-5: Role Services

5. Install the **RD Connection Broker** by adding the desired server from the **Server Pool**. Click on **Next**.

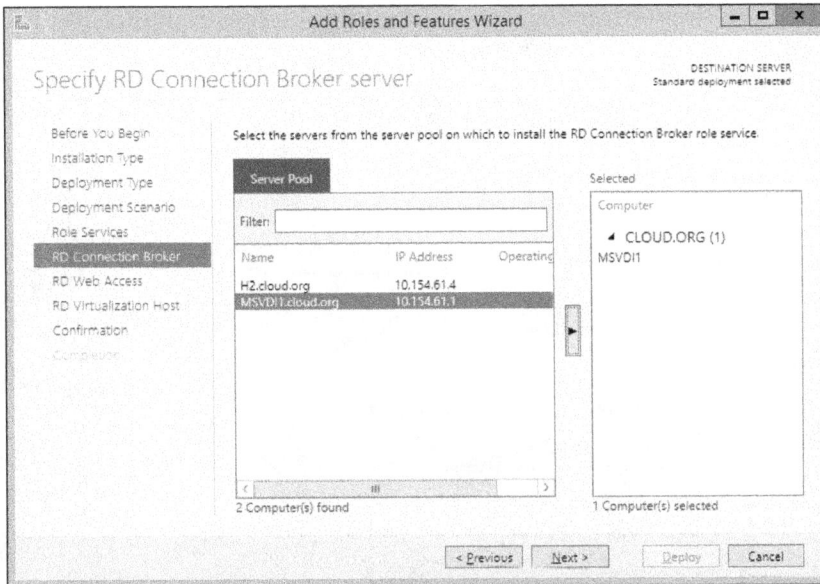

Figure 10-6: Installing RD Connection Broker

6. Install the **RD Web Access** role. You will see that an additional role, the IIS Web Server role, also gets installed along with RD Web Access. Not only that, it also creates the RD Web application for RD Web Access on the default website. Click on **Next**.

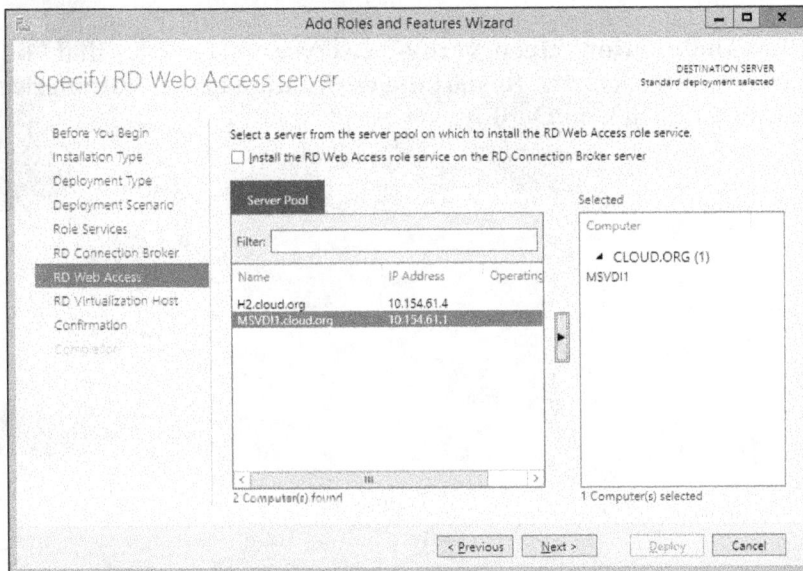

Figure 10-7: Installing RD Web Access

7. Install **RD Virtualization Host** on the selected server, which in turn will also install the Hyper-V role on the server. Click on **Next**.

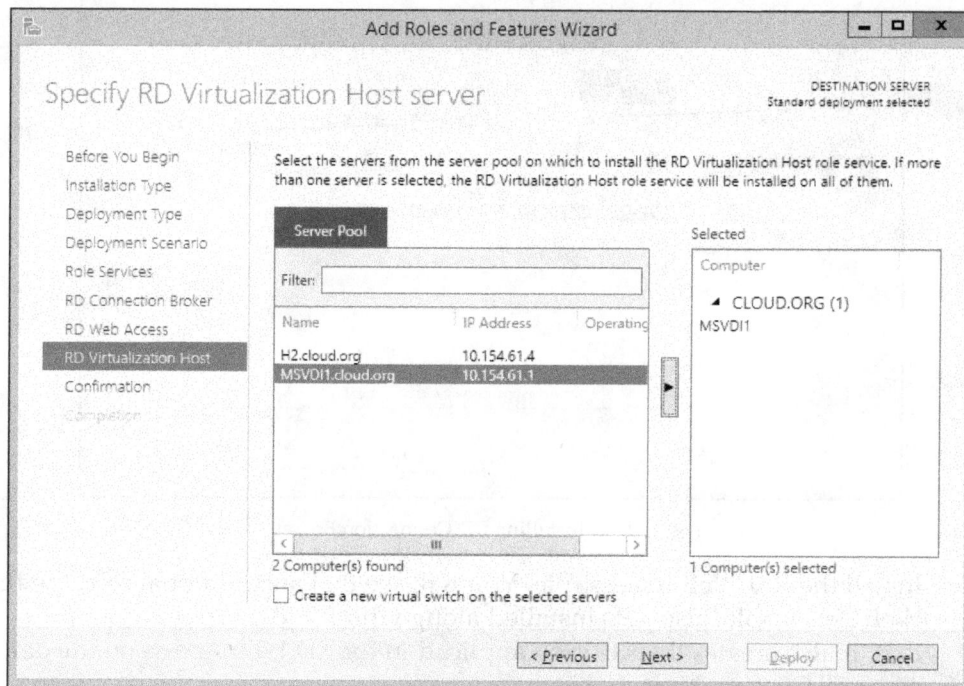

Figure 10-8: Installing RD Virtualization Host

8. On the **Confirmation** screen, verify the server and changes that you are going to commit, and check the **Restart the destination server automatically if required** box. Click on **Deploy**.

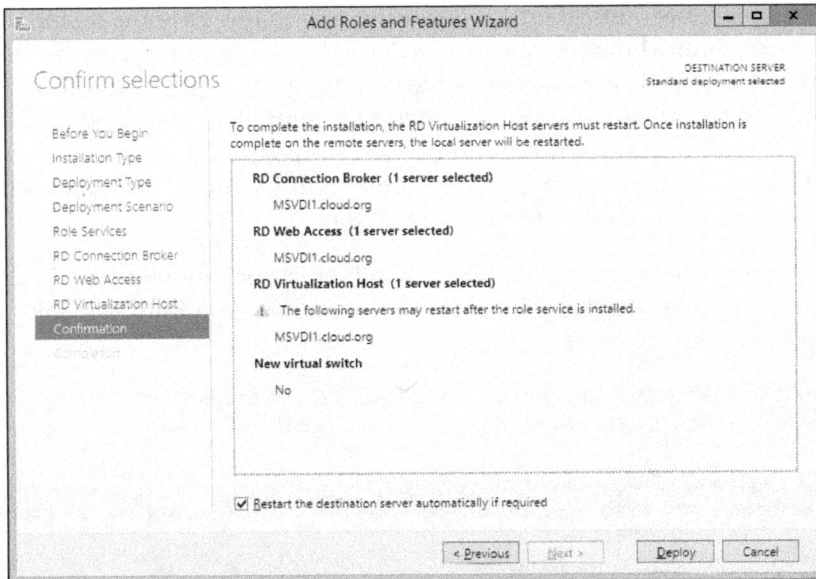

Figure 10-9: Confirmation

9. The next screen in the wizard is the **Completion** page, which depicts the state of three roles being installed. If you are installing the RD Virtualization role locally, it will reboot the server to complete the Hyper-V role installation and return to the **Completion** screen after the login to finalize the virtualization host installation.

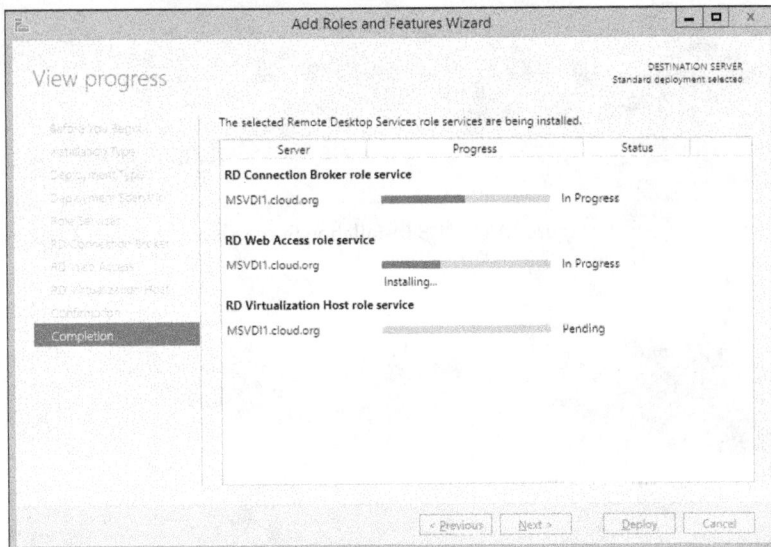

Figure 10-10: Completion

Once the roles have been installed successfully, you may verify the installation by reverting to Server Manager, and you will see the Remote Desktop Services plugin on the left pane. If you highlight the plugin on the right pane, you can see the **Overview** page enlisting two frames: **Deployment Overview** and **Deployment Servers**. The former shows a graphical chart of the installed roles, and the latter shows your servers, which are part of the deployment with the installed services. The *figure 10-11* offers a handy illustration for this.

It may not be necessary to share the PowerShell assist for the mentioned action, as you will be versed with the same by now. However, in good faith, the following should help bypass the screens:

```
Add-WindowsFeature RDS-Virtualization, RDS-Connection-Broker, RDS-
Web-Access -IncludeManagementTools
```

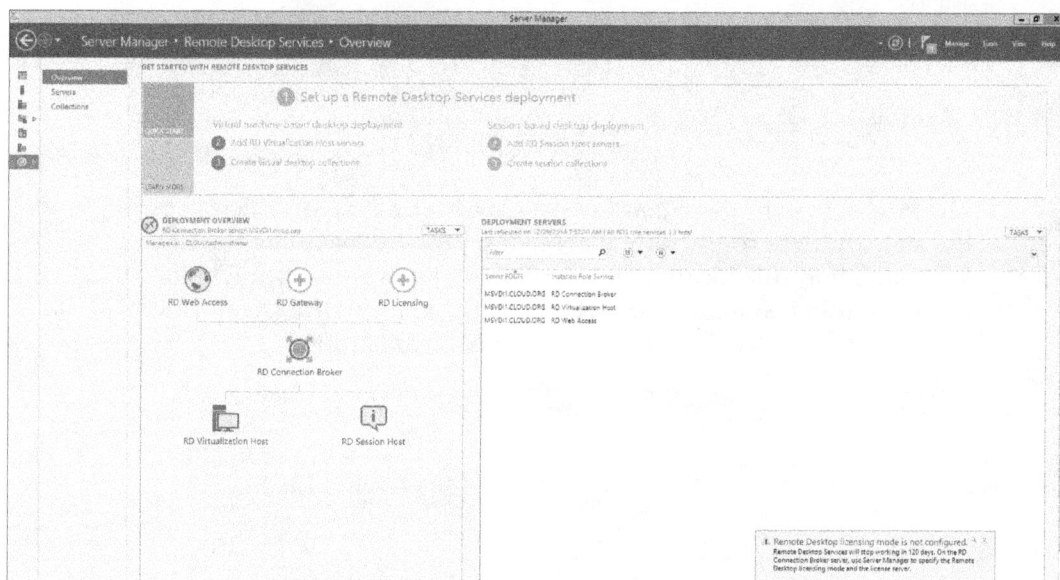

Figure 10-11: RDS Installation Succeeded

Post RDS installation actions

Once the base RDS framework is installed, you may customize or configure the deployment accordingly to build a more secure and highly available infrastructure. The **Deployment Overview** and **Deployment Properties** applets come in handy for further actions. There's a lot that can be done from the perspective of **Active Directory Domain Services (ADDS)** and **Active Directory Certificate Services (ADCS)**. You may create a dedicated OU for virtual desktops and assign it to the deployment properties, which authorizes the connection broker server to join the virtual desktops to the domain, and moves the computer objects to the desired OU. You may deploy certificates from your In-house issuing certification authority and design a single sign-on and preferred server authentication on the RDS roles.

From a VDI perspective, you may scale up your VDI infrastructure by adding more hosts, and create collections and edit collection properties. You can also configure the RDS Licensing, (rather you should, as there's no escaping from that) and the RDS Gateway, and configure high availability as well.

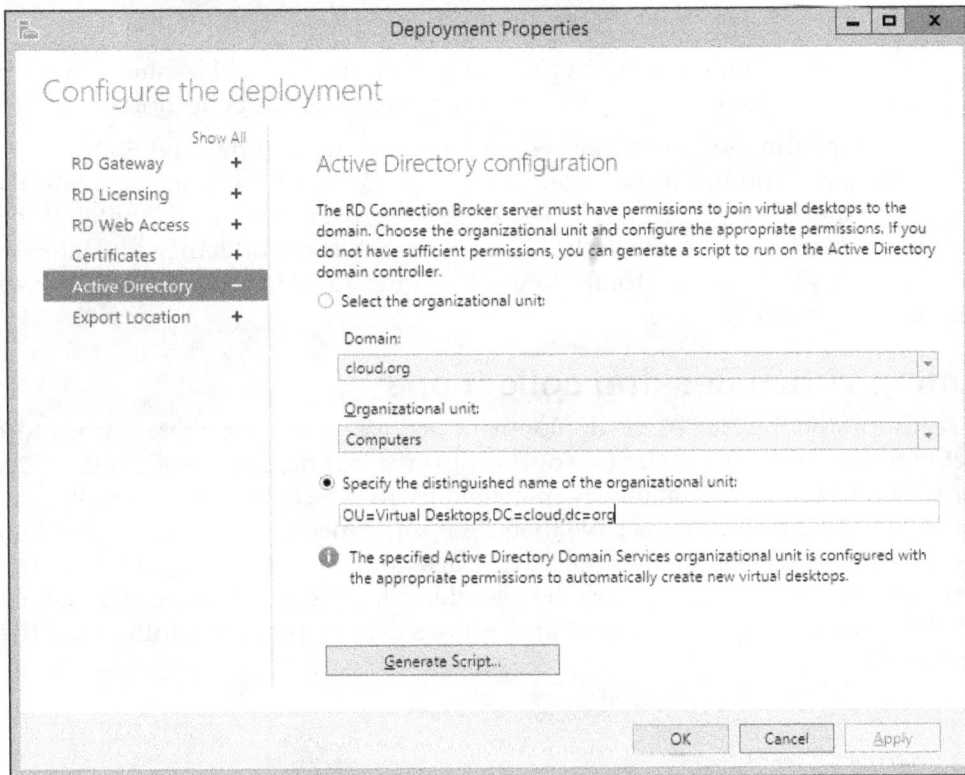

Figure 10-12: Deployment Properties

Deploying virtual desktops

After the installation and additional configuration, you will now learn how to create the virtual desktop pool. There is one prior action before we go ahead and create a collection. We need to prepare a gold image that will be used as a template for virtual machine deployment. Following are the steps to create a gold or master image:

1. Invoke the Hyper-V Manager from **Tools** menu, in Server Manager.

2. Create a new virtual machine and install the supported client operating system.

3. Install all the enterprise applications.

4. In the VM settings, configure RemoteFX if the Hyper-V host has the relevant graphics adapter.

5. **Sysprep (Generalize)** the virtual machine. The following command with the relevant switches will be invoked from an elevated command prompt in the sysprep directory (C:\Windows\system32\sysprep):

   ```
   sysprep.exe /generalize /oobe /shutdown /mode:vm
   ```

   Once the system preparation process is over, the VM will be shut down, and can now be used as a template virtual machine for the collection.

   Sysprep with the Generalize switch purges all the settings and SID from the previous Windows installation, and sets the Windows to boot the **Out-Of-BoxExperience (OOBE)**. Another interesting observation was switch/mode: vm, which is not visible in the Sysprep help. It turns off hardware detection, and the VM image continues to use the same virtual hardware profile prior to the Sysprep process.

Creating virtual desktop collections

We are now at the final leg of the deployment process. However, there is one more aspect to the process. VDI offers two options from a VM management perspective; either the pools can be automatically managed by RDMS, or we can manually manage them-and both options have their own set of merits and demerits. Managed pools allow the automatic creation of virtual desktops, based on the gold image and support for user-profile disk, where the user data stays consistent across the pooled desktops. Unmanaged, on the other hand, allows a more granular control over the pooled desktops.

Here, we will create a managed pooled desktop collection:

1. To begin, we use the RDS snap-in from the Server Manager. Then, there are two ways to start the process of creating a collection:

   ○ First, we can do it from the **Overview** pane by selecting the third option—**Create Virtual Desktop Collections**.

   ○ Second, select **Collections** option in the left pane for Remote Desktop Services, and under **Collections** drop-down **Tasks** and click on **Create Virtual Desktop Collection**.

   Both the options invoke the **Create Collection** wizard. On the **Before you Begin** screen, click on **Next**.

2. The next screen is **Collection Name**. You may update a suitable name for your VDI pool. Click on **Next**.

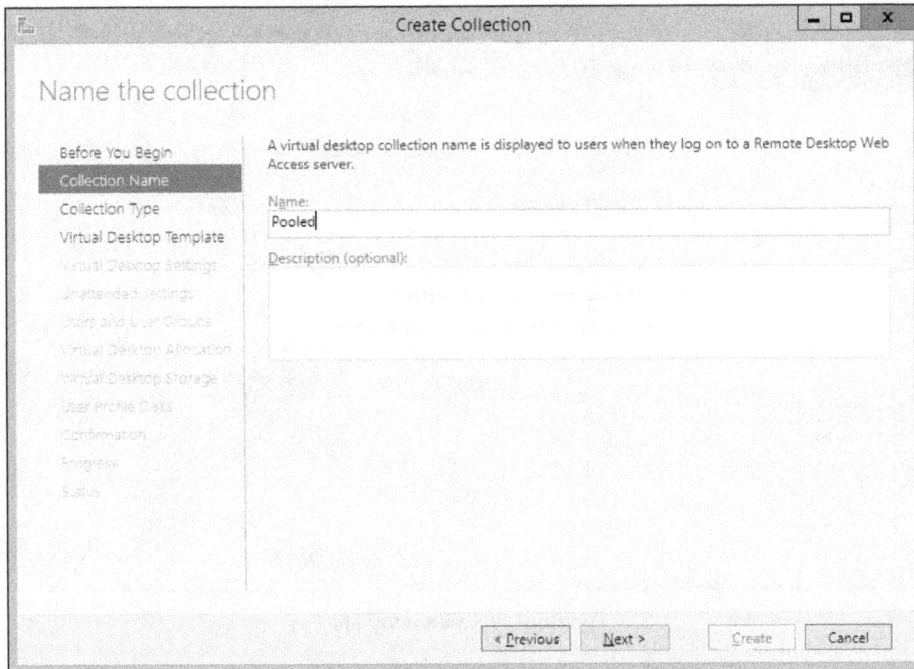

Figure 10-13: Collection Name

3. The next screen is **Collection Type**. Here, you have to update whether you wish to opt for **Pooled virtual desktop collection** or **Personal virtual desktop collection**. Right after the radio buttons, there is an **Automatically create and manage virtual desktops** checkbox. This is the same feature flag that we discussed at the beginning of this section. If you leave the box checked, it stays flagged for a managed pool; otherwise, it is an unmanaged pool. You may also find it interesting to see how the beneath options with green checks are flagged on and off when you toggle with the options.

We are going to opt for the managed pooled virtual desktop collection. Click on **Next**.

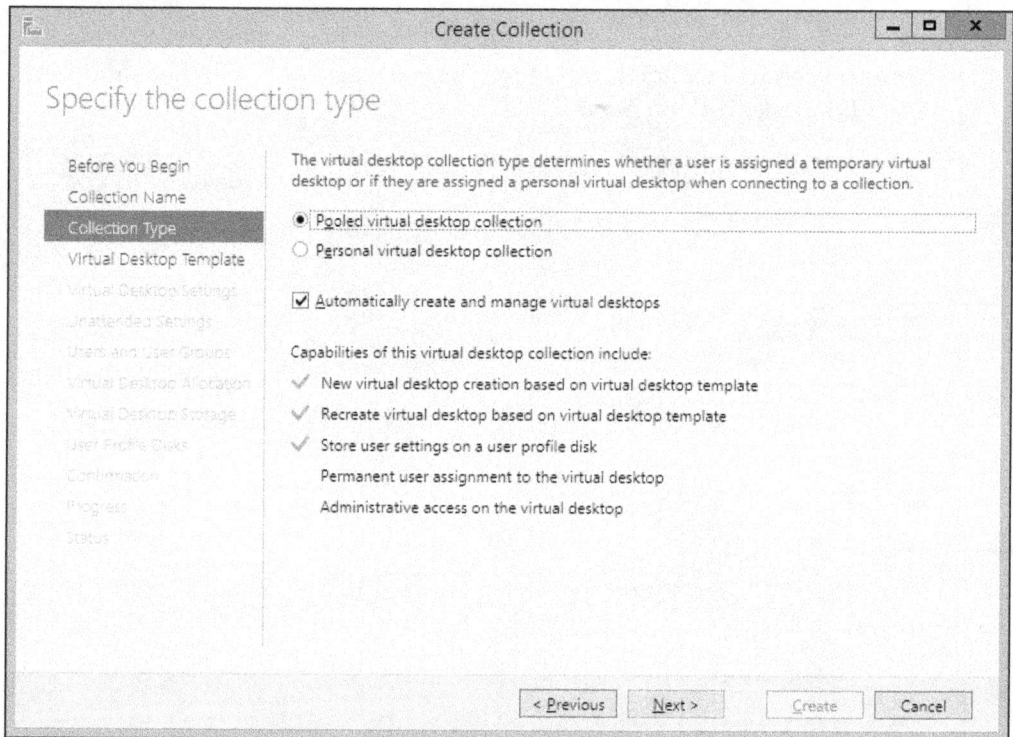

Figure 10-14: Collection Type

4. The next screen, **Virtual Desktop Template**, prompts you to select the gold
    or master image, which will be used as a template to deploy virtual desktops.
    RDMS automatically detects and enlists the images on the host. Select the
    preferred one, and then click on **Next**.

> Generation 2 virtual machines are not supported for virtual
> desktop collections for now.

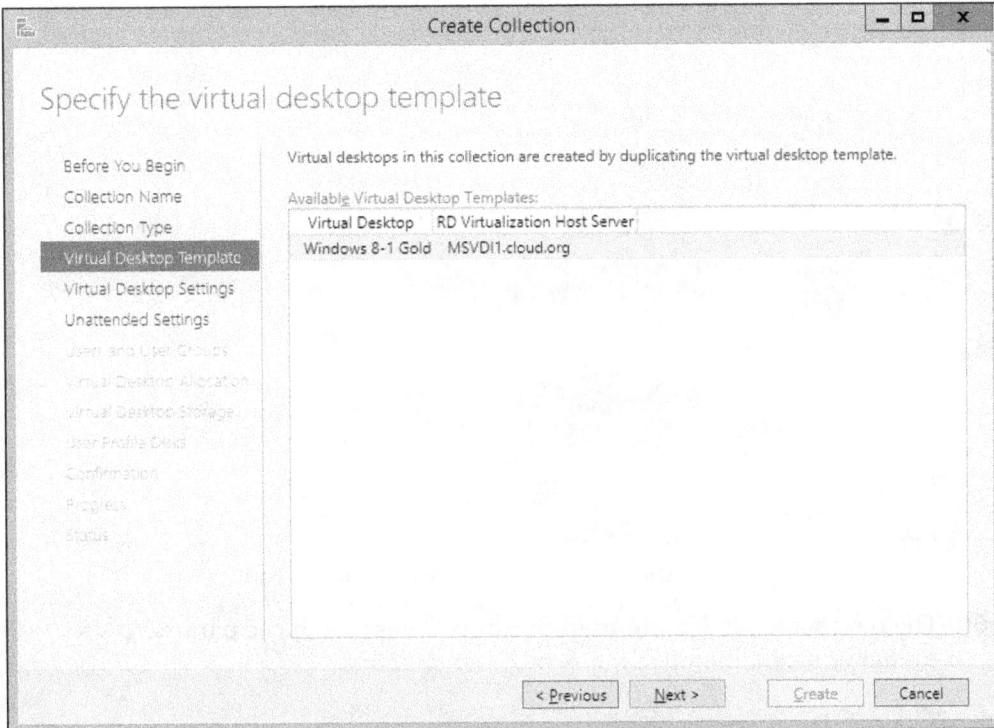

Figure 10-15: Virtual Desktop Template

5. The next screen is **Virtual Desktop Settings**. Select and apply **Provide unattended installation settings** that instructs the wizard to generate an answer file for the VM. You may also select the second option **Use an existing Sysprep answer file**. Click on **Next**.

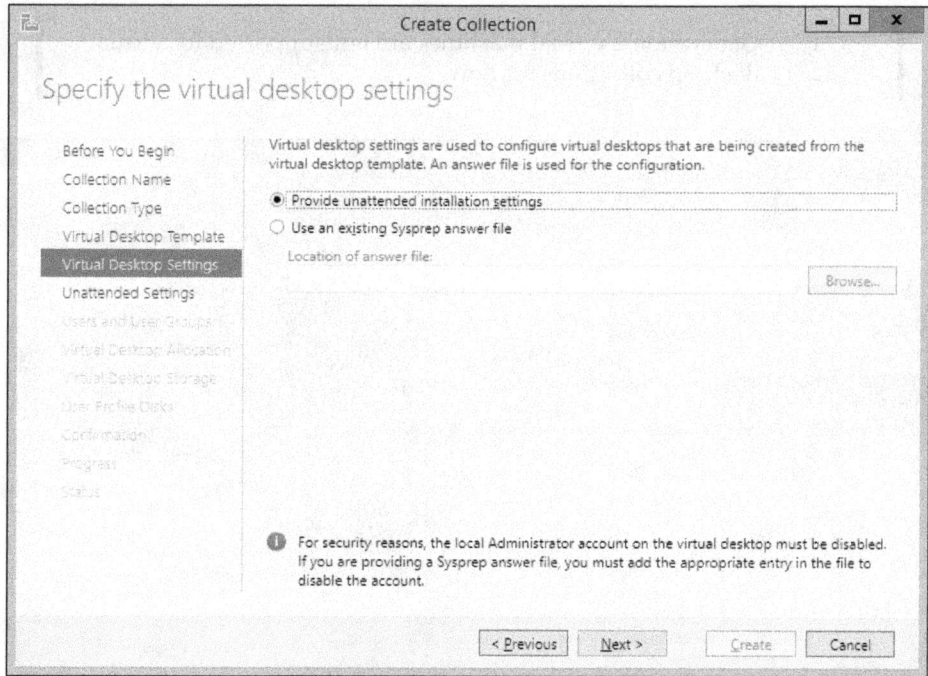

Figure 10-16: Virtual Desktop Settings

6. The next screen is **Unattended Settings**. These are basic parameters for domain placement and time zone. Click on **Next**.

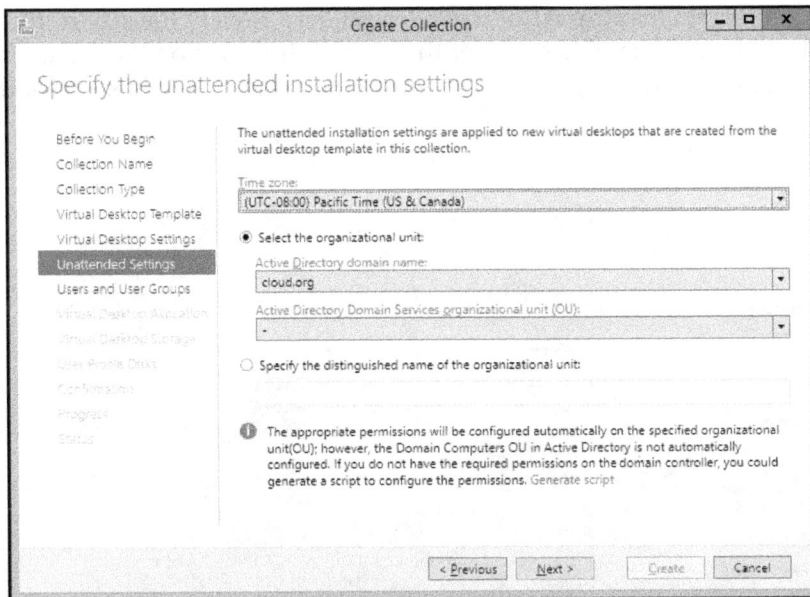

Figure 10-17: Unattended Settings

7. On the **Users and User Groups** page, you have to update the users or user groups that will have access to the collection. Also, specify the number of virtual desktops that will be generated under the collection to determine the collection size. Then, set the prefix of the virtual machine in the collections. Click on **Next**.

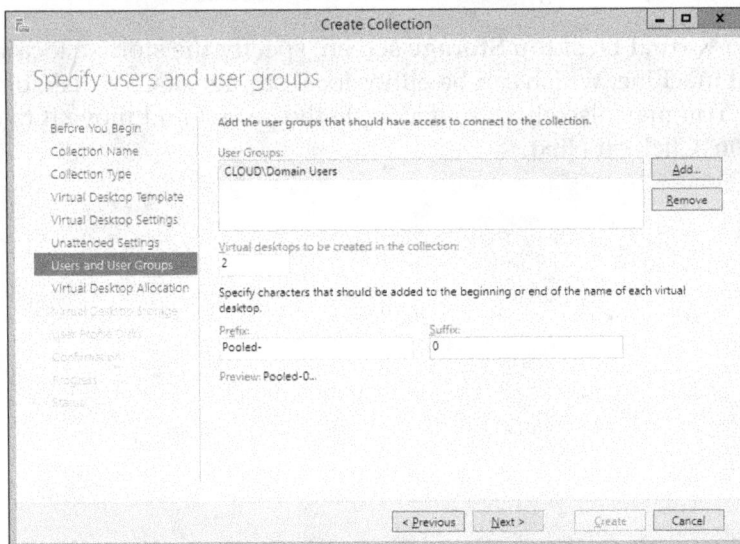

Figure 10-18: Users and User Groups

8. On a **Virtual Desktop Allocation** screen, let's review the size of the collection, and the placement of the virtual desktops on the virtualization host. You may deploy the VM on more than one host. Click on **Next**.

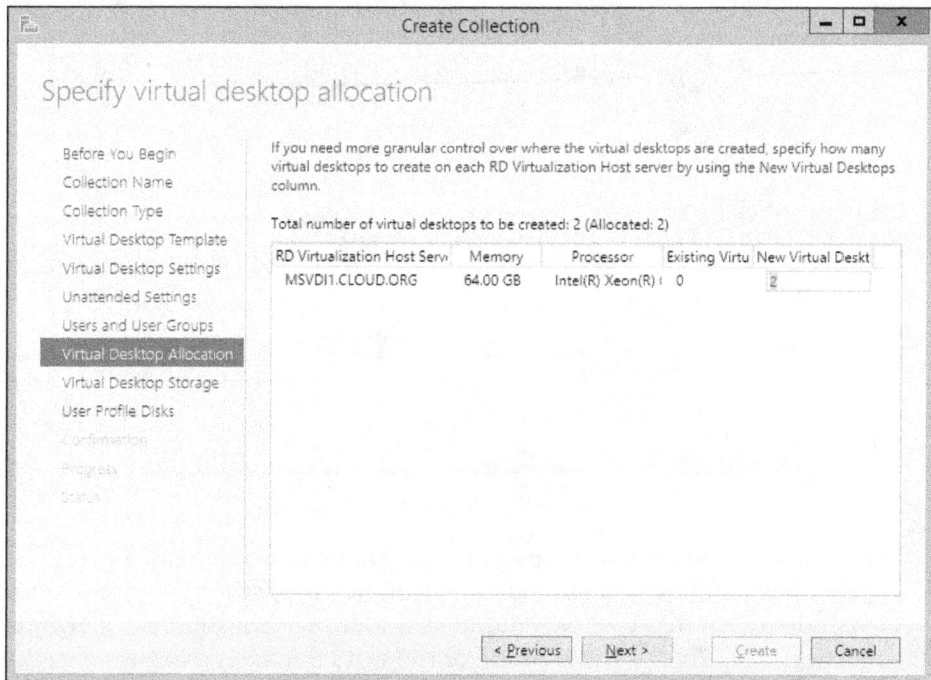

Figure 10-19: Virtual Desktop Allocation

9. On the **Virtual Desktop Storage** screen, specify the storage location for the virtual machine, which can be either local storage, a CSV disk, or an SMB share. You may also chose to decouple the parent and move it to a different location. Click on **Next**.

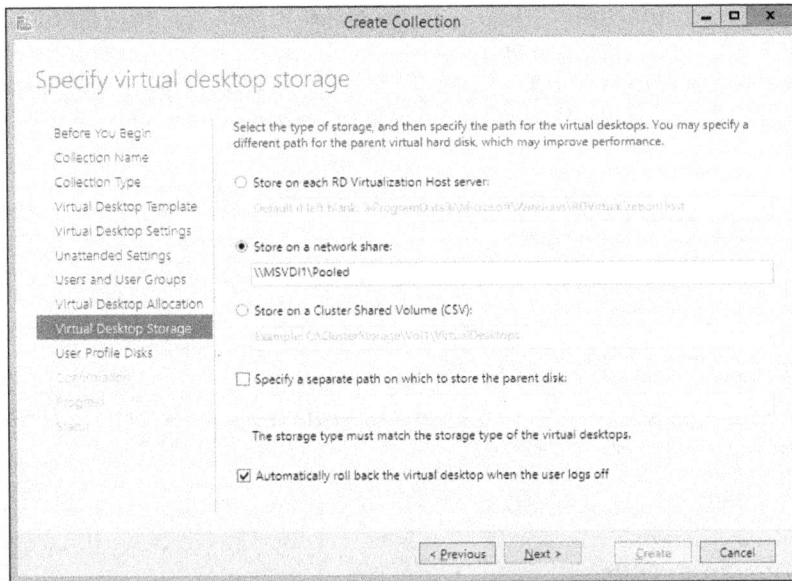

Figure 10-20: Virtual Desktop Storage

10. On the **User Profile Disks** screen, specify the share location where you will retain the user data. Ensure that the share will be prestaged. Click on **Next**.

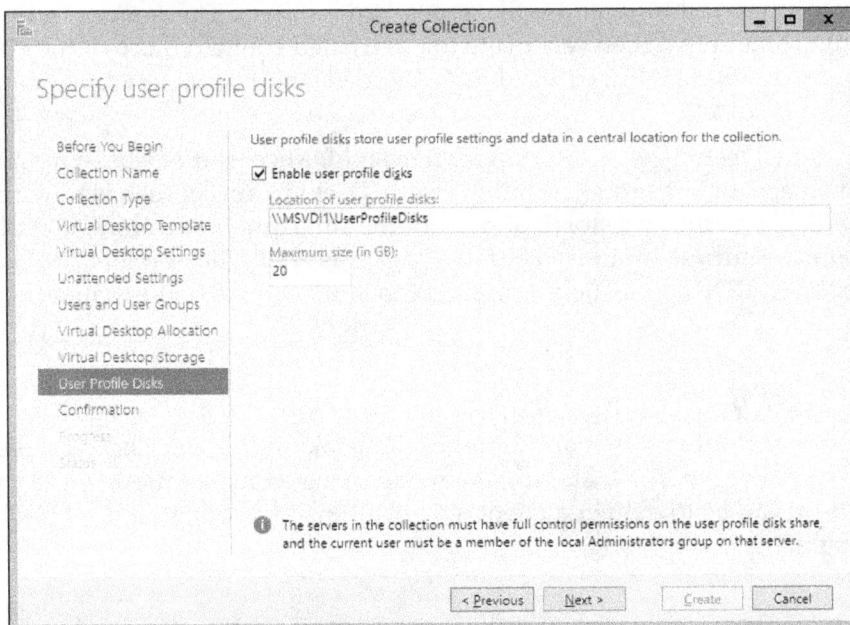

Figure 10-21: User Profile Disks

11. On the **Confirmation** screen, click on **Next**. It will take you through the progress page where the staging can be tracked, as the virtual desktop template is exported and pooled VMs are created. When the entire process is over, your will see that the VMs are populated in the Remote Desktop Services snap-in.

Creating a personal pool is almost the same. All we need to do is follow the prerequisites, and switch the radio option to **Personal Virtual Desktop Collection** on the **Collection Type** screen when running the **Create Collection** wizard.

RDS Access methods

There are many ways to access a VDI environment, and they work for both the desktop virtualization options. Let's consider these options:

- **RDC**: RDC version 8.0 (KB 2592687) or 8.1 (KB 2923545) should be used on Windows 7 client machine, as it has been tuned up to benefit from the latest RDS enhancements.

- **RD Web portal**: The RD Web portal provisions connections to RemoteApp and virtual desktops over HTTPS. When RD Web Access role is installed, it is enabled for SSL connections, and uses a self-signed certificate by default. When users connect to RD Web portal, they will be prompted with untrusted certificate Warnings, and will have to bypass them. The remedy is to either import the self-signed certificate to the trusted root CA store of the clients, or use an internal CA or a public CA issued cert. `https://FQDN ofRDWA Server/RDWeb`

- **Remote Desktop App**: With BYOD in sight, Microsoft has been up for the challenge and has rolled out its Remote Desktop app, which is now readily available on the app stores of most of the smartphone vendors, including Apple, Android, and for Windows phone as well. The app lets you make seamless RDP connection to the session and virtual desktops alike.

Summary

Here, we are concluding the final chapter of the book. In this chapter, we covered a different aspect of Hyper-V by taking it beyond server consolidation, and depicting how feasible it can be to deliver a client-side solution—Microsoft Virtual Desktop Infrastructure.

At the onset, we considered the various options that are available under desktop virtualization from Microsoft, including the old and reliable session desktops from the terminal server era, and the fairly new kid on the block virtual desktops. Virtual desktops has two sub-offerings: namely pooled and personal desktop collections.

Pooled desktops are a pool of virtual machines as a resource and when a user connects to the collection, he/she gets a VM dynamically assigned to them. The changes made to the VM are purged on the logoff and the VM is returned back to the pool. Hence, no personalization is saved. Ideal means maintaining a user-state personalization for remote user profiles and Folder Redirection. However, with Windows Server 2012 MS introduced, a new user state virtualization method called User Profile Disk (UPD) (which gets linked to a user logon in a pooled virtual desktop or session desktop) ensures the user state personalization and retention of user and application data. A personal or private virtual desktop collection, on the other hand, ensures a one-to-one user and VM assignment, and delivers performance and personalization similar to a physical desktop.

We also studied the features and technical aspects of Hyper-V, Windows Server 2012, and R2, which aid in deploying a stable and feature-rich VDI environment. RemoteFX offers excellent graphics and desktop to a virtual desktop, which is nothing short of a high-end PC. Memory management methods, dynamic memory, and smart paging ensure effective system memory utilization and high VM density per virtualization host. There were many storage enhancements in Windows Server 2012 and R2 that assisted in using storage resources in a cost-effective and optimized way—storage spaces, SMB3.0, CSV, SOFS, storage tiering, and online deduplication, to name a few.

Next, you learned about VDI components and server roles and requirements. The information is imperative for anyone who wishes to invest in VDI. You will understand the nitty-gritty of the technology before you move ahead with designing and deploying a VDI. We then reviewed the various RDS roles and understood their purpose. You may or may not need all of them, as not all of the roles are essential. Moreover, depending on your budget and availability tradeoffs, you may prefer to use them on a single server, or get the roles that are more highly available.

Finally, you learned how to deploy a simple VDI environment with both pooled and personal desktop collections, and how to customize the collections and make good use of the RDMS console.

Index

[PACKT] enterprise
PUBLISHING
professional expertise distilled

Thank you for buying
Designing Hyper-V Solutions

About Packt Publishing

Packt, pronounced 'packed', published its first book, *Mastering phpMyAdmin for Effective MySQL Management*, in April 2004, and subsequently continued to specialize in publishing highly focused books on specific technologies and solutions.

Our books and publications share the experiences of your fellow IT professionals in adapting and customizing today's systems, applications, and frameworks. Our solution-based books give you the knowledge and power to customize the software and technologies you're using to get the job done. Packt books are more specific and less general than the IT books you have seen in the past. Our unique business model allows us to bring you more focused information, giving you more of what you need to know, and less of what you don't.

Packt is a modern yet unique publishing company that focuses on producing quality, cutting-edge books for communities of developers, administrators, and newbies alike. For more information, please visit our website at www.packtpub.com.

About Packt Enterprise

In 2010, Packt launched two new brands, Packt Enterprise and Packt Open Source, in order to continue its focus on specialization. This book is part of the Packt Enterprise brand, home to books published on enterprise software – software created by major vendors, including (but not limited to) IBM, Microsoft, and Oracle, often for use in other corporations. Its titles will offer information relevant to a range of users of this software, including administrators, developers, architects, and end users.

Writing for Packt

We welcome all inquiries from people who are interested in authoring. Book proposals should be sent to author@packtpub.com. If your book idea is still at an early stage and you would like to discuss it first before writing a formal book proposal, then please contact us; one of our commissioning editors will get in touch with you.

We're not just looking for published authors; if you have strong technical skills but no writing experience, our experienced editors can help you develop a writing career, or simply get some additional reward for your expertise.

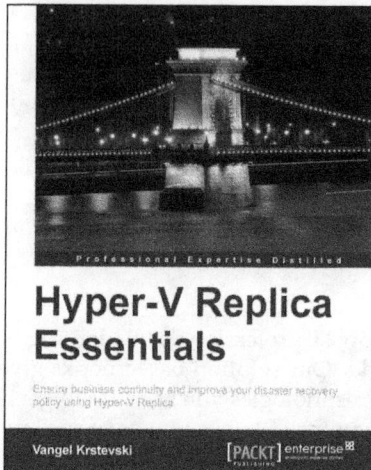

Hyper-V Replica Essentials

ISBN: 978-1-78217-188-1   Paperback: 96 pages

Ensure business continuity and improve your disaster recovery policy using Hyper-V Replica

1. A practical step-by-step guide that goes beyond theory and focuses on getting hands-on.

2. Ensure business continuity and faster disaster recovery.

3. Learn how to deploy a failover cluster and encrypt communication traffic.

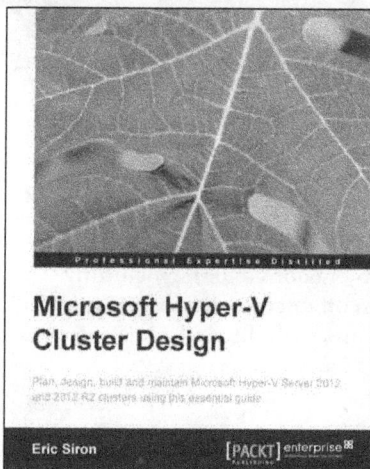

Microsoft Hyper-V Cluster Design

ISBN: 978-1-78217-768-5   Paperback: 462 pages

Plan, design, build and maintain Microsoft Hyper-V Server 2012 and 2012 R2 clusters using this essential guide

1. Successfully deploy a Microsoft Hyper-V cluster.

2. Select and use the right tools for building and maintaining a Hyper-V cluster.

3. Explore the labyrinth of storage and networking options and come out with a solution.

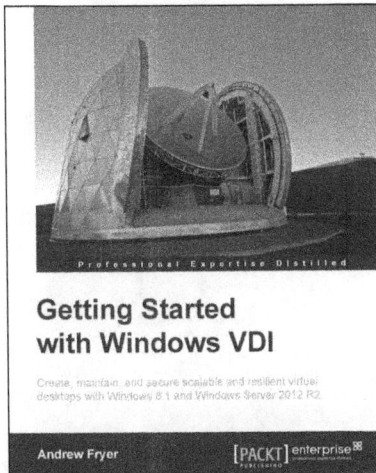

Getting Started with Windows VDI

ISBN: 978-1-78217-146-1   Paperback: 302 pages

Create, maintain, and secure scalable and resilient virtual desktops with Windows 8.1 and Windows Server 2012 R2

1. Explore the various parts of the VDI infrastructure such as the broker, web access server, and virtualization host.

2. Provide access for remote workers via any supported device.

3. Using a step-by-step approach, quickly grasp the complexities of VDI and learn to deploy its features.

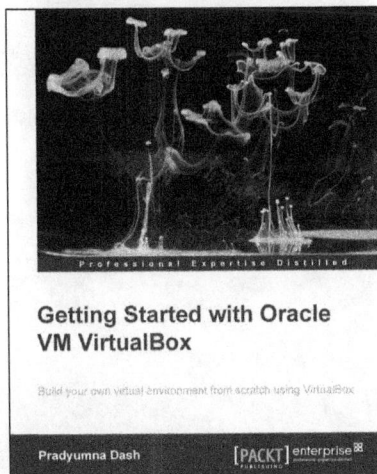

Getting Started with Oracle VM VirtualBox

ISBN: 978-1-78217-782-1   Paperback: 86 pages

Build your own virtual environment from scratch using VirtualBox

1. Learn how to install, configure, and manage VirtualBox.

2. A step-by-step guide which will teach you how to build your own virtual environment from scratch.

3. Discover advanced features of VirtualBox.

Please check **www.PacktPub.com** for information on our titles

* 9 7 8 1 7 8 2 1 7 1 4 4 7 *